Middle East Conflict

Primary Sources

SECOND EDITION

Middle East Conflict

Primary Sources

SECOND EDITION

Terri Schell
Sonia G. Benson, Contributing Writer
Jennifer Stock, Project Editor

U·X·L
A part of Gale, Cengage Learning

GALE
CENGAGE Learning·

Detroit • New York • San Francisco • New Haven, Conn • Waterville, Maine • London

GALE
CENGAGE Learning·

Middle East Conflict: Primary Sources, 2nd Edition
Terri Schell

Project Editor: Jennifer Stock

Rights Acquisition and Management: Christine Myaskvoksy

Composition: Evi Abou-El-Seoud

Manufacturing: Wendy Blurton

Imaging: John Watkins

Product Design: Kristine Julien

For product information and technology assistance, contact us at
Gale Customer Support, 1-800-877-4253.
For permission to use material from this text or product, submit all requests online at **www.cengage.com/permissions.**
Further permissions questions can be emailed to
permissionrequest@cengage.com

Cover photographs reproduced by permission of Hannibal Hanschkeepa/Corbis (protestors in Tahrir Square in Cairo, Egypt, in February 2011) and Reuters/Gary Hershorn/Getty Images (Bill Clinton watches as Yitzhak Rabin and Yasser Arafat shake hands after signing the Oslo Accords). Cover art reproduced by permission of Shutterstock.com (border image and arabic classical ornament).

While every effort has been made to ensure the reliability of the information presented in this publication, Gale, a part of Cengage Learning, does not guarantee the accuracy of the data contained herein. Gale accepts no payment for listing; and inclusion in the publication of any organization, agency, institution, publication, service, or individual does not imply endorsement of the editors or publisher. Errors brought to the attention of the publisher and verified to the satisfaction of the publisher will be corrected in future editions.

Library of Congress Cataloging-in-Publication Data

Middle East conflict reference library / [Jennifer Stock, project editor]. -- 2nd ed.
    v. cm.
    "U-X-L Reference Library".
    Includes bibliographical references and index.
    Contents: 1. Almanac / Sonia Benson -- 2. Biographies / Carol Brennan -- 3. Primary sources / Terri Schell.
    ISBN 978-1-4144-8607-9 (set) -- ISBN 978-1-4144-8608-6 (almanac) -- ISBN 978-1-4144-8609-3 (biographies) -- ISBN 978-1-4144-8610-9 (primary sources)
    1. Arab-Israeli conflict--Sources--Juvenile literature. 2. Arab-Israeli conflict--Juvenile literature. 3. Middle East--History--Juvenile literature. I. Stock, Jennifer York, 1974- II. Benson, Sonia. Almanac. III. Brennan, Carol, 1966- Biographies. IV. Schell, Terri, 1968- Primary sources.
    DS119.7.M4713 2012
    956.04--dc23   2011050994

Gale
27500 Drake Rd.
Farmington Hills, MI, 48331-3535

ISBN-13: 978-1-4144-8607-9 (set)	ISBN-10: 1-4144-8607-3 (set)
ISBN-13: 978-1-4144-8608-6 (Almanac)	ISBN-10: 1-4144-8608-1 (Almanac)
ISBN-13: 978-1-4144-8609-3 (Biographies)	ISBN-10: 1-4144-8609-X (Biographies)
ISBN-13: 978-1-4144-8610-9 (Primary Sources)	ISBN-10: 1-4144-8610-3 (Primary Sources)
ISBN-13: 978-1-4144-8612-3 (Cumulative Index)	ISBN-10: 1-4144-8612-X (Cumulative Index)

This title is also available as an e-book.
ISBN-13: 978-1-4144-9087-8 ISBN-10: 1-4144-9087-9
Contact your Gale, a part of Cengage Learning sales representative for ordering information.

Printed in China
1 2 3 4 5 6 7 16 15 14 13 12

Table of Contents

Reader's Guide

From the early twentieth century to present times, no region in the world has been so badly torn by conflict as the Middle East and North Africa. What is most striking about the many conflicts that have occurred in the Middle East is their complexity. For many years differences over religion, cultural identity, and political philosophy have combined with tribal and ethnic biases to fan the flames of conflict. Western imperialism and influence, as well as the struggle between modernization and traditionalism, have also played important roles in Middle East conflict. Untangling these numerous and overlapping elements presents a challenge to even the most experienced scholars and diplomats.

Even the term "Middle East" is somewhat complicated. Because the region is not strictly defined by geography, culture, or language, its definition has never been precise. The term was originally coined by Europeans (for whom Asia lies to the east). In the nineteenth century Europeans used the term "Near East" to distinguish areas of western Asia that were closer to Europe than the "Far East," the area that includes Southeast Asia, China, Japan, and Korea. In the twentieth century, the newer term "Middle East" came to replace "Near East," denoting the same basic area of Western Asia.

The nations that are most often included as part of the Middle East in the twenty-first century are: Saudi Arabia, Yemen, Oman, Qatar, Kuwait, Bahrain, the United Arab Emirates, Israel, the Palestinian territories, Jordan, Lebanon, Syria, Iraq, and Iran. Turkey, which is located in western Asia and also in Europe, is considered part of the Middle East due to its location and its many cultural and historical connections to the region. Egypt, although geographically part of North Africa, is also considered a Middle Eastern nation. Other North African states, notably Libya, Algeria, Tunisia, Morocco, and sometimes Sudan, are included as part of the Middle East by many authorities.

To understand the conflicts that have shaped the Middle East, one must keep in mind a variety of important forces that have shaped the region. The oldest and most enduring force is that of religion. The Middle East is home to three of the world's great monotheistic (belief in one god) religions—Judaism, Christianity, and Islam. Each of these religions has deep roots in the Middle East and places great importance on religious shrines and temples that continue to exist in the region, especially in the fiercely contested city of Jerusalem, in present-day Israel. Religious differences, both those between the religions and those that arise among sects (groups) within the same religion, such as followers of the Sunni and Shiite branches of Islam, continue to play an important role in the Middle East.

Other sources of conflict are based in the Middle East's long political history. The region's ancient cultures were shaped and influenced by the rule of the Islamic empires, whose great caliphs were the spiritual, political, and military leaders of the world's Muslims from the seventh to the thirteenth century, and then by the Ottoman Empire, whose sultans ruled over an area encompassing most of the Middle East and North Africa and a large part of southeastern Europe for six hundred years, from 1299 to 1923. After the relatively stable rule of these great Muslim empires, many Middle East countries came under the rule of Western governments in the early twentieth century. Foreigners divided the Middle East into separate countries without regard to the cultures and politics of the inhabitants. The internal politics of the new nations often arose in opposition to foreign rule. After gaining independence from Western rule, many of the countries of the Middle East fell under the power of authoritarian leaders with powerful security forces.

In addition to the enduring influence of religion and Western power, other hostilities have contributed to conflict in the Middle East. Ethnic differences have often resulted in wars among groups such as the Arabs, Persians, and Turks, to name a few. Armenians and Kurds (a non-Arab ethnic group) struggled to establish self-rule over their own territories. The Armenians have been successful, but the Kurds remain the largest ethnic group in the world without a country of their own.

The flashpoint for much of the conflict in the Middle East has been the area of present-day Israel and the Palestinian territories. This region, known historically as Palestine, was home to the ancient Jewish kingdom.

The Jews were expelled from Palestine as other ancient empires took control of the region, especially the Romans. As the centuries passed they faced anti-Semitism (prejudice against Jews) throughout the world. Then, in the nineteenth century, the Zionist movement arose calling for the creation of an independent Jewish state in Palestine. By this time Palestine had been home to Arabs for hundreds of years, and both groups pressed their claim to this land. The Jews were better organized, both politically and militarily, and in 1948 they declared the creation of the state of Israel. In the mid–twentieth century, Arabs fought against the Jewish state of Israel in a series of Arab-Israeli Wars. Arab Palestinians continue to claim the land that they believe was stolen from them, and they have sought various means—ranging from terrorism to political negotiation—to express their political will.

One of the driving forces of the conflicts in the Middle East since the mid–twentieth century has been oil. Oil has dramatically increased the wealth of those countries that produce it—especially Iran, Iraq, Kuwait, and Saudi Arabia—but it has not brought those countries peace, democracy, or political stability. In each of these countries, oil wealth has been controlled by a select few who hold power in the government. Foreign powers have worked aggressively to ensure that the oil-producing countries behave in ways that do not threaten foreign access to oil. Tensions created between various parties vying for control of oil in these countries causes ongoing conflict.

In 2011, the nature of Middle East conflict took a sudden, unexpected, and far-reaching turn when a series of prodemocracy uprisings rapidly spread throughout countries of the Middle East and North Africa that had long been suppressed by authoritarian rulers. Through their courageous efforts, the people of several Middle Eastern countries have overthrown their authoritarian leaders and worked create democratic governments. The place in history that this powerful prodemocracy movement, known as the Arab Spring, will take may be better understood in future times, but it has provided enormous insight into the causes and consequences of Middle East conflicts in modern times.

Coverage and features

Middle East Conflict: Primary Sources, 2nd Edition presents twenty-nine full or excerpted written works, poems, proclamations, or other documents relating to conflict in the Middle East and North Africa, divided into eight thematically organized chapters. Among the historic documents included are the Peel Commission Report of 1937, which recommended the division of Palestine into Arab and Jewish states; the 1948 declaration establishing the nation of Israel; and the 1968 Palestinian National Charter, which stated the goals of the Palestinian people. The volume also features personal accounts and artistic works, including an account by journalist Terry Anderson describing his time as a hostage in Lebanon and excerpts from the graphic novels *Palestine* and *Persepolis*. Also included are documents relating to the Arab Spring uprisings. More than eighty photographs and illustrations, a timeline, sources for further reading, and an index supplement the volume.

Middle East Conflict Reference Library, 2nd Edition

Middle East Conflict: Almanac, 2nd Edition examines the historical events that have contributed to conflicts in the in the Middle East and North Africa and traces developments to the present day. The volume's sixteen chapters cover the ancient Middle East, the rise and fall of the Ottoman Empire, the creation of Israel, the Palestinian Authority, the rise of Hezbollah in Lebanon, the Gulf Wars, terrorism, the Arab Spring uprisings, and more. Each chapter features informative sidebar boxes highlighting glossary terms and issues discussed in the text. Also included are more than one hundred photographs and illustrations, a timeline, a glossary, a list of research and activity ideas, sources for further reading, and an index providing easy access to subjects discussed throughout the volume.

Middle East Conflict: Biographies, 2nd Edition profiles thirty-five of the most influential figures from throughout the Middle East and North Africa. The volume profiles kings, presidents, and other political leaders, as well as activists and militants. Included are Iranian president Mahmoud Ahmadinejad, Lebanese politician Pierre Gemayel, Jewish author and activist Theodor Herzl, Libyan leader Mu'ammar al-Qaddaffi, Israeli prime minister Benjamin Netanyahu, and Egyptian president Anwar Sadat. Also included are prominent female leaders Golda Meir and Tzipporah Livni of Israel and Palestinian activist Hanan Ashrawi. The volume includes more than ninety photographs and illustrations, a timeline, sources for further reading, and an index.

A cumulative index of all three volumes in *Middle East Conflict Reference Library, 2nd Edition* is also available.

Acknowledgements

The editors would like to thank the advisor for *Middle East Conflict Reference Library, 2nd Edition*, Michael R. Fischbach, PhD. Dr. Fischbach is a Professor of History at Randolph-Macon College, in Ashland, Virginia. He specializes in the history of the modern Middle East, especially Palestine, Israel, Jordan, and the Arab-Israeli conflict.

The editors also would like to acknowledge Tom and Sara Pendergast, authors of the first edition of *Middle East Conflict Reference Library*.

Comments and suggestions

We welcome your comments on *Middle East Conflict: Primary Sources, 2nd Edition* and suggestions for other topics to consider. Please write: Editors, *Middle East Conflict: Primary Sources, 2nd Edition*, Gale Cengage Learning, 27500 Drake Road, Farmington Hills, Michigan 48331-3535; call toll free: 1-800-877-4253; fax to 248-699-8097; or send e-mail via http://www.gale.cengage.com.

Timeline of Events

7000 BCE: The first-known human civilizations begin to form in Mesopotamia, the site of present-day Iraq and parts of Syria, Turkey, and Iran.

2700 BCE: Egyptian society has developed into a sophisticated civilization.

c. 1030 BCE: Israelites, descendants of the Hebrew patriarch Abraham and ancestors of the Jews, take control of Canaan and call their kingdom Eretz Yisrael.

970–931 BCE: The First Temple of Solomon, which will become the center of the Jewish faith, is built in Jerusalem.

587–518 BCE: The First Temple of Solomon is destroyed by Babylonians and a second temple is built on the site.

146 BCE–476 CE: Most of the Mediterranean region comes under the control of the Roman Empire.

66–73 CE: In the Great Revolt, the Jews rise up against Roman rule; the Romans, in return, destroy the Second Temple.

c. 312: Constantine I, emperor of the Eastern Roman (later Byzantine) Empire, embraces Christianity and proclaims it the official religion of the empire.

632: The Muslim prophet Muhammad dies.

635–750: Muslims create the caliphate, the entire community of Muslims under the leadership of the caliph. The Islamic Empire spreads to Damascus, Syria, Mesopotamia, Palestine, and Egypt, and then on to North Africa, across Persia toward India and China, and westward beyond present-day Turkey, toward Italy, and Spain.

750–1050: The Islamic empire experiences a golden age in the arts and sciences.

1095–1291: The Crusades begin when the pope urges thousands of Roman Catholic men to join military campaigns to take control of the Holy Land from Muslims.

1204: The crusaders conquer the Christian Byzantine capital city of Constantinople, sharpening divisions between the Eastern Orthodox Church and the Roman Catholic Church.

1243: Mongol armies led by Genghis Khan conquer much of central Asia and the Middle East, including Anatolia.

1299: Turkish leader Osman I begins to conquer new territories around Anatolia, establishing the Ottoman Empire.

1453: Constantinople is conquered by the Ottoman Empire, which has grown to include the Balkan Peninsula, as well as Albania, Greece, and Hungary.

1500s: Under Ottoman sultans Selim I and his son Süleyman I, the Ottoman Empire attains worldwide supremacy, expanding from its base in Anatolia and Europe to include Syria, Egypt, and the western Arabian Peninsula, as well as North Africa.

1744: Wahhabi religious leader Muhammad ibn Abd al-Wahhab allies with Arab leader Mohammad ibn Saud and together they take power in the southern Arabian Peninsula. Though eventually forced to retreat by the Ottomans, Ibn Saud and his family maintain control in the desert regions of Arabia.

1768–1774: The Russo-Ottoman War results in Russia gaining control of the Crimea and other Ottoman territory.

1785: The Qahar dynasty begins in Iran.

1798–1801: The French invade and occupy Egypt.

1805–1848: Reign of Muhammad Ali in Egypt.

1839: A series of reforms known as Tanzimat, based mainly on the European style of government, are instituted in the Ottoman Empire.

1858–1860: Civil unrest in Lebanon and Syria leads to European intervention.

1869: Construction is completed on Egypt's Suez Canal, linking the Mediterranean Sea to the Red Sea.

1878: European powers convene the Congress of Berlin to settle territorial questions of the weakening Ottoman Empire; they grant independence to several Balkan countries, humiliating the fiercely proud Ottomans.

1881: France declares Tunisia a protectorate.

1881–1884: A vicious series of pogroms directed against Jews sweeps through Russia.

1882–1922: Great Britain invades and occupies Egypt.

1896: Theodor Herzl publishes *The Jewish State*, drawing attention to the ideas of Zionism, and promoting the immigration of Jews to Palestine. By the twentieth century, thousands of Jews had moved to the region.

1908–1909: The Young Turks overthrow the Ottoman sultan, announcing their intentions to separate government from religion and to make the Turkish language the official language of the empire.

1912: Italy begins its rule of Libya. Most of Morocco becomes a French protectorate, while a small part goes to Spain.

1914–1918: World War I; the Ottoman Empire joins the Central Powers of Germany and Austria-Hungary against the Allies: Great Britain, France, Russia, and the United States. Defeated, the Ottoman Empire collapses at war's end.

1914: At the outbreak of World War I, Great Britain declares Egypt to be a protectorate of the British Empire.

1915–1923: The Turkish leaders of the Ottoman Empire order the mass killing and displacement of the Armenians living in the empire; between 600,000 and 1.5 million Armenians die.

1916–1918: Arabs revolt against the Ottomans under an agreement with the British, hoping for Arab independence after World War I.

1917: The Balfour Declaration is approved by the British war cabinet, promising British support for the Zionist cause in Palestine.

1919: Iran becomes a British protectorate when it signs the Anglo-Persian Agreement of 1919.

1919–1922: Under several international treaties, a large portion of former Ottoman lands are divided up into mandates, to be administered by European nations under the supervision of the League of Nations. France receives control of Syria and Lebanon, and Great Britain receives control of Palestine and Iraq.

1922: Great Britain declares Egypt a constitutional monarchy.

1923: The independent Republic of Turkey is recognized by the international community.

1925: Reza Khan establishes the Pahlavi dynasty in Iran.

1928: The Muslim Brotherhood, an Islamist group that seeks to promote Islam and rid Egypt of foreign influence, is established in Egypt.

1931: Zionists in the mandate of Palestine form one of the first contemporary terrorist groups in the Middle East: Irgun Zvai Leumi, better known as Irgun, which attacks Arab civilians and British authorities.

1932: Iraq gains independence from Great Britain.

1932: Ibn Saud unites large portions of the Arabian Peninsula under his rule and calls his kingdom Saudi Arabia.

1935: The German government under the Nazis passes the Nuremberg Laws, which take away the civil rights of German Jews.

1935–1939: Thousands of Zionist immigrants pour into Palestine.

1936–1939: The Arab Revolt in Palestine is organized to protest British rule and Jewish immigration.

1937: **The Palestine Royal (Peel) Commission Report** makes the first recommendation for two separate independent nations on Palestinian land, one for Jews and one for Arabs.

1938: Vast quantities of oil are discovered in Saudi Arabia.

1939–1945: During World War II, the German Nazis initiate the systematic murder of Jewish people and several other groups, an act of genocide that will become known as the Holocaust.

1942: With the horrors of the Holocaust being revealed, **The Biltmore Program**, a statement created by American Zionists, pressures world powers to support an independent Jewish state in Palestine.

1943: As France withdraws from Lebanon, it frames the National Pact, a sectarian system of government that calls for a ratio of six Christians to every five Muslims in the Lebanese government.

1944: **The Alexandria Protocol** creates the framework for the Arab League, a regional political alliance of Arab nations.

1945: The leaders of Egypt, Iraq, Lebanon, Transjordan, Saudi Arabia, Syria, and Yemen join to form the Arab League to promote cooperation within the Arab world. In the initial agreement, members pledge to preserve the rights of the Palestinians.

1946: France withdraws from its mandatory rule of Syria after decades of bitter resistance to its rule. With France gone, Syria faces many internal divisions.

1947: The United Nations Special Committee on Palestine (UNSCOP) calls for the partition of Palestine into two separate states, a Jewish one and an Arab one. The Palestinians reject this plan.

1947: The Ba'ath Party is founded with the objective of bringing about a rebirth of Arab power. It is popular in Syria and Iraq.

1947–1948: Civil war breaks out between the Palestinians and the Jews in the British Mandate of Palestine.

May 14, 1948: The **Declaration of the Establishment of the State of Israel** creates an independent Jewish state on Palestinian land.

May 15, 1948: Following the **Statement Issued by the Governments of the Arab League States on the Occasion of the Entry of the Arab Armies in Palestine,** the armies of Egypt, Iraq, Lebanon, Syria, and Transjordan invade the former mandate of Palestine in an attempt to stop the creation of the new state of Israel, beginning the 1948 Arab-Israeli War.

August 1948: The 1948 Arab-Israeli War concludes with the defeat of the Arab forces. Israeli forces significantly expand their territory and ensure Israeli independence. An estimated 750,000 Palestinians are either forced to, or willingly, leave their homes and become refugees. Arabs refer to the events of 1948 as *al-Nakba* ("the catastrophe").

1952–1953: The Free Officers launch a military coup that overthrows the Egyptian monarchy.

1954: The United States helps Iranians stage a coup to return the ousted Mohammad Reza Pahlavi to power as shah of Iran.

1954–1962: In the eight-year Algerian war for independence from France nearly one million people are killed. Algeria declares its independence in 1962.

1956: Gamal Abdel Nasser becomes president of Egypt; he soon announces the nationalization of the Suez Canal, resulting in the Suez Crisis, a brief armed conflict with Great Britain, France, and Israel.

1956: France grants Tunisia independence.

1958–1961: In an attempt at creating a pan-Arab state, Gamal Abdel Nasser organizes the United Arab Republic (UAR), initially a political union between Egypt and Syria. Problems arise immediately, and a military coup in 1961 restores Syria's independence and disbands the UAR.

1959: Fatah, a Palestinian militant group dedicated to the establishment of an independent Palestinian state, is founded.

1959: Egyptian president Nasser makes his **Speech to the Officers' Club** in which he stresses the need for a united group of Arab countries and for the military of these countries to pursue common goals.

1964: The Palestine Liberation Organization (PLO) is founded.

1967: The 1967 Arab-Israeli War begins when Israel, fearing an attack from the Arab countries, attacks first, striking Egypt, Syria, and Jordan decisively. Israel nearly triples its size by taking the Golan Heights, the West Bank, the Gaza Strip, and the Sinai Peninsula. Israel establishes military rule in the captured regions, which come to be known as the occupied territories.

November 22, 1967: UN Security Council Resolution 242 outlines the principles that will guide Arab-Israeli negotiations after the war.

1968: The Palestine Liberation Organization revises **The Palestinian National Charter** to declare the purpose of warfare against Israel and to solidify the PLO's right to represent the Palestinian people.

1968: The Popular Front for the Liberation of Palestine (PFLP) hijacks an Israeli jetliner and diverts it to Algeria. The international attention gained by the hijacking encourages the PFLP and similar groups to continue to stage terrorist acts.

1969: Yasser Arafat becomes the chairman of the PLO, which has grown increasingly radical and violent. Palestinian militants launch constant guerrilla attacks against Israel in order to retake Palestinian land and return refugees to their homes.

1969: A group of military officers headed by Colonel Mu'ammar al-Qaddafi overthrows the Libyan king; al-Qaddafi establishes the Libyan Arab Republic and becomes its leader.

1970: The king of Jordan expels the PLO from his country in a bloody event known as Black September, in which three thousand Palestinians are killed. PLO leadership, forced out of the country, relocates to southern Lebanon.

1970: Syria's Ba'athist Party places Hafez Assad in power.

1972: At the Olympic Games in Munich, Germany, eight armed members of a Palestinian group calling itself Black September storm the apartments of the Israeli Olympic team, killing two team members and taking nine others hostage. During a rescue attempt, Black September murders the hostages.

1973: The brief 1973 Arab-Israeli War is launched by Egypt and Syria-led Arab forces against Israel. Arabs experience some initial success, although Israel successfully defends itself.

1973: Arabs and Arab members of the Organization of Petroleum Exporting Countries (OPEC), furious at U.S. interference in the 1973 Arab-Israel War, organize an embargo of oil shipments to the United States, effectively cutting off the majority of the U.S. oil supply.

1975: The fifteen-year Civil War in Lebanon begins.

1975: The Iraqi government tries to evict the Kurds from the country, forcing residents out of eight hundred Kurdish villages near the Iran-Iraq border.

1976: The Arab League grants Syria permission to station forty thousand Syrian troops in Lebanon as part of a peace agreement.

November 1977: Accepting the invitation of Israeli prime minister Menachem Begin, Egyptian president Anwar Sadat becomes the first Arab leader to visit Jerusalem since the creation of Israel. Both give **Speeches to the Knesset**, discussing their plans for peace between the two countries.

1978: The Camp David Accords are signed by Egyptian President Anwar Sadat and Israeli Prime Minister Menachem Begin at Camp David, setting the framework for Egypt to become the first Arab nation to recognize Israel as a state. Sadat and Begin are awarded Nobel Peace Prizes for their contributions to peace in the Middle East.

1978: Fatah members hijack an Israeli tourist bus, resulting in the deaths of thirty-eight Israelis. Outraged Israeli leaders launch Operation Litani, sending more than twenty thousand troops into southern Lebanon in an attempt to destroy the PLO.

1979: The Iranian Revolution (also known as the Islamic Revolution) transforms Iran from a secular (nonreligious) country into an Islamic country, in which the social, political, and economic institutions of the country are based on Islamic holy law.

1979: Saddam Hussein becomes president of Iraq and begins immediately to use his power to destroy opponents and establish an authoritarian government.

1979: The U.S. embassy in Iran is overtaken by a group of Iranian students. Fifty-two Americans are held hostage for 444 days.

1980s: Sumaya Farhat-Naser begins her search for peaceful solutions to the Palestinian-Israeli conflict, which she documents in *Daughter of the Olive Trees*.

June 2, 1980: A bomb planted by Era Rapaport destroys the legs of Bassam Shaka, the mayor of Nablus, a town about thirty miles north of Jerusalem. Rapaport would serve prison time for his attack on the Palestinian and would write about his views on Israeli-Palestinian relations in *Letters from Tel Mond Prison: An Israeli Settler Defends His Act of Terror*.

September 1980: Iraq invades Iran, beginning the brutal, eight-year Iran-Iraq War.

1981: Egyptian president Anwar Sadat is assassinated; the militant group Egyptian Islamic Jihad is responsible.

1982: Israel launches an attack on Lebanon called Operation Peace for Galilee to push the PLO in southern Lebanon back from the Israeli borders. With international intervention, the fighting is stopped; the PLO leadership moves to Tunisia.

1982: The Phalangists militia enter the Sabra and Shatila Palestinian refugee camps outside Beirut and massacre approximately one thousand Palestinian men, women, and children. During the massacre, Israeli troops surround the camps, doing little to stop the massacre.

1982: Syrian president Hafez Assad orders a brutal attack on the city of Hama, where the Muslim Brotherhood is headquartered. His forces kill more than ten thousand innocent inhabitants of the city.

1983: Small, militant Shiite Lebanese groups protesting the 1982 Israeli invasion of Lebanon launch a deadly series of suicide bombings: the first at the Beirut airport, which kills 241 U.S. Marines; a second that kills 58 French paratroopers; and a third that strikes an Israeli headquarters in southern Lebanon, killing 29 Israeli troops.

1984: Meir Kahane's Kach Party wins seats in the Israeli Knesset, but his controversial politics trouble many Israelis, including his book *They Must Go*, which demands that all Palestinians must be deported from any lands that Israelis live on.

1985: Lebanese Shiite militant groups merge into a new Islamist group called Hezbollah. Hezbollah's immediate purpose is to drive Israeli forces, and all Western influences, out of Lebanon.

March 1985: Journalist Terry Anderson is kidnapped by Hezbollah militants in Lebanon. His seven years as a hostage are documented in *Den of Lions*.

1987: The Palestinians in the West Bank and the Gaza Strip launch the First Intifada, an extended protest against Israeli occupation.

1988: Yasser Arafat promises to recognize Israel and to renounce terrorism.

1988: Iraq launches Anfal, an operation designed to destroy the Kurdish population in Iraq that includes bombing Kurdish villages, destroying Kurdish homes and farmlands, and forcing tens of thousands of Kurds to flee. One of the Anfal attacks is on the Kurdish town of Halabja, and it makes use of poison gases, such as sarin and mustard gas, killing and wounding thousands of Kurds.

1988: A terrorist bomb blows up Pan Am Flight 103 from London to New York over Lockerbie, Scotland, killing 243 passengers and 16 crew members. Libya's leader al-Qaddafi is suspected of being responsible.

1988: Soha Bechara is arrested by the South Lebanon Army for her activities against Israeli forces. She would document these actions and her time in prison in her book *Resistance: My Life for Lebanon*.

1989: Osama bin Laden establishes al-Qaeda headquarters in Sudan and begins to train warriors to carry out terrorist acts.

1989: Islamic Jihad, a militant Palestinian group, claims responsibility for the first known suicide bombing of the Israeli-Palestinian conflict.

1989: Lebanese lawmakers convene in Taif, Saudi Arabia, to restructure Lebanon's sectarian government, allowing for better representation for Muslims.

1990: The Lebanese Civil War ends, but Syria's forces remain in Lebanon. The Lebanese government grants Syria control of Lebanon's internal affairs and management of its foreign policy and security issues.

1990: North Yemen and South Yemen unify, becoming the Republic of Yemen.

1990–1991: The Persian Gulf War begins with Iraq's invasion of Kuwait. A U.S.-led coalition of more than thirty countries challenges and defeats Iraq but leaves Saddam Hussein in power. International sanctions on trade with Iraq cause great suffering in the country in the decade after the war.

1992: Lebanon holds its first parliamentary elections since 1972 and elects Rafiq Hariri as prime minister.

1993: The Oslo Accords, a set of agreements between the Israelis and the Palestinians, outlines a process in which Palestinians can achieve self-rule under an elected body called the Palestinian Authority (PA).

1993: Four radical Islamist conspirators explode a powerful bomb in the underground parking garage in one of the towers of New York City's World Trade Center, killing six and injuring more than one thousand people.

1993: Palestinian leader Yasser Arafat and Israeli prime minister Yitzhak Rabin shake hands on the lawn of the White House in Washington, D.C., in celebration of the **Israeli-PLO Declaration of Principles** signed at the Oslo Accords, which provides a framework for further peace negotiations and creates the Palestinian Authority, the main governing body of the Palestinian people.

1993: Joe Sacco publishes his first comic book about his time in the Middle East and his experiences with the Israeli-Palestinian conflicts. This and other comics would be grouped in a graphic novel called *Palestine*.

1998: Osama bin Laden and the World Islamic Front issue their **"Jihad Against Jews and Crusaders"**, which declares that it is the duty of all Muslims to kill Americans, both military and civilian.

2000: Yasser Arafat and Israeli Prime Minister Ehud Barak meet at Camp David to prepare for a Palestinian state, but the negotiations fail.

2000: The Second Intifada begins in the occupied Palestinian territories, with more violence than the first.

2000: The eighteen-year Israeli occupation of Lebanon ends with the withdrawal of Israeli soldiers, a huge victory for Hezbollah.

2000: Marjane Satrapi publishes the graphic novel *Perseoplis*, about her experiences as a young girl growing up during the Iranian Revolution.

2001: Following the death of president Hafez Assad in 2000, a period called Damascus Spring begins in Syria. Assad's son, Bashar Assad, promises reforms and eventual democracy, but quickly breaks his word and crushes democratic movements.

September 11, 2001: Al-Qaeda terrorists use passenger jets to destroy the World Trade Center towers in New York and damage the Pentagon building in Virginia. Nearly three thousand people are killed in the attack. The United States declares a war on terror.

2002: Israel launches Operation Defensive Shield, a military offensive against several West Bank cities. Yasser Arafat's compound in Ramallah is surrounded and the city is devastated.

2002: The United States claims that Iraq is secretly manufacturing weapons of mass destruction.

March 2003: A U.S.-led coalition makes air strikes on Baghdad, Iraq, starting the Iraq War.

2003: *Unfortunately, It Was Paradise*, a collection of poems by Palestinian poet **Mahmoud Darwish**, is published.

2003: Manal M. Omar joins the Women to Women International humanitarian mission in Iraq. She will later write about her experiences there in **Barefoot in Baghdad: A Story of Identity—My Own—and What It Means To Be a Woman in Chaos.**

2004: Photos are released to the public showing Iraqi prisoners being beaten and sexually humiliated by U.S. soldiers at Abu Ghraib, a prison in Baghdad where the United States is holding its detainees.

2004: Yasser Arafat dies.

2004: Israeli prime minister Ariel Sharon announces **Israel's Revised Disengagement Plan**, under which Israel agrees to withdraw Jewish settlements from the West Bank and the and parts of the Gaza Strip.

2005: Fatah leader Mahmoud Abbas is elected president of the Palestinian Authority.

2005: Israeli Prime Minister Ariel Sharon orders the evacuation all of Israel's twenty-one settlements in the Gaza Strip and four in the West Bank.

2005: Former Lebanese prime minister Rafiq Hariri is assassinated in Beirut. Blaming Syria for the murder, an estimated one million Lebanese people demonstrate against Syria's oppressive presence in their country. Syria is forced to end its twenty-nine-year occupation of Lebanon.

2005: Ghada Shahbandar, Bosayna Kamel, Engi Haddad, and other Egyptian activists form Shayfeen.com (also known as Shafeencom or Shayfeen) to monitor rights abuses Egypt's elections. Shahbander will write about the organization's creation in **"Taking to the Street."**

October 15, 2005: The ***Damascus Declaration for Democratic National Change*** is issued as a formal protest to government repression in Syria.

October 20, 2005: Iranian activist and lawyer Shrin Ebadi delivers her **"The Contribution of Islam to a Global Ethic"** speech at the University of Tübingen, Germany.

2006: The Palestinian Authority holds its first national legislative elections to choose members of the Palestinian Legislative Council. Hamas, a militant Islamist group wins the majority of the seats in the council.

2006: War erupts between Israel and Hezbollah in Lebanon. Thirty-three days of fighting devastate Lebanon but the war also harms Israel.

2006: A group of al-Qaeda-in-Iraq and Sunni extremists bomb the Askariya Mosque in Samarra, Iraq. Outraged Shiites blamed the Sunnis and form militias that sweep into Sunni neighborhoods, beating and killing Sunnis. Sunnis bomb and attack Shiites in revenge. An estimated one thousand deaths ensue, and hundreds of thousands of Iraqis flee their homes as the sectarian violence escalates.

December 2006: Iraqi President Saddam Hussein is executed for crimes against humanity.

2007: Fighting breaks out between Hamas and Fatah. After a violent split, Hamas serves as the sole ruler of the Gaza Strip and Fatah rules in the West Bank for the next four years. Under Hamas, the Gaza Strip continues to be a site for launching rockets into Israel.

2007: Israel labels the Gaza Strip a hostile entity and establishes a blockade of the territory that causes great suffering among the Gaza Strip's inhabitants.

2007: Mahmoud Abbas declares a state of emergency in the Palestinian Authority and creates a new government with moderate economist Salam Fayyad as prime minister.

2008: In response to attacks from Hamas, Israel launches Operation Cast Lead, a strike against the Gaza Strip that leaves thirteen hundred people dead and causes massive destruction.

2008: Hezbollah achieves a majority in the Lebanese government.

2009: In large numbers, Iranians protest what appear to be rigged elections, demanding the resignation of the president and democratic reforms. A government crackdown ends the demonstrations that come to be known as the Green Movement.

2009: The UN Human Rights Council releases the ***Report of the United Nations Fact Finding Mission on the Gaza Conflict*** (***The Goldstone Report***) after investigating possible human rights abuses during the Gaza War (2008–9).

June 4, 2009: U.S. president Barack Obama delivers his **Cairo Speech**, addressing the strained relations between the United States and many nations in the Middle East.

August 19, 2010: U.S. president Barack Obama declares the U.S. combat mission in Iraq over. All troops are scheduled to leave Iraq by the end of 2011.

December 17, 2010: In Sidi Bouzid, Tunisia, Mohamed Bouazizi sets himself on fire to protest poor treatment at the hands of officials, igniting a revolt against the authoritarian government in Tunisia. The revolt quickly leads to the Arab Spring, a series of prodemocracy uprisings throughout the Middle East.

2011: Fatah and Hamas reach a reconciliation agreement under which they agree to form a coalition government for the Palestinian Authority and then hold new elections in the Gaza Strip and the West Bank.

2011: The United Nation's Special Tribunal for Lebanon officially indicts four Hezbollah members in the assassination of Rafik Hariri; Hezbollah will not allow them to be arrested.

January 25, 2011: Tens of thousands of protesters position themselves in Tahrir Square in Cairo, Egypt, denouncing police brutality and demanding an end to president Hosni Mubarak's rule.

April 2011: Richard Goldstone publishes **"Reconsidering the Goldstone Report on Israel and War Crimes,"** publicly reversing his previous position that Israel intentionally targeted civilians during the Gaza War.

May 2, 2011: Osama bin Laden is killed by a U.S. Navy SEAL team in Pakistan.

June 2011: Journalist Asne Seierstad publishes **"Out of the Shadow of Fear,"** an article about the Arab Spring uprising in Syria.

October 20, 2011: Mu'ammar al-Qaddafi is killed by rebel forces while fleeing. The Libyan civil war is over.

March 18, 2011: Syrian security forces arrest, beat, and torture fifteen teenagers for painting graffiti on a school wall in Dara'a, setting off a protest that soon spreads to other cities. Within weeks, the Syrian government launches a violent crackdown.

Words to Know

Alawis: Also spelled Alawites; followers of a sect of Shia Islam that live in Syria. Their belief system and practices vary from Shiites in several ways, particularly in the belief that Ali, the son-in-law of the prophet Muhammad, was the human form of Allah (the Arabic word for God).

aliyah: The immigration of Jews to the historic Eretz Yisrael (Land of Israel).

anti-Semitism: Prejudice against Jews.

Arab League: A regional political alliance of Arab nations formed in 1945 to promote political, military, and economic cooperation within the Arab world.

Arabs: People of the Middle East and North Africa who speak the Arabic language or who live in countries in which Arabic is the dominant language.

Arab Spring: A series of prodemocracy uprisings in the Middle East and North Africa.

authoritarianism: A type of leadership in which power is consolidated under one strong leader, or a small group of elite leaders, who do not answer to the will of the people.

ayatollah: A high-ranking Shiite religious leader.

Ba'ath Party: A secular (nonreligious) political party founded in the 1940s with the goal of uniting the Arab world and creating one powerful Arab state.

Byzantine Empire: The eastern part of the Roman Empire, which thrived for one thousand years after the collapse of Rome in 476.

C

caliph: The spiritual, political, and military leader of the world's Muslims from the death of Muhammad in 632 until the caliphate was abolished in 1924.

caliphate: The entire community of Muslims under the leadership of the caliph.

chemical weapons: Toxic chemical substances used during armed conflict to kill, injure, or incapacitate an enemy.

Christianity: A religion based on the teachings of Jesus Christ.

cleric: An ordained religious official.

Cold War: A period of intense political and economic rivalry between the United States and the Soviet Union that lasted from 1945 to 1991.

Communism: A system of government in which the state plans and controls the economy and a single political party holds power.

Crusades: A series of military campaigns ordered by the Roman Catholic Church between 1095 and 1291 with the main goal of taking the Holy Land from the Muslims.

crucifixion: A form of execution in which a person is nailed or bound to a cross and left to die.

D

Druze: Members of a small sect of Islam who believe that the ninth-century caliph Tariq al-Hakim was God.

dynasty: A series of rulers from the same family.

E

Eretz Yisrael: "Land of Israel" in Hebrew; the ancient kingdom of the Jews.

emir: A ruler, chief, or commander in some Islamic countries.

ethnicity: Groupings of people in a society according to their common racial, national, tribal, religious, language, or cultural backgrounds.

evangelist: A Christian follower dedicated to converting others to Christianity.

excommunication: The official exclusion of a person from membership in the church.

F

Fatah: A Palestinian militant group and political party dedicated to the establishment of an independent Palestinian state.

fatwa: A statement of religious law issued by Islamic clerics.

fedayeen: An Arabic term meaning one who sacrifices for a cause; used to describe several distinct militant groups that have formed in the Arab world at different times. Opponents of the fedayeen use the term to describe members of Arab terrorist groups.

fundamentalism: A movement stressing adherence to a strict or literal interpretation of religious principles.

G

Gaza Strip: A narrow strip of land along the eastern shore of the Mediterranean Sea, west of Israel and bordering Egypt in the southwest. The region was occupied by Israel after the 1967 Arab-Israeli War.

Geneva Conventions: A series of international agreements that establish how prisoners of war and civilians in wartime are to be treated.

genocide: The deliberate and systematic destruction of a group of people based on religion, ethnicity, or nationality.

Golan Heights: A mountainous region located on the border of Syria and Israel, northwest of the Sea of Galilee. The region was occupied by Israel after the 1967 Arab-Israeli War and annexed in 1981.

guerilla warfare: Combat tactics used by a smaller, less equipped fighting force against a more powerful foe.

H

Haganah: The underground defense force of Zionists in Palestine from 1920 to 1948. It became the basis for the Israeli army.

hajj: The annual Muslim pilgrimage to Mecca that takes place in the last month of the year, which every Muslim is expected to perform at least once during their lifetime if they are able.

Hamas: A Palestinian Islamic fundamentalist group and political party operating primarily in the West Bank and the Gaza Strip with the goal of establishing a Palestinian state and opposing the existence of Israel. It has been labeled a terrorist organization by several countries.

Hebrew: The ancient language of the Jewish people and the official language of present-day Israel.

Hejaz: A coastal region on the western Arabian Peninsula that includes the Muslim holy cities of Mecca and Medina.

heretic: Someone whose opinions or beliefs oppose official church doctrine.

heresy: Opinions or beliefs that oppose official church doctrine.

Hezbollah: A Shiite militant group and political party based in Lebanon.

Holocaust: The mass murder of European Jews and other groups by the Nazis during World War II.

Holy Land: Roughly the present-day territory of Israel, the Palestinian territories, and parts of Jordan and Lebanon. This area includes sacred sites for Jews, Christians, and Muslims.

I

insurgency: An uprising, or rebellion, against a political authority.

Intifada: The Palestinian uprising against Israeli occupation in the West Bank and the Gaza Strip.

Irgun Zvai Leumi: A militant underground group founded in 1931 that worked to secure Israeli independence by staging violent attacks on British and Arab targets. Also known simply as Irgun.

Islam: The religious faith followed by Muslims based on a belief in Allah as the sole god and in Muhammad as his prophet.

Islamism: A fundamentalist movement characterized by the belief that Islam should provide the basis for political, social, and cultural life in Muslim nations.

jihad: An armed struggle against unbelievers, in defense of Islam; often interpreted to mean holy war. The term also refers to the spiritual struggle of Muslims against sin.

Jews: People who practice the religion of Judaism.

Judaism: The religion of the Jewish people based on the belief in one god and the teachings the Talmud.

K

kibbutz: A Jewish communal farming settlement in Israel, where settlers share all property and work collaboratively together. Plural is kibbutzim.

Koran: Also spelled Qur'an or Quran; the holy book of Islam.

Kurds: A non-Arab ethnic group who live mainly in present-day Turkey, Iraq, and Iran.

L

League of Nations: An international organization of sovereign countries established after World War I to promote peace.

M

mandate: A commission granting one country the authority to administer the affairs of another country. Also describes the territory entrusted to foreign administration.

mandate system: The system established after World War I to administer former territories of Germany and the Ottoman Empire.

Maronites: Members of an Arabic-speaking group of Christians, living mainly in Lebanon, who are in communion (share essential doctrines) with the Roman Catholic Church.

martyr: A person who dies for his or her religion.

militia: Armed civilian military forces.

millet: A community for non-Muslims in the Ottoman Empire, organized by religious group and headed by a religious leader.

Muslim Brotherhood: An Islamic fundamentalist group organized in opposition to Western influence and in support of Islamic principles.

Muslims: People who practice the religion of Islam.

mosque: A Muslim place of worship.

N

nationalism: The belief that a people with shared ethnic, cultural, and/or religious identities have the right to form their own nation. In established nations nationalism is devotion and loyalty to the nation and its culture.

nationalization: The practice of bringing private industry under the ownership and control of the government.

North Atlantic Treaty Organization (NATO): An international organization created in 1949 for purposes of collective security.

O

occupation: The physical and political control of an area seized by a foreign military force.

occupied territories: The lands under the political and military control of Israel, especially the West Bank and the Gaza Strip.

Organization of Petroleum Exporting Countries (OPEC): An organization formed in 1960 by the world's major oil-producing nations to coordinate policies and ensure stable oil prices in world markets.

Ottoman Empire: The vast empire of the Ottoman Turks which included southwest Asia, northeast Africa, and southeast Europe, and lasted from the thirteenth century to the early twentieth century.

P

Palestine: A historical region in the Middle East on the eastern shore of the Mediterranean Sea, comprising parts of present-day Israel and Jordan.

Palestine Liberation Organization (PLO): A political and military organization formed to unite various Palestinian Arab groups with the goal of establishing an independent Palestinian state.

Palestinian Authority (PA): The recognized governing institution for Palestinians in the West Bank and the Gaza Strip, established in 1993. Also known as the Palestinian National Authority.

Palestinians: An Arab people whose ancestors lived in the historical region of Palestine and who continue to lay claim to that land.

Pan-Arabism: A movement for the unification of Arab peoples and the political alliance of Arab states.

Pan-Islamism: A movement for the unification of Muslims under a single Islamic state where Islam provides the basis for political, social, and cultural life.

pasha: A provincial governor or powerful official of the Ottoman Empire.

pilgrim: A person who travels to a sacred place for religious reasons.

pilgrimage: A journey to a sacred place for religious reasons.

pogrom: A racially-motivated riot in which mobs, usually organized and sanctioned by the state, attack a minority group, most often Jews.

R

rabbi: A Jewish scholar, teacher, and religious leader.

refugees: People who flee their country to escape violence or persecution.

right of return: The right, claimed by a dispossessed people, to return to their historic homeland.

S

sanctions: Punitive measures adopted by the international community against a nation that has violated international law, usually in the form of diplomatic, economic, or social restrictions.

sect: A social unit within a society that is defined by its distinct beliefs or customs.

sectarian government: A government that distributes political and institutional power among its various religious sects and ethnic communities on a proportional basis.

settlements: Communities established and inhabited in order to claim land.

sharia: A system of Islamic law based on the Koran and other sacred writings. Sharia attempts to create the perfect social order, based on God's will and justice, and covers a wide range of human activities, including acts of religious worship, the law of contracts and obligations, personal status law, and public law.

sharif: A nobleman and political leader chosen from among descendants of the Muslim prophet Muhammad.

sheikh: An Arab tribal leader.

Shiites: Followers of the Shia branch of Islam. Shiites believe that only direct descendants of the prophet Muhammad are qualified to lead the Islamic faith.

socialism: A system in which the government owns the means of production and controls the distribution of goods and services.

Suez Canal: A shipping canal that connects the Mediterranean Sea with the Red Sea.

suicide bombing: An attack intended to kill others and cause widespread damage, carried about by someone who does not hope to survive the attack.

sultan: A ruler of a Muslim state, especially the Ottoman Empire.

Sunnis: Followers of the Sunni branch of Islam. Sunnis believe that elected officials, regardless of their heritage, are qualified to lead the Islamic faith.

synagogue: A Jewish place of worship.

T

Taliban: An Islamic militant and political group that controlled Afghanistan from 1996 to 2001.

Talmud: The authoritative, ancient body of Jewish teachings and tradition.

Tanakh: The Jewish Bible.

Temple Mount: A contested religious site in Jerusalem. It is the holiest site in Judaism, the third holiest site in Islam, and also important to the Christian faith.

Torah: A Hebrew word meaning teaching or instruction, it literally refers to the first five books of the Jewish Bible. The term is often used to refer to the body of wisdom held in Jewish scriptures and sacred literature.

tribute: Payment from one ruler of a state to another, usually for protection or to acknowledge submission.

U

United Nations: An international organization of countries founded in 1945 to promote international peace, security, and cooperation.

W

weapons of mass destruction: Any nuclear, chemical, or biological weapons capable of killing or injuring large numbers of people.

West Bank: An area between Israel and Jordan on the west bank of the Jordan River, populated largely by Palestinians. The region was occupied by Israel after the 1967 Arab-Israeli War.

World War I: 1914–18; a global war between the Allies (Great Britain, France, and Russia, joined later by the United States) and the Central Powers (Germany, Austria-Hungary, and their allies).

World War II: 1939–45; a war in which the Allies (Great Britain, France, the Soviet Union, the United States, and China) defeated the Axis Powers (Germany, Italy, and Japan).

Zionism: An international political movement originating in the late nineteenth century that called for the creation of an independent Jewish state in Palestine.

Zionists: Supporters of an international political movement that called for the creation of an independent Jewish state in Palestine.

Text Credits

The following is a list of the copyright holders who have granted us permission to reproduce excerpts from primary source documents in *Middle East Conflict: Primary Sources, 2nd Edition*. Every effort has been made to trace copyright; if omissions have been made, please contact us.

Copyrighted excerpts reproduced from the following books:

- Anderson, Terry A. From *Den of Lions: Memoirs of Seven Years.* Crown Publishers, Inc., 1993. Copyright © 1993 by TMS Corporation. Reproduced by permission of the author.
- Bechara, Soha. From "Excerpts from Resistance," in *Resistance: My Life for Lebanon.* Edited by Gabriel Levine. Soft Skull Press, 2003. Copyright © 2003 Soha Bechara. Translation © 2003 Gabriel Levine. Reproduced by permission.
- Darwish, Mahmoud. From "On This Earth," in *Unfortunately, It Was Paradise.* Edited by Munir Akash and Carolyn Forche. University of California Press, 2003. Copyright © 2003 by The Regents of the University of California. Reproduced by permission.
- Darwish, Mahmoud. From "I Belong There," in *Unfortunately, It Was Paradise.* Edited by Munir Akash and Carolyn Forche. University of Califronia Press, 2003. Copyright © 2003 by The Regents of the University of California. Reproduced by permission.

- Darwish, Mahmoud. From "Athens Airport," in *Unfortunately, It Was Paradise*. Edited by Munir Akash and Carolyn Forche. University of California Press, 2003. Copyright © 2003 by The Regents of the University of California. Reproduced by permission.

- Darwish, Mahmoud. From "As He Walks Away," in *The Adam of Two Edens*. Edited by Munir Akash and Daniel Moore. Translated by Sargon Boulos. Syracuse University Press, 2000. Copyright © 2000 by Syracuse University Press. Reproduced by permission of the publisher and the author.

- Darwish, Mahmoud. From "I Talk Too Much," in *Unfortunately, It Was Paradise*. Edited by Munir Akash and Carolyn Forche. University of Califronia Press, 2003. Copyright © 2003 by The Regents of the University of California. Reproduced by permission.

- Farhat-Naser, Sumaya. From excerpts in *Daughter of the Olive Trees: A Palestinian Woman's Struggle for Peace*. Edited by Dorothee Wilhelm, Manuela Reimann, and Chudi Burgi. Translated by Hilary Kilpatrick. Lenos Verlag, Basel, 2003. English translation copyright © 2003 by Lenos Verlag, Basel. All rights reserved. Reproduced by permission.

- Herzl, Theodor. From *The Jewish State: An Attempt at a Modern Solution of the Jewish Question*. American Zionist Emergency Council, 1946. Reproduced by permission.

- Kahane, Meir. From *They Must Go*. Grosset & Dunlap, 1981. Copyright © 1981 by Meir Kahane. Reproduced by permission of the Literary Estate of Meir Kahane.

- Khalil, Muhammad. From *The Arab States and the Arab League: A Documentary Record, Vol II*.

- Khayats, 1962. Copyright Muhammad Khalil 1962. All rights reserved. Reproduced by permission of the author.

- From *Barefoot in Baghdad* copyright 2010 by Manal M. Omar. Used by permission of Sourcebooks.

- Reprinted with the permission of Free Press, a Division of Simon & Schuster, Inc., from *Letters from Tel Mond Prison: An Israeli Settler Defends His Act of Terror* by Era Rapaport, edited by William B. Helmreich. Copyright © 1996 by William B. Helmreich. All rights reserved.

- From *Persepolis: The Story of a Childhood* by Marjane Satrapi, translated by Mattias Ripa & Blake Ferris, translation copyright © 2003 by L'Association, Paris, France. Used by permission of Pantheon Books, a division of Random House, Inc.

Copyrighted excerpts reproduced from the following periodicals:

- Bin Laden, Osama. From *Al-Quds al-Arabia*. Reproduced by permission.
- Ebadi, Shrin. "The Contribution of Islam to a Global Ethic," *Global Ethic Foundation*, October 20, 2005. Reproduced by permission.
- *Newsweek*, June 5, 2011. Copyright © 2011 Newsweek, Inc. All rights reserved. Reprinted by permission.
- Shahbender, Ghada. "Taking to the Street." *Al Ahram Weekly* (Cairo), March 14, 2007. Reproduced by permission of the author.
- *The Washtington Post*, April 1, 2011, for "Reconsidering the Goldstone Report on Israel and War Crimes" by Richard Goldstone. Reproduced by permission of the author.

Copyrighted excerpts reproduced from the following other sources:

- *The Balfour Declaration*, November 2, 1917. Letter by Arthur James Lord Balfour to Lord Rothschild. Israel Ministry of Foreign Affairs, 1917. Reproduced by permission.
- *The Cabinet Resolution Regarding the Disengagement Plan.* Prime Minister's Office of Israel, 2004. Reproduced by permission.
- *Declaration of the Establishment of the State of Israel, May 14, 1948.* Israel Ministry of Foreign Affairs, 1948. Reproduced by permission.
- *Declaration of Principles on Interim Self-Government Arrangements September 13, 1993.* Israel Ministry of Foreign Affair, 1993. Reproduced by permission. "The Damascus Declaration for Democratic National Change," *SyriaComment.com*, October 15, 2005. Reproduced by permission.
- *The Khartoum Resolutions*, September 1, 1967. Israel Ministry of Foreign Affairs, 1967. Reproduced by permission.

- *Palestine Royal (Peel) Commission Report,* July 1937. The National Archives (UK), 1937. Reproduced by permission.

- *The Palestinian National Charter: Resolutions of the Palestine National Council - July 1-17, 1968.* Israel Ministry of Foreign Affairs, 1968. Reproduced by permission.

- *Remarks by the President on a New Beginning,* Cairo University, Cairo, Egypt, June 4, 2009. The White House, 2009. Reproduced by permission.

- *Report of the United Nations Fact Finding Mission on the Gaza Conflict,* September 15, 2009. © United Nations, 2009. Reproduced with permission.

- *Statement to the Knesset by President Sadat - 20 November 1977.* Israel Ministry of Foreign Affairs, 1977. Reproduced with permission.

- *Statement to the Knesset by Prime Minister Begin, 20 November 1977.* Israel Ministry of Foreign Affairs, 1977. Reproduced with permission.

- *U.N. Security Council Resolution 242 - November 22, 1967.* Israel Ministry of Foreign Affairs, 1967. Reproduced by permission.

Vying for Power: Dividing Palestine

In the years leading up to World War I (1914–18; a global war between the Allies [Great Britain, France, and Russia, joined later by the United States] and the Central Powers [Germany, Austria-Hungary, and their allies]), the Ottoman Empire held control over much of what is known today as the Middle East. (The Ottoman Empire was the vast empire of the Ottoman Turks which included southwest Asia, northeast Africa, and southeast Europe, and lasted from the thirteenth century to the early twentieth century.) The modern nations of the Middle East were then territories within the empire, their populations loosely governed and not overly prosperous in this time before oil wealth transformed the region.

World War I brought sweeping change. The Ottoman Empire was defeated by Allied forces, and after the war, the Allies began the process of redrawing the map of the region. Under the authority of the League of Nations (an international organization of sovereign countries established after World War I to promote peace), Great Britain and France divided much of the former Ottoman territory into regions ruled under their mandate, or administrative authority. The areas operating under French mandate were Lebanon and Syria; those under British control were Palestine (a historical region comprising parts of present-day Israel and Jordan), Transjordan (present-day Jordan), and Iraq.

Palestine lay on the eastern shore of the Mediterranean Sea, and it stretched inland about 50 miles (80.47 kilometers) to the banks of the Jordan River and the Dead Sea. Much of the area was desert, and only one-third of the territory could support agriculture. However, the area was home to some of the holiest sites of Judaism, Christianity, and Islam, especially in the city of Jerusalem. In the mid–nineteenth century, Palestine had been home to about 500,000 people, approximately 80 percent of them Arab Muslims, 10 percent Christians, 4 percent Jews, and 1 percent Druze (a small sect of Islam).

In the 1880s, a new force began to reshape Palestine. That force was known as Zionism, an international political movement that called for the creation of an independent Jewish state in Palestine. Zionists declared that Jews had a claim to land in Palestine, which had been home to the ancient Jewish kindgom thousands of years before, and they encouraged Jews to move to Palestine. In the mid–nineteenth century, small numbers of Jews fleeing discrimination and persecution because of their religious beliefs in Europe and Russia began to settle in Palestine. In the late 1890s, Theodor Herzl (1860–1904), author of *The Jewish State*, created the World Zionist Organization to promote increased Jewish immigration to Palestine, and the number of immigrants increased. Zionism attracted the support of wealthy and influential Jews in Europe and the United States, including Herbert Samuel (1870–1963), a British diplomat and politician. By 1917, Samuel and other supporters of Zionism urged the British government to express its qualified support for the movement. That support came in the form of a letter, known as the Balfour Declaration, that expressed the British position.

The Balfour Declaration, named after British foreign secretary Lord Arthur Balfour (1848–1930), is perhaps the single most important document in the history of the century-long conflict between Jews and Arabs in the Middle East. It reads:

> His Majesty's Government view with favour the establishment in Palestine of a national home for the Jewish people, and will use their best endeavours to facilitate the achievement of this object, it being understood that nothing shall be done which may prejudice the civil and religious rights of the existing non-Jewish communities in Palestine, or the rights and political status enjoyed by Jews in any other country.

The dual promise implied in this declaration—the promise that Great Britain would support both Jewish and Arab interests in Palestine—proved nearly impossible to fulfill, as successive British administrations discovered through the 1920s, 1930s, and 1940s. Jews and Arabs who lived in Palestine fought repeatedly and sometimes violently over control of land and access to holy sites in Jerusalem. Increasingly, both sides became committed to the idea that the other was the enemy and that they must fight to remove the enemy's influence from Palestine.

The documents that make up this chapter show how the various players in this conflict—the British, the Zionists, and the Arabs—struggled to develop policies and strategies to address their interests in Palestine. The

Arthur Balfour, author of the Balfour Declaration.
© ARCHIVE PICS/ALAMY.

Palestine Royal Commission Report, often called the Peel Commission Report, was issued in 1937 by the British in an attempt to provide a framework for cooperation between Jews and Arabs in Palestine. (It proved so unpopular that a British government report called the White Paper, issued in 1939, reversed several of its suggestions.) The Biltmore Program was an argument made by American Zionists that Palestine should attain independence as a Jewish state, and it argued against British policy. Finally, the Alexandria Protocol, issued in 1944 during World War II (1939–45; a war in which the Allies [Great Britain, France, the Soviet Union, the United States, and China] defeated the Axis Powers [Germany, Italy, and Japan]), was the founding document of the League of Arab States (commonly known as the Arab League), a coalition of Arab nations to promote political, military, and economic cooperation within the Arab world. The Arab League joined together to oppose Zionism and to argue that Palestine should attain independence as an Arab state.

The Peel Commission Report

Excerpt from the Palestine Royal (Peel) Commission Report
(July 7, 1937)

Reprinted in Palestine and the Arab-Israeli Conflict

Edited by Charles D. Smith

Published in 2001

"Manifestly the problem cannot be solved by giving either the Arabs or the Jews all they want. The answer to the question 'Which of them in the end will govern Palestine?' must surely be 'Neither.'"

In 1917, in the midst of World War I (1914–18; a global war between the Allies [Great Britain, France, and Russia, joined later by the United States] and the Central Powers [Germany, Austria-Hungary, and their allies]), the British government issued the Balfour Declaration, changing the lives of many of the people in Palestine. The Balfour Declaration, issued in the form of a letter from diplomat Arthur Balfour (1848–1930), tried to clarify Great Britain's official position toward two groups who were vying for power in Palestine. These groups were the Arab Palestinians, primarily farmers and small-scale traders who had lived in the region for centuries, and Zionist Jews, recent immigrants whose mission was to establish an independent Jewish state in Palestine. Great Britain believed that the two groups could live alongside one another. Therefore, the Balfour Declaration stated that Britain would support the creation of a Jewish homeland in Palestine, but that it would also protect Arab rights in the region. It was a dual promise that proved impossible to keep.

Before World War I, the Ottoman Empire (the vast empire of the Ottoman Turks which included southwest Asia, northeast Africa, and southeast Europe, and lasted from the thirteenth century to the early twentieth century) had been the main power in the region. However, the Ottomans were defeated in the war and the Allies divided the land into new territories, based upon historical precedents. The Allies worked to establish a system of governance in the region with assistance from the League of Nations, an international organization of sovereign countries established after World War I to promote peace. The system they devised was called the mandate system, for it gave Western nations a mandate, or administrative authority, to provide governance for these new territories until such time as they could become independent nations. Great Britain took control of Palestine, and in 1920, Herbert Samuel (1870–1963) was named the first high commissioner for Palestine.

From the very beginning, Palestine proved a difficult place to rule. The native Arabs resented the way that Zionists established settlements on Arab land. They accused the Zionists of using their superior wealth to buy up large tracts of land and force Palestinian peasants to leave the lands they had tended for generations. They also resented the newcomers' claims to rights to visit holy sites. Zionists, by contrast, were single-minded in their desire to give Palestine a Jewish identity. They created their own school systems and labor unions, and they gave preferential treatment to Jews over Arab Palestinians. Zionists argued that the Arabs could move to other nearby countries that had an Arab character, such as Transjordan (present-day Jordan) or Syria. Palestine, they believed, was fated to be a Jewish state.

These competing claims to control in Palestine led to nearly constant conflict between Jews and Arabs. In May 1921, anti-Jewish riots broke out in the town of Jaffa and surrounding villages, leaving forty-seven Jews and forty-eight Arabs dead. In 1929, riots broke out over access to a holy site called the Western Wall (also known as the Wailing Wall; a surviving section of an ancient Jewish temple and one of Judaism's most sacred landmarks). This time, 133 Jews and at least 113 Arabs died.

By 1936, many Arabs had decided that the only way to protect their rights was to rise up in a general revolt against both the British and the Jews. This Arab Revolt lasted until 1939. The British were forced to send large numbers of troops to Palestine during the revolt to keep order, but changing politics in Europe—especially the rise of the Nazi Party in Germany—made Palestine seem like an unwanted diversion, and the

British government began to look for a way to peacefully give up control of Palestine.

Late in 1936 the British appointed a commission, headed by William Robert Wellesley (1867–1937), the first Earl of Peel, to investigate the situation in Palestine and make recommendations to the British government. The commission, often known as the Peel Commission, issued its report on July 7, 1937, after nearly six months of lengthy investigations and hearings, including interviews with people on all sides of the conflict. The report, technically called Command Paper 5479, is best known as the Palestine Royal Commission (or Peel Commission) Report, and it is reproduced below.

Members of the Peel Commission prepare to leave London, England, for Jerusalem in 1936. The head of the commission, William Robert Wellesley, is pictured on the far right. DEREK BERWIN/FOX PHOTOS/GETTY IMAGES.

Things to remember while reading the excerpt from the "Palestine Royal (Peel) Commission Report"

- Both Jews and Arabs made historical claims to Palestine. Jews claimed that their ancestors had roots to Palestine that dated from ancient times up to 70 CE, when Romans destroyed a Jewish temple and drove Jews from the region. Arabs had lived in Palestine for centuries and could point to hundreds of years of history living and farming in the region.

- One of the key ideas to come out of this document was the idea of partition (division). Under this concept, Palestine would be partitioned into two independent states—one for Arabs and one for Jews.

- The events in Palestine were deeply influenced by the rise of the Nazi Party in Germany. When Adolf Hitler (1889–1945), the head of the Nazi Party, came to power in 1933, he immediately passed laws that discriminated against Jews. Many Jews immigrated to Palestine to escape this discrimination. The increased Jewish immigration only added to tensions in Palestine.

• • •

Palestine Royal (Peel) Commission Report (July 7, 1937)

1. Before submitting the proposals we have to offer for its drastic treatment we will briefly restate the problem of Palestine.

2. Under the stress of the **World War** the British Government made promises to Arabs and Jews in order to obtain their support. On the strength of those promises both parties formed certain expectations.

3. The application to Palestine of the **Mandate System** in general and of the specific mandate in particular implied the belief that the obligations thus undertaken towards the Arabs and the Jews respectively would prove in course of time to be mutually compatible owing to the **conciliatory** effect on the Arab Palestinians of the material prosperity which Jewish immigration would bring in Palestine as a whole. That belief has not been justified, and we see no hope of its being justified in the future....

5. What are the existing circumstances?

An irrepressible conflict has arisen between two national communities within the narrow bounds of one small country. About 1,000,000 Arabs are in strife, open or **latent**, with some 400,000 Jews. There is no common ground between them. The Arab community is predominantly **Asiatic** in character,

World War: World War I (1914–18).

Mandate System: The system established after World War I which granted one country the authority to administer the affairs of another country.

Conciliatory: Appeasing; peace-making.

Latent: Hidden.

Asiatic: Asian; non-Western.

the Jewish community predominantly European. They differ in religion and in language. Their cultural and social life, their ways of thought and conduct, are as incompatible as their national aspirations. These last are the greatest bar to peace. Arabs and Jews might possibly learn to live and work together in Palestine if they would make a genuine effort to reconcile and combine their national ideals and so build up in time a joint or dual nationality. But this they cannot do. The War and its sequel have inspired all Arabs with the hope of reviving in a free and united Arab world the traditions of the Arab golden age. The Jews similarly are inspired by their historic past. They mean to show what the Jewish nation can achieve when restored to the land of its birth. National **assimilation** between Arabs and Jews is thus ruled out. In the Arab picture the Jews could only occupy the place they occupied in Arab Egypt or Arab Spain. The Arabs would be as much outside the Jewish picture as the **Canaanites** in the old land of Israel. The National Home, as we have said before, cannot be half-national. In these circumstances to maintain that Palestinian citizenship has any moral meaning is a mischievous pretence. Neither Arab nor Jew has any sense of service to a single State.

6. This conflict was inherent in the situation from the outset. The terms of the mandate tended to confirm it. If the Government had adopted a more rigorous and consistent policy it might have repressed the conflict for a time, but it could not have resolved it.

7. The conflict has grown steadily more bitter. It has been marked by a series of five Arab outbreaks, culminating in the rebellion of last year. In the earlier period hostility to the Jews was not widespread among the **fellaheen**. It is now general. The first three outbreaks, again, were directed only against the Jews. The last two were directed against the [British] Government as well.

8. This intensification of the conflict will continue. The **estranging** force of conditions inside Palestine is growing year by year. The educational systems, Arab and Jewish, are schools of **nationalism**, and they have only existed for a short time. Their full effect on the rising generation has yet to be felt. And patriotic "youth-movements," so familiar a feature of present-day politics in other countries of Europe or Asia, are afoot in Palestine. As each community grows, moreover, the rivalry between them deepens. The more numerous and prosperous and better-educated the Arabs become, the more insistent will be their demand for national independence and the more bitter their hatred of the obstacle that bars the way to it. As the Jewish National Home grows older and more firmly rooted, so will grow its self-confidence and political ambition.

9. The conflict is primarily political, though the fear of economic **subjection** to the Jews is also in Arab minds. The mandate, it is supposed, will terminate sooner or later. The Arabs would **hasten** the day, the Jews **retard** it, for obvious reasons in each case. Meanwhile the whole situation is darkened by uncertainty as to the future. The conflict, indeed, is as much about the future as about the present. Every intelligent Arab and Jew is forced to ask the question "Who in the end will govern Palestine?" This uncertainty is doubtless

Assimilation: The blending of one cultural group in harmony with another.

Canaanites: Ancient tribe of non-Jews.

Fellaheen: Arab peasants.

Estranging: Isolating.

Nationalism: The belief that a people with shared ethnic, cultural, and/or religious identities have the right to form their own nation.

Subjection: Control taken by force or domination.

Hasten: Hurry; bring about more quickly.

Retard: Slow.

aggravated by the fact that Palestine is a mandated territory; but, in the light of nationalist movements elsewhere, we do not think the situation would be very different if Palestine had been a British Colony.

10. Meantime the "external factors" will continue to play the part they have played with steadily increasing force from the beginning. On the one hand, Saudi Arabia, the Yemen, Iraq and Egypt are already recognized as sovereign states, and Trans-Jordan as an "independent government." In less than three years' time Syria and the Lebanon will attain their national sovereignty. The claim of the Palestine Arabs to share in the freedom of all Asiatic Arabia will thus be reinforced. Before the War they were linked for centuries past with Syria and the Lebanon. They already exceed the Lebanese in numbers. That they are as well qualified for self-government as the Arabs of neighbouring countries has been admitted.

11. On the other hand, the hardships and anxieties of the Jews in Europe are not likely to grow less in the near future. The pressure on Palestine will continue and might at any time be accentuated. The appeal to the good faith and humanity of the British people will lose none of its force. The Mandatory will be urged unceasingly to admit as many Jews into Palestine as the National Home can provide with a livelihood and to protect them when admitted from Arab attacks.

12. Thus, for internal and external reasons, it seems probable that the situation, bad as it now is, will grow worse. The conflict will go on, the gulf between Arabs and Jews will widen. . . .

14. In these circumstances, we are convinced that peace, order and good government can only be maintained in Palestine for any length of time by a rigorous system of repression. Throughout this Report we have been careful not to overstate the facts as we see them: but understatement is no less reprehensible; and we should be failing in our duty if we said anything to encourage a hopeful outlook for the future peace of Palestine under the existing system or anything akin to it. . . .

To put it in one sentence, we cannot—in Palestine as it now is—both concede the Arab claim to self-government and secure the establishment of the Jewish National Home. And this conflict between the two obligations is the more unfortunate because each of them, taken separately, accords with British sentiment and British interest. On the one hand, the application of the Mandate System to Arab Palestine as a means of advancement to self-government was in harmony with British principles—the same principles as have been put into practice since the War in different circumstances in India, Iraq and Egypt. British public opinion is wholly sympathetic with Arab aspirations towards a new age of unity and prosperity in the Arab world. Conversely, the task of governing without the consent or even the acquiescence of the governed is one for which, we believe, the British people have little heart. On the other hand, there is a strong British tradition of friendship with the Jewish people. Nowhere have Jews found it easier to live and prosper than in Britain. Nowhere is there a more genuine desire to do what can be done to help them in their present difficulties. Nowhere, again, was Zionism better understood before the War or given such practical proofs of sympathy. And British interest coincides with British sentiment. From the earliest days of the British **connexion** with India and beyond, the peace of the Middle East has been a cardinal principle of our foreign policy; and for the maintenance of that peace British statesmanship can show an almost unbroken record of friendship with the Arabs. . . .

A continuance or rather an aggravation—for that is what continuance will be—of the present situation cannot be contemplated without the gravest misgivings. It will mean constant unrest and disturbance in peace and potential danger in the event of war. It will mean a steady decline in our prestige. . . .

19. **Manifestly** the problem cannot be solved by giving either the Arabs or the Jews all they want. The answer to the question "Which of them in the end will govern Palestine?" must surely be "Neither." We do not think that any fair-minded statesman would suppose, now that the hope of harmony between the races has proved **untenable**, that Britain ought either to hand over to Arab rule 400,000 Jews, whose entry into Palestine has been for the most part facilitated by the British Government and approved by the League of Nations; or that, if the Jews should become a majority, a million or so of Arabs should be handed over to their rule. But, while neither race can justly rule all Palestine, we see no reason why, if it were practicable, each race should not rule part of it. . . .

Partition seems to offer at least a chance of ultimate peace. We can see none in any other plan. . . .

1. Treaty System

6. Treaties of Alliance should be negotiated by the **Mandatory** with the Government of Trans-Jordan and representatives of the Arabs of Palestine on the one hand and with the Zionist Organisation on the other. These Treaties would declare that, within as short a period as may be convenient, two sovereign independent States would be established—the one an Arab State, consisting of Trans-Jordan united with that part of Palestine which lies to the east and south of a frontier such as we suggest in Section 3 below; the other a Jewish State consisting of that part of Palestine which lies to the north and west of that frontier. . . .

2. The Holy Places

12. We regard the protection of the **Holy Places** as a permanent trust, unique in its character and purpose, and not contemplated by Article 22 of the Covenant of the League of Nations. We submit for consideration that, in order to avoid misunderstanding, it might frankly be stated that this trust will

Connexion: Connection.

Manifestly: Clearly.

Untenable: Not capable of being maintained.

Partition: Division of Palestine into two independent states.

Mandatory: The Mandate of Palestine.

Holy Places: Religious sites located in the city of Jerusalem.

only terminate if and when the League of Nations and the United States desire it to do so, and that, while it would be the trustee's duty to promote the well-being and development of the local population concerned, it is not intended that in course of time they should stand by themselves as a wholly self-governing community. . . .

10. Exchange of Land and Population

35. We have left to the last the two-fold question which, after that of the **Frontier**, is the most important and most difficult of all the questions which Partition in any shape involves.

36. If Partition is to be effective in promoting a final settlement it must mean more than drawing a frontier and establishing two States. Sooner or later there should be a transfer of land and, as far as possible, an exchange of population. . . .

Conclusion

1. "Half a loaf is better than no bread" is a peculiarly English proverb; and, considering the attitude which both the Arab and the Jewish representatives adopted in giving evidence before us, we think it improbable that either party will be satisfied at first sight with the proposals we have submitted for the adjustment of their rival claims. For Partition means that neither will get all it wants. It means that the Arabs must acquiesce in the exclusion from their sovereignty of a piece of territory, long occupied and once ruled by them. It means that the Jews must be content with less than the Land of Israel they once ruled and have hoped to rule again. But it seems to us possible that on reflection both parties will come to realize that the drawbacks of Partition are outweighed by its advantages. For, if it offers neither party all it wants, it offers each what it wants most, namely freedom and security. . . .

• • •

What happened next . . .

As the authors of the report predicted, neither side was happy with the recommendations of the Commission. The Jews, represented by a government-like organization called the Jewish Agency, accepted the idea of partition, but they believed that the portion of Palestine allotted to the Jews should be much larger, and they wanted Great Britain to pay to evict Palestinians from what would become Jewish territory. The Arabs, however, rejected the idea of partition altogether. They argued that since 70 percent of the population was Arabic, and 90 percent of the

Frontier: Borders.

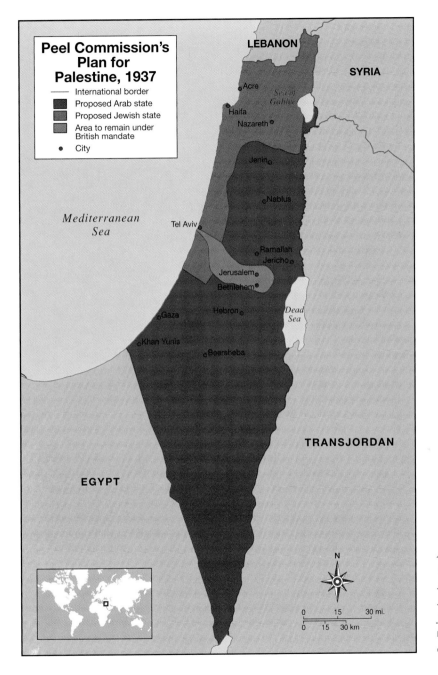

Peel Commission's Plan for Palestine, 1937

- —— International border
- ■ Proposed Arab state
- ■ Proposed Jewish state
- ■ Area to remain under British mandate
- ● City

LEBANON

SYRIA

Acre

Sea of Galilee

Haifa

Nazareth

Jenin

Nablus

Mediterranean Sea

Tel Aviv

Ramallah

Jericho

Jerusalem

Bethlehem

Gaza

Hebron

Dead Sea

Khan Yunis

Beersheba

TRANSJORDAN

EGYPT

N

0   15   30 mi.
0   15   30 km

A map showing the Peel Commission's plan for separating Palestine into two states, one for Arabs and one for Jews. MAP BY XNR PRODUCTIONS, INC./ CENGAGE LEARNING.

land was owned by Arabs, that the state should be Arab. The Arab Higher Committee, which spoke for the Arabs at the time, rejected the idea that a Jewish state should be forced upon Palestinians and

Middle East Conflict: Primary Sources, 2nd Edition

Iraqis demonstrating against the Peel Commission's recommended partition of Palestine. The Arabs in Palestine and neighboring nations rejected the idea of partition altogether. KEYSTONE-FRANCE/GAMMA-KEYSTONE VIA GETTY IMAGES.

called for the British to restrict Jewish immigration to Palestine. Arab uprisings continued in violent protest, and the situation did not improve.

Soon even the British agreed that partition was impossible and that they could not create a Jewish national home without the consent of the Arabs. Over the next several years, the British backtracked in their policy. As early as 1938, they issued another Command Paper, number 5893, that called the creation of independent Arab and Jewish states impractical. They also placed limits on Jewish immigration, despite the increased oppression that Jews faced in Germany and elsewhere in Europe. Finally, the British officially reversed parts of their policy when they issued a government document known as the 1939 White Paper.

The White Paper rejected the idea of partition, instead calling for the creation of an "independent Palestine state" in "which the two peoples in Palestine, Arabs and Jews, share authority in government in such a way that the essential interests of each are secured." Hoping to appease Arab anger at the growth in the Jewish population, the White Paper restricted Jewish immigration to Palestine for the next ten years and made future immigration subject to the consent of the Arabs. The White Paper pleased the Arabs enough to stop the organized uprising against British rule, but it angered the Jews. They felt that Great Britain had betrayed them by limiting immigration and backtracking on their support for a Jewish national home, which many Jews were beginning to think of as an independent state. Despite all the diplomacy, the situation in Palestine improved very little in the 1940s. Arabs and Jews continued to build separate cultures and fight against each other for control of the land they both claimed. Meanwhile, the rest of the world became absorbed in the fighting of World War II (1939–45; a war in which the Allies [Great Britain, France, the Soviet Union, the United States, and China] defeated the Axis Powers [Germany, Italy, and Japan]).

Though the Peel Commission Report and the White Paper seemed to cancel each other out, the Peel Report has become an important historical document. It is the first official document to acknowledge the possibility that Palestine might be divided into two independent states, one Jewish and the other Arab. In the early 2000s, this remained a widely accepted solution to the enduring conflict over control of the region. Negotiations continue over exactly what borders that state would take. In 2011 Palestinian president Mahmoud Abbas (1935–) appeared before the United Nations (an international organization of countries founded in 1945 to promote international peace, security, and cooperation) requesting recognition of an independent Palestinian state. The bid stalled, however, when the UN Security Council committee charged with reviewing the Palestinian application for UN membership failed to reach an agreement.

Did you know...

- The population of Palestine doubled over the course of the British mandate period, jumping from 750,000 to 1.8 million from 1922 to 1946. In 1922, 89 percent of the population was Arab and

11 percent Jewish. By 1946, just 69 percent was Arab and 31 percent Jewish.

- It is estimated that in the mid–1930s, over 90 percent of Jews in Palestine were literate, while only 30 percent of Arabs were literate.
- In 1936, per household income for Jews in Palestine was 44 Palestinian pounds, while that of Arabs was 17 Palestinian pounds.

Consider the following . . .

- Based on the conflicting claims to regions of Palestine in the 1930s, what would have been the best recommendation for Jews and Arabs to resolve their differences? How would this recommendation provide for the very different needs and perceived injustices of each side?
- Were the recommendations made by the Peel Commission fair? Explain why or why not.
- Diplomatic papers such as the Peel Commission Report are often dry and impersonal. What is the tone of this report? Do the writers sympathize with either side in the conflict? Use quotations to make a case for either side.

For More Information

BOOKS

Encyclopedia of the Modern Middle East and North Africa. 4 vols. New York: Macmillan Reference USA, 2004.

Farsoun, Samih K., and Naseer Aruri. *Palestine and the Palestinians: A Social and Political History.* 2nd ed. Boulder, CO: Westview Press, 2006.

Pappe, Ilan, ed. *A History of Modern Palestine: One Land, Two Peoples.* 2nd ed. Cambridge: Cambridge University Press, 2006.

Smith, Charles D., ed. *Palestine and the Arab-Israeli Conflict: A History with Documents*, 4th ed. Boston MA: Bedford/St. Martin's, 2001.

WEB SITES

"The Origins and Evolution of the Palestine Problem: 1917–1988." *United Nations Information System on the Question of Palestine* (June 30, 1978). http://unispal.un.org/unispal.nsf/0/AEAC80E740C782E4852561150071 FDB0 (accessed on November 30, 2011).

The Biltmore Program

The Biltmore Program (May 11, 1942)

> *Reprinted in* The Arab States and the Arab League
>
> *Edited by Muhammad Khalil*
>
> *Published in 1962*

"The Conference declares that the new world order that will follow victory cannot be established on foundations of peace, justice and equality, unless the problem of Jewish homelessness is finally solved."

Since 1917, the year that Great Britain had pledged in the Balfour Declaration to support the creation of a national home for Jews in Palestine (a historical region in the Middle East on the eastern shore of the Mediterranean Sea, comprising parts of present-day Israel and Jordan), Zionists looked to Britain to defend their cause. (Zionists are supporters of an international political movement that called for the creation of an independent Jewish state in Palestine.) Throughout the 1920s and into the 1930s, the British government, which administered Palestine, allowed Jewish immigrants to enter Palestine, where they built farms, businesses, and communities. This created a distinct Jewish society that existed alongside—but separate from—the Arab community in Palestine. (Arabs are people who speak the Arabic language or who live in countries in which Arabic is the dominant language.)

British support for the Zionist cause weakened considerably in the late 1930s, however, after protests, riots, and violent attacks by Arabs on both Jews and British officials made it clear that Arab Palestinians did not intend to give control of Palestine to the growing Jewish population. In 1939, the British released a new statement of policy, called the White Paper, that placed numerical limits on Jewish immigration to Palestine and promised Arabs the leading role in a future independent Palestine.

This White Paper enraged Zionists, who charged that the British had abandoned their support for a Jewish national home in Palestine. After 1939, Zionists began to look beyond Great Britain for support for their ultimate goal of making Palestine a secure site for the development of a Jewish homeland. European countries were out of the question, for most of them were caught up in the fighting of World War II (1939–45; a war in which the Allies [Great Britain, France, the Soviet Union, the United States, and China] defeated the Axis Powers [Germany, Italy, and Japan]). Increasingly, Zionist leaders looked to the United States, which did not enter the war until 1941, for support. The United States had a sizable Jewish population, including many wealthy supporters of Zionist causes, and it did not have a history of persecuting Jews.

During World War II, Germany was controlled by the Nazi Party leader Adolf Hitler (1889–1945), who in the 1930s had promoted anti-Semitism (prejudice against Jews) in Germany, including laws restricting Jewish activities. By 1939, German soldiers began to round up Jews in Germany and in conquered territories and send them to concentration camps, complexes built by the Germans for the confinement and extermination of political opponents and ethnic minorities, especially Jews. By the early 1940s, rumors began to circulate that Jews were being killed in great numbers as part of Hitler's plan, known as the "Final Solution," to rid Europe of Jews. At the time, however, these claims remained rumors; it was not until November 1942 that hard evidence of mass killings began to emerge. Still, these rumors contributed to the sense that something must be done to open Palestine to greater immigration of Jews.

Under these circumstances, about six hundred American Zionists and numerous Zionist leaders from Europe and Palestine gathered at the Biltmore Hotel in New York City from May 6 to May 11, 1942. The result of their meeting was the creation of the Biltmore Program, an eight-part statement of goals for the Zionist movement.

Things to remember while reading the "Biltmore Program"

- Zionists had long spoken of a Jewish homeland in Palestine, but the political status of that homeland was often left unstated. Some Zionists felt that a homeland could exist within a non-Jewish nation

The Biltmore Hotel in New York was the site of the meeting in 1942 where the Biltmore Program was drafted.
© BETTMANN/CORBIS.

that recognized and accepted Jewish immigrants. Others believed that the only safe homeland would be in an independent Jewish state.

• Among the participants at the conference were Chaim Weizmann (1874–1952), the head of the World Zionist Organization and a moderate who wanted to seek cooperation with the British, and

David Ben-Gurion (1886–1973), the leader of the Jewish Agency (the government-like organization for Jews in Palestine) who wanted to break decisively with the British and seek an independent Jewish state.

• • •

The Biltmore Program (May 11, 1942)

1. American Zionists assembled in this Extraordinary Conference reaffirm their **unequivocal** devotion to the cause of democratic freedom and international justice to which the people of the United States, allied with the other United Nations, have dedicated themselves, and give expression to their faith in the ultimate victory of humanity and justice over lawlessness and brute force.

2. This Conference offers a message of hope and encouragement to their fellow Jews in the **Ghettos** and **concentration camps** of Hitler-dominated Europe and prays that their hour of liberation may not be far distant.

3. The Conference sends its warmest greetings to the Jewish Agency Executive in Jerusalem, to the **Va'ad Leumi**, and to the whole **Yishuv** in Palestine, and expresses its profound admiration for their steadfastness and achievements in the face of peril and great difficulties. The Jewish men and women in field and factory, and the thousands of Jewish soldiers of Palestine in the Near East who have **acquitted** themselves with honor and distinction in Greece, Ethiopia, Syria, Libya and on other battlefields, have shown themselves worthy of their people and ready to resume the rights and responsibilities of nationhood.

4. In our generation, and in particular in the course of the past twenty years, the Jewish people have awakened and transformed their ancient homeland; from 50,000 at the end of the last war their numbers have increased to more than 500,000. They have made the waste places to bear fruit and the desert to blossom. Their pioneering achievements in agriculture and in industry, embodying new patterns of cooperative endeavor, have written a notable page in the history of colonization.

5. In the new values thus created, their Arab neighbors in Palestine have shared. The Jewish people in its own work of national redemption welcomes the economic, agricultural and national development of the Arab peoples and states. The Conference reaffirms the stand previously adopted at Congresses of the **World Zionist Organization**, expressing the readiness and the desire of the Jewish people for full cooperation of their Arab neighbors.

6. The Conference calls for the fulfillment of the original purpose of the Balfour Declaration and the mandate which "recognizing the historical connection

Unequivocal: Clear and without misunderstanding.

Ghetto: A poor part of a city occupied by minority groups.

Concentration camps: Complexes built by the Germans for the confinement and extermination of political opponents and ethnic minorities, especially Jews.

Va'ad Leumi: Executive body of the elected Jewish assembly in Palestine.

Yishuv: Jewish community.

Acquitted: Conducted.

World Zionist Organization: An organization devoted to promoting Jewish settlement in Palestine.

of the Jewish people with Palestine" was to afford them the opportunity, as stated by **President Wilson**, to found there a Jewish Commonwealth.

The Conference affirms its unalterable rejection of the White Paper of May 1939 and denies its moral or legal validity. The White Paper seeks to limit, and in fact to nullify Jewish rights to immigration and settlement in Palestine, and, as stated by Mr. **Winston Churchill** in the House of Commons in May 1939, constitutes a "breach and repudiation of the Balfour Declaration." The policy of the White Paper is cruel and indefensible in its denial of sanctuary to Jews fleeing from Nazi persecution; and at a time when Palestine has become a focal point in the war front of the United Nations, and the Palestine Jewry must provide all available manpower for farm and factory and camp, it is in direct conflict with the interests of the allied war effort.

7. In the struggle against the forces of aggression and **tyranny**, of which Jews were the earliest victims, and which now menace the Jewish National Home, recognition must be given to the right of the Jews of Palestine to play their full part in the war effort and in the defense of their own country, through a Jewish military force fighting under its own flag and under the high command of the United Nations.

8. The Conference declares that the new world order that will follow victory cannot be established on foundations of peace, justice and equality, unless the problem of Jewish homelessness is finally solved.

The Conference urges that the gates of Palestine be opened; that the Jewish Agency be vested with control of immigration into Palestine and with the necessary authority for **upbuilding** the country, including the development of its unoccupied and uncultivated lands; and that Palestine be established as a Jewish Commonwealth integrated in the structure of the new democratic world.

Then and only then will the age-old wrong to the Jewish people be righted.

• • •

What happened next...

Despite the fact that the group assembled at the Biltmore Hotel had no official status, the Biltmore Program had a significant impact on events in the United States and, eventually, in Palestine. As a means of increasing American support for Zionism, wrote Charles D. Smith, author of *Palestine and the Arab-Israeli Conflict*, "the Biltmore declarations were extraordinarily successful, especially once news of the Holocaust [the mass killing of European Jews and others by the Nazis during World War II] began to spread in the latter half of 1942. Membership in Zionist

President Wilson: U.S. president Woodrow Wilson (1856–1924).

Winston Churchill: British politician and later prime minister of Great Britain (1874–1965).

Tyranny: Absolute power, especially when exercised unjustly or cruelly.

Upbuilding: Building up.

organizations increased substantially. Publicity for the Zionist cause was pursued, including books published and distributed with Jewish financial aid." As a result, American politicians and the public became increasingly sympathetic to the idea of increasing immigration to Palestine and creating a Jewish commonwealth. In 1944, according to Smith, both major American political parties endorsed the ideas contained in the Biltmore Program. Thus the United States was well on its way to becoming a major supporter of the Zionist cause in Palestine.

The publication of the Biltmore Program also represented a victory for radical Zionists in their internal battle with moderate Zionists. Moderate Zionists had always advocated gradual diplomacy and placed faith in Great Britain's efforts to protect Jewish interests. Radical Zionists believed that Britain was too eager to please Arabs and that Zionists must distance themselves from Britain and pursue independent statehood. The Biltmore Program thus satisfied the radical Zionists, for it announced for the first time the goal of creating a Jewish independent state and also directly challenged British policy as contained in the White Paper of 1939. As world opinion shifted to support the Zionist cause announced in the Biltmore Program, Great Britain became even more determined to remove itself from political control over Palestine. In 1947 the United Nations (an international organization of countries founded in 1945 to promote international peace, security, and cooperation) announced a plan to create a Jewish state. In 1948 the British withdrew from Palestine and Jewish leaders declared the existence of Israel as an independent Jewish state.

What the Biltmore Program could not do, however, was solve the crisis facing Jews in Europe. The Biltmore statement drew some attention to German violence against Jews, and attention grew even more intense after the appearance in August 1942 of a document called the Riegner Cable. The Riegner Cable provided the first clear evidence of the German plan to exterminate European Jews. But governments were slow to react to the news. Neither the United States nor Great Britain opened its doors to Jewish refugees (people who flee their country to escape violence or persecution) from Europe; moreover, Great Britain continued to limit immigration to Palestine. It was not until 1944 that widespread efforts to aid Jewish refugees from Europe were undertaken— too late to save several million Jews who were killed in the Holocaust, mass murder of European Jews and other groups by the Nazis during World War II.

Jews arriving at the Auschwitz concentration camp in Poland. The Biltmore Program helped draw attention to the German violence against Jews; however, widespread efforts to aid Jewish refugees from Europe were not undertaken until 1942. © WORLD HISTORY ARCHIVE/ALAMY.

Did you know...

- The Biltmore Program was one of the key documents used to build support for the Zionist cause in the United States, support which grew large enough that the United States used its power to convince the United Nations to authorize the creation of a Jewish state in Palestine in 1947.

- David Ben-Gurion, one of the authors of the Biltmore Program, wrote the final draft of Israel's Declaration of Independence in 1947 and went on to become the first prime minister of the state of Israel.

Consider the following . . .

- Zionists were in a difficult position when it came to British policy. They were frustrated by the parts of the 1939 White Paper that limited Jewish immigration to Palestine and granted Arabs the power to deny the formation of a Jewish state. Yet they supported British efforts to defeat Germany in World War II. In what ways is this conflicting position reflected in the text of the Biltmore Program?
- The tragedy of the ongoing extermination of Jews that was underway in Germany and other Germany-controlled areas was part of the reason for creating the Biltmore Program. In what ways is this tragedy reflected in the document?
- One of the troubling questions of World War II is why the British and U.S. governments acted so slowly to address the problems of the Holocaust. As a way of understanding their inaction, research what was known about the Holocaust at the time of the Biltmore conference. Did policy makers have enough information to act? What should they have done?

For More Information

BOOKS

Encyclopedia of the Modern Middle East and North Africa. 4 vols. New York: Macmillan Reference USA, 2004.

Khalil, Muhammad, ed. *The Arab States and the Arab League: A Documentary Record.* Vol. 2, *International Affairs.* Beirut: Khayats, 1962.

Pasachoff, Naomi. *Links in the Chain: Shapers of the Jewish Tradition.* New York: Oxford University Press, 1997.

Raider, Mark A. *The Emergence of American Zionism.* New York: New York University Press, 1998.

Shapiro, David H. *From Philanthropy to Activism: The Political Transformation of American Zionism in the Holocaust Years, 1933–1945.* New York: Pergamon Press, 1994.

Smith, Charles D., ed. *Palestine and the Arab-Israeli Conflict: A History with Documents,* 4th ed. Boston MA: Bedford/St. Martin's, 2001.

Urofsky, Melvin I. *American Zionism from Herzl to the Holocaust.* Lincoln: University of Nebraska Press, 1995.

The Alexandria Protocol

The Alexandria Protocol (October 7, 1944)

Issued by representatives of Egypt, Iraq, Lebanon, Syria,
and Transjordan
Reprinted in The Arab States and the Arab League
Edited by Muhammad Khalil
Published in 1962

"A League will be formed of the independent Arab States which consent to join the League.... The object of the League will be ... to insure their [Arab States'] cooperation, and protect their independence and sovereignty against every aggression by suitable means."

When the British were granted a mandate (administrative authority) over Palestine in the early 1920s, they intended to create a society that would eventually be self-supporting. (Palestine is a historical region in the Middle East on the eastern shore of the Mediterranean Sea, comprising parts of present-day Israel and Jordan.) However, Palestine was a land divided by two cultures: Jewish immigrants who hoped to establish a homeland there, free from the discrimination they had faced in Europe and other parts of the world, and Arabs (people who speak the Arabic language or who live in countries in which Arabic is the dominant language) who were predominantly Muslim and had lived in Palestine for centuries. Jews embraced Zionism, an international political movement originating in the late nineteenth century that called for the creation of an independent Jewish state in Palestine. Arab Palestinians believed that Palestine was their land, and they did not welcome the Jews who came in growing numbers, buying land and building homes and businesses. From the 1920s onward, Jews and Arabs clashed over control of Palestine.

By the 1930s, conflicts between Jews and Arabs in Palestine had become frequent and increasingly violent. Both sides wanted to extend their range of control, and each side felt that the British administrators were favoring the other side. Arab revolts held between 1936 and 1939, which killed and wounded hundreds on both sides, brought open fighting between Arabs, Jews, and British forces. Years of conflict in Palestine, combined with the entry of Great Britain into World War II (1939–45; a war in which the Allies [Great Britain, France, the Soviet Union, the United States, and China] defeated the Axis Powers [Germany, Italy, and Japan]), had overextended British forces. In the early 1940s, the British prepared to leave Palestine. It was not clear what would happen in Palestine once the British left.

The uncertain future of Palestine in the early and mid–1940s had sharpened the organization and focus of Zionist groups in Palestine. Jews had built well-disciplined militias (amateur military forces) and had systems in place to provide water, power, education, and other services to their communities. No such organization and infrastructure existed within the Arab Palestinian community. The Grand Mufti (Muslim religious leader) Amin al-Husayni (also spelled Haj Āmin al-Husayni; 1895–1974) had been the dominant political and religious leader among Arab Palestinians in the 1930s, but his exile from the country in 1939 left a vacuum of power that no one else was prepared to fill. Political groups in Palestine were more involved in fighting each other than joining together to combat Zionism. Moreover, Arab communities were generally poor, with inadequate social systems. Palestinians were ill-prepared to govern in the absence of the British administration.

The leaders of neighboring Arab countries recognized that there was no organized Palestinian plan to take control of Palestine in the event of British withdrawal. Moreover, many Arab leaders felt that the end of World War II might provide Arab countries with an opportunity to assert greater political independence from the Western countries that had once claimed them as colonies. As the war went on, Arab countries began frequent talks aimed at increasing cooperation among Arab nations and at supporting the Palestinians' efforts to resist Zionist domination. In the fall of 1944, representatives of five of these nations—Egypt, Iraq, Lebanon, Syria, and Transjordan (present-day Jordan)—met in Alexandria, Egypt, and took the initial steps to organize themselves into a political union and establish a clear position on the question of Palestine. The document they signed on October 7, 1944, was called the Alexandria Protocol.

A riot in Palestine. By the 1930s, clashes between Jews and Arabs had become frequent and increasingly violent. © HULTON-DEUTSCH COLLECTION/CORBIS.

Things to remember while reading the "Alexandria Protocol"

- At the same time that Arab leaders were crafting this document, Jews in Europe were enduring the events of the Holocaust, the mass murder of European Jews and other groups by the Nazis during

World War II (1939–45). Despite the history of violence between Arabs and Jews, the document acknowledges and expresses regret for the fate of European Jews during World War II.

- The "Alexandria Protocol" refers to the establishment of an "Arab National Fund" to counter the efforts of the Jewish National Fund, which was established in 1901 by Zionists looking to purchase land in Palestine.

• • •

The Alexandria Protocol (October 7, 1944)

Anxious to strengthen and consolidate the ties which bind all Arab countries and to direct them toward the welfare of the Arab world, to improve its conditions, insure its future, and realize its hopes and aspirations,

And in response to Arab public opinion in all Arab countries,

Have met at Alexandria from **Shawwal 8, 1363** (September 25, 1944) to Shawwal 20, 1363 (October 7, 1944) in the form of a Preliminary Committee of the General Arab Conference, and have agreed as follows:

1. LEAGUE OF ARAB STATES

A League will be formed of the independent Arab States which consent to join the League. It will have a council which will be known as the "Council of the League of Arab States" in which all participating states will be represented on an equal footing.

The object of the League will be to control the execution of the agreements which the above states will conclude; to hold periodic meetings which will strengthen the relations between those states; to coordinate their political plans so as to insure their cooperation, and protect their independence and sovereignty against every aggression by suitable means; and to supervise in a general way the affairs and interests of the Arab countries.

The decisions of the Council will be binding on those who have accepted them except in cases where a disagreement arises between two member states of the League in which the two parties shall refer their dispute to the Council for solution. In this case the decision of the Council of the League will be binding.

In no case will resort to force to settle a dispute between any two member states of the League be allowed. But every state shall be free to conclude with any other member state of the League, or other powers, special agreements which do not contradict the text or spirit of the present dispositions.

Shawwal 8, 1363: Dates in this document are from the Islamic calendar.

In no case will the adoption of a foreign policy which may be prejudicial to the policy of the League or an individual member state be allowed.

The Council will intervene in every dispute which may lead to war between a member state of the League and any other member state or power, so as to reconcile them.

A subcommittee will be formed of the members of the Preliminary Committee to prepare a draft of the statutes of the Council of the League and to examine the political questions which may be the object of agreement among Arab States.

2. COOPERATION IN ECONOMIC, CULTURAL, SOCIAL, AND OTHER MATTERS

A. The Arab States represented on the Preliminary Committee shall closely cooperate in the following matters:

(1) Economic and financial matters, i.e., commercial exchange, customs, currency, agriculture, and industry.

(2) Communications, i.e., railways, roads, aviation, negation, posts and telegraphs.

(3) Cultural matters.

(4) Questions of nationality, passports, visas, execution of judgments, extradition of criminals, etc.

(5) Social questions.

(6) Questions of public health.

B. A subcommittee of experts for each of the above subjects will be formed in which the states which have participated in the Preliminary Committee will be represented. This subcommittee will prepare draft regulations for cooperation in the above matters, describing the extent and means of that collaboration.

C. A committee for coordination and editing will be formed whose object will be to control the work of the other subcommittees, to coordinate that part of the work which is accomplished, and to prepare drafts of agreement which will be submitted to the various governments.

D. When all the subcommittees have accomplished their work, the Preliminary Committee will meet to examine the work of the subcommittees as a preliminary step toward the holding of a General Arab Conference.

3. CONSOLIDATION OF THESE TIES IN THE FUTURE

While expressing its satisfaction at such a happy step, the Committee hopes that Arab States will be able in the future to consolidate that step by other steps, especially if post-war events should result in institutions which will bind various Powers more closely together.

4. SPECIAL RESOLUTION CONCERNING LEBANON

The Arab States represented on the Preliminary Committee emphasize their respect of the independence and sovereignty of Lebanon in its present frontiers, which the governments of the above States have already recognized in consequence of Lebanon's adoption of an independent policy, which the

Government of that country announced in its program of October 7, 1943, unanimously approved by the Lebanese Chamber of Deputies.

5. SPECIAL RESOLUTION CONCERNING PALESTINE

A. The Committee is of the opinion that Palestine constitutes an important part of the Arab World and that the rights of the Arabs in Palestine cannot be touched without prejudice to peace and stability in the Arab World.

The Committee also is of the opinion that the pledges binding the British Government and providing for the **cessation** of Jewish immigration, the preservation of Arab lands, and the achievement of independence for Palestine are permanent Arab rights whose prompt implementation would constitute a step toward the desired goal and toward the stabilization of peace and security.

The Committee declares its support of the cause of the Arabs of Palestine and its willingness to work for the achievement of their legitimate aims and the safeguarding of their just rights.

The Committee also declares that it is second to none in regretting the woes which have been inflicted upon the Jews of Europe by European dictatorial states. But the question of these Jews should not be confused with Zionism, for there can be no greater injustice and aggression than solving the problem of the Jews of Europe by another injustice, i.e., by inflicting injustice on the Arabs of Palestine of various religions and denominations.

B. The special proposal concerning the participation of the Arab Governments and peoples in the "Arab National Fund" to safeguard the lands of the Arabs of Palestine shall be referred to the committee of financial and economic affairs to examine it from all its angles and to submit the result of that examination to the Preliminary Committee in its next meeting.

In faith of which this protocol has been signed at Faruq I University at Alexandria on Saturday, Shawwal 20, 1363 (October 7, 1944).

• • •

What happened next . . .

The signing of the Alexandria Protocol represented the first time that Arab nations had joined together to further their political interests, and it expressed the hope that in the future those nations could work together to address the political and economic issues that faced them. Less than a year later, the League of Arab States called for by the Alexandria Protocol came into being. On March 22, 1945, Yemen and Saudi Arabia joined the five Protocol states in signing the Covenant of the League of Arab States, which mirrored the Protocol in most areas.

Cessation: Stopping.

An Arab Foreign Ministers' meeting at the Arab League headquarters in Cairo, Egypt. The Alexandria Protocol established the Arab League, which started with only five members and has grown over time to include many countries and organizations. © MONA SHARAF/REUTERS/CORBIS.

The League of Arab States, often called simply the Arab League, has been a durable organization, if not a terribly effective one. Though it continues to exist—in 2011, it had twenty-two members in the Middle East and Northern Africa, including Palestine—the Arab League has never succeeded at encouraging the kinds of economic and political cooperation achieved by such regional organizing bodies as the Organ- ization of American States (OAS; an association of countries in South and Central America and the Caribbean) or the European Union (EU; an economic and political association of European countries). Although the reasons behind the failure of Arab states to cooperate are a matter of substantial dispute, observers point to the fact that most Arab states are led by authoritarian figures, who are accustomed to absolute authority, as a key obstacle to effective joint action.

One point that Arab nations agreed on, however, was their desire that Palestine achieve independence as an Arab nation. The Arab League Covenant strengthened the call for Palestinian independence, declaring that Palestine's "existence and *de jure* [by right] national independence is a matter on which there is no doubt as there is no doubt about the independence of the other Arab countries." Just as the Zionists had used the Biltmore Program to stake a claim for an independent Jewish Palestine, Arab countries used the Alexandria Protocol and the Covenant of the League of Arab States to stake a similar claim for an Arab Palestine. (For more information, see **The Biltmore Program**.) Ever since that time, Arab nations have supported the rights of Palestinians to create an independent state. Several times over the years Arab nations have gone to war with Israel—the Jewish state that was created in Palestine in 1948—to try to achieve that goal.

Did you know...

- In 1947 the United Nations proposed a plan to partition (divide) Palestine into two independent states, one Arab and one Jewish. Arabs, unwilling to give up land to the Jews, did not respond favorably to this proposal.
- Violence between Arabs and Jews in Palestine occurred continuously throughout the 1930s and 1940s, but open and organized warfare did not happen until 1948, after Jews declared the independence of the state of Israel and Arab countries joined together to battle the Jews in the 1948 Arab-Israeli War.
- The Covenant of the League of Arab States declared that its primary purpose was to provide for "the general good of the Arab States, the improvement of their circumstances, the security of their future, and the realization of their hopes and aspirations."

Consider the following...

- Both the Biltmore Program and the Alexandria Protocol make claims about the right of Palestine to become independent. Compare and contrast these opposing claims. Are the assertions of both sides accurate? How do the documents attempt to discuss history so as to support their position?
- Are there ways that the Alexandria Protocol could have been written that would have encouraged greater Arab cooperation or assured that Palestinian independence was achieved?

- The Alexandria Protocol was written with the events of World War II in mind. Find examples of how the document reflects the uncertain shape of the postwar world.

For More Information

BOOKS

Encyclopedia of the Modern Middle East and North Africa. 4 vols. New York: Macmillan Reference USA, 2004.

Gomaa, Ahmed M. *The Foundation of the League of Arab States: Wartime Diplomacy and Inter-Arab Politics, 1941 to 1945.* New York: Longman, 1977.

Khalil, Muhammad, ed. *The Arab States and the Arab League: A Documentary Record.* Vol. 2, *International Affairs.* Beirut: Khayats, 1962.

WEB SITES

League of Arab States. http://www.arableagueonline.org/ (accessed on November 30, 2011).

2

Forming a State: The Birth of Israel and the Arab Response

In the 1920s the League of Nations (an international organization of sovereign countries established after World War I [1914–18] to promote peace) established a mandate (a commission granting one country the authority to administer the affairs of another country) for Great Britain in Palestine, a historical region in the Middle East on the eastern shore of the Mediterranean Sea, comprising parts of present-day Israel and Jordan. Under this system, Britain served as the ruling power of Palestine. This region was populated primarily by Arabs (people who speak the Arabic language) who were predominantly Muslim and had lived in the region for centuries. Jewish immigrants had begun arriving in Palestine, the site of the ancient Jewish kingdom, in increasing numbers in order to escape the discrimination they were facing in Europe and other parts of the world. Both Arabs and Jews made claims for the same land, and leaders of the two sides vied for power. Tensions rose, but no solution to the problem was found.

Many Jews adhered to Zionism, an international political movement originating in the late nineteenth century that called for the creation of an independent Jewish state in Palestine. The British initially supported Zionism, and Jews immigrated to Palestine in larger numbers in the 1920s and 1930s with the goal of settling the land and establishing their nation. The new Jewish settlers clashed with Arab Palestinians over ownership of land and resources. The two sides came into increasing conflict, which the British government was unable to resolve.

During World War II (1939–45; a war in which the Allies [Great Britain, France, the Soviet Union, the United States, and China] defeated the Axis Powers [Germany, Italy, and Japan]), German leader Adolf Hitler (1889–1945) sought to accomplish the mass extermination of

American school children waving Israeli flags in celebration the creation of the state of Israel in 1948. Many Jewish people around the world supported the creation of the nation of Israel. © BETTMANN/CORBIS.

European Jews and other groups. Millions of Jews were killed, and the Holocaust made Jews increasingly intent on establishing their own nation. Although the British had restricted the number of Jews who could immigrate to Palestine to appease Arab leaders in the late 1930s, many Jews already there smuggled in those fleeing persecution in Europe. These illegal activities generated hostility between the British government and the Jewish activists, and the rise of Jewish immigrants intensified tensions between Jews and Arabs.

By the end of World War II, Jews and Arabs in Palestine were both working to gain independence from British rule. Each group wanted its own nation. In 1947 the United Nations, an international organization of countries founded in 1945 to promote international peace, security, and cooperation, devised a plan to partition (divide) Palestine into two states, one Jewish and one Arab.

While Jewish leaders in Palestine accepted the partition plan, Arab Palestinian leaders rejected it, calling for Arab control over all of Palestine. Arabs turned to the Arab League for direction. (The Arab League is a regional political alliance of Arab nations formed in 1945 to promote political, military, and economic cooperation within the Arab world.) The organization decided to protect Palestine from the threat of Zionism, but infighting between Arab leaders for ultimate control of the league weakened its effectiveness in responding to the problem.

In May 1948, the British officially withdrew from Palestine. Jews in Palestine declared the establishment of the independent state of Israel, issuing the "Declaration of Israel's Independence." Neighboring Arab nations contested the newly created Jewish state of Israel and supported the Arab Palestinians. Arab armies attacked Israel, marking the start of the 1948 Arab-Israeli War, and the Arab League released the "Statement Issued by the Governments of the Arab League States on the Occasion of the Entry of the Arab Armies in Palestine."

Israel, backed by the United States and other Western European countries, proved to be stronger in the conflict, and thousands of Arabs fled Palestine, becoming refugees in surrounding Arab-controlled countries such as Jordan, Syria, and Egypt, where refugee camps were created. (Refugees are people who flee their country to escape violence or persecution.) Each of these documents makes a strong case for why its group is entitled to the land of Palestine, arguments that explain why conflicts continue in the Middle East into the twenty-first century.

Declaration of the Establishment of the State of Israel

Declaration of the Establishment of the State of Israel
(May 14, 1948)

Issued by Israel's Provisional Council of State in Tel Aviv
Reprinted in Palestine and the Arab-Israeli Conflict
Edited by Charles D. Smith
Published in 2001

"This right is the natural right of the Jewish people to be masters of their own fate, like all other nations, in their own sovereign state."

The declaration of Israel's statehood on May 14, 1948, served as the culmination of many decades of work around the world on the part of Zionists, supporters of an international political movement that called for the creation of an independent Jewish state in Palestine. (Palestine is a historical region in the Middle East on the eastern shore of the Mediterranean Sea, comprising parts of present-day Israel and Jordan.) Beginning in the late nineteenth century, Zionists promoted Jewish settlement in Palestine and coordinated several fund-raising drives in Great Britain and the United States. Zionists realized that to continue their efforts to create a Jewish state in Palestine, they needed to be organized and efficient. To this end, the World Zionist Organization established the Jewish Agency in 1929. The agency started as an effort to link Zionist fund-raising efforts with the governing bodies distributing those funds to Jews in Palestine, but was redesigned to serve the economic and social needs of Jewish settlement in Palestine. The agency evolved into a fully functioning governing body of the Jewish people in Palestine.

With its first offices in Jerusalem, the Jewish Agency soon had branch offices in London, England; Geneva, Switzerland; and New York City. As the official representative of Jews in Palestine, the agency negotiated with Arab Palestinian leadership, foreign governments, and the United Nations (UN; an international organization of countries founded in 1945 to promote international peace, security, and cooperation.) It also coordinated the efforts of Jewish militias, or amateur military groups.

From the 1920s to 1948, Palestine was under British mandate (administrative authority). The eventual goal of the mandate was to establish self-rule in Palestine. This goal was not easily achieved, however, given that two groups laid claim to the region. Jews had begun immigrating to Palestine, the site of the ancient Jewish kingdom, to escape the discrimination they faced throughout the world. Arab Palestinians also claimed the land, for they had lived in Palestine for centuries. (Arabs are people who speak the Arabic language or who live in countries in which Arabic is the dominant language.)

In 1947 the UN investigated the question of which group should rule in Palestine, and members of the Jewish Agency presented their pleas for an independent state, which they would call Israel. The UN proposed a plan to partition (divide) Palestine into two separate states for the Arabs and the Jews, a plan that the Arabs rejected. The British withdrew from Palestine in on May 14, 1948, and that same day Jewish leader David Ben-Gurion (1886–1973) declared the establishment of the state of Israel. Confident that the international community of Europe and the United States would quickly recognize the legitimacy of its claim to independence, Israel's only concern was how the Arabs in Palestine and other countries of the Middle East would react.

Things to remember while reading the "Declaration of the Establishment of the State of Israel"

- The "Declaration of the Establishment of the State of Israel" mentions the resolution of the United Nations General Assembly of November 29, 1947. This resolution called for the partition (division) of Palestine into separate Jewish and Arab states.
- In February 1948, the Jewish Agency mobilized its defense forces to control the areas of the proposed Jewish state, as presented in UN partition plan, and to move into areas assigned to the Arab state. The operation sparked a mass evacuation of Arab

David Ben-Gurion reads the Declaration of the Establishment of Israel to the newly formed Israeli government in May 1948.
© BETTMANN/CORBIS.

Palestinians, and by May nearly 300,000 had fled from these areas.

- Note how carefully the document explains why Israel should be an independent state.
- The "Declaration of the Establishment of the State of Israel" extends an offer of invitation to all Jews wishing to immigrant to the land.

• • •

Declaration of the Establishment of the State of Israel (May 14, 1948)

Eretz-Israel: "Land of Israel" in Hebrew; the ancient kingdom of the Jews.

Eretz-Israel was the birthplace of the Jewish people. Here their spiritual, religious and political identity was shaped. Here they first attained to statehood, created cultural values of national and universal significance and gave to the world the eternal **Book of Books**.

After being forcibly exiled from their land, the people kept faith with it throughout their dispersion and never ceased to pray and hope for their return to it and for the restoration in it of their political freedom.

Impelled by this historic and traditional attachment, Jews strove in every successive generation to re-establish themselves in their ancient homeland. In recent decades they returned in their masses. Pioneers, **Ma'apilim** and defenders, they made deserts bloom, revived the Hebrew language, built villages and towns, and created a thriving community controlling its own economy and culture, loving peace but knowing how to defend itself, bringing the blessings of progress to all the country's inhabitants, and aspiring towards independent nationhood.

In the year **5657**, at the summons of the spiritual father of the Jewish State, Theodor Herzl, the First Zionist Congress convened and proclaimed the right of the Jewish people to national rebirth in its own country.

This right was recognized in the Balfour Declaration of 2 November, 1917, and reaffirmed in the mandate of the League of Nations which, in particular, gave international sanction to the historic connection between the Jewish people and Eretz-Israel and to the right of the Jewish people to rebuild its national home.

The catastrophe which recently befell the Jewish people—the massacre of millions of Jews in Europe—was another clear demonstration of the urgency of solving the problem of its homelessness by re-establishing in Eretz-Israel the Jewish State, which would open the gates of the homeland wide to every Jew and confer upon the Jewish people the status of a fully privileged member of the comity of nations.

Survivors of the Nazi **holocaust** in Europe, as well as Jews from other parts of the world, continued to migrate to Eretz-Israel, undaunted by difficulties, restrictions and dangers, and never ceased to assert their right to a life of dignity, freedom and honest toil in their national homeland.

In the second world war, the Jewish community of this country contributed its full share to the struggle of the freedom—and peace-loving nations against the forces of Nazi wickedness and, by the blood of its soldiers and its war effort, gained the right to be reckoned among the peoples who founded the United Nations.

On 29 November, 1947, the United Nations General Assembly passed a resolution calling for the establishment of a Jewish state in Eretz-Israel; the General Assembly required the inhabitants of Eretz-Israel to take such steps as were necessary on their part for the implementation of that resolution. This recognition by the United Nations of the right of the Jewish people to establish their state is **irrevocable**.

This right is the natural right of the Jewish people to be masters of their own fate, like all other nations, in their own sovereign state.

Book of Books: The Bible.

Ma'apilim: Immigrants coming to Israel in defiance of British policy.

5657: Reference to the Jewish calendar corresponding to the year 1897.

Holocaust: The mass murder of European Jews and other groups by the Nazis during World War II (1939–45).

Irrevocable: Impossible to take back.

Accordingly we, members of the People's Council, representatives of the Jewish community of Eretz-Israel and of the Zionist movement, are here assembled on the day of the termination of the British mandate over Eretz-Israel and, by virtue of our natural and historic right and on the strength of the resolution of the United Nations General Assembly, hereby declare the establishment of a Jewish state in Eretz-Israel, to be known as the State of Israel.

We declare that, with effect from the moment of the termination of the mandate being tonight, the eve of **Sabbath,** the 6th Iyar, 5708 (15 May 1948), until the establishment of the elected, regular authorities of the state in accordance with the constitution which shall be adopted by the elected Constituent Assembly not later than 1 October 1948, the People's Council shall act as a provisional Council of State, and its executive organ, the People's Administration, shall be the Provisional Government of the Jewish state, to be called "Israel".

The State of Israel will be open for Jewish immigration and for the ingathering of the exiles; it will foster the development of the country for the benefit of all its inhabitants; it will be based on freedom, justice and peace as envisaged by the Prophets of Israel; it will ensure complete equality of social and political rights to all its inhabitants irrespective of religion, race or sex; it will guarantee freedom of religion, conscience, language, education and culture; it will safeguard the **Holy Places** of all religions; and it will be faithful to the principles of the Charter of the United Nations.

The State of Israel is prepared to cooperate with the agencies and representatives of the United Nations in implementing the resolution of the General Assembly of 29 November 1947, and will take steps to bring about the economic union of the whole of Eretz-Israel.

We appeal to the United Nations to assist the Jewish people in the building-up of its state and to receive the State of Israel into the **comity** of nations.

We appeal—in the very midst of the onslaught launched against us now for months—to the Arab inhabitants of the State of Israel to preserve peace and participate in the upbuilding of the state on the basis of full and equal citizenship and due representation in all its provisional and permanent institutions.

We extend our hand to all neighboring states and their peoples in an offer of peace and good neighborliness, and appeal to them to establish bonds of cooperation and mutual help with the sovereign Jewish people settled in its own land. The State of Israel is prepared to do its share in a common effort for the advancement of the entire Middle East.

We appeal to the Jewish people throughout the **diaspora** to rally round the Jews of Eretz-Israel in the tasks of immigration and upbuilding and to stand by them in the great struggle for the realization of the age-old dream— the redemption of Israel.

Placing our trust in the Almighty, we affix our signatures to this proclamation at this session of the Provisional Council of State, on the soil

Sabbath: Day of rest and worship for the Jewish people; from sundown on Friday to sundown on Saturday.

Holy Places: Religious sites located in the city of Jerusalem.

Comity: Friendship.

Diaspora: The Jewish community living throughout the world.

Jews in Tel Aviv celebrating the creation of the new state of Israel in 1948. STR/AFP/ GETTY IMAGES.

of the homeland, in the city of Tel-Aviv, on this Sabbath eve, the 5th day of Iyar, 5708 (14 May 1948).

• • •

What happened next...

Israel did secure the international recognition it had hoped for. The United States and the Soviet Union were the first to recognize Israel's independence, and all the other Western states quickly followed. But the

Arab states did not. The day after Israel declared its independence, several Arab nations mobilized forces against the new country.

Military forces from Egypt, Iraq, Jordan, Lebanon, and Syria advanced on Israel to take back the land that they believed rightfully belonged to Arab Palestinians. Arab forces also moved into areas of the proposed Arab state (as set forth by the UN partition plan) in an effort to defend the Palestinians from Israeli attacks, which had been occurring since earlier in the spring as the Israelis prepared to take control of this territory. Although the Arabs had superior weaponry at the beginning of the war, the efficient organization and greater manpower of the Israeli forces prevailed. The Arab-Israeli War of 1948 (known in Israel as the War of Independence) ended in 1949 with the defeat of the Arabs. By the end of the war, Israel occupied all the territory the UN had assigned to it under the partition plan of 1947, including land that the UN had allotted for the Arab state in Palestine, as well as parts of Lebanon and Egypt. The Arab Palestinians who had been living in the areas now claimed by Israel found themselves without a land of their own. Many Palestinians became refugees (people who flee their country to escape violence or persecution), settling in refugee camps in neighboring Arab states.

Did you know . . .

- The Arab-Israeli War of 1948 resulted in the division of Jerusalem into Jewish and Arab sectors.
- After the war, Israel immediately began to build itself as a nation, and within twenty years, it had become the most technologically advanced country in the Middle East.
- Unlike Jews, who were governed in Palestine by the Jewish Agency, Arab Palestinians never had a government. After Israel declared its existence as a nation, the League of Arab States (commonly called the Arab League; a regional political alliance of Arab nations formed in 1945 to promote political, military, and economic cooperation within the Arab world) served as the governing body speaking for the population of Arabs in Palestine, issuing the "Statement Issued by the Governments of the Arab League States on the Occasion of the Entry of the Arab Armies in Palestine."
- After the war, many Arab Palestinians living in the newly created state of Israel lost their rights, including the right to own land. This change caused many Arab Palestinians to become refugees.

Consider the following...

- The "Declaration of the Establishment of the State of Israel" notes that the land was the birthplace of the Jewish people. Why would this fact give the Jewish people a claim to the land? Are there peoples in other countries who might use this same claim for their own purposes?
- The "Declaration of the Establishment of the State of Israel" offers a hand of peace to Arabs, but the Jewish Agency had been working for nearly a year to organize military takeovers of several Arab Palestinian areas. How might Arab Palestinians who had been forced from their homes by the Jews feel about the "Declaration of the Establishment of the State of Israel"?
- The "Declaration of the Establishment of the State of Israel" states that UN recognition of the right of the Jewish people to establish their state is "irrevocable." Explain why the authors of the declaration made this claim. Also consider: If the UN had resolved that the Jewish people did not have the right to establish a self-ruled state, would that particular decision have been "irrevocable" as well?

For More Information

BOOKS

Louis, W. Roger. *The British Empire in the Middle East, 1945–1951: Arab Nationalism, the United States and Postwar Imperialism.* New York: Oxford University Press, 1984.

Miller, Debra A. *The Arab-Israeli Conflict.* San Diego, CA: Lucent Books, 2005.

Shindler, Colin. *A History of Modern Israel.* Cambridge: Cambridge University Press, 2008.

Smith, Charles D., ed. *Palestine and the Arab-Israeli Conflict: A History with Documents.* 7th ed. Boston: Bedford/St. Martin's Press, 2009.

Wagner, Heather Lehr. *Israel and the Arab World.* Philadelphia: Chelsea House, 2002.

WEB SITES

"Facts about Israel: History." *Israel Ministry of Foreign Affairs* (November 28, 2010). http://www.mfa.gov.il/MFA/Facts+About+Israel/History/Facts+about+Israel-+History.htm (accessed November 30, 2011).

"The History of the Jewish Agency for Israel." *Jewish Agency for Israel.* http://www.jafi.org.il/JewishAgency/English/About/History (accessed on November 30, 2011).

"Zionism and the Creation of Israel." *MidEast Web.* http://www.mideastweb.org/zionism.htm (accessed November 3, 2011).

Statement Issued on the Occasion of the Entry of the Arab Armies in Palestine

Statement Issued by the Governments of the Arab League States on the Occasion of the Entry of the Arab Armies in Palestine (May 15, 1948)

Reprinted in The Arab States and the Arab League:
A Documentary Record *Vol. 2*
Edited by Muhmmad Khalil
Published in 1962

"The events which have taken place in Palestine have unmasked the aggressive intentions and the imperialistic designs of the Zionists . . . ."

In 1947, as the United Nations (an international organization of countries founded in 1945 to promote international peace, security, and cooperation) considered the idea of partitioning, or dividing, Palestine into Jewish and Arab (Arabic-speaking) states, Arab Palestinians were living without an organized self-government. (Palestine is a historical region in the Middle East on the eastern shore of the Mediterranean Sea, comprising parts of present-day Israel and Jordan.) The Arab Higher Committee (AHC) had been form in 1936 to resist Jewish immigration and British administration in Palestine. But the AHC was never formally recognized by the British, as the Jewish Agency (the governing body of Jews in Palestine) had been. (For more information, see **Declaration of the Establishment of the State of Israel**.) The AHC was dissolved by the

British in 1937, and its leaders had been deported as a result of the ongoing Arab revolts in Palestine.

The Arab Palestinians' political weakness made them dependent on the League of Arab States. Commonly known as the Arab League, this organization was a regional political alliance of Arab nations formed in 1945 to promote political, military, and economic cooperation within the Arab world. The Arab League enabled Arab states to work together while maintaining their separate identities. The first members were Egypt, Saudi Arabia, Yemen, Transjordan (present-day Jordan), Syria, Lebanon, and Iraq. In an attempt to help establish an Arab Palestinian government, the Arab League reestablished the AHC in 1946, naming

Members of the Arab Higher Committee, c. 1948. The Arab League sponsored the Arab Higher Committee and named exiled Palestinian leaders to the top positions, but Palestinians had little true power in the Arab League. © HULTON-DEUTSCH COL-LECTION/CORBIS.

the exiled Palestinian leaders to the top positions. However, the Palestinians in the AHC and the leaders of the Arab League could not agree on the future of Palestine, and the AHC was reduced to an insignificant, powerless part of the Arab League.

When Israel declared its independence on May 14, 1948, the Arab Palestinians, having no government and no unified military of their own, were completely reliant on the Arab League. On May 15, 1948, the governments of the Arab League member states issued the "Statement Issued by the Governments of the Arab League States on the Occasion of the Entry of the Arab Armies in Palestine." Their support, both politically and militarily, of the Palestinians broadened the Arab-Israeli conflict beyond the disputed region of Palestine (now the newly formed state of Israel) to include neighboring Arab states.

Things to remember while reading the "Statement Issued by the Governments of the Arab League States on the Occasion of the Entry of the Arab Armies in Palestine"

- A surge of Arab nationalism (the belief that a people with shared ethnic, cultural, and/or religious identities have the right to form their own nation) rose in the early 1900s against the Ottoman Empire (the vast empire of the Ottoman Turks which included southwest Asia, northeast Africa, and southeast Europe, and lasted from the thirteenth century to the early twentieth century), which ruled over much of the Middle East.

- European domination of the Middle East after World War I (1914–18; a global war between the Allies [Great Britain, France, and Russia, joined later by the United States] and the Central Powers [Germany, Austria-Hungary, and their allies]) provoked resentment among Arabs, many of whom had been promised autonomy for helping the Europeans overthrow the Ottoman Empire.

- Both Great Britain and France granted many Arab nations their independence as World War II (1939–45; a war in which the Allies [Great Britain, France, the Soviet Union, the United States, and China] defeated the Axis Powers [Germany, Italy, and Japan]) came to a close.

- The Arab League was united in its opposition to Jewish claims to Palestine.

• • •

Statement Issued by the Governments of the Arab League States on the Occasion of the Entry of the Arab Armies in Palestine (May 15, 1948)

1. Palestine was part of the former **Ottoman Empire**, subject to its law and represented in its parliament. The overwhelming majority of the population of Palestine were Arabs. There was in it a small minority of Jews that enjoyed the same rights and bore the same responsibilities as the [other] inhabitants, and did not suffer any ill-treatment on account of its religious beliefs. The **holy places** were **inviolable** and the freedom of access to them was guaranteed.

2. The Arabs have always asked for their freedom and independence. On the outbreak of the **First World War**, and when the **Allies** declared that they were fighting for the liberation of peoples, the Arabs joined them and fought on their side with a view to realizing their national aspirations and obtaining their independence. England pledged herself to recognize the independence of the Arab countries in Asia, including Palestine. The Arabs played a remarkable part in the achievement of final victory and the Allies have admitted this.

3. In 1917 England issued a **declaration** in which she expressed her sympathy with the establishment of a national home for the Jews in Palestine. When the Arabs knew of this they protested against it, but England reassured them by affirming to them that this would not prejudice the right of their countries to freedom and independence or affect the political status of the Arabs in Palestine. **Notwithstanding** the legally void character of this declaration, it was interpreted by England to aim at no more than the establishment of a spiritual centre for the Jews in Palestine, and to conceal no ulterior political aims, such as the establishment of a Jewish State. The same thing was declared by the Jewish leaders.

4. When the war came to an end England did not keep her promise. Indeed, the Allies placed Palestine under the **mandate system** and entrusted England with [the task of carrying it out], in accordance with a document providing for the administration of the country, in the interests of its inhabitants and its preparation for the independence which the Covenant of the **League of Nations** recognized that Palestine was qualified to have.

5. England administered Palestine in a manner which enabled the Jews to flood it with immigrants and helped them to settle in the country. [This was so] notwithstanding the fact that it was proved that the density of the population in Palestine had exceeded the economic capacity of the country to absorb additional immigrants. England did not pay regard to the interests or rights of the Arab inhabitants, the lawful owners of the country. Although they used to express, by various means, their concern and **indignation** on account of this state of affairs which was harmful to their being and their

Ottoman Empire: The vast empire of the Ottoman Turks which included southwest Asia, northeast Africa, and southeast Europe, and lasted from the thirteenth century to the early twentieth century.

Holy places: Religious sites located in the city of Jerusalem.

Inviolable: Secure from attack.

First World War: World War I (1914–18).

Allies: The nations who joined together to win World War I; Great Britain, France, Russia, and the United States

Declaration: The Balfour Declaration.

Notwithstanding: Despite.

Mandate system: The system established after World War I to administer former territories of Germany and the Ottoman Empire.

League of Nations: An international organization of sovereign countries established after World War I to promote peace.

Indignation: Anger aroused by something unjust.

future, they [invariably] were met by indifference, imprisonment and oppression.

6. As Palestine is an Arab country, situated in the heart of the Arab countries and attached to the Arab world by various ties—spiritual, historical, and strategic—the Arab countries, and even the Eastern ones, governments as well as peoples, have concerned themselves with the problem of Palestine and have raised it to the international level; [they have also raised the problem] with England, asking for its solution in accordance with the pledges made and with democratic principles. The Round Table Conference was held in London in 1939 in order to discuss the Palestine question and to arrive at the just solution thereof. The Governments of the Arab States participated in [this conference] and asked for the preservation of the Arab character of Palestine and the proclamation of its independence. This conference ended with the issue of a White Paper in which England defined her policy towards Palestine, recognized its independence, and undertook to set up the institutions that would lead to its exercise of the characteristics of [this independence]. She [also] declared that her obligations concerning the establishment of a Jewish national home had been fulfilled, since that home had actually been established. But the policy defined in that [White] paper was not carried out. This, therefore, led to the deterioration of the situation and the **aggravation of matters** contrary to the interests of the Arabs.

7. While the **Second World War** was still in progress, the Governments of the Arab States began to hold consultations regarding the reinforcement of their co-operation and the increasing of the means of their collaboration and their **solidarity**, with a view to safeguarding their present and their future and to participating in the erection of the **edifice** of the new world on firm foundations. Palestine had its [worthy] share of consideration and attention in these conversations. These conversations led to the establishment of the **League of Arab States** as an instrument for the co-operation of the Arab States for their security, peace and well-being.

The Pact of the League of Arab States declared that Palestine has been an independent country since its separation from the Ottoman Empire, but the manifestations of this independence have been suppressed due to reasons which were out of the control of its inhabitants. The establishment of the United Nations shortly afterwards was an event about which the Arabs had the greatest hopes. Their belief in the ideals on which that organization was based made them participate in its establishment and membership.

8. Since then the Arab League and its [member] Governments have not spared any effort to pursue any course, whether with the Mandatory Power or with the United Nations, in order to bring about a just solution of the Palestine problem: [a solution] based upon true democratic principles and compatible with the provisions of the Covenant of the League of Nations and the [Charter] of the United Nations, and which would [at the same time] be lasting, guarantee peace and security in the country and prepare it for

Aggravation of matters: Increasing irritation over issues.

Second World War: World War II (1939–45).

Solidarity: Common interests within a group.

Edifice: Bulding of large size.

League of Arab States: A regional political alliance of Arab nations formed in 1945 to promote political, military, and economic cooperation within the Arab world.

progress and prosperity. But **Zionist** claims were always an obstacle to finding such a solution, [as the Zionists], having prepared themselves with armed forces, strongholds and fortifications to face by force anyone standing in their way, publicly declared [their intention] to establish a Jewish State.

9. When the General Assembly of the United Nations issued, on 29 November 1947, its recommendation concerning the solution of the Palestine problem, on the basis of the establishment of an Arab State and of another Jewish [state] in [Palestine] together with placing the City of Jerusalem under the trusteeship of the United Nations, the Arab States drew attention to the injustice implied in this solution [affecting] the right of the people of Palestine to immediate independence, as well as democratic principles and the provisions of the Covenant of the League of Nations and [the Charter] of the United Nations. [These States also] declared the Arabs' rejection of [that solution] and that it would not be possible to carry it out by peaceful means, and that its forcible imposition would **constitute** a threat to peace and security in this area.

The warnings and expectations of the Arab States have, indeed, proved to be true, as disturbances were soon widespread throughout Palestine. The Arabs clashed with the Jews, and the two [parties] proceeded to fight each other and shed each other's blood. Whereupon the United Nations began to realize the danger of recommending the partition [of Palestine] and is still looking for a way out of this state of affairs.

10. Now that the British mandate over Palestine has come to an end, without there being a legitimate constitutional authority in the country, which would safeguard the maintenance of security and respect for law and which would protect the lives and properties of the inhabitants, the Governments of the Arab States declare the following:—

First: That the rule of Palestine should revert to its inhabitants, in accordance with the provisions of the Covenant of the League of Nations and [the Charter] of the United Nations and that [the Palestinians] should alone have the right to determine their future.

Second: Security and order in Palestine have become disrupted. The Zionist aggression resulted in the **exodus** of more than a quarter of a million of its Arab inhabitants from their homes and in their taking refuge in the neighbouring Arab countries.

The events which have taken place in Palestine have unmasked the aggressive intentions and the **imperialistic** designs of the Zionists, including the atrocities committed by them against the peace-loving Arab inhabitants, especially in **Dayr Yasin, Tiberias and others**. Nor have they respected the inviolability of **consuls**, as they have attacked the consulates of the Arab States in Jerusalem. After the termination of the British mandate over Palestine the British authorities are no longer responsible for security in the country, except to the degree affecting their withdrawing forces, and [only] in the areas in which these forces happen to be at the time of withdrawal as announced by [these authorities]. This state of affairs would render Palestine without any

Zionist: Supporters of the creation of an independent Jewish state in Palestine.

Constitute: Be.

Exodus: Departure of a large number of people.

Imperialistic: Displaying a belief in nation building.

Dayr Yasin, Tiberias and others: Arab villages in which Jews attacked and killed numerous Arabs.

Consuls: Government representatives.

governmental machinery capable of restoring order and the rule of law to the country, and of protecting the lives and properties of the inhabitants.

Third: This state of affairs is threatening to spread to the neighbouring Arab countries, where feeling is running high because of the events in Palestine. The Governments of the Member States of the Arab League and of the United Nations are exceedingly worried and deeply concerned about this state of affairs.

Fourth: These Governments had hoped that the United Nations would have succeeded in finding a peaceful and just solution of the problem of Palestine, in accordance with democratic principles and the **provisions** of the Covenant of the League of Nations and [the Charter] of the United Nations, so that peace, security and prosperity would prevail in this part of the world.

Fifth: The Governments of the Arab States, as members of the Arab League, a regional organization within the meaning of the provisions of Chapter VIII of the Charter of the United Nations, are responsible for maintaining peace and security in their area. These Governments view the events taking place in Palestine as a threat to peace and security in the area as a whole and [also] in each of them taken separately.

Sixth: Therefore, as security in Palestine is a sacred trust in the hands of the Arab States, and in order to put an end to this state of affairs and to prevent it from becoming aggravated or from turning into [a state of] chaos, the extent of which no one can foretell; in order to stop the spreading of disturbances and disorder in Palestine to the neighbouring Arab countries; in order to fill the gap brought about in the governmental machinery in Palestine as a result of the termination of the mandate and the non-establishment of a lawful successor authority, the Governments of the Arab States have found themselves compelled to intervene in Palestine solely in order to help its inhabitants restore peace and security and the rule of justice and law to their country, and in order to prevent bloodshed.

Seventh: The Governments of the Arab States recognize that the independence of Palestine, which has so far been suppressed by the British mandate, has become an accomplished fact for the lawful inhabitants of Palestine. They alone, by virtue of their **absolute sovereignty**, have the right to provide their country with laws and governmental institutions. They alone should exercise the attributes of their independence, through their own means and without any kind of foreign interference, immediately after peace, security and the rule of law have been restored to the country.

At that time the intervention of the Arab states will cease, and the independent State of Palestine will co-operate with the [other member] States of the Arab League in order to bring peace, security and prosperity to this part of the world.

The Governments of the Arab States emphasize, on this occasion, what they have already declared before the London Conference and the United Nations, that the only solution of the Palestine problem is the establishment

Provisions: Agreement between parties regarding some aspect of a legal matter.

Absolute sovereignty: Supreme power or authority

of a unitary Palestinian State, in accordance with democratic principles, whereby its inhabitants will enjoy complete equality before the law, [and whereby] minorities will be assured of all the guarantees recognized in democratic constitutional countries, and [whereby] the holy places will be preserved and the right of access thereto guaranteed.

Eighth: The Arab States most **emphatically** declare that [their] intervention in Palestine was due only to these considerations and objectives, and that they aim at nothing more than to put an end to the prevailing conditions in [Palestine]. For this reason, they have great confidence that their action will have the support of the United Nations; [that it will be] considered as an action aiming at the realization of its aims and at promoting its principles, as provided for in its Charter.

• • •

What happened next...

Members of the Arab League mobilized their armies and invaded Israel in May 1948. They also advanced into areas that the UN had proposed to be part of an Arab state, in order to defend Palestinians after weeks of attacks by the Israelis attempting to take control of these areas. Arabs outnumbered the Jewish residents in Palestine by more than two to one, and the Arab military forces outnumbered those of the Jews. However, the Arab invaders lacked strong organization. The Arab forces—including forces from Egypt, Iraq, Jordan, Lebanon, Saudi Arabia, and Syria—were not motivated by a common goal or directed by a centralized command. The Jewish forces were. The Jews had developed a highly organized underground army before declaring independence, called Haganah; that group became the country's official army in 1948. Although the Arabs initially had superior weaponry, Israel soon gained access to weapons from the Soviet bloc (communist nations closely aligned with the Soviet Union), specifically Czechoslovakia, as well as from the United States and Western European countries, thus securing the necessary equipment to overcome its deficiencies. In addition, Israel remained focused on its task of pushing Arabs out, while Arab infighting led to distracting skirmishes between Arab armies during the war.

By 1949, Israel had won the war and expanded its territory. Much of the land the United Nations had proposed for the independent Arab state in 1947 had become either part of Israel or was annexed by Jordan. Approximately 750,000 Palestinians fled out of fear or were forced off land captured by Israel during the war. Some of these Palestinians moved to neighboring Arab countries, but most gathered in refugee camps in

Emphatically: Forcefully.

Arab fighters in a foxhole outside of Jerusalem. Arab League members mobilized their armies and invaded Israel in May 1948.
© BETTMANN/CORBIS.

hopes of returning to their homes. (Refugees are people who flee their country to escape violence or persecution.) The inability of the peoples of Israel and Palestine to find lasting peace kept over 1.4 million Palestinians languishing in refugee camps as of 2011, according to statistics maintained by the United Nations Relief and Works Agency for Palestine Refugees.

Did you know . . .

- The conflict between the newly declared state of Israel and the Arab nations is called the 1948 Arab-Israeli War.

- Of Palestine's 1.3 million Arab inhabitants before the 1948 Arab-Israeli War, almost half became refugees, living in refugee camps in the West Bank, the Gaza Strip, or in neighboring Arab countries, by war's end.
- In September 1948, the Arab League announced the formation of an All-Palestine Government, but Arab infighting, especially between Egypt and Jordan, destroyed the power of the new government, and it endured as a powerless department of the Arab League until 1959.
- Palestinians refer to the 1948 Arab-Israeli War and the refugee crisis that followed as *al-Nakba* (an Arabic word meaning "the catastrophe").
- Neither Israel nor the Arab states agreed to negotiate a lasting peace after the 1948 Arab-Israeli War.

Consider the following . . .

- Could the 1948 Arab-Israeli War have been avoided if the Arab states had agreed to the Jewish state's existence? What might Palestine have looked like in this case?
- In what other diplomatic ways might the Arab states have reacted to the declaration of Israel's independence? Was war the only recourse left to them?
- Does the "Statement Issued by the Governments of the Arab League States on the Occasion of the Entry of the Arab Armies in Palestine" provide any insight into the continued difficulties between Arab countries and Israel?

For More Information

BOOKS

Diller, Daniel, ed. *The Middle East*. 8th ed. Washington, DC: Congressional Quarterly, 1995.

Frank, Mitch. *Understanding the Holy Land: Answering Questions about the Israeli-Palestinian Conflict*. New York: Viking, 2005.

Khalil, Muhammad, ed. *The Arab States and the Arab League: A Documentary Record*. Vol. 2, *International Affairs*. Beirut: Khayats, 1962.

WEB SITES

"The Palestinian Refugees." *MidEast Web*. http://www.mideastweb.org/refugees1.htm (accessedon November 30, 2011).

The Question of Palestine & the United Nations. http://www.un.org/Depts/dpi/palestine/ (accessed on November 30, 2011).

3

Conflict in the Middle East after the 1967 Arab-Israeli War

On May 14, 1948, the state of Israel declared its independence, thus achieving the long-held goal of the world Jewish community for a national homeland. Israel then fought a war for its existence, defeating the combined forces of the Arab nations of Egypt, Iraq, Jordan, Lebanon, and Syria. The end of this war in 1949 did not bring peace to the Middle East, however. It drove approximately 750,000 native Arab inhabitants out of Israel and into neighboring countries, especially Lebanon and Jordan. (Approximately 260,000 Jews living in Arab nations relocated to Israel. From the 1950s to the early 1970s, about 340,000 more Jews moved to Israel.) Palestinians were deeply angered at what they saw as the Jewish theft of their nation. (Palestinians are an Arab people whose ancestors lived in the historical region of Palestine, comprising parts of present-day Israel and Jordan, and who continue to lay claim to that land.) Neighboring Arab nations resented their military defeat. Like the Palestinians, these nations violently objected to the existence of Israel. In addition, they found the Palestinian refugee populations that lived in their countries to be a constant source of trouble. (Refugees are people who flee their country to escape violence or persecution.)

For most of the 1950s and early 1960s, Israel and its neighbors managed to live together in relative peace. One exception was the 1956 Suez Crisis in which joint British-French-Israeli forces invaded Egypt. The invasion was launched after Egypt nationalized (brought under government control) the Suez Canal, a shipping canal that connects the Mediterranean Sea with the Red Sea, in a failed attempt to reestablish Western control of the canal.

During these years, Arab nations were engaged in an ongoing dispute over whose view of the Arab future would prevail. In Egypt, President Gamal Abdel Nasser (1918–1970) promoted Pan-Arabism (a movement

The Israeli army securing a position in the Golan Heights in Syria near the end of the 1967 Arab-Israeli War. © BETTMANN/ CORBIS.

for the unification of Arab peoples and the political alliance of Arab states), arguing that Arab nations should join together to combat Western control and influence, due to the support of Western nations for the Jewish nation of Israel. In Syria and Iraq, members of the Ba'ath Party (a secular [nonreligious] political party founded in the 1940s with the goal of uniting the Arab world and creating one powerful Arab state) embraced Pan-Arabism, but they wanted a socialist system. (Socialism is a system in which the government owns the means of production and controls the distribution of goods and services). In Jordan and Saudi Arabia, hereditary monarchs (the leaders in a system of rule where

The Occupied Territories

As a result of the 1967 Arab-Israeli War, fought between June 5 and June 10, 1967, Israel occupied territories formerly held by its neighbors. From Egypt, Israel seized the Sinai Peninsula and the Gaza Strip; from Syria, it took the Golan Heights; and from Jordan, it seized the West Bank. From that time on, the occupied territories have been the source of nearly continual dispute between Israel and those neighbors. Arab governments and the Palestine Liberation Organization (PLO; a political and military organization formed to unite various Palestinian Arab groups with the goal of establishing an independent Palestinian state) released official statements demanding the return of these lands. UN Security Council Resolution 242, along with most of the world community, also demanded the return of these captured territories. However, the Israeli government generally refused to make direct statements about its plans for these areas.

Israel did not take a consistent official position primarily because the country was deeply divided over what to do with these territories. Some believed in the idea of a so-called Greater Israel. They wanted to make these territories a permanent part of their nation. They began to build Jewish settlements in these territories, in the hopes that if these settlements became large enough, Israel would be unable to give back the land. Others did not want Israel to claim these territories, especially the Gaza Strip and the West Bank, because they contained huge Palestinian populations. If these Palestinians became citizens of Israel, they would become a majority and could affect Israel's politics. These Israelis believed that the territories should be used instead as bargaining chips in Israel's efforts to gain permanent peace settlements with its Arab neighbors.

Israel began returning the Sinai Peninsula to Egypt in the 1970s and completed doing so in 1982; these actions were part of the peace process with Egypt. In 2005, under Israeli prime minister Ariel Sharon's (1928–) disengagement plan, Israel withdrew its settlers from the Gaza Strip, as well as from four West Bank settlements. The West Bank remains a source of negotiation with Palestinians. In Israel, the argument over what to do with these territories continues.

power transfers from family member to family member) were comfortable with their own unquestioned rule. At this point in Arab history, the belief that Arabs should unite under sharia (Islamic religious law) was not widespread. In addition, there was continued pressure from Palestinians to address their claims against Israel. The disorder between Arab countries kept direct conflicts with Israel to a minimum, at least for a time.

War returned to the Middle East in 1967. Continual small-scale attacks on Israel by Palestinians based in neighboring Lebanon, Syria, and Jordan increased tensions between the countries, as did standoffs between Israeli and Egyptian forces in the Sinai Peninsula. By May 1967 Palestinian attacks on Israel were so persistent that many of the Arab countries in the region began to prepare for war. Israel, believing that war was imminent, decided to attack first, catching its Arab neighbors by surprise. On June 5, the Israelis launched a series of air strikes on Egyptian forces in Egypt and the Sinai Peninsula, followed shortly thereafter by offensive attacks in the Golan Heights, in Syria, and the West Bank, in Jordan. Ignoring calls from the United States for a cease-fire, the Israelis made stunning advances. When open fighting stopped six days later, the Arabs had been defeated. Israel occupied the entire Sinai Peninsula, the Golan Heights, the West Bank, and the Gaza Strip, narrow strip of land along the eastern shore of the Mediterranean Sea, west of Israel and bordering Egypt in the southwest. The 1967 Arab-Israeli War (known in Israel as the Six-Day War) left Israel in possession of vast new tracts of land and had a lasting impact on the nature of the conflict in the Middle East.

In the aftermath of the 1967 Arab-Israeli War, all sides in the conflict were forced to reconsider what they expected for the future. The United Nations (an international organization of countries founded in 1945 to promote international peace, security, and cooperation) tried to ease the conflict by passing resolutions that would provide a framework for peace. Among these resolutions was UN Security Council Resolution 242, which demanded that Israel return the territories it captured during the war.

The Palestinians, encouraged by Arab political support, arms, and money, recognized that they must become better organized if they were to make any advances in their pursuit of an independent state. To this end, in 1964, they formed the Palestine Liberation Organization (a political and military organization formed to unite various Palestinian Arab groups with the goal of establishing an independent Palestinian state) and issued a National Charter in 1968.

United Nations Resolution 242

United Nations Security Council Resolution 242
(November 22, 1967)

Reprinted in Palestine and the Arab-Israeli Conflict
Edited by Charles D. Smith
Published in 2001

"The Security Council, expressing its continuing concern with the grave situation in the Middle East . . . and the need to work for a just and lasting peace in which every state in the area can live in security. . . . . "

Since its founding in 1945, the United Nations (UN; an international organization of countries founded to promote international peace, security, and cooperation) has had a special relationship with Palestine and the problems the country faced. (Palestine is a historical region in the Middle East on the eastern shore of the Mediterranean Sea, comprising parts of present-day Israel and Jordan.) Among its first actions as an organization was the creation of the United Nations Special Committee on Palestine (UNSCOP), which in 1947 recommended the division of Palestine into two independent states, one Jewish and one Arab. On November 29, 1947, the UN General Assembly adopted Resolution 181, which set in place a plan to partition (divide) Palestine into two states. Arab Palestinians rejected the partition. (Arabs are people who speak the Arabic language or who live in countries in which Arabic is the dominant language.) In May 1948 the Jews declared the establishment of the state of Israel, and in 1949 Israel was admitted as a member of the UN.

Over time, the UN sought to play a mediating role in the conflict that existed between Israel and Arabs, both within Israel and in neighboring countries. In 1948 the UN passed Resolution 194, which called on Israel to allow Palestinian refugees to return to homes that they had fled during the war or to compensate those who did not wish to return. In the 1950s and 1960s the UN appointed special mediators to help resolve minor conflicts, and in 1956, it created a United Nations Emergency Force to help keep peace between Israelis and Egyptians in the Sinai Peninsula. When the 1967 Arab-Israeli War broke out between Israel and the combined forces of Egypt, Jordan, and Syria, the UN scrambled to call a cease-fire to end the war.

The Israeli victory in the 1967 war was a decisive moment in the history of the Arab-Israeli conflict. With its capture of the West Bank, the Golan Heights, and the Sinai Peninsula, Israel felt that it had gained the security it had long lacked. These new territories gave Israel what it considered to be

A man holds a newspaper featuring a story about the start of the 1967 Arab-Israeli War, while a meeting of the United Nations Security Council takes place in the background. The United Nations attempted to be the peacemaker between the Arab countries of the Middle East and Israel. © BETTMANN/CORBIS.

The United Nations Security Council

The United Nations Security Council is the most powerful organization within the UN. It consists of five permanent members—the United States, Great Britian, France, the Russian Federation, and the People's Republic of China—and ten other member nations, half of which are replaced every year. The Security Council's purpose under the United Nations Charter is the maintenance of international peace and security. It is the only body of the UN that is authorized to use force against an aggressor nation. (As of 2011, the UN Security Council has authorized the use of force only twice in its existence: during the Korean War of 1950 and the Persian Gulf War of 1991.)

One of the primary ways that the UN Security Council notifies the world of its intentions is through numbered Security Council Resolutions. Security Council Resolutions can authorize the use of force, call on a member nation to perform an action, or establish a framework for the resolution of a conflict. Security Council Resolutions bear the force of law, but that does not mean that they are always followed.

The United Nations Security Council meeting room at UN headquarters in New York City. © BLICKWINKEL/ ALAMY.

buffer zones, or neutral areas separating two hostile countries, between major Israeli cities and enemy military positions. The war created problems, however. Israel had taken control of territories that were home to huge numbers of Palestinians. Although the UN had been unable to prevent the 1967 Arab-Israeli War, it worked to negotiate a resolution that would allow all sides to step away from the brink of continual conflict. Security Council Resolution 242 was the result.

Things to remember while reading "United Nations Security Council Resolution 242"

- UN Security Council Resolutions generally reflect the opinion of the major world powers. No resolution can pass over the objection of any one of the five permanent Security Council members: the

United States, Great Britain, France, the Russian Federation, and the People's Republic of China.

- During the course of the 1967 Arab-Israeli War, the UN Security Council passed five resolutions calling for an end to the war and for the reasonable treatment of civilians in war zones.

- In the aftermath of the 1967 Arab-Israeli War, the political status of the captured territories was unclear. Most of the land was classified as occupied territory, meaning it was controlled by the Israeli military forces but not officially part of the state of Israel. Only East Jerusalem was annexed, or claimed, as part of the state of Israel.

• • •

United Nations Security Council Resolution 242 (November 22, 1967)

The Security Council,

Expressing its continuing concern with the grave situation in the Middle East,

Emphasizing the **inadmissibility** of the acquisition of territory by war and the need to work for a just and lasting peace in which every state in the area can live in security,

Emphasizing further that all Member States in their acceptance of the Charter of the United Nations have undertaken a commitment to act in accordance with Article 2 of the Charter,

1. *Affirms* that the fulfillment of Charter principles requires the establishment of a just and lasting peace in the Middle East which should include the application of both the following principles:

(i) Withdrawal of Israel[i] armed forces from territories occupied in the recent conflict;

(ii) Termination of all claims or states of **belligerency** and respect for and acknowledgement of the sovereignty, territorial integrity and political independence of every State in the area and their right to live in peace within secure and recognized boundaries free from threats or acts of force.

2. *Affirms further* the necessity

(a) For guaranteeing freedom of navigation through international waterways in the area;

(b) For achieving a just settlement of the refugee problem;

(c) For guaranteeing the territorial **inviolability** and political independence of every State in the area, through measures including the establishment of **demilitarized zones**;

3. *Requests* the Secretary-General to designate a Special Representative to proceed to the Middle East to establish and maintain contact with the

Inadmissibility: Unacceptability.

Belligerency: Being at war.

Inviolability: Security from attack.

Demilitarized zones: Areas in which military troops, weapons, and military installments are not allowed.

States concerned in order to promote agreement and assist efforts to achieve a peaceful and accepted settlement in accordance with the provisions and principles in this resolution;

4. *Requests* the Secretary-General to report to the Security Council on the progress of the efforts of the Special Representative as soon as possible.

• • •

What happened next...

United Nations Security Council Resolution 242 did not bring immediate peace to the Middle East. Egypt and Jordan interpreted the resolution as a call for Israel to withdraw to pre–1967 borders before any peace negotiations could take place. Israel interpreted the resolution as calling for Arab states to enter into direct negotiations with Israel. Syria rejected the resolution altogether, according to a UN publication titled *The Question of Palestine and the United Nations,* "maintaining that the resolution had linked the central issue of Israeli withdrawal to concessions demanded from Arab countries." And the Palestine Liberation Organization (PLO; a political and military organization formed to unite various Palestinian Arab groups with the goal of establishing an independent Palestinian state) rejected the resolution for simplifying and downgrading the question of Palestine to the single issue of the refugee problem. In short, every country directly impacted by the resolution found fault with parts of it.

In the short term, the Arab-Israeli conflict continued. Arab states refused to recognize or negotiate with Israel until the mid–1970s. Periodic clashes along borders occurred through the late 1960s and early 1970s, and open warfare broke out again with the 1973 Arab-Israeli War, when Israel was attacked by Egypt and Syria. As in the past, the UN brokered a cease-fire, this time with Security Council Resolution 338, and established a second United Nations Emergency Force to resolve land claims resulting from the 1973 Arab-Israeli War. Because neither Israel nor the Arab countries had gained or lost any significant land in the 1973 war, the Emergency Force continued to focus on the territories taken by Israel in the 1967 war.

Resolution 242 did have important long-term effects, however. It helped initiate peace talks between Egypt and Israel that led to a peace agreement between those nations in 1979, and it was the basis for a peace agreement with Jordan that was signed in 1994. According to Charles Smith, author of *Palestine and the Arab-Israeli Conflict*, Resolution 242 "has remained the official basis of negotiating efforts to the present." Certain phrases from Resolution 242—"the need to work for a just and lasting peace," and "live in peace within secure and recognized boundaries free from threats or acts of force"—have been consistently referred to by all sides in the conflict during peace negotiations in the 1990s and early 2000s. Mahmoud Abbas (1935–), who became president of the Palestinian Authority (the recognized governing institution for Palestinians in the West Bank and the Gaza Strip) in 2005, has met regularly with a succession of Israeli prime ministers, including Ariel Sharon (1928–), Ehud Olmert (1945–), and Benjamin Netanyahu (1949–) for ongoing talks, which have sometimes involved other Arab leaders as well as those of Western nations.

U.S. president Bill Clinton watches as King Hussein of Jordan (left) and Israeli prime minister Yitzhak Rabin sign a peace treaty in 1994. UN Resolution 242 was the basis for this agreement. DAVID RUBINGER/TIME LIFE PICTURES/GETTY IMAGES.

Did you know . . .

- UN Security Council resolutions are numbered in the order that they are created. The first resolution was issued on January 25, 1946. To find the latest resolution, go to the UN Security Council Web site: http://www.un.org/Docs/sc/.

- The 1967 Arab-Israeli War occurred at a time of world crisis. Not only were the United States and the Soviet Union engaged in the Cold War (a period of intense political and economic rivalry between the United States and the Soviet Union that lasted from 1945 to 1991), but the United States had also committed its military to fighting the Vietnam War (1954–75; a war between the forces of North Vietnam supported by China and the Soviet Union and the forces of South Vietnam supported by the United States). Neither the United States nor the Soviet Union wanted to get drawn into further military conflicts in the Middle East, so they worked through the United Nations to try to bring about peace.

Consider the following . . .

- Critics sometimes complain that UN Security Council resolutions are ineffective in influencing a conflict or a nation's policies. Is this true in relation to Israel? What would motivate the countries involved in this conflict to pay attention to these resolutions?

- Historians sometimes try to understand the past by posing counter-historical questions—questions that ask what would have happened if conditions were different. For example, what would have happened if the Security Council had not urged Israel and the Arab states to end the 1967 Arab-Israeli War? Or, would peace have come more quickly to the Middle East without the involvement of the United Nations? Explore these questions, or invent your own counter-historical questions that explore other aspects of this conflict.

For More Information

BOOKS

Farsoun, Samih K., with Christina E. Zacharia. *Palestine and the Palestinians.* Boulder, CO: Westview Press, 1997.

Smith, Charles D., ed. *Palestine and the Arab-Israeli Conflict: A History with Documents*, 4th ed. Boston MA: Bedford/St. Martin's, 2001.

Wagner, Heather Lehr. *Israel and the Arab World.* Philadelphia: Chelsea House, 2002.

Worth, Richard. *Israel and the Arab States.* New York: F. Watts, 1983.

PERIODICALS

The Question of Palestine & the United Nations. United Nations Department of Public Information. (March 2003). Available online at http://www.un.org/Depts/dpi/palestine (accessed on November 30, 2011).

WEB SITES

UN Security Council. http://www.un.org/Docs/sc/ (accessed on November 30, 2011).

The Palestinian National Charter

The Palestinian National Charter: Resolutions of the
Palestine National Council (July 1–17, 1968)

Issued by the Palestine Liberation Organization

Reprinted in Palestine and the Arab-Israeli Conflict

Edited by Charles D. Smith

Published in 2001

"The Palestinians will have three mottoes: national unity,
national mobilization, and liberation."

For almost twenty years after the creation of the state of Israel in 1948, most of the world saw the conflict in the Middle East as an Arab-Israeli issue. (Arabs are people who speak the Arabic language or who live in countries in which Arabic is the dominant language.) Indeed, the major battles—from the 1948 Arab-Israeli War to the 1967 Arab-Israeli War—were between Israel and the Arab nations that surrounded it. During this period, the Palestinian people (Arabs whose ancestors lived in the historical region of Palestine, comprising parts of present-day Israel and Jordan, and who continue to lay claim to that land) played a secondary role in the conflict. Although their rights were always mentioned by the leading Arab nations as part of their justification for fighting against Israel, the Palestinians generally lacked political organizations that could give voice to their hopes and desires to reclaim their country. All that began to change after Israel's surprising defeat of the Arab nations in 1967.

"In the immediate wake of their dispossession and expulsion from Palestine in 1948, the Palestinian refugees were so traumatized and consumed with mere physical survival . . . that they were politically paralyzed," wrote Samih K. Farsoun and Naseer Aruri in *Palestine and the Palestinians.* But by the early 1960s, Palestinians were beginning to function again in organized groups. In the communities that they formed in Jordan, Lebanon, and Syria, Palestinians began to come together in women's groups, labor unions, charitable societies, and other groups. One of the most important forms of Palestinian organizing came in student groups, which formed at colleges and universities throughout the Arab world. Soon, a sense began to grow among the Palestinian people that they must work together to regain the land of Palestine, which they considered to be theirs by right.

Since most Palestinians lived in Arab nations, their actions against Israel could cause trouble for those countries if those actions were not controlled. Therefore, the leaders of Arab nations wanted to direct the way that Palestinians expressed their political goals. In 1964, the member nations of the League of Arab States (commonly called the Arab League; a regional political alliance of Arab nations formed in 1945 to promote political, military, and economic cooperation within the Arab world) created the Palestine Liberation Organization (PLO; a political and military organization formed to unite various Palestinian Arab groups with the goal of establishing an independent Palestinian state) to represent the interests of the Palestinians. The Arab League allowed for the creation of a legislative body, the Palestine National Council (PNC), and a military branch, the Palestine Liberation Army (PLA). The Arab states kept close control over the PLO and made sure that it adopted policies that did not threaten Arab League nations through most of the early 1960s.

Israel's defeat of the Arab nations in 1967 and its capture of the West Bank and the Gaza Strip—home to millions of Palestinians—forced the Arab nations to back off their attempts to reclaim territory from Israel and create an independent Palestinian state. But it did not kill the Palestinians' desire for independence. Instead, it encouraged the more radical Palestinians to become even stronger and more vocal. Such groups as Fatah (a Palestinian militant group and political party dedicated to the establishment of an independent Palestinian state), under the leadership of Yasser Arafat (1929–2004), and the Popular Front for the Liberation of Palestine (PFLP), under the leadership of George Habash (1926–2008), called on the Palestinians to take a new approach to combating Israel. They supported the idea that Palestinians should not rely on Arab nations to win their independence but that they should join in a people's struggle for

The Khartoum Arab Summit Resolutions

The Israeli victory in the 1967 Arab-Israeli War was a setback for the members of the Arab League. Even when the Arab nations combined their forces, and although they had more soldiers, they could not defeat the armies of Israel on the field of battle. That did not mean, however, that the Arab League was ready to give up its efforts to restore Arab control over Palestine. At a meeting of the Arab League in Khartoum, Sudan, in August 1967, the Arab nations—except Syria, which boycotted the meeting—signed resolutions asserting Arab unity and military cooperation. The third resolution established Arab policy toward Israel. It read:

The Arab Heads of State have agreed to unite their political efforts at the international and diplomatic level to eliminate the effects of the aggression and to ensure the withdrawal of the aggressive Israeli forces from the Arab lands which have been occupied since the aggression of June 5 [1967]. This will be done within the framework of the main principles by which the Arab States abide, namely, no peace with Israel, no recognition of Israel, no negotiations with it, and insistence on the rights of the Palestinian people in their own country.

This statement quickly became known as the "Three NOs," for the Arabs had declared that they would have no peace with Israel, no recognition of Israel, and no negotiations with Israel. In effect, the Arab nations wanted to deny Israel a right to participate in the regional issues facing the Middle East. Eventually, this policy would fall apart, as first Egypt (1978–79) and then Jordan (1994) signed peace agreements with Israel.

"THE KHARTOUM RESOLUTIONS." ISRAEL MINISTRY OF FOREIGN AFFAIRS. HTTP://WWW.MFA.GOV.IL/MFA/ PEACE+ PROCESS/GUIDE+TO+THE+ PEACE+ PROCESS/THE+KHARTOUM+ RESOLUTIONS.HTM (ACCESSED ON NOVEMBER 30, 2011).

victory. By 1968, these more radical groups, especially Fatah, had joined the PLO. Arafat became chairman of the PLO.

In July 1968, the PNC delegates met in Cairo, Egypt, and revised Palestinian National Charter, the document that states the goals of the Palestinian people.

Things to remember while reading the "Palestinian National Charter"

- The Charter refers to the diaspora, which means the scattering of a people by a disastrous event. The Palestinian diaspora began with Israel's declaration of independence in 1948, when Palestinians dispersed to countries throughout the Middle East and beyond.

- The authors of the Charter were deeply influenced by other revolutionary movements of the 1960s, including those in Algeria, Cuba, China, and Vietnam. They believed that the only way to regain Palestine was through armed struggle not through negotiation.
- The authors of the Charter did not wish to deny the popular Pan-Arab for the unification of Arab peoples and the political alliance of Arab states. There are frequent references to Arab unity in the Charter.
- Zionism—referred to repeatedly in the Charter—was an international political movement originating in the late nineteenth century that called for the creation of an independent Jewish state in Palestine. Once Israel was established, Zionism evolved into a movement in support of maintaining (and sometimes expanding) that Jewish homeland.

Young Palestinian refugees in a makeshift tent classroom at their refugee camp, in 1949, The Palestinian National Charter refers to the diaspora, which began with Israel's declaration of independence in 1948, when Palestinians dispersed to countries throughout the Middle East and beyond. © HULTON-DEUTSCH COLLECTION/CORBIS.

• • •

The Palestinian National Charter: Resolutions of the Palestine National Council (July 1–17, 1968)

Article 1:

Palestine is the homeland of the Arab Palestinian people; it is an indivisible part of the Arab homeland, and the Palestinian people are an integral part of the Arab nation.

Article 2:

Palestine, with the boundaries it had during the **British mandate**, is an indivisible territorial unit.

Article 3:

The Arab Palestinian people possess the legal right to their homeland and have the right to determine their destiny after achieving the **liberation** of their country in accordance with their wishes and entirely of their own accord and will.

Article 4:

The Palestinian identity is a genuine, essential, and inherent characteristic; it is transmitted from parents to children. The **Zionist** occupation and the dispersal of the Arab Palestinian people, through the disasters which befell them, do not make them lose their Palestinian identity and their membership in the Palestinian community, nor do they negate them.

Article 5:

The Palestinians are those Arab nationals who, until 1947, normally resided in Palestine regardless of whether they were evicted from it or have stayed there. Anyone born, after that date, of a Palestinian father—whether inside Palestine or outside it—is also a Palestinian.

Article 6:

The Jews who had normally resided in Palestine until the beginning of the Zionist invasion will be considered Palestinians.

Article 7:

There is a Palestinian community and that it has material, spiritual, and historical connection with Palestine are indisputable facts. It is a national duty to bring up individual Palestinians in an Arab revolutionary manner. All means of information and education must be adopted in order to acquaint the Palestinian with his country in the most profound manner, both spiritual and material, that is possible. He must be prepared for the armed struggle and ready to sacrifice his wealth and his life in order to win back his homeland and bring about its liberation.

Article 8:

The phase in their history, through which the Palestinian people are now living, is that of national struggle for the liberation of Palestine. Thus the

British mandate: A commission granting Great Britain the authority to administer the affairs of Palestine.

Liberation: Freedom.

Zionist: Supporters of an international political movement that called for the creation of an independent Jewish state in Palestine.

conflicts among the Palestinian national forces are secondary, and should be ended for the sake of the basic conflict that exists between the forces of Zionism and of **imperialism** on the one hand, and the Arab Palestinian people on the other. On this basis the Palestinian masses, regardless of whether they are residing in the national homeland or in **diaspora** constitute—both their organizations and the individuals—one national front working for the retrieval of Palestine and its liberation through armed struggle.

Article 9:

Armed struggle is the only way to liberate Palestine. Thus it is the overall strategy, not merely a tactical phase. The Arab Palestinian people assert their absolute determination and firm resolution to continue their armed struggle and to work for an armed popular revolution for the liberation of their country and their return to it. They also assert their right to normal life in Palestine and to exercise their right to **self-determination** and sovereignty over it.

Article 10:

Commando action constitutes the nucleus of the Palestinian popular liberation war. This requires its escalation, comprehensiveness, and the mobilization of all the Palestinian popular and educational efforts and their organization and involvement in the armed Palestinian revolution. It also requires the achieving of unity for the national struggle among the different groupings of the Palestinian people, and between the Palestinian people and the Arab masses, so as to secure the continuation of the revolution, its escalation, and victory.

Article 11:

The Palestinians will have three mottoes: national unity, national mobilization, and liberation.

Article 12:

The Palestinian people believe in Arab unity. In order to contribute their share toward the attainment of that objective, however, they must, at the present stage of their struggle, safeguard their Palestinian identity and develop their consciousness of that identity, and oppose any plan that may dissolve or impair it.

Article 13:

Arab unity and the liberation of Palestine are two complementary goals, the attainment of either of which facilitates the attainment of the other. Thus, Arab unity leads to the liberation of Palestine, the liberation of Palestine leads to Arab unity; and work toward the realization of one objective proceeds side by side with work toward the realization of the other.

Article 14:

The destiny of the Arab nation, and indeed Arab existence itself, depend upon the destiny of the Palestine cause. From this interdependence springs the Arab nation's pursuit of, and striving for, the liberation of Palestine. The

Imperialism: The practice of expanding the power of one country by taking control of other nations or creating colonies.

Diaspora: The scattering of a people by a disastrous event.

Self-determination: The right of a people to determine their own political status.

Commando action: Military action characterized by surprise and sudden strikes.

people of Palestine play the role of the **vanguard** in the realization of this sacred national goal.

Article 15:

The liberation of Palestine, from an Arab viewpoint, is a national duty and it attempts to repel the Zionist and **imperialist** aggression against the Arab homeland, and aims at the elimination of Zionism in Palestine. Absolute responsibility for this falls upon the Arab nation—peoples and governments—with the Arab people of Palestine in the vanguard. Accordingly, the Arab nation must mobilize all its military, human, moral, and spiritual capabilities to participate actively with the Palestinian people in the liberation of Palestine. It must, particularly in the phase of the armed Palestinian revolution, offer and furnish the Palestinian people with all possible help, and material and human support, and make available to them the means and opportunities that will enable them to continue to carry out their leading role in the armed revolution, until they liberate their homeland.

Article 16:

The liberation of Palestine, from a spiritual point of view, will provide the Holy Land with an atmosphere of safety and tranquility, which in turn will safeguard the country's religious sanctuaries and guarantee freedom of worship and of visit to all, without discrimination of race, color, language, or religion. Accordingly, the people of Palestine look to all spiritual forces in the world for support.

Article 17:

The liberation of Palestine, from a human point of view, will restore to the Palestinian individual his dignity, pride, and freedom. Accordingly the Arab Palestinian people look forward to the support of all those who believe in the dignity of man and his freedom in the world.

Article 18:

The liberation of Palestine, from an international point of view, is a defensive action necessitated by the demands of self-defense. Accordingly the Palestinian people, desirous as they are of the friendship of all people, look to freedom-loving, and peace-loving states for support in order to restore their legitimate rights in Palestine, to re-establish peace and security in the country, and to enable its people to exercise national sovereignty and freedom.

Article 19:

The partition of Palestine in 1947 and the establishment of the state of Israel are entirely illegal, regardless of the passage of time, because they were contrary to the will of the Palestinian people and to their natural right in their homeland, and inconsistent with the principles embodied in the Charter of the United Nations; particularly the right to self-determination.

Article 20:

The Balfour Declaration, the mandate for Palestine, and everything that has been based upon them, are deemed null and void. Claims of historical or

Vanguard: Leading position.

Imperialist: Having the characteristic of increasing a nation's authority and power by taking over territory or by dominating another nation's politics and economy.

religious ties of Jews with Palestine are incompatible with the facts of history and the true conception of what constitutes statehood. **Judaism,** being a religion, is not an independent nationality. Nor do Jews constitute a single nation with an identity of its own; they are citizens of the states to which they belong.

Article 21:

The Arab Palestinian people, expressing themselves by the armed Palestinian revolution, reject all solutions which are substitutes for the total liberation of Palestine and reject all proposals aiming at the liquidation of the Palestinian problem, or its internationalization.

Article 22:

Zionism is a political movement organically associated with international imperialism and **antagonistic** to all action for liberation and to progressive movements in the world. It is racist and fanatic in its nature, aggressive, expansionist, and colonial in its aims, and **fascist** in its methods. Israel is the instrument of the Zionist movement, and a geographical base for world imperialism placed strategically in the midst of the Arab homeland to combat the hopes of the Arab nation for liberation, unity, and progress. Israel is a constant source of threat **vis-á-vis** peace in the Middle East and the whole world. Since the liberation of Palestine will destroy the Zionist and imperialist presence and will contribute to the establishment of peace in the Middle East, the Palestinian people look for the support of all the progressive and peaceful forces and urge them all, irrespective of their affiliations and beliefs, to offer the Palestinian people all aid and support in their just struggle for the liberation of their homeland.

Article 23:

The demand of security and peace, as well as the demand of right and justice, require all states to consider Zionism an **illegitimate** movement, to outlaw its existence, and to ban its operations, in order that friendly relations among peoples may be preserved, and the loyalty of citizens to their respective homelands safeguarded.

Article 24:

The Palestinian people believe in the principles of justice, freedom, sovereignty, self-determination, human dignity, and in the right of all peoples to exercise them.

Article 25:

For the realization of the goals of this Charter and its principles, the Palestine Liberation Organization will perform its role in the liberation of Palestine in accordance with the Constitution of this Organization.

Article 26:

The Palestine Liberation Organization, representative of the Palestinian revolutionary forces, is responsible for the Arab Palestinian peoples' movement in its struggle—to retrieve its homeland, liberate and return to it

Judaism: The religion of the Jewish people based on the belief in one god and the teachings the Talmud.

Zionism: An international political movement originating in the late nineteenth century that called for the creation of an independent Jewish state in Palestine.

Antagonistic: Opposed.

Fascist: Supportive of or advocating of a system of government characterized by dictatorship, centralized control of private enterprise, repression of all opposition, and extreme nationalism.

Vis-á-vis: Face-to-face with.

Illegitimate: Illegal.

and exercise the right to self-determination in it—in all military, political, and financial fields and also for whatever may be required by the Palestine case on the inter-Arab and international levels.

Article 27:

The Palestine Liberation Organization shall cooperate with all Arab states, each according to its potentialities; and will adopt a neutral policy among them in the light of the requirements of the battle of liberation; and on this basis does not interfere in the internal affairs of any Arab state.

Article 28:

The Arab Palestinian people assert the genuineness and independence of their national revolution and reject all forms of intervention, trusteeship, and subordination.

Article 29:

The Palestinian people possess the fundamental and genuine legal right to liberate and retrieve their homeland. The Palestinian people determine their attitude toward all states and forces on the basis of the stands they adopt *vis-á-vis* to the Palestinian revolution to fulfill the aims of the Palestinian people.

Article 30:

Fighters and carriers of arms in the war of liberation are the nucleus of the popular army which will be the protective force for the gains of the Arab Palestinian people.

Article 31:

The Organization shall have a flag, an oath of allegiance, and an anthem. All this shall be decided upon in accordance with a special regulation.

Article 32:

A law, known as the Basic Statute of the Palestine Liberation Organization, shall be **annexed** to this Covenant. It will lay down the manner in which the Organization, and its organs and institutions, shall be constituted; the respective competence of each; and the requirements of its obligation under the Charter.

Article 33:

This Charter shall not be amended save by [vote of] a majority of two-thirds of the total membership of the National Congress of the Palestine Liberation Organization [taken] at a special session convened for that purpose.

● ● ●

What happened next . . .

The emergence of the Palestine Liberation Organization as an aggressive and vocal representative of the Palestinian people forever changed the politics of the Middle East. No longer did Palestinians have to look to

Annexed: Added or attached.

Arab nations to protect their interests; with the PLO, they had an organization dedicated to reclaiming Palestine for Palestinians. In the 1970s the PLO was granted observer status by the United Nations General Assembly, and, eventually, recognized by more than one hundred countries around the world.

The goals the Palestinians set for themselves in the revised charter of 1968 have been difficult to achieve, however, for a variety of reasons. By setting themselves up as a movement committed to waging armed struggle against Israel, the PLO became a problem for any Arab nation that hosted the organization. Jordan forcibly evicted the PLO in 1970, because the group was the source of many political and social problems between Jordanians who supported the PLO's violent attacks against Israel and others who did not. The PLO moved to Lebanon, which was driven into civil war by the PLO's frequent attacks on Israel; as a result, the PLO leadership was exiled to Tunisia in 1982. The PLO's encouragement of violence against Israel led to it being branded as a terrorist organization by the United States for many years until its reform in the 1990s, during which the PLO and Israel sought peaceful ways to end the long-standing conflict.

Over time, the PLO has had to drop some of its most radical positions. It no longer calls for the utter destruction of Israel, for example, nor does it

Yasser Arafat, the leader of the PLO, explains the goals of Palestinians to the United Nations in 1974, in the hopes of securing aid for the Palestinian people. KEYSTONE-FRANCE/ GAMMA-KEYSTONE VIA GETTY IMAGES.

anticipate that an independent Palestine will exist within the borders that existed during the years of British administration (1920–48). In fact, in the late 1990s and early 2000s, the political activities of the Palestinians were increasingly represented by the Palestinian Authority (the recognized governing institution for Palestinians in the West Bank and the Gaza Strip), which continues to pursue the goal of establishing a small but independent Palestine in the West Bank and the Gaza Strip.

Did you know...

- Although the end of the 1967 Arab-Israeli War brought a decrease in battles between Israel and the Arab nations, conflicts with Palestinians in Jordan increased dramatically, from 97 incidents in 1967 to 916 incidents in 1968; 2,432 in 1969; and 1,887 in 1970.
- Many of the elements of the revised Palestinian National Charter, such as those calling for the destruction of Israel, were abandoned in 1993 during peace talks that led to the signing of the Oslo Accords, an agreement between Israel and the PLO to accept the rights of both Israelis and Palestinians to exist and to create an independent Palestinian country in the West Bank territory that Israel had taken over during the 1967 war. However, as of 2011, a new text of the charter has not been prepared.

Consider the following...

- Compare and contrast the revised Palestinian National Charter with the "Declaration of Independence of the State of Israel." What are the essential facts about which they disagree? How do these documents depict the claims made by the other? Is there a basis for common ground to be found in these two documents?
- In 1974, PLO leader Yasser Arafat appeared before the United Nations and said: "Today I have come bearing an olive branch and a freedom-fighter's gun." In what ways does the Palestinian National Charter offer both the olive branch of peace and the prospect of further war?
- The revised Palestinian National Charter is an aggressive and strongly worded document. Was this confrontational stance an effective way to organize opposition to Israeli rule? Was there a different path the Palestinians could have taken in trying to reach their goals?

For More Information

BOOKS

Carew-Miller, Anna. *Palestinians.* Philadelphia: Mason Crest, 2010.

Farsoun, Samih K., and Naseer Aruri. *Palestine and the Palestinians: A Social and Political History.* 2nd ed. Boulder, CO: Westview Press, 2006.

Sharp, Anne Wallace. *The Palestinians.* Detroit: Lucent Books, 2005.

Smith, Charles D., ed. *Palestine and the Arab-Israeli Conflict: A History with Documents,* 4th ed. Boston MA: Bedford/St. Martin's, 2001.

PERIODICALS

The Question of Palestine & the United Nations. United Nations Department of Public Information. (March 2003). Available online at http://www.un.org/Depts/dpi/palestine (accessed on November 30, 2011).

WEB SITES

"The Khartoum Resolutions.' *Israel Ministry of Foreign Affairs.* http://www.mfa.gov.il/MFA/Peace+Process/Guide+to+the+Peace+Process/The+Khartoum+Resolutions.htm (accessed on November 30, 2011).

Permanent Observer Mission of Palestine to the United Nations. http://www.un.int/wcm/content/site/palestine/ (accessed on November 30, 2011).

The Road to Peace

The ongoing conflict between Arabs (people who speak the Arabic language) and Israelis has a long and complex history. In the early nineteenth century, the Zionist movement called for the creation of an independent Jewish state in Palestine, a historical region in the Middle East on the eastern shore of the Mediterranean Sea, comprising parts of present-day Israel and Jordan. Jews began immigrating to this region, which was the site of the ancient Jewish kingdom. But Palestine was already populated by Arabs, who were predominantly Muslim and had lived there for centuries. After World War I (1914–18) Great Britain was granted a mandate (administrative authority) over the region, with the ultimate goal of establishing self-rule in Palestine. Conflicts arose, however, over who should assume power. Both Arabs and Jews made claim to the land.

In May 1948, the British withdrew from Palestine, and Jews declared the establishment of the state of Israel. Palestinians (an Arab people whose ancestors lived in the historical region of Palestine and who continue to lay claim to that land) did not have the ability or the means to fight the new Jewish state, which had a well-organized government and a highly trained militia. Neighboring Arab states supported the Palestinians. They did not recognize Israel as a legitimate nation, and attacked Israel in the 1948 Arab-Israeli War. Israel emerged the victor in this and two other wars in 1967 and 1973. In the 1967 Arab-Israeli War, Israel captured of large amounts of land from Arab states. These occupied territories (lands under the political and military control of Israel, especially the West Bank and Gaza Strip) have remained an additional point of conflict between Israel and Arab nations. Palestinians, many of whom became refugees after the various Arab-Israeli Wars, continue to assert their claim to territory, calling for the creation of an independent Palestinian state. With this history of conflict and disagreement, learning to live in peace with each other has been difficult for Arabs and Israelis.

The larger disagreements between Arabs and Israelis, and the more specific disputes between Israel and individual Arab countries or with the Palestinians, are complicated and often difficult to resolve. They involve control of disputed territory, the rights of people driven from their land by armed conflict, and complex differences of religion and ethnicity. The documents contained in this section represent a variety of resolutions presented by Middle Eastern leaders, activist groups, and others who are hopeful of creating permanent peace and who are involved in sorting out the details of the conflict when peace efforts fall short.

Included is the historic address to the Israeli Knesset (legislature) by Egyptian president Anwar Sadat (also spelled al-Sadat; 1918–1981), as well as the response given by Israeli prime minister Menachem Begin (1913–1992). Also included is the disengagement plan offered by Israel in 2004 to kick-start a peace process that had once again been delayed.

A sign expressing a wish for peace in both English and Hebrew overlooks an orchard in Galilee, Israel. There are many challenges in negotiating and sustaining peace in the Middle East. © ANNIE GRIFFITHS BELT/CORBIS.

The final two documents, however, regarding the United Nations Human Rights Council's efforts to investigate the treatment of civilians during the Gaza War (2008-9) show how determining accountability and truth is politically complex. (The United Nations is an international organization of countries founded in 1945 to promote international peace, security, and cooperation.)

This selection of documents is a small sampling of various steps toward peace in the Middle East. Each document offers insight into the difficulties of negotiating and sustaining peace in the Middle East. Peace has not yet been achieved; however, Arabs and Israelis continue to demonstrate a commitment to pursuing a solution that works.

Speeches to the Knesset

Excerpt from Anwar Sadat's Speech to the Israeli Knesset
(November 20, 1977)

> *Reprinted in* Palestine and the Arab-Israeli Conflict
> *Edited by Charles D. Smith*
> *Published in 2001*

Excerpt from Menachem Begin's Reply to President Sadat
(November 20, 1977)

> *Reprinted in* Palestine and the Arab-Israeli Conflict
> *Edited by Charles D. Smith*
> *Published in 2001*

"What is peace to Israel? To live in the region, together with her Arab neighbours, in security and safety—this is a logic to which I say: 'Yes.'"

— Egyptian president Anwar Sadat.

Relations between Israel and its Arab neighbors were strained after the 1967 Arab-Israeli War. (Arabs are people who speak the Arabic language or who live in countries in which Arabic is the dominant language.) At the end of the war, Israel controlled huge tracts of land once ruled by Arabs, including the Sinai Peninsula and the Gaza Strip from Egypt, the Golan Heights from Syria, and the West Bank from Jordan. Emerging from the war as the dominant power in the Middle East, Israel dictated new areas of negotiation between itself and Arab nations. In addition to the location of Israel's permanent borders and the question of how to deal with Palestinian refugees (people who flee their country to escape violence or persecution), negotiations would now include consideration of whether captured Arab lands would be returned. (Palestinians are an Arab people whose ancestors lived in the historical region of Palestine, comprising parts of present-day Israel and Jordan, and who continue to lay claim to that land.) In response, in 1967, the Arab states held a summit in Khartoum, Sudan, and officially declared that Arab states would accept "no peace with Israel, no recognition of Israel, no negotiations with it" and would insist "on the rights of the Palestinian people in their own country."

These circumstances influenced the next decade of Arab-Israeli relations. Egypt launched a War of Attrition against Israel in 1969, gaining valuable aid from the Soviet Union. Although the United States negotiated a cease-fire in 1970, the negotiations were difficult and incomplete. When Anwar Sadat (also spelled al-Sadat; 1918–1981) became the president of Egypt in 1970, he was eager to finalize a peace agreement with Israel, and he agreed to a solution proposed by United Nations ambassador Gunnar Jarring (1907–2002) in 1971. However, Israel rejected it, not wanting to give up the land it had taken during the 1967 Arab-Israeli War, and tensions continued.

Sadat soon became convinced that diplomacy would not help Egypt regain the Sinai Peninsula or other Arab nations their lost land. On October 6, 1973, Sadat, with the cooperation of Syria, launched the 1973 Arab-Israeli War. Despite early Arab victories, the war ended in late October 1973 with neither side having achieved definite success. Because the Israelis and Arabs were unwilling to negotiate directly with each other, U.S. secretary of state Henry Kissinger (1923–) became instrumental in negotiating a plan to stop the fighting between Israel and the Arab states by traveling back and forth between Israel and various Arab capitals. By 1975, he had successfully concluded a plan for Egypt to gain some land, but the question of what to do with the Palestinian refugees became a roadblock (Palestinians wanted to be reimbursed for or allowed to return to their land, whereas Israelis believed the land rightfully belonged to them).

Frustrated with the stalemate and wanting peace to progress, Sadat announced on November 9, 1977, to the surprise of most of the world, that he would be willing to travel to Israel to pursue peace. At the time, Israel's prime minister was Menachem Begin (1913–1992), a man who had rejected the idea that Israel should return any land to the Arabs and who refused to acknowledge the Palestine Liberation Organization (PLO; a political and military organization formed to unite various Palestinian Arab groups with the goal of establishing an independent Palestinian state). Although hostile toward

Arabs, Begin accepted Sadat's proposal and invited him to visit a session of the Knesset, Israel's legislative body. The following are excerpts from the speeches Sadat and Begin gave to the Israeli Knesset on November 20, 1977.

Things to remember while reading the excerpts from Anwar Sadat's "Speech to the Israeli Knesset" and Menachem Begin's "Reply to President Sadat":

- Before Sadat expressed his willingness to visit Israel for peace, few would have expected Begin to be a man who would offer compromises. Begin was known as one of Israel's most aggressive and stubborn leaders.
- Notice the difference between Sadat and Begin's comments about the Palestinians.

Egyptian president Anwar Sadat making his historic speech to the Knesset on November 20, 1977. YA'AKOV SA'AR/GPO VIA GETTY IMAGES.

• • •

Excerpt from Anwar Sadat's Speech to the Israeli Knesset (November 20, 1977)

In the Name of God, Mr. Speaker of the Knesset, ladies and gentlemen . . . .

God's peace and mercy be with you. God willing, peace for us all. Peace for us in the Arab land and in Israel and in every part of the land of this wide world, this world which is made complex by its bloody conflicts and which is made tense by its sharp contradictions and which is threatened every now and then by destructive wars—wars made by man to kill his brother man and, in the end, amid the debris and mutilated bodies of men, there is neither victor nor **vanquished**. . . .

All of us in this land, the land of God, **Moslems**, Christians and Jews, worship God and no other god. God's decrees and commandments are: love, honesty, chastity and peace. . . .

Ladies and gentlemen: There are moments in the life of nations and peoples when those who are known for their wisdom and foresight are required to look beyond the past, with all its complications and remnants, for the sake of a courageous **upsurge** towards new horizons. . . .

We must rise above all forms of **fanaticism** and self-deception and obsolete theories of superiority. It is important that we should never forget that virtue is God's alone. If I say that I want to protect the Arab people from the terrors of new, terrifying wars, I declare before you with all sincerity that I have the same feelings and I carry the same responsibility for every human being in the world and, most certainly, for the Israeli people.

A life which is taken away in war is the life of a human being, whether it is an Arab or an Israeli life. The wife who becomes a widow is a human being and has the right to live in a happy family environment whether she is an Arab or an Israeli. The innocent children who lose the care and love of their parents are all our children; they are all our children, whether in the land of the Arabs or in Israel; we have a great responsibility to provide them with a prosperous present and a better future. . . .

Ladies and gentlemen, let us be frank with each other, using straightforward words and clear thoughts which cannot be twisted. . . . How can we achieve a just and lasting peace? . . .

Firstly, I did not come to you with a view to concluding a separate agreement between Egypt and Israel, this is not provided for in Egypt's policy. The problem does not lie just between Egypt and Israel; moreover, no separate peace between Egypt and Israel—or between any **confrontation state** and Israel—could secure a lasting and just peace in the region as a whole. Even if a peace agreement was achieved between all the confrontation states and Israel, without a just solution to the Palestinian problem it would never ensure the establishment of the durable, lasting peace the entire world is now trying to achieve. . . .

I have come to you so that together we can build a lasting and just peace, so that not one more drop of the blood of either side may be shed. . . .

Vanquished: Defeated.

Moslems: Muslims; people who practice the religion of Islam.

Upsurge: Rapid rise.

Fanaticism: Extreme commitment to a cause.

Confrontation state: Country at war with Israel.

This in itself forms a giant turning-point, a decisive landmark of an historic transformation. We used to reject you, and we had our reasons and **grievances**. Yes, we used to reject meeting you anywhere. Yes, we used to describe you as "so-called Israel." Yes, conferences and international organizations used to bring us together. Our representatives have never and still do not exchange greetings and **salaams**. Yes, this is what happened, and it still goes on. . . . But I say to you today and I say to the whole world that we accept that we should live with you in a lasting and just peace. We do not want to surround you or to be surrounded ourselves with missiles which are ready to destroy, with the missiles of hatred and bitterness.

More than once, I have said that Israel has become a living reality. The world recognized it and the **two superpowers** shouldered the responsibility of its security and the defense of its existence. And when we want peace both in theory and in practice we welcome you to live amongst us in security and peace, in theory and practice. . . .

Ladies and gentlemen, the truth is—and it is the truth that I am telling you—that there can be no peace in the true sense of the word, unless this peace is based on justice and not on the occupation of the territory of others. It is not right that you seek for yourselves what you deny to others. In all frankness and in the spirit which prompted me to come to you, I say to you: You have finally to abandon the dreams of tomorrow and you have also to abandon the belief that force is the best means of dealing with the Arabs. You have to absorb very well the lessons of confrontation between ourselves and you; expansion will be of no avail to you. . . .

To put it clearly, our territory is not a subject of bargaining; it is not a topic for wrangling. . . .

What is peace to Israel? To live in the region, together with her Arab neighbours, in security and safety—this is a logic to which I say: "Yes." For Israel to live within her borders secure from any aggression—this is a logic to which I say: "Yes." For Israel to get all kinds of assurances that ensure for her these two facts—this is a demand to which I say "YES." . . .

But how can this be achieved? How can we arrive at this result so that it can take us to a permanent and just peace? There are facts that must be confronted with all courage and clarity. There is Arab land which Israel has occupied and still occupies by armed force. And we insist that complete withdrawal from this land be undertaken and this includes Arab Jerusalem, Jerusalem to which I have come, as it is considered the city of peace and which has been and will always be the living embodiment of coexistence between believers of the **three religions**. It is inadmissible for anyone to think of Jerusalem's special position within the context of **annexation** and expansion. It must be made a free city, open to all the faithful. What is more important is that the city must not be closed to those who have chosen it as a place of residence for several centuries. . . .

Let me tell you without hesitation that I have not come to you, under this dome, to beg you to withdraw your forces from the occupied territory. This is

Grievances: Complaints and resentments.

Salaams: Deep bows with the right palm pressed to the forehead as a sign of greeting and respect; a customary greeting gesture in Islamic countries.

Two superpowers: The United States and the Soviet Union.

Three religions: Islam, Judaism, and Christianity, all of which claim holy sites within the city of Jerusalem.

Annexation: The state of being added or attached.

because complete withdrawal from the Arab territories occupied after 1967 is a matter that goes without saying, over which we accept no controversy and in respect of which there is no begging to anyone or from anyone. There will be no meaning to talk about a lasting, just peace and there will be no meaning to any step to guarantee our lives together in this part of the world in peace and security while you occupy an Arab land by armed forces. There can never be peace established or built with the occupation of others' land. . . .

As regards the Palestine question, nobody denies that it is the essence of the entire problem. Nobody throughout the entire world accepts today slogans raised here in Israel which disregard the existence of the people of Palestine and even ask where the people of Palestine are. The problem of the Palestinian people, and the legitimate rights of the Palestinian people are now no longer ignored or rejected by anybody; no thinking mind supposes that they could be ignored or rejected; they are facts that meet with the support and recognition of the international community both in the West and the East and in international documents and official declarations. . . .

Even the USA—your first ally, which is the most committed to the protection of the existence and security of Israel . . . has opted for facing up to the reality and to facts, to recognize that the Palestinian people have legitimate rights, and that the Palestine question is the **crux** and essence of the conflict. . . .

In all sincerity, I tell you that peace cannot be achieved without the Palestinians, and that it would be a great mistake, the effect of which no one knows, to turn a blind eye to this question or to set it aside. . . .

When the bells of peace ring, there will be no hand to beat the drums of war; should such a hand exist, it will not be heard. Imagine with me the peace agreement in Geneva, the good news of which we herald to a world thirsty for peace: (Firstly) a peace agreement based on ending the Israeli occupation of the Arab territory occupied in 1967; (secondly) the realization of basic rights of the Palestinian people and this people's right to **self-determination**, including their right to setting up their own state; thirdly, the right of all the countries of the region to live in peace within their secure and guaranteed borders, through agreed measures for the appropriate security of international borders, in addition to the appropriate international guarantees; fourthly, all the States in the region will undertake to administer relations among themselves in accordance with the principles and aims of the UN Charter, in particular **eschewing** the use of force and settling differences among them by peaceful means; and fifthly, ending the state of war that exists in the region. . . .

The experiences of past and contemporary history teach us all that missiles, warships and nuclear weapons, perhaps, cannot establish security. On the contrary, they destroy all that was built by security. For the sake of our peoples, for the sake of a civilization made by man, we must protect man in every place from the rule of the force of arms. We must raise high the rule of humanity with the full force of principles and values which hold man high. . . .

Crux: Crucial or essential point.

Self-determination: The right to decide for oneself without interference from others.

Eschewing: Avoiding.

Israeli prime minister Menachem Begin (left) speaks to the Israeli parliament following Anwar Sadat's address. Begin surprised many people when he accepted Sadat's proposal for peace talks.
© BETTMANN/CORBIS.

Excerpt from Menachem Begin's Reply to President Sadat (November 20, 1977)

Knesset: Legislative body of the Israeli government.

Id al-Adha: Also spelled Eid al-Adha; Islamic religious holiday commemorating the willingness of Abraham to sacrifice his son Issac in obedience to God.

Isaac: The son of Abraham, whom God asked Abraham to sacrifice. Abraham bound Isaac to the altar in preparation for sacrificing him.

Our common forefather: According to the Koran and the Hebrew Bible, Abraham is the forefather of many tribes, including the Ishmaelites and the Israelites. Muslims believe Muhammad was descended from Ishmael; Jews believe they descended from the Israelites.

Mr. Speaker, Mr. President of the State of Israel, Mr. President of the Arab Republic of Egypt, Ladies and Gentlemen, members of the **Knesset**, we send our greetings to the President and to all the people of the Islamic religion in our country, and wherever they may be, on the occasion of the Feast, the Festival of the Sacrifice, **Id al-Adha**. This feast reminds us of the binding of **Isaac**. This was the way in which the Creator of the World tested our forefather, Abraham—**our common forefather**—to test his faith, and Abraham passed this test. . . . Thus we contributed, the people of Israel and the Arab people, to the progress of mankind, and thus we are continuing to contribute to human civilization to this day.

I greet and welcome the President of Egypt for coming to our country and on his participating in the Knesset session. The flight time between Cairo and Jerusalem is short, but the distance between Cairo and Jerusalem was until last night almost endless. President Sadat crossed the distance courageously. We, the Jews, know how to appreciate such courage, and we know how to appreciate it in our guest, because it is with courage that we are here and this is how we continue to exist, and we shall continue to exist.

Mr. Speaker, this small nation, the remaining refuge of the Jewish People which returned to its historic homeland—has always wanted peace and, since the dawn of our independence, on 14 May 1948 . . . in the Declaration of

Independence in the founding scroll of our national freedom, **David Ben-Gurion** said: We extend a hand of peace and good-neighbourliness to all neighbouring countries and their peoples. We call upon them to cooperate, to help each other, with the Hebrew people independent in its own country. One year earlier, even from the underground, when we were in the midst of the fateful struggle for the liberation of the country and the redemption of the people, we called on our neighbours in these terms: In this country we shall live together and we shall advance together and we shall live a life of freedom and happiness. Our Arab neighbours: Do not reject the hand stretched out to you in peace.

But it is my **bounden** duty, Mr. Speaker, and not only my right, not to pass over the truth, that our hand outstretched for peace was not grasped and, one day after we had renewed our independence—as was our right, eternal right, which cannot be disputed—we were attacked on three fronts and we stood almost without arms, the few against many, the weak against the strong, while an attempt was made, one day after the Declaration of Independence, to strangle it at birth, to put an end to the last hope of the Jewish People, the yearning renewed after the years of destruction and **holocaust**.

No, we do not believe in might and we have never based our attitude to the Arab people on might; quite the contrary, force was used against us. Over all the years of this generation we have never stopped being attacked by might, the might of the strong arm stretched out to exterminate our people, to destroy our independence, to deny our rights. We defended ourselves, it is true. . . . With the help of Almighty God, we overcame the forces of aggression, and we have guaranteed the existence of our nation, not only for this generation, but for the coming generations too. We do not believe in might; we believe in right, only in right and therefore our aspiration, from the depth of our hearts, has always been, to this very day, for peace. . . .

Therefore, permit me, today, to set out the peace programme as we understand it. We want full, real peace, with absolute reconciliation between the Jewish and the Arab peoples. . . .

The first clause of a peace treaty is **cessation** of the state of war, for ever. We want to establish normal relations between us, as they exist between all nations, even after wars. . . .

Let us sign a peace treaty and let us establish this situation forever, both in Jerusalem and in Cairo. . . .

Mr. Speaker, it is my duty today to tell our guest and all the peoples watching us and listening to our words about the link between our people and this land. The President [of Egypt] recalled the **Balfour Declaration**. No, sir, we did not take over any strange land; we returned to our homeland. The link between our people and this land is eternal. It arose in the earliest days of humanity and was never altered. In this country we developed our civilization. . . . And when we were expelled from our land, when force was

David Ben-Gurion: First prime minister of Israel (1886–1973).

Bounden: Required.

Holocaust: The mass murder of European Jews and other groups by the Nazis during World War II.

Cessation: Stoppage.

Balfour Declaration: A 1917 declaration by Great Britain, which supported the creation of a Jewish homeland in Palestine and asserted at the same time that nothing ought to be done to reduce the rights and political status of non-Jews in Palestine.

used against us, no matter how far we went from our land, we never forgot it for even one day. We prayed for it; we longed for it; we have believed in our return to it. . . .

This, our right, was recognized. The Balfour Declaration was included in the **mandate** laid down by the **nations of the world**, including the United States of America, and the preface to this recognized international document says: Whereas recognition has the bible given to the historical connection of the Jewish people with Palestine and to the grounds for reconstituting their national home in that country, the historic connection between the Jewish people and Palestine or, in Hebrew Eretz Yisra'el, was given reconfirmation—reconfirmation—as the national homeland in that country, that is in Eretz Yisra'el. . . .

President Sadat knows and he knew from us before he came to Jerusalem that we have a different position from his with regard to the permanent borders between us and our neighbours. However, I say to the President of Egypt and to all our neighbours: Do not say there is not, there will not be negotiations about any particular issue. I propose, with the agreement of the decisive majority of this parliament, that everything will be open to negotiation. Anyone who says, with reference to relations between the Arab people, or the Arab peoples around us, and the State of Israel, that there are things which should be omitted from negotiations is taking upon himself a grave responsibility, everything can be negotiated. No side will say the contrary. No side will present prior conditions. We will conduct the negotiations honourably. If there are differences of opinion between us, this is not unusual. Anyone who has studied the history of wars and the signing of peace treaties knows that all negotiations over a peace treaty began with differences of opinion between the sides. And in the course of the negotiations they came to an agreement which permitted the signing of peace treaties and agreements. And this is the road we propose to take.

• • •

What happened next . . .

After unsuccessful attempts to conduct peace negotiations, Anwar Sadat and Menachem Begin met with U.S. president Jimmy Carter (1924–) at Camp David, the presidential retreat in Maryland, in September 1978. The meeting resulted in two agreements known as the Camp David Accords. The first agreement outlined a compromise over the Sinai Peninsula, which had been captured from Egypt by Israel in the 1967 Arab-Israeli War. The second established a framework in which negotiations about the future of the West Bank and the Gaza Strip would be conducted. The Camp David Accords generated further negotiations that

Mandate: A commission granting one country the authority to administer the affairs of another country. Also describes the territory entrusted to foreign administration.

Nations of the world: Reference to the League of Nations, an international organization of sovereign countries established after World War I to promote peace.

Egyptian president Anwar Sadat, U.S. president Jimmy Carter, and Israeli prime minister Menachem Begin sign a peace treaty in 1979. © WALLY MCNAMEE/CORBIS.

culminated in the Israel-Egypt peace treaty, which was signed in Washington, D.C., on March 26, 1979.

Did you know . . .

- Although Anwar Sadat had noted that the Palestinians were central to peace in the Middle East, the Israel-Egypt peace treaty signed in 1979 did not include a plan for lasting peace with the Palestinians.
- The Arab League (a regional political alliance of Arab nations formed in 1945 to promote political, military, and economic cooperation within the Arab world), expelled Egypt from its membership and issued political and economic sanctions against Egypt as punishment for signing the peace agreement with Israel. Arab League members, except for Oman and Sudan, refused to conduct diplomatic relations with Egypt after it signed the peace agreement.

- The Israeli-Egyptian peace agreement did not include guarantees for Palestinian refugees. The PLO broke off relations with Egypt after it signed the agreement.
- Anwar Sadat was assassinated in 1981 by activists opposed to Egypt's peace with Israel.

Consider the following...

- Sadat's trip to Israel cost him diplomatic ties with other Arab states. Why do you think he felt his trip was worth the price? Why might a peace agreement with Israel be more important to Egypt than maintaining its place as a leader among Arab nations? Look for items in the text of his speech to support your ideas.
- Sadat and Begin had very different opinions about how to achieve lasting peace in the Middle East. What is the biggest difference of opinion as stated in these two speeches?
- In the two speeches, are there clues as to why a solution regarding the Arab Palestinians was ultimately left out of the final peace agreement?

For More Information

BOOKS

Brackett, Virginia. *Menachem Begin*. Philadelphia: Chelsea House, 2003.

Kras, Sara Louise. *Anwar Sadat*. Philadelphia: Chelsea House, 2003.

Smith, Charles D., ed. *Palestine and the Arab-Israeli Conflict: A History with Documents*, 4th ed. Boston MA: Bedford/St. Martin's, 2001.

Wagner, Heather Lehr. *Anwar Sadat and Menachem Begin: Negotiating Peace in the Middle East*. New York: Chelsea House, 2007.

WEB SITES

"Guide to the Middle East Peace Process." *Israeli Ministry of Foreign Affairs.* http://www.mfa.gov.il/MFA/Peace+Process/Guide+to+the+Peace+Process/ (accessed on November 30, 2011).

"The Khartoum Resolutions.' *Israel Ministry of Foreign Affairs.* http://www.mfa.gov.il/MFA/Peace+Process/Guide+to+the+Peace+Process/The+Khartoum+Resolutions.htm (accessed on November 30, 2011).

The Oslo Accords

Excerpt from the Israeli-PLO Declaration of Principles
(September 13, 1993)

Reprinted in Palestine and the Arab-Israeli Conflict

Edited by Charles D. Smith

Published in 2001

"The Government of the State of Israel and the PLO team . . . agree that it is time to put an end to decades of confrontation and conflict . . . and achieve a just, lasting and comprehensive peace. . . . "

During rounds of negotiations between Israel and its Arab neighbors in the early 1990s, the role of the Palestine Liberation Organization (PLO; a political and military organization formed to unite various Palestinian Arab groups with the goal of establishing an independent Palestinian state) became increasingly important. Previously, Israel had considered the PLO to be a terrorist group and refused diplomatic relations with it. However, as Israel conducted negotiations with Syria, Jordan, and Lebanon, the authority of the PLO as a representative of Palestinians (an Arab people whose ancestors lived in the historical region of Palestine, comprising parts of present-day Israel and Jordan, and who continue to lay claim to that land) was firmly established when delegates from Arab countries refused to make decisions regarding Palestinians without first consulting with the PLO.

In 1993 the world was shocked by the announcement of an agreement between Israel and the PLO that had been negotiated in secret discussions in Oslo, Norway. On September 13, 1993, Arafat and prime minister Yitzhak Rabin (1922–1995) shook hands to seal the agreement. The event took place on the lawn of the White House in Washington,

The Palestine Liberation Organization

The Palestine Liberation Organization (PLO) emerged as the representative of the Palestinian people in 1964, under the leadership of the dynamic chairman Yasser Arafat (1929–2004). The charter, or stated set of laws and beliefs, of the organization committed the PLO to waging armed struggle against Israel in order to reclaim Palestine (a historical region in the Middle East on the eastern shore of the Mediterranean Sea, comprising parts of present-day Israel and Jordan) from the Israelis for Palestinians. These policies caused several conflicts in the Middle East for many years.

The PLO originally organized its military forces in Jordan and launched attacks on Israel from positions along the border. But the attacks the PLO launched on Israel prompted the Jordanian government to remove the organization from the country in 1970. By the 1980s, similar PLO activities in Lebanon had prompted an invasion by Israel, which eventually led to the PLO leadership being expelled from Lebanon in 1982. The PLO next relocated to Tunisia.

For its violent attacks on Israel, the PLO was branded as a terrorist organization by many countries. However, by the 1990s, the power of the PLO among Palestinians was such that neither the Arab nations nor Israel and its allies could deny the legitimate role of the PLO as representative of the Palestinian people.

D.C. In the "Israeli-PLO Declaration of Principles, September 13, 1993," more commonly known as the Oslo Accords, Israel and the PLO agreed on the principles upon which the two political entities would begin to set up an interim (temporary) self-government for Palestinians that would be recognized by Israel. The Oslo Accords established the Palestinian Authority, an elected governing institution for Palestinians in the West Bank and the Gaza Strip; outlined the terms of Israeli withdrawal from some of the occupied territories (lands under the political and military control of Israel, especially the West Bank and Gaza Strip); and detailed the terms of the transition of power from Israel to the Palestinians.

Things to remember while reading the excerpt from "Israeli-PLO Declaration of Principles, September 13, 1993"

- The Oslo Accords marked a historic moment in the Arab-Israeli conflict, because it is a formal document in which Israel recognizes the authority of the PLO to speak for the Palestinian people and the PLO accepts Israel as an independent nation.
- For their efforts in the Oslo Accords, Israeli prime minister Yitzhak Rabin, Israeli foreign minister Shimon Peres (1923–), and PLO leader Yasser Arafat shared the Nobel Peace Prize in 1994.
- Notice that the Oslo Accords left several issues for future negotiations, including Israel's permanent borders, the accepted areas for Jewish settlements, the permanent home of Palestinian refugees, and the political authority over Jerusalem.

Israeli prime minister Yitzhak Rabin and PLO leader Yasser Arafat shake hands as a symbol of peace between Israel and the Palestinians after the signing of the Oslo Peace Accords. J. DAVID AKE/AFP/GETTY IMAGES.

• • •

Israeli-PLO Declaration of Principles (September 13, 1993)

Declaration of Principles on Interim Self-Government Arrangements:

The Government of the State of Israel and the PLO team (in the Jordanian-Palestinian delegation to the Middle East Peace Conference) (the "Palestinian Delegation"), representing the Palestinian people, agree that it is time to put an end to decades of confrontation and conflict, recognise their mutual legitimate and political rights, and strive to live in peaceful coexistence and mutual dignity and security and achieve a just, lasting and comprehensive peace settlement and historic reconciliation through the agreed political process. Accordingly, the two sides agree to the following principles:

Article I

Aim of Negotiations

The aim of the Israeli-Palestinian negotiations within the current Middle East peace process is, among other things, to establish a Palestinian **Interim** Self-Government Authority, the elected Council (the "Council"), for the Palestinian people in the West Bank and the Gaza Strip, for a transitional period not exceeding five years, leading to a permanent settlement based on **Security Council resolutions 242 (1967) and 338 (1973)**.

It is understood that the interim arrangements are an integral part of the whole peace process and that the negotiations on the permanent status will lead to the implementation of Security Council resolutions 242 (1967) and 338 (1973). . . .

Article IV

Jurisdiction

Jurisdiction of the Council will cover West Bank and Gaza Strip territory, except for issues that will be negotiated in the permanent status negotiations. The two sides view the West Bank and the Gaza Strip as a single territorial unit, whose integrity will be preserved during the interim period.

2. Permanent status negotiations will commence as soon as possible, but not later than the beginning of the third year of the interim period, between the Government of Israel and the Palestinian people's representatives.

3. It is understood that these negotiations shall cover remaining issues, including: Jerusalem, refugees, settlements, security arrangements, borders, relations and co-operation with other neighbours, and other issues of common interest.

4. The two parties agree that the outcome of the permanent status negotiations should not be prejudiced or pre-empted by agreements reached for the interim period.

Interim: Temporary.

Security Council resolutions 242 and 338: Two recommendations made by the United Nations Security Council on how to resolve matters between Israel and the Palestinians and bring peace to the region.

Jurisdiction: The territorial range of authority or control.

Article VI

Preparatory transfer of powers and responsibilities . . .

2. Immediately after the entry into force of this Declaration of Principles and the withdrawal from the Gaza Strip and Jericho area, with the view to promoting economic development in the West Bank and Gaza Strip, authority will be transferred to the Palestinians in the following spheres: education and culture, health, social welfare, direct taxation and tourism. The Palestinian side will commence in building the Palestinian police force, as agreed upon. Pending the inauguration of the Council, the two parties may negotiate the transfer of additional powers and responsibilities, as agreed upon.

Article VII

Interim agreement

1. The Israeli and Palestinian delegations will negotiate an agreement on the interim period (the "Interim Agreement").

2. The Interim Agreement shall specify, among other things, the structure of the Council, the number of its members, and the transfer of powers and responsibilities from the Israeli military government and its Civil Administration to the Council. The Interim Agreement shall also specify the Council's executive authority, legislative authority in accordance with Article IX below, and the independent Palestinian judicial organs.

3. The Interim Agreement shall include arrangements, to be implemented upon the inauguration of the Council, for the assumption by the Council of all of the powers and responsibilities transferred previously in accordance with Article VI above.

4. In order to enable the Council to promote economic growth, upon its **inauguration**, the Council will establish, among other things, a Palestinian Electricity Authority, a Gaza Sea Port Authority, a Palestinian Development Bank, a Palestinian Export Promotion Board, a Palestinian Environmental Authority, a Palestinian Land Authority and a Palestinian Water Administration Authority and any other Authorities agreed upon, in accordance with the Interim Agreement, that will specify their powers and responsibilities.

5. After the inauguration of the Council, the Civil Administration will be dissolved, and the Israeli military government will be withdrawn.

Article VIII

Public Order and Security

In order to guarantee public order and internal security for the Palestinians of the West Bank and the Gaza Strip, the Council will establish a strong police force, while Israel will continue to carry the responsibility for defending against external threats, as well as the responsibility for overall security of Israelis for the purpose of safeguarding their internal security and public order. . . .

Article XIII

Redeployment of Israeli Forces

1. After the entry into force of this Declaration of Principles, and not later than the eve of elections for the Council, a **redeployment** of Israeli military forces in the West Bank and the Gaza Strip will take place, in addition to withdrawal of Israeli forces carried out in accordance with Article XIV.

Inauguration: Beginning.

Redeployment: To move military forces from one combat zone to another.

2. In redeploying its military forces, Israel will be guided by the principle that its military forces should be redeployed outside populated areas.

3. Further redeployments to specified locations will be gradually implemented **commensurate** with the assumption of responsibility for public order and internal security by the Palestinian police force pursuant to Article VIII above.

Article XIV

Israeli Withdrawal from the Gaza Strip and Jericho Area

Israel will withdraw from the Gaza Strip and Jericho area, as detailed in the protocol attached as Annex II.

Article XV

Resolution of Disputes

[. . .]

3. The parties may agree to submit to **arbitration** disputes relating to the interim period, which cannot be settled through **conciliation.** To this end, upon the agreement of both parties, the parties will establish an Arbitration Committee. . . .

Annex I

Protocol on the Mode and Conditions of Elections

1. Palestinians of Jerusalem who live there will have the right to participate in the election process, according to an agreement between the two sides.

2. In addition, the election agreement should cover, among other things, the following issues:

(a) The system of elections;

(b) The mode of the agreed supervision and international observation and their personal composition;

(c) Rules and regulations regarding election campaigns, including agreed arrangements for the organizing of mass media, and the possibility of licensing a broadcasting and television station.

3. The future status of displaced Palestinians who were registered on 4 June 1967 will not be prejudiced because they are unable to participate in the election process owing to practical reasons.

Annex II

Protocol on Withdrawal of Israeli Forces from the Gaza Strip and Jericho Area

Commensurate: Corresponding in size, extent, or degree.

Arbitration: The hearing and determination of a case in controversy.

Conciliation: To make compatible or reconcile.

1. The two sides will conclude and sign within two months from the date of entry into force of this Declaration of Principles an agreement on the withdrawal of Israeli military forces from the Gaza Strip and Jericho area. This agreement will include comprehensive arrangements to apply in the Gaza Strip and the Jericho area **subsequent to** the Israeli withdrawal.

2. Israel will implement an accelerated and scheduled withdrawal of Israeli military forces from the Gaza Strip and Jericho area, beginning immediately with the signing of the agreement on the Gaza Strip and Jericho area and to be completed within a period not exceeding four months after the signing of this agreement.

3. The above agreement will include, among other things:

(a) Arrangements for a smooth and peaceful transfer of authority from the Israeli military government and its Civil Administration to the Palestinian representatives.

(b) Structure, powers and responsibilities of the Palestinian authority in these areas, except: external security, settlements, Israelis, foreign relations and other mutually agreed matters.

(c) Arrangements for the assumption of internal security and public order by the Palestinian police force consisting of police officers recruited locally and from abroad (holding Jordanian passports and Palestinian documents issued by Egypt). Those who will participate in the Palestinian police force coming from abroad should be trained as police and police officers.

(d) A temporary international or foreign presence, as agreed upon.

(e) Establishment of a joint Palestinian-Israeli Co-ordination and Co-operation Committee for mutual security purposes.

(f) An economic development and **stabilization** program, including the establishment of an Emergency Fund, to encourage foreign investment and financial and economic support. Both sides will co-ordinate and co-operate jointly and unilaterally with regional and international parties to support these aims.

(g) Arrangements for a safe passage for persons and transportation between the Gaza Strip and Jericho area. . . .

Article IV

It is understood that:

1. Jurisdiction of the Council will cover West Bank and Gaza Strip territory, except for issues that will be negotiated in the permanent status negotiations: Jerusalem, settlements, military locations and Israelis.

2. The Council's jurisdiction will apply with regard to the agreed powers, responsibilities, spheres and authorities transferred to it. . . .

Subsequent to: Following.

Stabilization: Making stable or steady.

Article VII (5):

The withdrawal of the military government will not prevent Israel from exercising the powers and responsibilities not transferred to the Council. . . .

Annex II:

It is understood that, subsequent to the Israeli withdrawal, Israel will continue to be responsible for external security, and for internal security and public order of settlements and Israelis. Israeli military forces and civilians may continue to use roads freely within the Gaza Strip and the Jericho area.

• • •

What happened next . . .

Although many of the provisions, or requirements, detailed in the Declaration of Principles were fulfilled, they did not result in a lasting peace. The successes of the Oslo Accords were the establishment of the Palestinian Authority, Palestinian control over portions of the occupied territories, and the organization of a Palestinian police force.

Despite these gains, Palestinians and Israelis remained unable to agree on how Jerusalem should be controlled, the nature of permanent borders, or what to do about the Palestinian refugees. By 2000, frustration among Palestinians culminated in the Second Intifada, or uprising against Israeli occupation. Over the next decade, violence would alternate with negotiations, but there was still no peace in the region in 2011.

Did you know . . .

- The five-year transitional period called for in the Oslo Accords was to begin upon Israeli withdrawal from the Gaza Strip and Jericho area, which occurred in September 2005.
- The Oslo Accords called for a Palestinian civil administration to take over governing authority from the Israeli military government upon Israeli withdrawal from the Gaza Strip and the Jericho area, after which time a Palestinian Council would be elected. This occurred in January 2006, with members of the Hamas political party winning a majority of the legislative seats over those from the rival Fatah political faction. After the Battle of Gaza in 2007, in which Hamas defeated Fatah forces, Hamas took control of the region.

A man lifts his son into the air as Palestinians in Gaza celebrate the signing of the Oslo Accords. © PETER TURNLEY/ CORBIS.

- It was hoped that the Oslo Accords would provide an opening for negotiations about economic cooperation with Egypt and Jordan, as well as an opportunity for all sides to negotiate regional development programs.

Consider the following . . .

- Why were the Oslo Accords inadequate as a solution to the Israeli-Arab conflict?
- Describe the features of the Oslo Accords that were most important in continuing the peace process.
- Identify the parts of the Oslo Accords that were the most difficult for Israeli citizens to accept, as well as those most difficult for Palestinians to accept. Explain why these were the most difficult parts for each side.

For More Information

BOOKS

Freedman, Robert O., ed. *The Middle East and the Peace Process: The Impact of the Oslo Accords.* Gainesville: University Press of Florida, 1998.

Smith, Charles D., ed. *Palestine and the Arab-Israeli Conflict: A History with Documents*, 4th ed. Boston MA: Bedford/St. Martin's, 2001.

Watson, Geoffrey R. *The Oslo Accords: International Law and the Israeli-Palestinian Peace Agreements.* New York: Oxford University Press, 2000.

Weinberger, Peter Ezra. *Co-Opting the PLO: A Critical Reconstruction of the Oslo Accords, 1993–1995.* Lanham, MD: Lexington Books, 2007.

WEB SITES

"Oslo Accords." *The Knesset.* http://www.knesset.gov.il/lexicon/eng/oslo_eng.htm (accessed on November 30, 2011).

"Shattered Dreams of Peace: The Road from Oslo." *Frontline* (June 2002). http://www.pbs.org/wgbh/pages/frontline/shows/oslo/ (accessed on November 30, 2011).

Israel's Revised Disengagement Plan

Excerpt from Israel's Revised Disengagement Plan—Main
Principles (June 6, 2004)

Published by the Israeli Prime Minister's Office

"The purpose of the plan is to lead to a better security,
political, economic and demographic situation."

By the early 2000s, relations between Israelis and Palestinians living in
the occupied territories (lands under the political and military control
of Israel, especially the West Bank and Gaza Strip) had once again
deteriorated. Despite several peace conferences and numerous rounds of
negotiations, as well as signed resolutions and accords (formal agreements), Israelis and Palestinians could not establish and maintain peace
between them. In 2000, Palestinians erupted in sustained popular violence. The Second Intifada, or uprising, which began in September 2000,
led Israel to cut off diplomatic relations with the Palestinians.

Unable and unwilling to work together, Israelis and Palestinians
appealed to the international community. United Nations secretary-
general Kofi Annan (1938–), U.S. secretary of state Colin Powell
(1937–), Russian foreign minister Igor Ivanov (1945–), Danish foreign
minister Per Stig Moeller (1942–), High Representative for European
Common Foreign and Security Policy Javier Solana (1942–), and European Commissioner for External Affairs Chris Patten (1944–) met to
establish a workable Israeli-Palestinian peace plan in 2002. On September 17, 2002, the group, called the Quartet because it included representatives from the European Union (EU; an economic and political
association of European countries), Russia, the United States, and the
United Nations (an international organization of countries founded in

Israeli prime minister Ariel Sharon. In 2004 Sharon announced that Israel would withdraw military personnel and remove selected settlements from the Gaza Strip and portions of the West Bank. © RICKI ROSEN/CORBIS.

1945 to promote international peace, security, and cooperation), issued a document referred to as the Roadmap to Peace. The Roadmap was a political plan that would implement a lasting peace in the Middle East after a three-year transition period. The transitional stages included a Palestinian cease-fire and an Israeli army withdrawal from the occupied territories, followed by the establishment of a provisional (temporary)

Palestinian state in 2005 and then negotiations to resolve the future of Jerusalem, Palestinian refugees (people who flee their country to escape violence or persecution), and permanent borders for Israel and the Palestinian state—all long-standing unresolved issues in the conflict. The plan was greeted by the Israelis and Palestinians with varying degrees of acceptance, yet at the time, it stood as the most complete plan to end the Arab-Israeli conflict. However, continued violence in the region prevented any progress toward peace.

Israeli prime minister Ariel Sharon (1928–) knew that either Israel or the Palestinians had to take action if peace was ever to be a reality in the region. Unable to negotiate a satisfactory peace with the Palestinians, Sharon decided to have Israel take the first step toward peace on its own. In 2004, he announced that Israel would withdraw military personnel and remove selected settlements (communities established and inhabited in order to claim land) from the Gaza Strip and portions of the West Bank, without requiring the Palestinian Authority, the recognized governing institution for Palestinians in the West Bank and the Gaza Strip, to yield any land or resources. The following document is a portion of the Israeli disengagement plan to remove Israel's army and settlers from parts of the occupied territories.

Things to remember while reading the excerpt from "Israel's Revised Disengagement Plan— Main Principles, June 6, 2004"

- The disengagement plan does not replace the Roadmap to Peace proposed by the Quartet.
- At stake in the plan are twenty-one settlements in the Gaza Strip and another four settlements in the West Bank. Approximately 9,000 Jewish settlers would ultimately be affected by the dismantling of those settlements.

• • •

Israel's Revised Disengagement Plan—Main Principles (June 6, 2004)

1. Background—Political and Security Implications

The State of Israel is committed to the peace process.... The State of Israel has come to the conclusion that there is currently no reliable Palestinian partner with which it can make progress in a two-sided peace process. Accordingly, it has developed a plan of revised disengagement (hereinafter—the plan), based on the following considerations:

One. The **stalemate** dictated by the current situation is harmful. In order to break out of this stalemate, the State of Israel is required to initiate moves not dependent on Palestinian cooperation.

Two. The purpose of the plan is to lead to a better security, political, economic and demographic situation.

Three. In any future permanent status arrangement, there will be no Israeli towns and villages in the Gaza Strip. On the other hand, it is clear that in the West Bank, there are areas which will be part of the State of Israel, including major Israeli population centers, cities, towns and villages, security areas and other places of special interest to Israel.

Four. The State of Israel supports the efforts of the United States, operating alongside the international community, to promote the reform process, the construction of institutions and the improvement of the economy and welfare of the Palestinian residents, in order that a new Palestinian leadership will emerge and prove itself capable of fulfilling its commitments under the Roadmap.

Five. Relocation from the Gaza Strip and from an area in **Northern Samaria** should reduce friction with the Palestinian population.

Six. The completion of the plan will serve to dispel the claims regarding Israel's responsibility for the Palestinians in the Gaza Strip.

Seven. The process set forth in the plan is without prejudice to the relevant agreements between the State of Israel and the Palestinians. Relevant arrangements shall continue to apply.

Eight. International support for this plan is widespread and important. This support is essential in order to bring the Palestinians to **implement** in practice their obligations to combat terrorism and **effect** reforms as required by the Roadmap, thus enabling the parties to return to the path of negotiation . . . .

3.1 The Gaza Strip

1) The State of Israel will evacuate the Gaza Strip, including all existing Israeli towns and villages, and will **redeploy** outside the Strip. This will not include military deployment in the area of the border between the Gaza Strip and Egypt ("the **Philadelphi Route**") as detailed below.

2) Upon completion of this process, there shall no longer be any permanent presence of Israeli security forces in the areas of Gaza Strip territory which have been evacuated.

3.2 The West Bank

3) The State of Israel will evacuate an area in Northern Samaria (Ganim, Kadim, Sa-Nur and Homesh), and all military installations in this area, and will redeploy outside the vacated area.

Stalemate: Situation in which in which no progress can be made.

Northern Samaria: An area in the northern half of the West Bank.

Implement: Put into action, carry out.

Effect: Cause.

Redeploy: Move military forces.

Philadelphi Route: A narrow strip of land along the border between Gaza and Egypt that is controlled and patrolled by Israeli forces.

4) Upon completion of this process, there shall no longer be any permanent presence of Israeli security forces in this area.

5) The move will enable **territorial contiguity** for Palestinians in the Northern Samaria area.

6) The State of Israel will assist, together with the international community, in improving the transportation **infrastructure** in the West Bank in order to facilitate the contiguity of Palestinian transportation.

7) The process will facilitate normal life and Palestinian economic and commercial activity in the West Bank.

3.3 The intention is to complete the planned relocation process by the end of 2005 . . . .

10. Economic Arrangements

. . . In the longer term, and in line with Israel's interest in encouraging greater Palestinian economic independence, the State of Israel expects to reduce the number of Palestinian workers entering Israel, to the point that it ceases completely. The State of Israel supports the development of sources of employment in the Gaza Strip and in Palestinian areas of the West Bank, by international elements . . . .

13. Conclusion

The goal is that implementation of the plan will lead to improving the situation and breaking the current **deadlock**. If and when there is evidence from the Palestinian side of its willingness, capability and implementation in practice of the fight against terrorism, full cessation of terrorism and violence and the institution of reform as required by the Roadmap, it will be possible to return to the track of negotiation and dialogue.

• • •

What happened next . . .

On February 8, 2005, at the Sharm el-Sheik summit in Egypt, Palestinian and Israeli leaders met for the first time in four years. Newly elected Palestinian Authority president Mahmoud Abbas (1935–) met with Sharon to formalize a truce between Israelis and Palestinians. Although both Israeli and Palestinian leaders acknowledged that the violence and division between their peoples would continue for a time, both were hopeful of eventual peace as neighbors.

Israel's Cabinet (the committee of senior ministers responsible for controlling government policy) approved the plan for the removal of the Israeli army and settlements in the occupied territories on February 20, 2005. It also announced a revised route for a separation barrier, under

Territorial contiguity: A continuous stretch of land.

Infrastructure: The basic structure of a system; in this case, roads.

Deadlock: A situation in which no progress can be made; a stalemate.

A Palestinian family watches an Israeli bulldozer demolishing houses in one of the West Bank settlements evacuated by Israel as part of Ariel Sharon's disengagement plan. SAIF DAHLAH/AFP/GETTY IMAGES.

construction since 2002, to guard the Jewish settlements remaining in the West Bank. The day after the vote, 500 Palestinian prisoners were released. The Israeli government then sent eviction notices to approximately 8,500 Jewish settlers in the Gaza Strip and in four settlements in the northern portion of the West Bank. Those who refused to vacate by mid–August 2005 were forcibly removed by Israeli security forces, and by the end of September, the Israeli withdrawal was complete.

Did you know...

- The disengagement plan was the first Israeli proposal to evacuate settlements in the occupied territories since occupation started in 1967.
- Many ordinary Israelis and government leaders were against the disengagement plan. Opponents held several mass demonstrations

in the months leading up to the withdrawal from Gaza, and finance minister Benjamin Netanyahu (1949–) resigned his post in protest (Netanyahu was elected prime minister of Israel in 2009).

- Observers noted that Ariel Sharon's plan removed settlers from areas of the occupied territories that were the most difficult to defend.

Consider the following . . .

- What advantages did Israel gain by making this decision to withdraw from certain portions of the occupied territories without requiring anything in return from the Palestinians? Explain.
- Describe the disadvantages of the disengagement plan for both Israelis and the Arab Palestinians.
- Could the Palestinians have made a decision that would have made a similar impact on efforts for peace as the Israeli disengagement plan? Explain.
- Think about the Israeli strategy behind its disengagement plan. What benefits to the Israelis are there in the plan?
- The Palestinians argued for Israeli withdrawal from the occupied territories for many years. Why might Israel agree that this is a good policy?

For More Information

BOOKS

Gelvin, James L. *The Israel-Palestine Conflict: 100 Years of War.* 2nd ed. Cambridge: Cambridge University Press, 2007.

Gunderson, Cory Gideon. *The Israeli-Palestinian Conflict.* Edina, MN: Abdo, 2004.

Sharp, Anne Wallace. *The Palestinians.* Detroit: Lucent Books, 2005.

Smith, Charles D., ed. *Palestine and the Arab-Israeli Conflict: A History with Documents,* 4th ed. Boston MA: Bedford/St. Martin's, 2001.

Tessler, Mark. *A History of the Israeli-Palestinian Conflict.* 2nd ed. Bloomington: Indiana University Press, 2009.

WEB SITES

"Address to the Fourth Herzliya Conference." *Israeli Ministry of Foreign Affairs* (December 18, 2003). http://www.mfa.gov.il/MFA/Government/ Speeches+by+Israeli+leaders/2003/Address+by+PM+Ariel+Sharon+at+the+ Fourth+Herzliya.htm (accessed on November 30, 2011).

"The Cabinet Resolution Regarding the Disengagement Plan." *Israeli Ministry of Foreign Affairs* (June 6, 2004). http://www.mfa.gov.il/MFA/ Peace+Process/Reference+Documents/Revised+Disengagement+Plan+6 -June-2004.htm (accessed on November 30, 2011).

"Q&A: The Middle East Summit and Its Aftermath." *NPR* (February 24, 2005). http://www.npr.org/templates/story/story.php?storyId=4502428 (accessed on November 30, 2011).

The Goldstone Report

Excerpt from the Executive Summary of the *Report of the United Nations Fact Finding Mission on the Gaza Conflict* (*The Goldstone Report*)

By the UN Human Rights Council

September 15, 2009

"From the facts available to it, the Mission is of the view that some of the actions of the Government of Israel might justify a competent court finding that crimes against humanity have been committed."

The Gaza Strip, a narrow strip of land along the eastern shore of the Mediterranean Sea, west of Israel and bordering Egypt in the southwest, has for decades been a point of conflict in the Middle East. Gaza was part of Palestine, a historical region in the Middle East on the eastern shore of the Mediterranean Sea, comprising parts of present-day Israel and Jordan. After World War I (1914–18), Palestine was under British mandate, or administrative authority. Then, after the 1948 Arab-Israeli War, in which Arab nations attacked the newly-declared nation of Israel, Egypt took control of the Gaza Strip. Two decades later, Israel began its occupation (physical and political control of an area seized by a foreign military force) of the Gaza Strip following the 1967 Arab-Israeli War. In 1994, as directed by the Oslo Accords (an agreement outlining specific measures towards achieving peace between Israel and the Palestinians), the Gaza Strip came under the control of a Palestinian government body that came to be known as the Palestinian Authority, but Israel still maintained a military and civilian presence there. (For more information, see **The Oslo Accords**.) By 2005, however, Israel completed its withdrawal of troops and settlements from the region as part of its disengagement plan, another step in the peace process by which Israel ended its occupation of Gaza and reduced the number of settlements in the West Bank, an area between Israel and Jordan on the west bank of the Jordan River that was also occupied by Israel after the 1967 Arab-Israeli War. (For more information, see **Israel's Revised Disengagement Plan**.)

Despite these moves, the region remained a hotbed of conflict. Clashes between Israelis and Palestinians continued, and within the Palestinian Authority, rival political parties Hamas and Fatah battled for control. In 2007, violent fighting broke out between the two groups. Hamas emerged with control of the Gaza Strip, while Fatah ruled the West Bank. From Gaza, Hamas persistently launched rocket attacks against Israel. In September 2007 Israel began a blockade of the Gaza Strip, closing its borders and limiting the types of goods that could be brought into the region, including food, commercial items, fuel, weapons, and other goods and supplies. Egypt, which shares a 9-mile (14.5-kilometer) border with Gaza, supported the blockade, agreeing to only allow humanitarian supplies into Gaza. However, using secret tunnels between the Gaza Strip and Egypt, Hamas still managed to get materials to make rockets and their attacks on Israel continued. On December 27, 2008, Israel launched a series of air strikes against Hamas targets in Gaza, in a mission called Operation Cast Lead. A week later, Israeli ground troops invaded Gaza, and fighting ended with a cease-fire in mid–January 2009.

The Gaza War prompted the United Nations Human Rights Council (UNHRC), a unit made up of representatives from forty-seven member countries that is focused on human rights issues, to adopt a resolution that called for an investigation into allegations of "grave violations" of human rights during the conflict. (The United Nations is an international organization of countries founded in 1945 to promote international peace, security, and cooperation.) More than thirteen hundred Palestinians, including hundreds of civilians, and 13 Israelis were killed in the Gaza War. A four-person committee led by South African judge and former war crimes prosecutor Richard Goldstone (1938–) was established to investigate the actions of both Israeli and Hamas forces during the war. Other members of the team included Pakistani human rights lawyer Hina Jilani (1953–), former Irish colonel Desmond Travers (1941–), and British international law professor Christine Chinkin.

Richard Goldstone, head of the United Nations committee charged with investigating the actions of Israel and Hamas forces during the Gaza War.
© MARTIAL TREZZINI/EPA/ CORBIS.

The effort was controversial from the start. The UNHRC resolution called for specific attention to Israel's activities during the war, which angered Israel and its supporters and prompted them to refuse to cooperate with the effort. Although the UNHRC, which is largely made up of representatives from Muslim nations, agreed that the actions of the Palestinians would also be probed, the official resolution was not revised to reflect this change. Furthermore, some observers questioned whether Goldstone and his colleagues were appropriate choices to lead the effort, citing associations and comments prior to the investigation that were thought to indicate the possibility of bias against Israel.

Nevertheless, the Goldstone team began its fact-finding mission in May 2009. The members made two visits to the Gaza Strip in June 2009, touring damaged sites, conducting interviews, and reviewing documents and other evidence. The group also conducted public hearings to gather testimony from war victims. On September 15, 2009, the Goldstone team issued its findings.

The following excerpt from the *Report of the United Nations Fact Finding Mission on the Gaza Conflict*, also known as *The Goldstone Report*, details possible war crimes and crimes against humanity on the part of both Israel and Hamas. The report notes incidents in which it concludes that Israel used excessive force, purposely targeted civilians and destroyed

A Palestinian man surveys his neighborhood in Gaza City after Israeli bombings. Members of the United Nations Fact Finding Mission on the Gaza Conflict visited the Gaza Strip and toured damages sites as part of their investigation. © SHAWN BALDWIN/ CORBIS.

basic infrastructure such as sources of food and water, and used people as human shields. It concludes that Hamas also intentionally targeted the civilian population and inflicted terror with its attacks on southern Israel. In total, the full report was 574 pages long.

Things to remember while reading the excerpt from *The Goldstone Report*:

- The report refers to the Fourth Geneva Convention, which is a treaty adopted in 1949 that outlines standards for the treatment and protection of civilians during war. (The first three Geneva Conventions addressed standards of treatment for military personnel and prisoners of war.) Actions found to be in violation of the Geneva Conventions are considered war crimes.

- The report refers to Israel's use of bombs containing tungsten and white phosphorus, cancer-causing chemicals that cause severe injury or burns. While weapons containing tungsten and white phosphorus are not illegal, their use in a densely populated area like the Gaza Strip is considered by some to be a war crime.
- The findings that the document presents are not legal charges, nor do they represent conclusive evidence of criminal activity. Instead, the report's findings were intended to be the basis for further investigations to determine whether war crimes and crimes against humanity had been committed.

• • •

The Goldstone Report

The Occupied Palestinian Territory: the Gaza Strip . . .
2. Overview of Israel's military operations in the Gaza Strip and casualties

29. Israel deployed its navy, air force and army in the operation it codenamed "Operation Cast Lead". The military operations in the Gaza Strip included two main phases, the air phase and the air-land phase, and lasted from 27 December 2008 to 18 January 2009. The Israeli offensive began with a week-long air attack, from 27 December until 3 January 2009. The air force continued to play an important role in assisting and covering the ground forces from 3 January to 18 January 2009. The army was responsible for the ground invasion, which began on 3 January 2009 when ground troops entered Gaza from the north and from the east. The available information indicates that the Golani, Givati and Paratrooper Brigades and five Armoured Corps Brigades were involved. The navy was used in part to **shell** the Gaza coast during the operations. Chapter VI also locates the incidents investigated by the Mission, described in Chapters VII to XV, in the context of the military operations.

30. Statistics about Palestinians who lost their life during the military operations vary. Based on extensive field research, non-governmental organizations place the overall number of persons killed between 1,387 and 1,417. The Gaza authorities report 1,444 fatal casualties. The Government of Israel provides a figure of 1,166. The data provided by non-governmental sources with regard to the percentage of civilians among those killed are generally consistent and raise very serious concerns with regard to the way Israel conducted the military operations in Gaza.

31. According to the Government of Israel, during the military operations there were 4 Israeli fatal casualties in southern Israel, of whom 3 were civilians and one soldier, killed by rockets and mortars attacks by Palestinian armed

Shell: Bomb.

groups. In addition, 9 Israeli soldiers were killed during the fighting inside the Gaza strip, 4 of whom as a result of friendly fire.

3. Attacks by Israeli forces on government buildings and persons of the Gaza authorities, including police

32. Israeli armed forces launched numerous attacks against buildings and persons of the Gaza authorities. As far as attacks on buildings are concerned, the Mission examined the Israeli strikes against the Palestinian Legislative Council and the Gaza main prison (Chapter VII). Both buildings were destroyed to an extent that puts them out of use. Statements by Israeli Government and armed forces representatives justified the attacks arguing that political and administrative institutions in Gaza are part of the "Hamas terrorist infrastructure". The Mission rejects this position. It finds that there is no evidence that the Legislative Council building and the Gaza main prison made an effective contribution to military action. On the information available to it, the Mission finds that the attacks on these buildings constituted deliberate attacks on civilian objects in violation of the rule of customary international humanitarian law whereby attacks must be strictly limited to military objectives. These facts further indicate the commission of the grave breach of extensive destruction of property, not justified by military necessity and carried out unlawfully and **wantonly**.

33. The Mission examined the attacks against six police facilities, four of them during the first minutes of the military operations on 27 December 2008, resulting in the death of 99 policemen and nine members of the public. The overall around 240 policemen killed by Israeli forces constitute more than one sixth of the Palestinian casualties. The circumstances of the attacks and the Government of Israel July 2009 report on the military operations clarify that the policemen were deliberately targeted and killed on the ground that the police as an institution, or a large part of the policemen individually, are in the Government of Israel's view part of the Palestinian military forces in Gaza.

34. ....The Mission finds that, while a great number of the Gaza policemen were recruited among Hamas supporters or members of Palestinian armed groups, the Gaza police were a civilian law-enforcement agency. The Mission also concludes that the policemen killed on 27 December 2008 cannot be said to have been taking a direct part in hostilities and thus did not lose their civilian **immunity** from direct attack as civilians on this ground. The Mission accepts that there may be individual members of the Gaza police that were at the same time members of Palestinian armed groups and thus combatants. It concludes, however, that the attacks against the police facilities on the first day of the armed operations failed to strike an acceptable balance between the direct military advantage

Wantonly: Recklessly and with unprovoked cruelty.

Immunity: Protection.

anticipated (i.e. the killing of those policemen who may have been members of Palestinian armed groups) and the loss of civilian life (i.e. the other policemen killed and members of the public who would inevitably have been present or in the vicinity), and therefore violated international humanitarian law. . . .

7. Deliberate attacks against the civilian population

43. The Mission investigated eleven incidents in which Israeli forces launched direct attacks against civilians with lethal outcome (Chapter XI). The cases examined in this part of the report are, with one exception, all cases in which the facts indicate no justifiable military objective pursued by the attack. The first two incidents are attacks against houses in the Samouni neighbourhood south of Gaza City, including the shelling of a house in which Palestinian civilians had been forced to assemble by the Israeli forces. The following group of seven incidents concern the shooting of civilians while they were trying to leave their homes to walk to a safer place, waving white flags and, in some of the cases, following an **injunction** from the Israeli forces to do so. The facts gathered by the Mission indicate that all the attacks occurred under circumstances in which the Israeli forces were in control of the area and had previously entered into contact with or at least observed the persons they subsequently attacked, so that they must have been aware of their civilian status. In the majority of these incidents, the consequences of the Israeli attacks against civilians were **aggravated** by their subsequent refusal to allow the evacuation of the wounded or to permit access to ambulances.

44. These incidents indicate that the instructions given to the Israeli forces moving into Gaza provided for a low **threshold** for the use of lethal fire against the civilian population. The Mission found strong **corroboration** of this trend emerging from its fact-finding in the testimonies of Israeli soldiers collected in two publications it reviewed.

45. The Mission further examined an incident in which a mosque was targeted with a missile during the early evening prayer, resulting in the death of fifteen, and an attack with **flechette munitions** on a crowd of family and neighbours at a condolence tent, killing five. The Mission finds that both attacks constitute intentional attacks against the civilian population and civilian objects.

46. From the facts **ascertained** in all the above cases, the Mission finds that the conduct of the Israeli armed forces constitute grave breaches of the Fourth Geneva Convention in respect of willful [sic] killings and willfully [sic] causing great suffering to protected persons and as such give rise to individual criminal responsibility. It also finds that the direct targeting and **arbitrarily** killing of Palestinian civilians is a violation of the right to life. . . .

Injunction: Command.

Aggravated: Made worse.

Threshold: Level of tolerance.

Corroboration: Support or confirmation.

Flechette munitions: Small, sharp projectile weapons.

Ascertained: Discovered or learned.

Arbitrarily: Unnecessarily; without cause.

9. Attacks on the foundations of civilian life in Gaza: destruction of industrial infrastructure, food production, water installations, sewage treatment and housing

50. The Mission investigated several incidents involving the destruction of industrial infrastructure, food production, water installations, sewage treatment and housing (Chapter XIII). Already at the beginning of the military operations, the Al Bader flour mill was the only flour mill in the Gaza Strip still operating. The flour mill was hit by a series of air strikes on 9 January 2009 after several false warnings had been issued on previous days. The Mission finds that its destruction had no military justification. The nature of the strikes, in particular the precise targeting of crucial machinery, suggests that the intention was to disable the factory in terms of its productive capacity. From the facts it ascertained, the Mission finds that there has been a violation of the grave breaches provisions of the Fourth Geneva Convention. Unlawful and wanton destruction which is not justified by military necessity amounts to a war crime. The Mission also finds that the destruction of the mill was carried out for the purposes of denying **sustenance** to the civilian population, which is a violation of customary international law and may constitute a war crime. The strike on the flour mill further constitutes a violation of human rights provisions regarding the right to adequate food and means of **subsistence**.

51. The chicken farms of Mr. Sameh Sawafeary in the Zeitoun neighbourhood south of Gaza City reportedly supplied over 10 per cent of the Gaza egg market. Armoured bulldozers of the Israeli forces systematically flattened the chicken coops, killing all 31,000 chickens inside, and destroyed the plant and material necessary for the business. The Mission concludes that this was a deliberate act of wanton destruction not justified by any military necessity and draws the same legal conclusions as in the case of the destruction of the flour mill.

52. Israeli forces also carried out a strike against a wall of one of the raw sewage lagoons of the Gaza Waste Water Treatment Plant, which caused the outflow of more than 200,000 cubic metres of raw sewage into neighbouring farmland. The circumstances of the strike on the lagoon suggest that it was deliberate and premeditated. The Namar Wells complex in Jabalya consisted of two water wells, pumping machines, a generator, fuel storage, a reservoir chlorination unit, buildings and related equipment. All were destroyed by multiple air strikes on the first day of the Israeli aerial attack. The Mission considers it unlikely that a target the size of the Namar Wells could have been hit by multiple strikes in error. It found no grounds to suggest that there was any military advantage to be had by hitting the wells and noted that there was no suggestion that Palestinian armed groups had used the wells for any purpose. Considering that the right to drinking water is part of the right to adequate food, the Mission makes the same legal findings as in the case of the Al Bader flour mill. . . .

Sustenance: Items needed to stay alive; nourishment.

Subsistence: Staying alive; existence.

10. The use of Palestinian civilians as human shields

55. The Mission investigated four incidents in which Israeli forces **coerced** Palestinian civilian men at gun point to take part in house searches during the military operations (Chapter XIV). The Palestinian men were blindfolded and handcuffed as they were forced to enter houses ahead of the Israeli soldiers. In one of the incidents, Israeli forces repeatedly forced a man to enter a house in which Palestinian combatants were hiding. Published testimonies of Israeli soldiers who took part in the military operations confirm the continued use of this practice, in spite of clear orders from Israel's High Court to the armed forces to put an end to it and repeated public assurances from the armed forces that the practice had been discontinued. The Mission concludes that this practice amounts to the use of Palestinian civilians as human shields and is therefore prohibited by international humanitarian law. It puts the right to life of the civilians at risk in an arbitrary and unlawful manner and constitutes cruel and inhuman treatment. The use of human shields also is a war crime. The Palestinian men used as human shields were questioned under threat of death or injury to extract information about Hamas, Palestinian combatants and tunnels. This constitutes a further violation of international humanitarian law.

11. Deprivation of liberty: Gazans detained during the Israeli operation of 27 December 2008 to 18 January 2009

56. During the military operations Israeli armed forces rounded up large numbers of civilians and detained them in houses and open spaces in Gaza and, in the case of many Palestinian men, also took them to detention facilities in Israel. In the cases investigated by the Mission, the facts gathered indicate that none of the civilians were armed or posed any apparent threat to the Israeli soldiers. Chapter XV of the report is based on the Mission's interviews with Palestinian men who were detained, as well as on the Mission's review of other relevant material, including interviews with relatives and statements from other victims submitted to the Mission.

57. From the facts gathered, the Mission finds that there were numerous violations of international humanitarian law and human rights law committed in the context of these detentions. Civilians, including women and children, were detained in degrading conditions, deprived of food, water and access to sanitary facilities, and exposed to the elements in January without any shelter. The men were handcuffed, blindfolded and repeatedly made to strip, sometimes naked, at different stages of their detention.

58. In the Al Atatra area in north-western Gaza Israeli troops had dug out sand pits in which Palestinian men, women and children were detained. Israeli tanks and artillery positions were located inside the sand pits and around them and fired from next to the detainees.

Coerced: Forced.

59. The Palestinian men who were taken to detention facilities in Israel were subjected to degrading conditions of detention, harsh interrogation, beatings and other physical and mental abuse. Some of them were charged with being unlawful **combatants**. Those interviewed by the Mission were released after the proceedings against them had apparently been discontinued.

60. In addition to arbitrary deprivation of liberty and violation of **due process rights**, the cases of the detained Palestinian civilians highlight a common thread of the interaction between Israeli soldiers and Palestinian civilians which emerged clearly also in many cases discussed in other parts of the Report: continuous and systematic abuse, outrages on personal dignity, humiliating and degrading treatment contrary to fundamental principles of international humanitarian law and human rights law. The Mission concludes that the treatment of these civilians constitutes the **infliction** of a collective penalty on those persons and amounts to measures of intimidation and terror. Such acts are grave breaches of the Geneva Conventions and constitute a war crime. . . .

13. The impact of the military operations and of the blockade on the Gaza population and their human rights

65. The Mission examined the combined impact of the military operations and of the blockade on the Gaza population and its enjoyment of human rights. The economy, employment opportunities and family livelihoods were already severely affected by the blockade when the Israeli offensive began. Insufficient supply of fuel for electricity generation had a negative impact on industrial activity, on the operation of hospitals, on water supply to households and on sewage treatment. Import restrictions and the ban on all exports from Gaza affected the industrial sector and agricultural production. Unemployment levels and the percentage of the population living in poverty and deep poverty were rising.

66. In this precarious situation, the military operations destroyed a substantial part of the economic infrastructure. As a large part of the factories were targeted and destroyed or damaged, poverty, unemployment and food insecurity further increased dramatically. The agricultural sector similarly suffered due to the destruction of agricultural land, water wells and fishing boats during the military operations. The continuation of the blockade impedes the reconstruction of the economic infrastructure destroyed.

67. As a result of the **razing** of farmland and destruction of greenhouses, food insecurity is expected to further worsen in spite of the increased quantities of food items allowed into Gaza since the beginning of the military operations. Dependence on food assistance increases. Levels of stunting and thinness in children and of **anaemia** prevalence in children and

Combatants: Fighters.

Due Process Rights: Rights guaranteed by law that protect a person from the state; these rights established by law are above the actions of a state.

Infliction: The act of imposing something.

Razing: Cutting down; flattening in order to destroy completely.

Anaemia: A blood condition that can be tied to malnutrition.

pregnant women were worrying already before the military operations. The hardship caused by the extensive destruction of shelter (UNDP reported 3,354 houses completely destroyed and 11,112 partially damaged) and resulting displacement particularly affects children and women. In the water and sanitation sector, the destruction of infrastructure (such as the destruction of the Namar wells and the attack against the water treatment plant described in Chapter XIII), aggravated the pre-existing situation. Already before the military operations, 80 percent of the water supplied in Gaza did not meet the WHO's standards for drinking water. The discharge of untreated or partially treated waste water into the sea is a further health hazard worsened by the military operations.

68. The military operations and resulting casualties subjected the **beleaguered** Gaza health sector to additional strain. Hospitals and ambulances were targeted by Israeli attacks. Patients with chronic health conditions could not be given priority in hospitals faced with the **influx** of patients with life-threatening injuries. Patients with hostilities-related injuries had often to be discharged as early as possible to free beds. The long term health impact of these early discharges, as well as of weapons containing substances such as tungsten and white phosphorous, remains a source of concern. While the exact number of people who will suffer permanent disabilities is still unknown, the Mission understands that many persons who sustained traumatic injuries during the conflict still face the risk of permanent disability due to complications and inadequate follow-up and physical **rehabilitation**. . . .

72. The Mission acknowledges that the supply of humanitarian goods, particularly foodstuffs, allowed into Gaza by Israel temporarily increased during the military operations. The level of goods allowed into Gaza before the military operations, however, was insufficient to meet the needs of the population even before hostilities started, and has again decreased after the end of the military operations. From the facts ascertained by it, the Mission believes that Israel has violated its obligation to allow free passage of all consignments of medical and hospital objects, food and clothing (article 23 of the Fourth Geneva Convention). The Mission also finds that Israel violated specific obligations it has as Occupying Power spelled out in the Fourth Geneva Convention, such as the duty to maintain medical and hospital establishments and services and to agree to relief schemes if the occupied territory is not well supplied.

73. The Mission also concludes that in the destruction by Israeli armed forces of private residential houses, water wells, water tanks, agricultural land and greenhouses there was a specific purpose of denying them for their sustenance to the population of the Gaza Strip. The Mission finds that Israel violated its duty to respect the right of the Gaza population to an adequate standard of living, including access to adequate food, water and housing. The Mission moreover finds violations of specific human rights provisions

Beleaguered: Troubled or harassed.

Influx: Arrival in large numbers.

Rehabilitation: Medical and psychological treatment to restore a person to health.

protecting the rights of children, particularly those who are victims of armed conflict, women and the disabled.

74. The conditions of life in Gaza, resulting from deliberate actions of the Israeli forces and the declared policies of the Government of Israel—as they were presented by its authorized and legitimate representatives—with regard to the Gaza Strip before, during and after the military operation, **cumulatively** indicate the intention to inflict collective punishment on the people of the Gaza Strip in violation of international humanitarian law.

75. Finally, the Mission considered whether the series of acts that deprive Palestinians in the Gaza Strip of their means of sustenance, employment, housing and water, that deny their freedom of movement and their right to leave and enter their own country, that limit their access a court of law and an effective remedy, could amount to persecution, a crime against humanity. From the facts available to it, the Mission is of the view that some of the actions of the Government of Israel might justify a competent court finding that crimes against humanity have been committed. . . .

Israel

20. Impact on civilians of rocket and mortar attacks by Palestinian armed groups on southern Israel

103. Palestinian armed groups have launched about 8000 rockets and mortars into southern Israel since 2001 (Chapter XIII). While communities such as Sderot and Kibbutz Nir-Am have been within the range of rocket and mortar fire since the beginning, the range of rocket fire increased to nearly 40 kilometres from the Gaza border, encompassing towns as far north as Ashdod, during the Israeli military operations in Gaza.

104. Since 18 June 2008, rockets fired by Palestinian armed groups in Gaza have killed 3 civilians inside Israel and 2 civilians in Gaza when a rocket landed short of the border on 26 December 2008. Reportedly, over 1000 civilians inside Israel were physically injured as a result of rocket and mortar attacks, 918 of which were injured during the time of the Israeli military operations in Gaza.

Cumulatively: When added together.

Post-traumatic stress disorder: A psychological condition found in some people who have experienced combat, violence, or other events that results in anxiety, depression, and other symptoms.

105. The Mission has taken particular note of the high level of psychological trauma suffered by the civilian population inside Israel. Data gathered by an Israeli organization in October 2007 found that 28.4% of adults and 72–94% of children in Sderot suffered from **Post-Traumatic Stress Disorder**. 1596 people were reportedly treated for stress-related injuries during the military operations in Gaza while over 500 people were treated following the end of the operations.

106. Rocket and mortars have damaged houses, schools and cars in southern Israel. On 5 March 2009, a rocket struck a synagogue in Netivot. The rocket and mortar fire has adversely impacted on the right to education

of children and adults living in southern Israel. This is a result of school closures and interruptions to classes by alerts and moving to shelters and also the diminished ability to learn that is witnessed in individual experiencing symptoms of psychological trauma.

107. The rocket and mortar fire has also adversely impacted on the economic and social life of the affected communities. For communities such as Ashdod, Yavne, Beer Sheba, which experienced rocket strikes for the first time during the Israeli military operations in Gaza, there was a brief interruption to their economy and cultural brought about by the temporary displacement of some of their residents. For towns closer to the Gaza border that have been under rocket and mortar fire since 2001, the recent **escalation** has added to the **exodus** of residents from these areas.

108. The Mission has determined that the rockets and, to a lesser extent, mortars, fired by the Palestinian armed groups are incapable of being directed towards specific military objectives and were fired into areas where civilian populations are based. The Mission has further determined that these attacks constitute **indiscriminate** attacks upon the civilian population of southern Israel and that where there is no intended military target and the rockets and mortars are launched into a civilian population, they constitute a *deliberate* attack against a civilian population. These acts would constitute war crimes and may amount to crimes against humanity. Given the seeming inability of the Palestinian armed groups to direct the rockets and mortars towards specific targets and given the fact that the attacks have caused very little damage to Israeli military assets, the Mission finds that there is significant evidence to suggest that one of the primary purposes of the rocket and mortar attacks is to spread terror amongst the Israeli civilian population, a violation of international law.

109. Noting that some of the Palestinian armed groups, along them Hamas, have publicly expressed an intention to target civilians as **reprisals** for the fatalities of civilians in Gaza as a result of Israeli military operations, the Mission is of the view that reprisals against civilians in armed hostilities are contrary to international humanitarian law.

110. The Mission notes that the relatively few casualties sustained by civilians inside Israel is due in large part to the precautions put into place by Israel. This includes an early warning system, the provision of public shelters and **fortifications** of schools and other public buildings at great financial cost—a projected USD 460 million between 2005 and 2011—to the Government of Israel. The Mission is greatly concerned, however, about the lack of an early warning system and a lack of public shelters and fortifications available to the Palestinian Israeli communities living unrecognised and in some of the recognised villages that are within the range of rocket and mortars being fired by Palestinian armed groups in Gaza. . . .

• • •

Escalation: Increase.

Exodus: Departure in large numbers.

Indiscriminate: Not based on careful distinctions, random.

Reprisals: Retaliation for injuries received.

Fortifications: Adding of structural features to make a building safe.

What happened next...

Overall, reaction to the report was mixed. The government of Israel and its supporters were outraged, criticizing the report as biased and full of errors, and considering it to be a major blow to the nation's image. In January 2010, a *New York Times* article quoted Israeli prime minister Benjamin Netanyahu (1949–) as saying, "We face three major strategic challenges, the Iranian nuclear program, rockets aimed at our citizens and Goldstone." Israel maintained that its actions in the Gaza War were based in its rights to defend itself from what it considered terrorist aggression, and it noted that Hamas's military tactics purposely endangered civilians. Hamas itself denied the report's accusations of war crimes. Internationally, reactions tended to be split along pro-Israel and pro-Arab lines, while several human rights groups praised the work of the Goldstone team. Goldstone himself vigorously defended the accuracy of his team's findings.

Both the report and the United Nations General Assembly recommended that Israel and Hamas conduct their own investigations into the incidents and accusations covered in the report, with the threat of intervention by the International Criminal Court if they failed to do so. (The International Criminal Court is a legal body with representatives from many nations that prosecutes those who commit war crimes and crimes against humanity.) A follow-up report issued by the United Nations in March 2011 noted that Israel had indeed conducted a thorough investigation of hundreds of questionable incidents during the Gaza War and had created new policies to lessen the chance of civilian deaths in the future. The report also chastised Hamas for failing to conduct any investigations of its own activities.

In a surprising turn of events, in April 2011, Goldstone published an op-ed piece in *The Washington Post* in which he reversed his previous position that Israel had intentionally targeted civilians during the Gaza War, based upon new information and evidence that had come to light since *The Goldstone Report* was issued. In the piece, Goldstone stated, "Although the Israeli evidence that has emerged since publication of our report doesn't negate the tragic loss of civilian life, I regret that our fact-finding mission did not have such evidence explaining the circumstances in which we said civilians in Gaza were targeted, because it probably would have influenced our findings about intentionality and war crimes." The three other members of the UNHRC's fact-finding team have issued

The United Nations Security Council meets to discuss the findings of the Goldstone Report. © JUSTIN LANE/EPA/CORBIS.

a statement critical of Goldstone's retraction and asserting that they continue to stand by the contents of the report. (For more information, see **Reconsidering Goldstone**.)

Did you know . . .

- Nearly 1.6 million people, over 99 percent of them Sunni Muslims, live in the Gaza Strip, which is roughly twice the size of Washington, D.C., according to statistics compiled by the U.S. Central Intelligence Agency. (Sunnis are followers of the Sunni branch of Islam.) Approximately 200,000 Palestinians sought refuge in Gaza after the 1948 Arab-Israeli War; currently, over 1.1 million of the Palestinians in Gaza are considered to be refugees (people who flee their country to escape violence or persecution), with half of them living in refugee camps, according to the United Nations Relief and Works Agency.

- Richard Goldstone, who is Jewish, is a former governor of Hebrew University in Jerusalem. He initially turned down the invitation to head up the UNHRC's investigative team because its original directive targeted only Israel's activities during the war. However, after the release of the report, he was criticized by the Jewish community in South Africa, and in 2010, protesters threatened to disrupt his grandson's bar mitzvah in Johannesburg. (A bar mitzvah is a religious initiation ceremony of a Jewish boy at age of thirteen.)

Consider the following...

- Israel refused to cooperate with the work of Goldstone's team and, in fact, went so far as to not allow the group access to the Gaza Strip through its borders. (The group entered Gaza via Egypt.) Do you agree with Israel's position not to cooperate with Goldstone's investigation? Do you think the contents of the report would have been different if Israel had cooperated from the start?
- The choice of Richard Goldstone to head the UNHRC's investigation into possible war crimes and crimes against humanity during the Gaza War was met with both praise and criticism. Research Goldstone's professional history, including his associations and public statements prior to beginning work for the UNHRC. Do you think he was a good choice to head the fact-finding mission? Why or why not?
- Research the impact that the U.S. military actions in Afghanistan and Iraq have had on civilian populations of those countries and compare that information to the examples and standards presented in *The Goldstone Report*. Considering the nature of incidents outlined in the report, could a case be made that the United States has committed war crimes?

For More Information

PERIODICALS

Bronner, Ethan. "As Talks Falter, Israel Warns of More Extensive Attacks." *New York Times* (January 11, 2009): A6.

Bronner, Ethan. "Israel Poised to Challenge a U.N. Report on Gaza." *New York Times* (January 20, 2010): A6.

Bronner, Ethan, and Isabel Kershner. "Head of U.N. Panel Regrets Saying Israel Intentionally Killed Gazans." *New York Times* (April 3, 2011): A10.

MacFarquhar, Neil. "Inquiry Finds Gaza War Crimes from Both Sides." *New York Times* (September 16, 2009): A1.

Mitnick, Joshua. "In Israel, Goldstone's Gaza War Retraction Triggers 'Earthquake' of Vindication." *Christian Science Monitor* (April 3, 2011).

Pinklington, Ed, and Conal Urquhart. "UN Gaza Report Co-Authors Round on Goldstone." *The Guardian* (London; April 14, 2011): 16.

Urquhart, Conal. "Judge Goldstone Expresses Regrets about His Report into Gaza War." *The Guardian* (London; April 3, 2011): 16.

United Nations Human Rights Council. *Report of the United Nations Fact Finding Mission on the Gaza Conflict* (September 15, 2009). Available online at http://www2.ohchr.org/english/bodies/hrcouncil/specialsession/9/docs/UNFFMGC_Report.PDF (accessed on November 30, 2011).

WEB SITES

Nebehay, Stephanie. "South African to Head U.N. Rights Inquiry in Gaza." *Reuters.com* (April 3, 2009). http://www.reuters.com/article/2009/04/03/us-palestinians-israel-inquiry-idUSTRE5321K820090403?sp=true (accessed on November 30, 2011).

Sharp, Heather. "Israel Debates Response to Gaza Report." *BBC News* (October 24, 2009). http://news.bbc.co.uk/2/hi/middle_east/8322584.stm (accessed on November 30, 2011).

"UN Condemns 'War Crimes' in Gaza." *BBC News* (September 16, 2009). http://news.bbc.co.uk/2/hi/middle_east/8257301.stm (accessed on November 30, 2011).

Reconsidering Goldstone

Excerpt from "Reconsidering the Goldstone Report on Israel and War Crimes"

By Richard Goldstone

Published in The Washington Post

April 1, 2011

"If I had known then what I know now, the Goldstone Report would have been a different document."

In January 2009, the United Nations Human Rights Commission (UNHRC) adopted a resolution that called for an investigation into allegations of human rights violations during the Gaza War. (The United Nations is an international organization of countries founded in 1945 to promote international peace, security, and cooperation.) The war began on December 27, 2008, when the Israeli military launched a major air and ground offensive in the Gaza Strip, in response to several months of rocket attacks by Hamas into southern Israel. (Hamas is a Palestinian Islamic fundamentalist group and political party operating primarily in the West Bank and the Gaza Strip with the goal of establishing a Palestinian state and opposing the existence of Israel.) According to the UNHRC, at issue was the treatment of civilians during the war. By the time a cease-fire was enacted on January 18, 2009, more than thirteen hundred Palestinians, hundreds of them civilians, were killed, as were 13 Israelis.

The original UNHRC directive met with criticism from Israel and its supporters for singling out for investigation only Israel's activities during the war and not those of Hamas. This prompted the UNHRC to acknowledge that allegations against Hamas would be looked into as well, but Israel still refused to cooperate with the investigation. A four-person committee

Smoke rising from Rafah, in the southern Gaza Strip, after an Israeli air strike in January 2009, during the Gaza War. Israel launched a major air and ground offensive in the Gaza Strip, in response to Hamas attacks on Israel. © WISSAM NASSAR/XINHUA PRESS/CORBIS.

led by South African judge and former war crimes prosecutor Richard Goldstone (1938–) was named to conduct a fact-finding mission. Other members of the team were Pakistani human rights lawyer Hina Jilani (1953–), former Irish colonel Desmond Travers (1941–), and British international law professor Christine Chinkin.

In June and July 2009, Goldstone and his team made two visits to the Gaza Strip to tour damaged sites, interview civilians and military personnel, and collect documents and other evidence. They also conducted public hearings to gather testimony from war victims. On September 15, 2009, the Goldstone team issued its findings in a document titled *Report of the United Nations Fact Finding Mission on the Gaza Conflict*, which has come to be known as *The Goldstone Report*. The report concluded that both Israel and Hamas committed possible war crimes and crimes against humanity during the Gaza War. The government of Israel and its supporters dismissed the report as biased and full of errors, and Hamas denied accusations that it committed war crimes. Internationally, reactions tended to be split along pro-Israel and pro-Arab lines, while several human rights groups praised the work of the Goldstone team. (For more information, see **The Goldstone Report**.)

Although Goldstone initially defended his team's conclusions, by April 2011 his opinion on the Israel's conduct in the Gaza War had changed. Following the recommendation of *The Goldstone Report* and the United Nations General Assembly, Israel had conducted a thorough investigation of its own actions during the war. In Goldstone's opinion, the results shed new light on many of the incidents that his team had previously reviewed without Israel's input. Citing information and evidence that emerged after *The Goldstone Report* was issued, he wrote an op-ed piece for *The Washington Post* titled "Reconsidering the Goldstone Report on Israel and War Crimes," which is excerpted below. In publishing the piece, Goldstone publicly reversed his previous position that Israel intentionally targeted civilians during the Gaza War.

Things to remember while reading the excerpt from "Reconsidering the Goldstone Report on Israel and War Crimes":

- Israel refused to cooperate with Goldstone's committee and, therefore, had no input into its investigation. The UNHRC is made up largely of representatives from forty-seven countries, the majority of them Muslim nations and their allies. Israel considered the motives of the UNHRC's call for an investigation to be biased.

- Israel claims a history of bias and mistreatment by the United Nations. The condemnation of Israel's actions during the Gaza War is one of many instances in response to which Israel has cited the UNHRC and its predecessor, the Commission for Human Rights, for singling out Israel for human rights violations while ignoring the actions of other countries.

- Goldstone refers to Hamas as a "non-state actor" to emphasize that Hamas is an organization that represents a political movement as part of the Palestinian Authority (the recognized governing institution for Palestinians in the West Bank and the Gaza Strip) but does not have the same status as a nation.

- Goldstone, who is Jewish, was the target of criticism by others in the Jewish community, including those in his native South Africa. In 2010, protesters threatened to disrupt his grandson's bar mitzvah in Johannesburg as a show of their ongoing anger over the contents of the Goldstone Report. (A bar mitzvah is a religious initiation ceremony of a Jewish boy at age of thirteen.)

• • •

Reconsidering the Goldstone Report on Israel and War Crimes

We know a lot more today about what happened in the Gaza war of 2008–09 than we did when I chaired the fact-finding mission appointed by the U.N. Human Rights Council that produced what has come to be known as the Goldstone Report. If I had known then what I know now, the Goldstone Report would have been a different document.

The final report by the U.N. committee of independent experts—chaired by former New York judge Mary McGowan Davis—that followed up on the recommendations of the Goldstone Report has found that "Israel has dedicated significant resources to investigate over 400 allegations of operational misconduct in Gaza" while "the **de facto** authorities (i.e., Hamas) have not conducted any investigations into the launching of rocket and mortar attacks against Israel."

Our report found evidence of potential war crimes and "possibly crimes against humanity" by both Israel and Hamas. That the crimes allegedly committed by Hamas were intentional goes without saying—its rockets were purposefully and indiscriminately aimed at civilian targets.

The allegations of intentionality by Israel were based on the deaths of and injuries to civilians in situations where our fact-finding mission had no evidence on which to draw any other reasonable conclusion. While the investigations published by the Israeli military and recognized in the U.N. committee's report have established the validity of some incidents that we investigated in cases involving individual soldiers, they also indicate that civilians were not intentionally targeted as a matter of policy.

For example, the most serious attack the Goldstone Report focused on was the killing of some 29 members of the al-Simouni family in their home. The **shelling** of the home was apparently the consequence of an Israeli commander's **erroneous** interpretation of a **drone image**, and an Israeli officer is under investigation for having ordered the attack. . . .

De Facto: Actual.

Shelling: Bombing.

Erroneous: Incorrect.

Drone Image: Surveillance photograph taken from an unmanned aircraft used in military operations.

While I welcome Israel's investigations into allegations, I share the concerns reflected in the McGowan Davis report that few of Israel's inquiries have been concluded and believe that the proceedings should have been held in a public forum. Although the Israeli evidence that has emerged since publication of our report doesn't **negate** the tragic loss of civilian life, I regret that our fact-finding mission did not have such evidence explaining the circumstances in which we said civilians in Gaza were targeted, because it probably would have influenced our findings about intentionality and war crimes. . . .

As I indicated from the very beginning, I would have welcomed Israel's cooperation. The purpose of the Goldstone Report was never to prove a foregone conclusion against Israel. I insisted on changing the original mandate adopted by the Human Rights Council, which was skewed against Israel. I have always been clear that Israel, like any other sovereign nation, has the right and obligation to defend itself and its citizens against attacks from abroad and within. Something that has not been recognized often enough is the fact that our report marked the first time illegal acts of terrorism from Hamas were being investigated and condemned by the United Nations. I had hoped that our inquiry into all aspects of the Gaza conflict would begin a new era of **evenhandedness** at the U.N. Human Rights Council, whose history of bias against Israel cannot be doubted. . . .

Some have suggested that it was absurd to expect Hamas, an organization that has a policy to destroy the state of Israel, to investigate what we said were serious war crimes. It was my hope, even if unrealistic, that Hamas would do so, especially if Israel conducted its own investigations. At minimum I hoped that in the face of a clear finding that its members were committing serious war crimes, Hamas would **curtail** its attacks. Sadly, that has not been the case. Hundreds more rockets and mortar rounds have been directed at civilian targets in southern Israel. That comparatively few Israelis have been killed by the unlawful rocket and mortar attacks from Gaza in no way minimizes the criminality. The U.N. Human Rights Council should condemn these **heinous** acts in the strongest terms. . . .

I continue to believe in the cause of establishing and applying international law to **protracted** and deadly conflicts. Our report has led to numerous "lessons learned" and policy changes, including the adoption of new Israel Defense Forces procedures for protecting civilians in cases of urban warfare and limiting the use of **white phosphorus** in civilian areas. The Palestinian Authority established an independent inquiry into our allegations of human rights abuses—assassinations, torture and illegal detentions—perpetrated by **Fatah** in the West Bank, especially against members of Hamas. Most of those allegations were confirmed by this inquiry. Regrettably, there has been no effort by Hamas in Gaza to investigate the allegations of its war crimes and possible crimes against humanity.

Negate: Make nonexistent or untrue.

Evenhandedness: Fairness; impartiality.

Curtail: Reduce or bring to an end.

Heinous: Deeply disturbing.

Protracted: Long-lasting; drawn out.

White phosphorus: A chemical that causes burns.

Fatah: A Palestinian militant group and political party dedicated to the establishment of an independent Palestinian state.

Simply put, the laws of armed conflict apply no less to non-state actors such as Hamas than they do to national armies. Ensuring that non-state actors respect these principles, and are investigated when they fail to do so, is one of the most significant challenges facing the law of armed conflict. Only if all parties to armed conflicts are held to these standards will we be able to protect civilians who, through no choice of their own, are caught up in war. . . .

• • •

What happened next . . .

Israel immediately praised Goldstone's retraction and set about conducting a campaign to fix the damage it felt the report had done to its image. A *New York Times* article on Israel's response to the retraction quotes Prime Minister Benjamin Netanyahu (1949–) as calling for "practical and public diplomacy measures in order to reverse and minimize the great damage that has been done by this campaign of denigration against the State of Israel." Netanyahu also hoped to convince the United Nations to nullify the report, but recognized that success would be difficult. According to an April 3, 2011, *Guardian* article, Netanyahu told his cabinet, "There are very few incidents in which false accusations are taken back, and this is the case with the Goldstone report." As a result, Israeli foreign ministers decided to take a less aggressive stance with the United Nations, urging it to recognize Goldstone's retraction as a position paper or appendage to the original report instead of nullification. On April 8, United Nations secretary general Ban Ki-moon (1944–) informed Israeli president Shimon Peres (1923–) that the United Nations would not retract the report despite Goldstone's statement.

Two weeks after the retraction was published, the other three authors of the Goldstone report, Hina Jilani, Christine Chinkin, and Desmond Travers, issued a statement published in a the *Guardian* in which they reaffirmed their commitment to their original findings. They speculated that Goldstone's reversal was the result of personal and political pressure, and they noted that "calls to reconsider or even retract the report, as well as attempts at misrepresenting its nature and purpose, disregard the rights of victims, Palestinians and Israeli, to truth and justice."

Israeli prime minister Benjamin Netanyahu delivers a statement responding to Goldstone's retraction. Netanyahu called for the Goldstone Report to be formally nullified. YUVAL CHEN-POOL/GETTY IMAGES.

Did you know . . .

- In July 2010, Israel announced that its chief military prosecutor was pursuing four separate cases of misconduct by several officers and soldiers for acts committed during the Gaza War. One of the cases, which involved allegations that a staff sergeant shot at Palestinian civilians waving white flags, was cited in *The Goldstone Report.*

- Goldstone was initially reluctant to serve on the UNHRC's team investigating human rights violations in the Gaza War, because the original directive targeted only Israel's activities. He only accepted the post after the focus of the investigation was widened to include an examination of Hamas's actions as well.

- Some observers suggested that Goldstone was pressured by pro-Israel supporters, including prominent members of the South African Jewish community, into making the retraction.

Consider the following . . .

- Review Goldstone's reasons for "reconsidering" his position on the Goldstone Report. Do you think that he makes a strong argument for changing his stance?
- In his retraction, Goldstone asserts that "the laws of armed conflict apply no less to non-state actors such as Hamas than they do to national armies." Research the terms of the Fourth Geneva Convention and other international agreements that outline the terms of warfare. What are the complexities of holding "non-state actors" accountable to these standards?
- Some critics accused Goldstone of a "blood libel," meaning a false accusation. This term stems from the false belief during the Middle Ages (c. 500–c. 1500) that Jews used the blood of Christian children to prepare the Passover feast. Research the history of the term and its significance to the Jewish community. Do you think this was a fair characterization of Goldstone's actions in issuing the original report? Why or why not?

For More Information

PERIODICALS

Bronner, Ethan. "Head of U.N. Panel Regrets Saying Israel Intentionally Killed Gazans." *New York Times* (April 3, 2011): A10.

Bronner, Ethan, and Isabel Kershner. "Israel Grapples with Retraction on U.N. Report." *New York Times* (April 4, 2011): A7.

Goldstone, Richard. "Reconsidering the Goldstone Report on Israel and War Crimes." *The Washington Post* (April 1, 2011). Avaiable online at http://www.washingtonpost.com/opinions/reconsidering-the-goldstone-report-on-israel-and-war-crimes/2011/04/01/AFg111JC_story.html (accessed on November 30, 2011).

Jilani, Hina, Christine Chinkin, and Desmond Travers. "Goldstone report: Statement issued by members of UN mission on Gaza war." *Guardian* (April 14, 2011) Available online at. http://www.guardian.co.uk/commentisfree/2011/apr/14/goldstone-report-statement-un-gaza (accessed on November 30, 2011).

Mitnick, Joshua. "In Israel, Goldstone's Gaza War Retraction Triggers 'Earthquake' of Vindication." *Christian Science Monitor* (April 3, 2011).

Pinklington, Ed, and Conal Urquhart. "UN Gaza Report Co-Authors Round on Goldstone." *Guardian* (April 14, 2011): 16.

Urquhart, Conal. "Judge Goldstone Expresses Regrets about His Report into Gaza War." *Guardian* (April 3, 2011): 16.

WEB SITES

Cohler-Esses, Larry, Gal Beckerman, and Claudia Braude. "Did a Private Meeting Prompt Goldstone to Change His Mind?" *The Jewish Daily Forward.* (April 6, 2011). http://www.forward.com/articles/136818/#ixzz1ZIWByks9 (accessed on November 30, 2011).

Nebehay, Stephanie. "South African to Head U.N. Rights Inquiry in Gaza." *Reuters.com* (April 3, 2009). http://www.reuters.com/article/2009/04/03/us-palestinians-israel-inquiry-idUSTRE5321K820090403?sp=true (accessed on November 30, 2011).

Ravid, Barak. "Israel to Launch Quiet Diplomatic Campaign in Wake of Goldstone Retraction." *Harretz.com* (April 6, 2011). http://www.haaretz.com/print-edition/news/israel-to-launch-quiet-diplomatic-campaign-in-wake-of-goldstone-retraction-1.354320 (accessed on November 30, 2011).

5

Competing Visions of the Middle East

Today, the Middle East is a region of the world characterized by nations with a wide variety of political systems. There are monarchies (a form of government in which the position of head of state is inherited), as in Saudi Arabia and Jordan; republics (governments ruled by representatives of the people), as in Egypt and Lebanon; Islamic republics (governments ruled by representatives of the Islamic faith), as in Iran; republics under military rule (governments ruled by representatives of the military), as in Syria; and democracies (governments ruled directly by the people), as in Israel and Turkey. There are militant organizations as well as pro-democracy movements within many states pushing for change, even revolution. Some nations are ruled primarily by sharia (Islamic religious law), as in Saudi Arabia and Iran, and most of the Arab nations show the influence of Islamic law. However, some nations' governments are primarily secular, or nonreligious, such as Egypt, Syria, and Israel. A few nations, such as Israel, have a multiparty democracy, similar to the form of government in the United States and most European nations. Most Middle Eastern nations have a single leader who severely limits the expression of political groups that do not support the current government. Egypt, for example, which is often considered one of the more progressive of the Middle Eastern countries, authorized its first multiparty elections in 2005. However, Egyptians who saw such a change as an empty gesture took to the streets in 2011 to demand true democratic reform, resulting in a revolution.

Not only do the political systems in the Middle Eastern nations show real variety, but so do their cultures. Some of the Arab (Arabic-speaking) countries—Iraq and Lebanon, for example—allow women full access to employment, education, and other civil rights. Others, such as Saudi Arabia, insist that women be strictly separated from men in most circumstances and restrict women's rights to drive or show their faces in public.

A protestor raises his rifle to the sky during a demonstration in Beirut, Lebanon. Differing beliefs in the Middle East have caused many groups to protest and commit acts of violence. © MAHER ATTAR/CORBIS SYGMA.

Most Middle Eastern countries experience friction between their Muslim and non-Muslim populations, and also—as in Iraq and Lebanon—between the Sunni and Shiite branches of Islam.

These great variations in political and cultural life indicate that the Middle East is a region where important questions about religion, government, and philosophy come up on a daily basis. In this chapter, some of the fundamental guiding visions for the nature of social and political life in the Middle East that have emerged since the late nineteenth century are presented. One of the most controversial issues in Middle Eastern history has been the influence of Zionism (an international political movement originating in the late nineteenth century that called for the creation of an independent Jewish state in Palestine). The Zionist movement succeeded when the state of Israel came into being in 1948. Included in this chapter are excerpts from

Theodor Herzl's *The Jewish State* (1896), which gave birth to the international Zionist movement.

Zionism was a nationalist movement. (Nationalism is the belief that a people with shared ethnic, cultural, and/or religious identities have the right to form their own nation. In established nations nationalism is devotion and loyalty to the nation and its culture.) Like all nationalist movements, it sought to create a nation that reflected the interests and culture of a particular social group, which in this case were Jews. Arab nations that came into being after the collapse of the Ottoman Empire (the vast empire of the Ottoman Turks which included southwest Asia, northeast Africa, and southeast Europe, and lasted from the thirteenth century to the early twentieth century) during World War I (1914–18) also embraced nationalism as they formed states and gained political independence. For many Arab leaders, however, nationalism was not enough. They wanted independent Arab nations to join together to increase their strength and promote their Arab identity. Their vision was called Pan-Arabism, and one of its greatest spokesmen was Gamal Abdel Nasser (1918–1970), the president of Egypt from 1956 to 1970 and one of the founders of the United Arab Republic, a short-lived effort to unite Arab nations. In 1959, Nasser laid out his vision in a speech to military officers; an excerpt from that important speech is included in this chapter.

The most extreme visions for the Middle East come from supporters of Islam who want to see a more radical transformation of Islamic societies, both in the Middle East and in any country with a large Muslim population. These people, often called Islamic fundamentalists, or simply Islamists, want to make Islam the basis for political, social, and cultural life in Muslim nations. (Fundamentalism is a movement stressing adherence to a strict or literal interpretation of religious principles.) They also want to eliminate all traces of Western influence in the Middle East. Some of them resort to acts of terrorism to try to achieve their goals. Osama bin Laden (1957–2011), best known as the mastermind of the September 11, 2001, terrorist attacks on the United States, proposed his violent vision for the triumph of Islamic fundamentalism in a statement attributed to the World Islamic Front.

These extreme examples of fundamentalism can be contrasted with those who see the possibilities of Islam existing along with other religions and cultures. Nobel Peace Prize winner Shirin Ebadi (1947–), an accomplished Iranian lawyer and judge whose career was halted when Islamists took control of her country in the 1979 Iranian Revolution (also known as the Islamic Revolution), advocates for a dynamic vision of Islam that promotes human rights and democracy, as an excerpt from a speech she gave before the Global Ethic Foundation in 2005 illustrates. A similar vision focused on overcoming a history of distrust and violence between the United States and the Muslim world can be found in the excerpt of a speech presented by U.S. president Barack Obama (1961–) in Cairo, Egypt, in 2009. Obama's speech emphasizes commonalities instead of differences and affirms U.S. commitment to human rights and democracy.

The documents in this chapter present ideas on how the Middle East region should be structured, both politically and religiously, or how the Middle East can achieve a positive role of influence and peace on a global level. Many of these documents continue to shape the politics and social organization of Middle Eastern countries today.

The Jewish State

Excerpt from *The Jewish State*
Written by Theodor Herzl
Originally published as Der Judenstaat in 1896
Translated in English as The Jewish State: An Attempt
at a Modern Solution of the Jewish Question
Published in 1946

"The Jews who wish for a State shall have it, and they will deserve to have it."

One cannot hope to understand the historic and ongoing conflict in the Middle East without understanding the role that Israel plays in the region, and one cannot understand Israel without first understanding Zionism. Zionism was, and still is, a political movement aimed at creating a national homeland for the Jewish people. Today, that homeland exists in the nation of Israel. Yet many feel that Jews are still not secure from the persecution they have faced in other countries, even in Israel. Many Arabs (people who speak the Arabic language or who live in nations where Arabic is the dominant language) in the Middle East who feel that some of their own land was taken from them have devoted themselves to the destruction of Israel. Moreover, anti-Semitism, or prejudice against Jews, continues to exist in many countries in the twenty-first century. To this day, Zionists insist that an independent Jewish nation is the key to the eventual end of Jewish persecution.

Zionism itself was the product of the anti-Semitic social conditions that existed in Europe and Russia during the nineteenth century. Although anti-Semitism among Christians traces its roots back to the time of the Roman Empire, it flourished again in the nineteenth century due to racial theories that held that the Jews, or Semites, were a distinct and inferior race. A series of events across Europe and Russia—including pogroms (racially motivated riots in which mobs, usually organized and sanctioned by the state, attack a minority group, most often Jews) in Russia and Poland, anti-Jewish publications in France and Great Britain, and attacks and riots against Jews in Germany—forced many Jews to acknowledge that despite their best efforts to assimilate (blend in) with European society, they were not truly welcomed as citizens of any major country. One Hungarian-born Jew who came to this conclusion was Theodor Herzl (1860–1904).

Herzl began to look for a solution to the problems facing Jews in Europe when he experienced anti-Semitic riots in France in the mid–1890s. He soon learned of a small movement to relocate Russian Jews to a place the Jews called Zion, an ancient name for holy sites near the city of Jerusalem, which was located in the territory known as Palestine, then part of the Ottoman Empire (the vast empire of the Ottoman Turks which included southwest Asia, northeast Africa, and southeast Europe, and lasted from the thirteenth century to the early twentieth century). Inspired by the promise of religious freedom that these small Jewish settlements seemed to offer, Herzl became an immediate convert to the cause. He expanded the ideas of Zionism by suggesting actual plans that Jewish people could use to create a true nation of their own and creating organizations to further this cause. These ideas were so integral in convincing the worldwide Jewish population that the goals of Zionism could become a reality that Herzl is often heralded as the father of Zionism. In 1896, Herzl published *Der Judenstaat* (later published in English as *The Jewish State*), which outlined his ideas for how Jews and other supporters of Zionism could work to create a national homeland for Jews.

Things to remember while reading the excerpt from *The Jewish State*:

- Herzl's book was predated by a work called *Autoemancipation* (1881), in which Polish Jew Leo Pinsker (1821–1891) suggested that all Jews relocate to Palestine. This book was not read by a large Jewish audience, and only a few copies of it were published. Herzl claimed not to have read the work prior to writing *The Jewish State*.

Theodor Herzl, Zionist leader and author of The Jewish State. © WORLD HISTORY ARCHIVE/ALAMY.

- *The Jewish State* was both an immediate and lasting publishing success. First published in Germany and Austria, it was later published in eighty editions and in eighteen different languages. The version that appears below was published in 1946, on the fiftieth anniversary of the original publication.

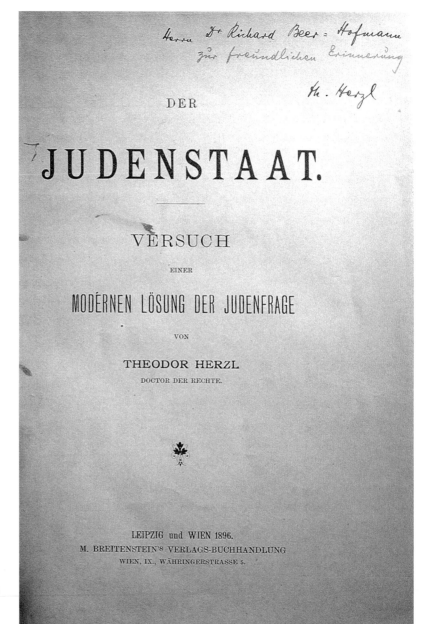

The cover of the first edition of Der Judenstaat (The Jewish State), *1896.* IMAGNO/GETTY IMAGES.

• • •

The Jewish State

Preface

The idea which I have developed in this pamphlet is a very old one: it is the restoration of the Jewish State.

The world resounds with outcries against the Jews, and these outcries have awakened the slumbering idea.

I wish it to be clearly understood from the outset that no portion of my argument is based on a new discovery. I have discovered neither the historic condition of the Jews nor the means to improve it. In fact, every man will see for himself that the materials of the structure I am designing are not only in existence, but actually already in hand. If, therefore, this attempt to solve the **Jewish Question** is to be designed by a single world, let it be said to be the result of an inescapable conclusion rather than that of a flighty imagination.

I must, in the first place, guard my scheme from being treated as **Utopian** by superficial critics who might commit this error of judgment if I did not warn them. I should obviously have done nothing to be ashamed of if I had described a Utopia on philanthropic lines; and I should also, in all probability, have obtained literary success more easily if I had set forth my plan in the irresponsible guise of a romantic tale. But this Utopia is far less attractive than any one of those portrayed by **Sir Thomas More** and his numerous forerunners and successors. . . .

Everything depends on our propelling force. And what is that force? The misery of the Jews.

Who would venture to deny its existence? We shall discuss it fully in the chapter on the causes of Anti-Semitism.

Everybody is familiar with the phenomenon of steam-power, generated by boiling water, which lifts the kettle-lid. Such tea-kettle phenomena are the attempts of Zionist and kindred associations to check Anti-Semitism.

I believe that this power, if rightly employed, is powerful enough to propel a large engine and to move passengers and goods: the engine having whatever form men may choose to give it. . . .

I shall therefore clearly and emphatically state that I believe in the practical outcome of my scheme, though without professing to have discovered the shape it may ultimately take. The Jewish State is essential to the world; it will therefore be created.

The plan would, of course, seem absurd if a single individual attempted to do it; but if worked by a number of Jews in co-operation it would appear perfectly rational, and its accomplishment would present no difficulties worth mentioning. The idea depends only on the number of its supporters. Perhaps our ambitious young men, to whom every road of progress is now closed,

Jewish Question: Question of what to do with the millions of Jews in Poland, Germany, and elsewhere.

Utopian: Impossibly ideal.

Sir Thomas More: British writer who penned the first Utopian novel (1779–1852).

seeing in this Jewish State a bright prospect of freedom, happiness and honors opening to them, will ensure the **propagation** of the idea. . . .

It depends on the Jews themselves whether this political pamphlet remains for the present a political romance. If the present generation is too dull to understand it rightly, a future, finer and a better generation will arise to understand it. The Jews who wish for a State shall have it, and they will deserve to have it.

I.—Introduction . . .

The Jewish Question still exists. It would be foolish to deny it. It is a remnant of the Middle Ages, which civilized nations do not even yet seem able to shake off, try as they will. They certainly showed a generous desire to do so when they **emancipated** us. The Jewish question exists wherever Jews live in perceptible numbers. Where it does not exist, it is carried by Jews in the course of their **migrations**. We naturally move to those places where we are not persecuted, and there our presence produces persecution. This is the case in every country, and will remain so, even in those highly civilized—for instance, France—until the Jewish question finds a solution on a political basis. The unfortunate Jews are now carrying the seeds of Anti-Semitism into England; they have already introduced it into America.

I believe that I understand Anti-Semitism, which is really a highly complex movement. I consider it from a Jewish standpoint, yet without fear or hatred. I believe that I can see what elements there are in it of vulgar sport, of common trade jealousy, of inherited prejudice, of religious intolerance, and also of pretended self-defence. I think the Jewish question is no more a social than a religious one, notwithstanding that it sometimes takes these and other forms. It is a national question, which can only be solved by making it a political world-question to be discussed and settled by the civilized nations of the world in council.

We are a people—one people.

We have honestly endeavored everywhere to merge ourselves in the social life of surrounding communities and to preserve the faith of our fathers. We are not permitted to do so. In vain are we loyal patriots, our loyalty in some places running to extremes; in vain do we make the same sacrifices of life and property as our fellow-citizens; in vain do we strive to increase the fame of our native land in science and art, or her wealth by trade and commerce. . . .

Oppression and persecution cannot **exterminate** us. No nation on earth has survived such struggles and sufferings as we have gone through. **Jew-baiting** has merely stripped off our weaklings; the strong among us were invariably true to their race when persecution broke out against them.[. . .]

No human being is wealthy or powerful enough to transplant a nation from one habitation to another. An idea alone can achieve that and this idea of a State may have the requisite power to do so. The Jews have dreamt this kingly dream all through the long nights of their history. "Next year in **Jerusalem**" is

Propagation: Spread.

Emancipated: Freed.

Migrations: Moves from one place or country to another.

Exterminate: Kill all members of a group.

Jew-baiting: The persecution or harassment of Jews.

Jerusalem: The capital city of Palestine, home to numerous holy sites.

our old phrase. It is now a question of showing that the dream can be converted into a living reality.

For this, many old, outgrown, confused and limited notions must first be entirely erased from the minds of men. Dull brains might, for instance, imagine that this **exodus** would be from civilized regions into the desert. That is not the case. It will be carried out in the midst of civilization. We shall not revert to a lower stage, we shall rise to a higher one. We shall not dwell in mud huts; we shall build new more beautiful and more modern houses, and possess them in safety. We shall not lose our acquired possessions; we shall realize them. We shall surrender our well earned rights only for better ones. We shall not sacrifice our beloved customs; we shall find them again. We shall not leave our old home before the new one is prepared for us. Those only will depart who are sure thereby to improve their position; those who are now desperate will go first, after them the poor; next the prosperous, and, last of all, the wealthy. Those who go in advance will raise themselves to a higher grade, equal to those whose representatives will shortly follow. Thus the exodus will be at the same time an ascent of the class.

The departure of the Jews will involve no economic disturbances, no crises, no persecutions; in fact, the countries they abandon will revive to a new period of prosperity. There will be an inner migration of Christian citizens into the positions evacuated by Jews. The outgoing current will be gradual, without any disturbance, and its initial movement will put an end to Anti-Semitism. The Jews will leave as honored friends, and if some of them return, they will receive the same favorable welcome and treatment at the hands of civilized nations as is accorded to all foreign visitors. Their exodus will have no resemblance to a flight, for it will be a well-regulated movement under control of public opinion. The movement will not only be **inaugurated** with absolute conformity to law, but it cannot even be carried out without the friendly cooperation of interested governments, who would derive considerable benefits from it.

Security for the integrity of the idea and the vigor of its **execution** will be found in the creation of a body corporate, or corporation. This corporation will be called "The Society of Jews." In addition to it there will be a Jewish company, an economically productive body.

An individual who attempted even to undertake this huge task alone would be either an impostor or a madman. The personal character of the members of the **corporation** will guarantee its integrity, and the adequate **capital of the Company** will prove its stability.

These **prefatory** remarks are merely intended as a hasty reply to the mass of objections which the very words "Jewish State" are certain to arouse. Henceforth we shall proceed more slowly to meet further objections and to explain in detail what has been as yet only indicated; and we shall try in the interests of this pamphlet to avoid making it a dull **exposition**. Short **aphoristic** chapters will therefore best answer the purpose.

Exodus: Mass departure.

Inaugurated: Started officially.

Execution: Being carried out.

Corporation: A legal entity or organization created under the laws of a state with its own rights and privileges; in this context used to mean an organized group.

Capital of the company: The money controlled by members of the group.

Prefatory: Introductory.

Exposition: Background information that appears at the beginning of a writing.

Aphoristic: Truthful and brief; in a concise fashion.

If I wish to substitute a new building for an old one, I must demolish before I construct. I shall therefore keep to this natural sequence. In the first and general part I shall explain my ideas, remove all prejudices, determine essential political and economic conditions, and develop the plan.

In the special part, which is divided into three principal sections, I shall describe its execution. These three sections are: The Jewish Company, Local Groups, and the Society of Jews. The Society is to be created first, the Company last; but in this exposition the reverse order is preferable, because it is the financial soundness of the enterprise which will chiefly be called into question, and doubts on this score must be removed first.

In the conclusion, I shall try to meet every further objection that could possibly be made. My Jewish readers will, I hope, follow me patiently to the end. Some will naturally make their objections in an order of succession other than that chosen for their **refutation**. But whoever finds his doubts dispelled should give allegiance to the cause.

Although I speak of reason, I am fully aware that reason alone will not suffice. Old prisoners do not willingly leave their cells. We shall see whether the youth whom we need are at our command—the youth, who irresistibly draw on the old, carry them forward on strong arms, and transform rational motives into enthusiasm.

II.—The Jewish Question . . .

THE PLAN: The whole plan is in its essence perfectly simple, as it must necessarily be if it is to come within the comprehension of all.

Let the **sovereignty** be granted us over a portion of the globe large enough to satisfy the rightful requirements of a nation; the rest we shall manage for ourselves.

The creation of a new State is neither ridiculous nor impossible. We have in our day witnessed the process in connection with nations which were not largely members of the middle class, but poorer, less educated, and consequently weaker than ourselves. The Governments of all countries **scourged** by Anti-Semitism will be keenly interested in assisting us to obtain the sovereignty we want.

The plan, simple in design, but complicated in execution, will be carried out by two agencies: The Society of Jews and the Jewish Company.

The Society of Jews will do the preparatory work in the domains of science and politics, which the Jewish Company will afterwards apply practically.

The Jewish Company will be the **liquidating agent** of the business interests of departing Jews, and will organize commerce and trade in the new country.

Refutation: Disproof; argument against.

Sovereignty: Supreme independent authority.

Scourged: Punished severely.

Liquidating agent: One charged with selling off material goods in order to accumulate cash.

PALESTINE OR ARGENTINE? Shall we choose Palestine or Argentine? We shall take what is given us, and what is selected by Jewish public opinion. The Society will determine both these points.

Argentine is one of the most fertile countries in the world, extends over a vast area, has a sparse population and a mild climate. The Argentine Republic would derive considerable profit from the **cession** of a portion of its territory to us. The present **infiltration** of Jews has certainly produced some discontent, and it would be necessary to enlighten the Republic on the intrinsic difference of our new movement.

Palestine is our ever-memorable historic home. The very name of Palestine would attract our people with a force of marvelous potency. If **His Majesty the Sultan** were to give us Palestine, we could in return undertake to regulate the whole finances of Turkey. We should there form a portion of a **rampart** of Europe against Asia, an outpost of civilization as opposed to barbarism. We should as a neutral State remain in contact with all Europe, which would have to guarantee our existence. The **sanctuaries of Christendom** would be safeguarded by assigning to them an extra-territorial status such as is well-known to the law of nations. We should form a guard of honor about these sanctuaries, answering for the fulfillment of this duty with our existence. This guard of honor would be the great symbol of the solution of the Jewish question after eighteen centuries of Jewish suffering. . . .

VI. Conclusion

How much has been left unexplained, how many defects, how many harmful **superficialities**, and how many useless repetitions in this pamphlet, which I have thought over so long and so often revised!

But a fair-minded reader, who has sufficient understanding to grasp the spirit of my words, will not be repelled by these defects. He will rather be roused thereby to cooperate with his intelligence and energy in a work which is not one man's task alone, and to improve it.

Have I not explained obvious things and overlooked important objections?

I have tried to meet certain objections; but I know that many more will be made, based on high grounds and low.

To the first class of objections belongs the remark that the Jews are not the only people in the world who are in a condition of distress. Here I would reply that we may as well begin by removing a little of this misery, even if it should at first be no more than our own.

It might further be said that we ought not to create new distinctions between people; we ought not to raise fresh barriers, we should rather make the old disappear. But men who think in this way are **amiable visionaries**; and the idea of a native land will still flourish when the dust of their bones will

Cession: Yielding control or rights to another.

Infiltration: Movement into a different group.

His Majesty the Sultan: The ruler of the Ottoman Empire.

Rampart: Protective barrier.

Sanctuaries of Christendom: Religious sites revered by Christians.

Superficialities: Thoughts and actions concerned only with what is apparent on the surface.

Amiable visionaries: Happy dreamers.

have vanished tracelessly in the winds. Universal brotherhood is not even a beautiful dream. **Antagonism** is essential to man's greatest efforts.

But the Jews, once settled in their own State, would probably have no more enemies. As for those who remain behind, since prosperity **enfeebles** and causes them to diminish, they would soon disappear altogether. I think the Jews will always have sufficient enemies, such as every nation has. But once fixed in their own land, it will no longer be possible for them to scatter all over the world. The **diaspora** cannot be reborn, unless the civilization of the whole earth should collapse; and such a consummation could be feared by none but foolish men. Our present civilization possesses weapons powerful enough for its self-defence.

Innumerable objections will be based on low grounds, for there are more low men than noble in this world. I have tried to remove some of these narrow-minded notions; and whoever is willing to fall in behind our white flag with its seven stars, must assist in this campaign of enlightenment. Perhaps we shall have to fight first of all against many an evil-disposed, narrow-hearted, short-sighted member of our own race.

Again, people will say that I am furnishing the Anti-Semites with weapons. Why so? Because I admit the truth? Because I do not maintain that there are none but excellent men amongst us?

Will not people say that I am showing our enemies the way to injure us? This I absolutely dispute. My proposal could only be carried out with the free consent of a majority of Jews. Action may be taken against individuals or even against groups of the most powerful Jews, but Governments will never take action against all Jews. The equal rights of the Jew before the law cannot be withdrawn where they have once been conceded; for the first attempt at withdrawal would immediately drive all Jews, rich and poor alike, into the ranks of revolutionary parties. The beginning of any official acts of injustice against the Jews invariably brings about economic crises. Therefore, no weapons can be effectually used against us, because these injure the hands that wield them. Meantime hatred grows apace. The rich do not feel it much, but our poor do. Let us ask our poor, who have been more severely **proletarized** since the last removal of Anti-Semitism than ever before.

Some of our prosperous men may say that the pressure is not yet severe enough to justify emigration, and that every forcible **expulsion** shows how unwilling our people are to depart. True, because they do not know where to go; because they only pass from one trouble into another. But we are showing them the way to the Promised Land; and the splendid force of enthusiasm must fight against the terrible force of habit.

Persecutions are no longer so **malignant** as they were in the Middle Ages? True, but our sensitiveness has increased, so that we feel no **diminution** in our sufferings; prolonged persecution has overstrained our nerves.

Antagonism: Hostility.

Enfeebles: Weakens.

Diaspora: Scattering of Jews from Palestine in about 600 BCE.

Proletarized: Made into the proletariat, or laboring class.

Expulsion: The act of expelling or casting out.

Malignant: Hurtful or evil.

Diminution: Reduction.

Will people say, again, that our enterprise is hopeless, because even if we obtained the land with supremacy over it, the poor only would go with us? It is precisely the poorest whom we need at first. Only the desperate make good conquerors.

Will some one say: Were it feasible it would have been done long ago?

It has never yet been possible; now it is possible. A hundred—or even fifty—years ago it would have been nothing more than a dream. Today it may become a reality. Our rich, who have a pleasurable acquaintance with all our technical achievements, know full well how much money can do. And thus it will be: just the poor and simple, who do not know what power man already exercises over the forces of Nature, just these will have the firmest faith in the new message. For these have never lost their hope of the Promised Land.

Here it is, fellow Jews! Neither fable nor deception! Every man may test its reality for himself, for every man will carry over with him a portion of the Promised Land—one in his head, another in his arms, another in his acquired possessions.

Now, all this may appear to be an **interminably** long affair. Even in the most favorable circumstances, many years might elapse before the commencement of the foundation of the State. In the meantime, Jews in a thousand different places would suffer insults, mortifications, abuse, blows, depredation, and death. No; if we only begin to carry out the plans, Anti-Semitism would stop at once and for ever. For it is the conclusion of peace.

The news of the formation of our Jewish Company will be carried in a single day to the remotest ends of the earth by the lightning speed of our telegraph wires.

And immediate relief will ensue. The intellects which we produce so superabundantly in our middle classes will find an outlet in our first organizations, as our first technicians, officers, professors, officials, lawyers, and doctors; and thus the movement will continue in swift but smooth progression.

Prayers will be offered up for the success of our work in temples and in churches also; for it will bring relief from an old burden, which all have suffered.

But we must first bring enlightenment to men's minds. The idea must make its way into the most distant, miserable holes where our people dwell. They will awaken from gloomy brooding, for into their lives will come a new significance. Every man need think only of himself, and the movement will assume vast proportions.

And what glory awaits those who fight unselfishly for the cause!

Therefore I believe that a wondrous generation of Jews will spring into existence. The **Maccabeans** will rise again.

Interminably: Endlessly.

Maccabeans: Family of Jewish patriots who revolted against Syrian rule in Judea in the first century BCE.

Let me repeat once more my opening words: The Jews who wish for a State will have it.

We shall live at last as free men on our own soil, and die peacefully in our own homes.

The world will be freed by our liberty, enriched by our wealth, magnified by our greatness.

And whatever we attempt there to accomplish for our own welfare, will react powerfully and beneficially for the good of humanity.

• • •

What happened next...

Rarely has the publication of a single book had such a large impact on the history of a people and a nation. *The Jewish State* ignited interest in the question of Jewish immigration from countries experiencing anti-Semitism. Almost immediately, Herzl became the figurehead of a growing movement to promote the ideas of Zionism. He published a newspaper, *Die Welt (The World)*, which helped to spread his ideas. He also organized the First Zionist Congress in Basle, Switzerland, in 1897, which attracted two hundred delegates from around the world. From that very first meeting, delegates stated their preference for Palestine as the destination for Jewish immigration. From that point on, Zionism's major efforts were directed toward creating a Jewish homeland in Palestine. In the years that followed, the Zionist Organization formed in Basle grew in wealth and influence, and Jewish immigration to Palestine increased.

The Zionist goal of creating a Jewish homeland in Palestine did not progress as easily as Herzl had predicted, however. From the beginning, Arabs living in the area resented the Zionists' claim that Palestine was a land awaiting proper management. Arab peasants were evicted from their homes and farms when wealthy Zionists bought up the land. From the early 1900s, Arabs resisted the Jewish presence in Palestine. To this day, many Arabs in the region feel that Palestine was stolen from its rightful inhabitants by ruthless Zionists willing to use their wealth and power to build a Jewish state.

Summing up the events of the First Zionist Congress in 1897, Herzl declared: "In Basle I created the Jewish State. Were I to say this aloud I would be greeted by universal laughter. But perhaps five years hence, in any case, certainly fifty years hence, everyone will perceive it. The state exists as essence in the will-to-the-state of a people," as quoted by Naomi

Pasachoff in *Links in the Chain: Shapers of the Jewish Tradition.* In fact, he was correct, almost to the year. In 1948, the nation of Israel declared its independence as a Jewish state. Herzl's vision had been realized, but not without consequences. Jews fought with Arabs in the region from the beginning of the Jewish immigration to Palestine, and since its establishment in 1948, Israel has engaged in several costly wars with its Arab neighbors. Today, fighting continues between Israelis and Palestinians, an Arab people whose ancestors lived in the historical region of Palestine and who continue to lay claim to that land, and their supporters. Certainly, Herzl did not anticipate that the realization of the Zionist dream would cause such lasting conflict.

Did you know...

- Among Jews, a period of large immigration to Israel is known by the Hebrew word "aliyah" (immigration of Jews to the historic Eretz Yisrael [Land of Israel]). The first aliyah occurred in the early 1880s, when some thirty-five thousand Russian Jews immigrated to Palestine. The second aliyah—encouraged by Herzl's Zionist organizing—drew about forty thousand Jews to Palestine between 1904 and 1914.
- One of the most common objections to early Jewish immigration to Palestine was that the arid (dry) region would not be able to support the increased population. Jewish settlers disproved this argument by developing successful dry-farming methods and building irrigation networks using a complicated system of canals.
- The nation of Israel offers Jews around the world the right to immigrate to Israel. This right is referred to as the "right of return."
- Theodor Herzl died in 1904, well before Zionists had secured their goal of creating a homeland for Jews.

Consider the following...

- Herzl imagined that Jewish migration to a national homeland would benefit the countries that these Jews were leaving because it would bring an end to the social unrest caused by anti-Semitism. Was this part of his dream realized?
- Herzl speaks of steam power with enough force to propel an engine. What is this a metaphor for? Does this metaphor work to explain the conditions Herzl describes?

A camp for immigrant Jews in Palestine in the 1920s. About forty thousand Jews immigrated to Palestine between 1904 and 1914.
© EVERETT COLLECTION INC./ALAMY.

- There are a number of statements in *The Jewish State* that seem prophetic. Identify these statements and the ways in which they have come to be fulfilled.

- Herzl proposes that Argentina might have been a reasonable place to create a Jewish state. How would history have been different if the Jewish national homeland had been created in Argentina? Some factors to consider are the political stability of that part of the world, the availability of natural resources, and the role played by race and religion.

- Compare and contrast *The Jewish State* to one or more of the other documents in this chapter. How do these visions for the Middle East differ? Are they compatible or contrary to each other? To what extent do these visions still shape politics in the region?

For More Information

BOOKS

Elon, Amos. *Herzl.* New York: Holt, Rinehart, and Winston, 1975.

Engel, David. *Zionism.* Harlow: Pearson/Longman, 2009.

Finkelstein, Norman H. *Theodor Herzl: Architect of a Nation.* Minneapolis, MN: Lerner, 1991.

Herzl, Theodor. *Der Judenstaat.* 1896. Translated in English as *The Jewish State: An Attempt at a Modern Solution of the Jewish Question.* New York: American Zionist Emergency Council, 1946.

Pasachoff, Naomi. *Links in the Chain: Shapers of the Jewish Tradition.* New York: Oxford University Press, 1997.

Vital, David. *The Origins of Zionism.* Oxford: Clarendon Press, 1975.

WEB SITES

"Immigration." *Jewish Virtual Library.* http://www.jewishvirtuallibrary.org/jsource/Immigration/immigtoc.html (accessed on November 30, 2011).

Israel, Steve. "The Story of Zionism." *Jewish Agency for Israel.* http://www.jewishagency.org/JewishAgency/English/Jewish+Education/Compelling+Content/Eye+on+Israel/Story_Zionism (accessed on November 30, 2011).

"Theodor (Binyamin Ze'ev) Herzl." *Jewish Virtual Library.* http://www.jewishvirtuallibrary.org/jsource/biography/Herzl.html (accessed on November 30, 2011).

Speech to the Officers' Club

Excerpt from Gamal Abdel Nasser's Speech to the Officers'
Club (April 25, 1959)

Speech given in Cairo, Egypt

Reprinted in The Arab States and the Arab League:
A Documentary Record

Published in 1962

"The obliteration of Arab nationalism from any Arab country
means that our turn will come to defend nationalism in our country."

For centuries, much of the Middle East was under the control of the
Ottoman Empire, the vast empire of the Ottoman Turks which
included southwest Asia, northeast Africa, and southeast Europe, and
lasted from the thirteenth century to the early twentieth century. As the
empire began to decline, Arabs in the Middle East dreamed that they
would attain political independence, perhaps in a single state encompassing the entire Arabian Peninsula. (Arabs are people of the Middle East
and North Africa who speak the Arabic language or who live in countries
in which Arabic is the dominant language.) Husayn ibn 'Ali (also spelled
Hussein bin Ali; c. 1854–1931), the sharif of Mecca (in present-day
Saudi Arabia), was the leading Muslim religious figure in the Arabian
Peninsula. After the beginning of World War I (1914–18; a global war
between the Allies [Great Britain, France, and Russia, joined later by the
United States] and the Central Powers [Germany, Austria-Hungary, and
their allies]) Husayn sought an alliance with the Great Britain, exchang-
ing letters with Sir Henry McMahon (1862–1949), the British high
commissioner in Egypt. In this correspondence, Husayn promised to
lead a rebellion against Ottoman rule in exchange for British recognition

of Arab independence after the war. (The Ottomans were fighting on the side of the Central Powers.) Husayn successfully led the Arab Revolt, which lasted from 1916 to 1919. However, after the Allies won World War I and the Ottoman Empire came to an end, the Allies divided most of the Middle East into territories under the mandate (administrative authority) of Great Britain and France. Arab dreams of independence were thus temporarily thwarted.

By the 1950s the Arab world had developed into a multinational region. The territories under British and French mandate had gained their independence and the Middle East—an area that had once been loosely defined by small emirates, or kingdoms—had become home to numerous nations, including the newly created Jewish state of Israel in the former British mandate of Palestine. (Palestine is a historical region in the Middle East on the eastern shore of the Mediterranean Sea, comprising parts of present-day Israel and Jordan.) Although these nations went about creating their own unique national identities upon gaining their independence, there remained a desire among many to unite all Arabs. This desire was known as Pan-Arabism, a movement for the unification of Arab peoples and the political alliance of Arab states.

The greatest proponent of Pan-Arabism was Egyptian president Gamal Abdel Nasser (1918–1970). Nasser had come to power in the early 1950s as part of a military coup (overthrow of the government) that removed the country's king. In 1956, he became the country's first president and soon emerged as a champion of Arab political causes and Arab nationalism. (Nationalism is devotion and loyalty to a nation and its culture, in this case the entire Arab world.)

Nasser's Pan-Arabism, sometimes called Nasserism, aspired to unify all the Arab countries into a single, powerful Arab state. That state would be secular (nonreligious), with the government not tied to any particular religion; it would be socialist, following a system by which the major means of production and distribution are owned, managed, and controlled by the government; and it would be anti-imperialist, meaning it would not ally itself with Western nations, especially the two major powers trying to exert political influence in the world, the United States and the Soviet Union. Finally, Nasser's Pan-Arabism encouraged Arabs to unite in opposition to Israel. Nasser and other Arabs resented the way that Israel had claimed what they considered to be Arab land. (When Israel declared its existence in the former territory of Palestine, that region was also home to Arab

Egyptian president Gamal Abdel Nasser was a proponent of Pan-Arabism. © EVERETT COLLECTION INC./ALAMY.

Palestinians, who had lived there for hundreds of years. However, the Jews had ancient ties to Palestine and thus believed that it was their rightful homeland.) Pan-Arabists also thought that Western countries used Israel as a means to spread their influence in the Middle East and to attack Arab and Islamic culture.

In 1958, Nasser joined with Syrian president Shukri al-Quwatli (1891–1967) to form the United Arab Republic, a political union intended as a first step toward further Arab unification. In 1959, Nasser spoke of his goals for the Pan-Arabist movement to a group of military and political leaders in Cairo, Egypt.

Things to remember while reading the excerpt from Gamal Abdel Nasser's "Speech to the Officers' Club"

- The key components of Nasser's beliefs are Pan-Arabism, anti-imperialism (being against large countries taking over smaller countries), and anti-Zionism (opposition to the creation of a Jewish state in Palestine). He refers to each of these key issues in his speech.
- Some of Nasser's longtime rivals for power in the Middle East were Jordan and Iraq. Look for the subtle ways that he criticizes his political enemies in his speech.
- Nasser's speech contains both a short version of recent Middle Eastern history and proposals for future action.

• • •

Gamal Abdel Nasser's Speech to the Officers' Club (April 25, 1959)

Brethren:

I extend my congratulations to you all and wish you success in the great work you undertake for the glory of our nation.

Circumstances and occasions often change, but whatever changes may occur, the men of the Armed Forces always bear the same eternal duty of protecting the **Fatherland** and the people's objectives. Moreover, they must always be ready at any time to protect the gains we make. . . .

When we look at the position we occupy in the world, this world in which we live and from which we cannot separate ourselves, we find that our zone is one of great strategic importance, that its history reflects all sorts of differences, particularly the struggles of the great powers for domination over the area on account of its vital and strategic importance.

We men of the Armed Forces therefore have a great responsibility, as our country has always been the target of the ambitions of the big powers, those big powers that always seek power and think they can have it through dominating our land.

However, we have resolved to follow an independent policy and to maintain the independence of our country. We made that known when we declared that our policy is based on positive neutrality and **non-alignment**, for this means that we shall not submit to power politics, and shall not, under any circumstances, accept the role of a **satellite** or allow our fate to be decided in a foreign country or our policy to be planned in a foreign capital. . . .

Fatherland: Egypt.

Non-alignment: The refusal to create a political alliance with any of the "big powers," i.e. the United States, Great Britain, France, or the Soviet Union.

Satellite: A country that is under the influence or control of another country.

Middle East Conflict: Primary Sources, 2nd Edition

As soon as **Cairo** achieved its independence through freeing the country from British occupation and domination . . . the banner of **Arab nationalism** and Arab **solidarity** was raised in Cairo and we felt that we could not really feel free or enjoy our independence until each and every Arab country became independent. The independence of all Arab countries is a closely knit entity and we consider that there is a serious threat to our independence if any Arab country remains under foreign domination. When both Egypt and Syria achieved their freedom and the two countries raised the banner of Arab nationalism, we find that the Arab people in Egypt and Syria united in defending and upholding the independence of the Arab world and Arab nationalism.

We felt that the armed forces were imperative in defending and safeguarding this freedom and this great call for Arab nationalism which now came to prove its existence. The call for Arab nationalism is not a racial call, it is not the call of any one person, neither is it a new call; the call of Arab nationalism rang throughout the centuries and showed its strength whenever the Arab countries were independent or whenever they felt the threat of danger. The banner of Arab nationalism was raised in the 10th Century— when the Arab countries were threatened with invasion and outside pressures they realized that their very existence depended on their strong belief in and adherence to Arab nationalism, to protect the Arab world and its civilization. The united Arab army was then able to defeat the **Crusaders** who occupied the Arab world for over 80 years. The Arab armies achieved this victory only when they felt that their unity brought them strength and that Arab nationalism was their shield of protection. The union between the armies of Egypt and Syria brought them success and they saved Syria and Egypt and Palestine and all the other Arab countries from the occupation of the Crusaders. In truth the call of Arab nationalism is not a new call, nor is it a newly discovered mission—indeed it is a deeply-rooted factor in the heart and mind of the Arab nation; the Arab nation was sometimes distracted from it but rallied round it and clung to it whenever it was faced with danger.

When the **Tartars** invaded this part of the world, occupying Baghdad and crossing the **Euphrates** into Syria and threatened Egypt, it became clear that the only way to repel this invasion was by rallying under the flag of Arab nationalism. Eventually the Syrian and Egyptian armies united and successfully pushed the Tartar forces back of the Euphrates. The Tartars had not met such a setback in their invasion until they reached Syria. Once again were the Arab armies by means of their united strength able to defeat the enemy and save the Arab nation and its civilization. This was by no means a racial mission, it was a mission of sacrifice for and defence of the Arab world.

During the **First World War**, when the Arabs wanted to rid themselves of the Ottoman occupation which lasted for over 500 years they resorted again to Arab nationalism and unity. The Arab revolution rallied round the banner

Cairo: The capital of Egypt.

Arab nationalism: Devotion and loyalty to a nation and its culture, in this case the entire Arab world.

Solidarity: Unity.

Crusaders: Christian soldiers who participated in a series of military campaigns ordered by the Roman Catholic Church between 1095 and 1291 with the main goal of taking the Holy Land from the Muslims.

Tartars: Muslims from Turkey and north central Asia.

Euphrates: A river in southwest Asia flowing from central Turkey into Syria.

First World War: World War I (1914–18).

of Arab nationalism but committed the error of allying itself with Britain instead of depending only on the Arab people to reach its goal of independence and freedom. It is inconceivable that any major power would desire us to achieve independence and unity. Britain exploited Arab nationalism and used it to defeat the **Ottoman Empire**. After the First World War Britain did not fulfill its promises to the Arab people—instead the Arab world was divided under British and French rule. But the people of the Arab nations rebelled against this foreign rule and fought for their independence until the **Palestine War** broke out. The Arab countries entered the Palestine War, not under the unified flag of Arab nationalism, but torn by internal feuds, jealousies and **rancour**. We were seven armies fighting in Palestine under 6 or 7 different and separate commands. The great tragedy which befell the Arab nation was a direct result of the jealous ambitions between the different commands. We all know how these battles were carried out and how Israel, exploiting our division upon ourselves and our jealous feuds, struck at one Arab army after another; we know the tragic end of the Palestine War. We know that the Arabs, the Palestinians, were kicked out of **Palestine** and became **refugees** after the victory of international **Zionism**. International Zionism constitutes a threat to all the Arab countries for Israel is not the outcome of Zionism's efforts in 1948 only—these efforts started a long time ago and stretched over the years until they achieved their first material victory, the **Balfour Declaration** of 1917. From 1917 until 1948 Zionism and **Imperialism** continued their efforts and intrigues to put this declaration into effect. We can say that 1948 is not the year in which the Palestine story started and ended—it started long before that and Zionist aims were not restricted to that part of Palestine which their forces occupied. The Zionists always claimed that their holy state extends from the Nile to the Euphrates. As they seized opportunities in the past, they will try to do the same in the future. We all know that when they **annexed** part of the Egyptian territory in the Sinai peninsula after their aggression against us, they did so in the hope of keeping it under their rule.

This does not suit in any way the interests of International Zionism, because it knows, together with Israel, that Arab Union, or Arab solidarity and military strength spells a quick end to their expansionist schemes in the Arab world. What it actually means for them is that with the springing up of a strong Arab community on their borders, it will be utterly impossible for them to realize their ambitions, or to go on violating the rights of the Palestinians Arabs who have been thrown out of their homeland in 1948, and who still are determined to regain their rights in their own country, their rights to their own land and their own properties which have long been **usurped** from them.

International Zionism, then, spared no efforts in its fight against Arab Nationalism, and its attempts at preventing the Arab countries from coming together in a military agreement. They used every possible means to achieve this end, through the influence they have in the imperialist countries, through

Ottoman Empire: The vast empire of the Ottoman Turks which included southwest Asia, northeast Africa, and southeast Europe, and lasted from the thirteenth century to the early twentieth century.

Palestine War: The 1948 Arab-Israeli War fought between Israel and surrounding Arab nations after Israel declared its statehood.

Rancour: Bitterness, resentment.

Palestine: A historical region in the Middle East on the eastern shore of the Mediterranean Sea, comprising parts of present-day Israel and Jordan.

Refugees: People who flee their country to escape violence or persecution.

Zionism: An international political movement originating in the late nineteenth century that called for the creation of an independent Jewish state in Palestine.

Balfour Declaration: Declaration by Britain which supported the creation of a Jewish homeland in Palestine.

Imperialism: Extending a country's power and influence by establishing economic and political dominance over other nations.

Annexed: Took possession of.

Usurped: Taken.

money, inducement and even through using traitors inside the Arab world, who were known to have betrayed their countries in the past.

Imperialism, on its part too, which long aspired to place this part of the world in its spheres of influence, in order to dominate it and usurp its wealth at the cheapest of prices, establish military and air bases on its soil so as to achieve military superiority, this same Western imperialism also felt it could never reach its goals as long as there was a strong Arab nation facing it; it also realised that it would not have a chance as long as it was encountered with the kind of solidarity that the Arabs now had, the solidarity that enabled them to have one strong unified army working for the sole purpose of protecting the Arab nation.

Imperialism therefore strove in every way it could to divide the Arab countries, and to sow the seeds of dissension and hatred among them, using the traitors and agents of imperialism who have always **collaborated** with it, and who already accepted to become stooges selling their countries at a cheap price.

Those are the treacherous statesmen who accepted to work as agents and **stooges** for imperialism, and for a **fifth column** against their own countries and against the freedom of their own peoples.

Western imperialism went along this road using every possible means; money, influence, **propaganda**, economic warfare and economic blockade. Relying on these agents, it attempted to spread **discord** between the Arab countries, fabricate crises so as to **disseminate** hatred among the Arabs.

Collaborated: Worked together.

Stooges: People who knowingly allow themselves to be used for another's profit.

Fifth Column: A group of people who secretly work to defeat a larger group of people, such as a nation, often from within.

Propaganda: Material distributed for the purpose promoting a cause or viewpoint.

Discord: Conflict.

Disseminate: Spread.

Obliteration: Destruction.

These were the bases of this alliance between Western imperialism and Zionism, the spreading of disunity and hatred among the Arab people. But the Arab awakening which made the people aware of all such methods, the Arab determination to achieve complete freedom and independence for their countries and their knowledge of the road that leads to the realization of their aspirations, defeated all these attempts of the Imperialist-Zionist alliance. . . .

But, to their misfortune, this hatred the imperialists hoped to disseminate among the Arab countries or among the sons of the Arab nation, was doomed to failure because the Arab people firmly believe in Arab nationalism and knew that in adhering to this nationalism lay their only salvation and their future security. They knew that the unity of the Arab countries and their solidarity were the only means to achieve Arab strength, dignity, freedom and independence. . . .

In all their struggles, the Arab people firmly believe in their armed forces, in the Arab army which had determined to protect this mission and to sacrifice everything for the cause of Arab nationalism. We all believe that our survival depends on the defence of every Arab country. The **obliteration** of Arab nationalism from any Arab country means that our turn will come to defend nationalism in our country. The obliteration of Arab nationalism in Palestine is a sign of danger to us. Should we slacken or weaken, our turn will come; we shall suffer the same fate as Palestine. . . .

But our victory over the attempts of imperialism would not bring us to the end of our road, for imperialism will never despair, and will continue its endeavours to bring this area into spheres of influence by all possible means, depending on the use of its agents.

In the meantime, new factors appeared, for at this stage, after we had gained our great victory over the forces of imperialism, the **Communists** in the Arab countries felt that the time had come for them to strike at the Arab nationalist movement and destroy it, because they saw in it an obstacle to their domination of the Arab countries.

And with this started a new phase in our Arab Nationalism battle.

The first phase was the struggle of Arab Nationalism with Zionism . . . coupled with the struggle against the imperialist powers and their efforts to bring the Arab countries into spheres of influence.

The new phase in the battle was the struggle against the activities of Communist parties in the area. This phase started after the outbreak of the **revolution in Iraq**.

This revolution broke out in order to do away with the agents of imperialism in the country. It adopted the call for Arab Nationalism. Then the Communist party in Iraq started to launch attacks against the United Arab Republic and its policy, one month after the Iraqi Revolution. . . .

Attacks were launched against the United Arab Republic, and the policy of Arab solidarity, in which the Arab people had put their faith. The Communists did not consider Zionism as the danger threatening the Arab states, but preferred to attack Arab Nationalism, for they believed that this nationalism and its appeal to the Arab nation constituted the real threat to their domination of the Arab countries. . . .

Brethren, it is not a matter of difference over a doctrine or idea, but of domination, of centres of political power, of the policy of the great powers, and whether we Arab countries are free, or satellites, lying within spheres of influence, and whether we shall follow a policy of positive neutrality or align ourselves with either camp.

It was the policy of Arab Nationalism which prevented the Communist Party in Syria from gaining control of the country, and which threatens the plans of the Communists in Iraq. And it is because of this Arab nationalism that world Zionism and Israel are violently fighting the United Arab Republic. World imperialism also is fighting the United Arab Republic, depending on agents, stooges and opportunists, as in Iraq, for imperialism sees in the success of the United Arab Republic and its policy a consolidation of the strength of the Arabs in the area, and the potentiality of creating an independent strong zone, which would render the return of Western Imperialism to the area, in an attempt to bring it within spheres of influence, a practical impossibility. Imperialism has been defeated in several rounds, but it has not despaired and continues its attempts to bring the area

Communists: Advocates of Communism, a system of government in which the state plans and controls the economy and a single political party holds power.

Revolution in Iraq: A reference to the 14 July Revolution in 1958, a coup that overthrew the king and established the Iraqi Republic.

within spheres of influence, by all possible means, in order to affect the international situation accordingly.

And then comes Communism . . . the aims of which were proclaimed by the Communist parties in our land. At the same time, the Eastern camp, or the Soviet Union, which had supported us in our struggle against Western imperialism, and when we declared that our policy would be built on positive neutrality and non-alignment, changed its policy. . . .

If the East intends to align the United Arab Republic to its side it will have no alternative but to fight us because the United Arab Republic is adamant in its refusal to be included in any sphere of influence. Likewise if the West desires to include this area in its sphere of influence, it will have to fight and subjugate us. The West has already waged all sorts of war against us; armed, economic, psychological and propaganda wars. Thus we find that there is perfect accord between these powers in their efforts to influence the people of the United Arab Republic. . . .

We have a long struggle ahead of us before we can complete our independence. The road to independence is strewn with sacrifices and requires firmness and constant protection. The price we are paying for the safeguarding of our freedom, independence and dignity does not compare in any way to the price being paid by those countries which accept the role of attendant countries to other bigger countries or which allow themselves to be **goaded** into spheres of influence. We are determined, rulers and people, to pursue a policy aiming at complete independence, non-alignment to either East or West and non-subjection to any foreign nation.

Anything we might sacrifice in pursuit of this policy is nothing compared to what the people would have to suffer if they fell under the **yoke** of a foreign power and had to live under its rule. We can see how the dominated nations cannot in any way have a will or character of their own.

You men of the armed forces are the guardians of this country as you carry a great responsibility for a noble cause on which depends the destiny of every individual in the Arab nation, as well as the destiny of the Arab nation at large. It is the mission of Arab nationalism.

This is why the nation and the people feel confident in their struggle as they feel that they are backed by a strong national army ready to sacrifice everything.

The people feel confident. We who have drawn this policy and determined to make it independent, must do our utmost and sacrifice everything to fulfill this mission, from the President of the Republic to the last soldier. We all work for the establishment of these principles and the achievement of these goals. All the people are one army working for this cause.

May God guide our steps.

Goaded: Provoked, pushed.

Yoke: Control.

● ● ●

What happened next...

Nasser's speech, and his larger Pan-Arabist political philosophy, caused quite a stir, both in the Middle East and around the world. Within the Arab community, it excited those who supported the prospects for a unified Arab world. They saw in Pan-Arabism a way to regain Arab dignity and improve the Arab economy. They also believed that the only way to defeat Israel and regain Palestine for Arab Palestinians was through united action. Others within the Arab community, however, did not embrace Nasser's vision. Saudi Arabia preferred its monarchy and its strict religious legal system. Jordan preferred to ally itself with Great Britain and the United States. Meanwhile, political factions within every Arab nation resisted Nasser's attempts to consolidate power in his hands.

Despite the fervor of Nasser's vision, Pan-Arab unity proved difficult to achieve. The alliance between Syria and Egypt was strained from the beginning, with Syrians feeling that they had given up too much power to Egypt. By September 1961, the Syrian military led Syria in leaving the United Arab Republic. Nasser did not wish to use the Egyptian military to fight against fellow Arabs, and the union dissolved. Egypt also formed a short-lived union with Yemen from 1958 to 1961. Pan-Arabism lost most of its supporters in 1967, when Israel defeated the combined but poorly organized troops of Egypt, Jordan, and Syria in the 1967 Arab-Israeli War. After that time, few seriously supported the idea of Arab unification, and Arab nations each pursued their own independent course into the future. It would take the passion of Islamic fundamentalism (a movement stressing adherence to a strict or literal interpretation of religious principles) to revive dreams of a unified Arab world in the later years.

Did you know...

- From the 1940s through the early 1970s, Egypt was the wealthiest and most powerful nation in the Middle East. However, the oil-producing capacity of nations such as Saudi Arabia and Iraq has since shifted the balance of economic power in the region.
- Though Syria withdrew from the United Arab Republic in 1961, Egypt continued to use the name until Nasser's death in 1970, when it was renamed the Arab Republic of Egypt.

Consider the following...

- Nasser offers a short version of Middle Eastern history. Is his history accurate? How has he shaped what he said to suit his political goals?
- What are the ways in which Nasser draws attention to the failings of other Arab nations? Point to those places in which he attacks his enemies, and identify those he attacks. (Hint: He does not refer to them directly.)
- Policy makers in the United States and Great Britain have often tried to depict Pan-Arabism as a radical, dangerous political philosophy. Is the tone of Nasser's speech one of a radical nature? Why might Nasser appear to be a threat to Western nations?
- Compare and contrast Nasser's speech to one or more of the other documents in this chapter. How do these visions for the Middle East differ? Are they compatible or contrary to each other? To what extent do these visions still shape politics in the region?

For More Information

BOOKS

Farah, Tawfic E., ed. *Pan-Arabism and Arab Nationalism: The Continuing Debate.* Boulder, CO: Westview Press, 1987.

Khalil, Muhammad, ed. *The Arab States and the Arab League: A Documentary Record.* Vol. 2. Beirut, Lebanon: Khayats, 1962.

Luciani, Giacomo, and Ghassan Salamé, eds. *The Politics of Arab Integration.* New York: Croom Helm, 1988.

Paparchontis, Kathleen. *100 Leaders Who Changed the World.* Milwaukee, WI: World Almanac, 2003.

Shemesh, Moshe. *Arab Politics, Palestinian Nationalism, and the Six Day War: The Crystallization of Arab Strategy and Nasir's Descent to War, 1957–1967.* Brighton: Sussex Academic Press, 2008.

WEB SITES

"Gamal Abdel Nasser." *Encyclopedia of the Middle East.* http://www.mideastweb.org/Middle-East-Encyclopedia/gamal_abdel_nasser.htm (accessed on November 30, 2011).

Jihad Against Jews and Crusaders

"Jihad Against Jews and Crusaders"
Written by the World Islamic Front
Published in Al-Quds al-Arabi, *February 23, 1998*

"All these crimes and sins committed by the Americans are clear declaration of war on Allah, his messenger, and Muslims."

For hundreds of years, Arabs in the Middle East did not hold full control over their own countries and governments. (Arabs are people of the Middle East and North Africa who speak the Arabic language or who live in countries in which Arabic is the dominant language.) Under the Ottoman Empire (the vast empire of the Ottoman Turks which included southwest Asia, northeast Africa, and southeast Europe, and lasted from the thirteenth century to the early twentieth century.), they had been forced to report to governors in the capital city of Constantinople (present-day Istanbul, Turkey). When the Ottoman Empire collapsed at the end of World War I (1914–18; a global war between the Allies [Great Britain, France, and Russia, joined later by the United States] and the Central Powers [Germany, Austria-Hungary, and their allies]), Arabs hoped they would achieve political independence. Instead, most of the Middle East was divided into territories under the mandate (administrative authority) of Great Britain and France. As the twentieth century progressed, these states gained political independence. Still, many Arabs felt that their countries were unduly influenced by the demands of other countries, either in the West (the United States, Great Britain, and France, for example) or in the East (the Soviet Union). Whether they admired the Pan-Arabism (a movement for the unification of Arab peoples and the political alliance of Arab states) promoted by Egyptian president Gamal Abdel Nasser (1918–1970) or took part in 1979 Iranian Revolution (also known as the Islamic Revolution), Arabs throughout the Middle East sought ways to limit outside influences and establish local control of their government and society. (For more information on Nasser and Pan-Arabism, see **Speech to the Officers' Club**.)

Religion has always played an enormous role in shaping Arabs' visions of their society. In most Western nations, institutions of religion and government are separated (a practice known as secularism). But in the Middle East many people believe that religion should directly influence governmental policy and law. Saudi Arabia, for example, has used sharia (Islamic religious law) as its legal system since the country's founding in 1932. Iran adopted sharia after its revolution in 1979, during which the Iranian people overthrew the secular (nonreligious) government and installed religious leaders as lawmakers. However, many of the governments established in Middle Eastern countries did not fully incorporate Islamic holy law into their governments, preferring to remain secular. Beginning in the 1960s, but gathering momentum especially after the 1980s, many Muslims in these countries began to call for Islam to play a greater role in their society. Osama bin Laden (1957–2011), a militant from a wealthy Saudi Arabian family, was a strong advocate for that change.

In the West, Osama bin Laden was labeled an Islamic fundamentalist (someone who believes in a strict or literal interpretation of religious teachings) and a terrorist. He was known for the numerous attacks made by his organization, al-Qaeda, especially on U.S. targets, such as the 1993 attack on the World Trade Center in New York City. (Al-Qaeda's deadliest attack would come on September 11, 2001, when two hijacked airplanes were flown into the World Trade Center, one was flown into the Pentagon, and a fourth crashed in Pennsylvania as passengers tried to retake control. Nearly three thousand people were killed.) Yet to his followers, bin Laden was a hero. By expressing his hatred of Western influences, his desire to destroy the Jewish nation of Israel, and his goal of establishing sharia as law in every predominantly Muslim nation, bin Laden became a figurehead for those who would like to permanently rid the Middle East of non-Islamic influences.

In 1998, bin Laden joined with several Muslim clerics (ordained religious officials) to issue a statement declaring their principles. This group called itself the World Islamic Front, though many believed that it was merely an extension of al-Qaeda. In the statement, reproduced below, the World Islamic Front tells Muslims that they have a duty to kill

Osama bin Laden (pictured) joined with several Muslim clerics in the World Islamic Front to issue a statement declaring their principles in 1998. AFP/GETTY IMAGES.

Americans. The statement was issued as a *fatwa*, a statement of religious law issued by an Islamic cleric and intended to instruct devout Muslims.

Things to remember while reading "Jihad Against Jews and Crusaders"

- Although Osama bin Laden, one of the heads of the World Islamic Front, was a member of a wealthy Saudi Arabian family, he was banned from his native country in 1991. He lived for a time in Sudan and went into hiding after the September 11, 2001, attacks on the United States. He was discovered and killed in a compound in Pakistan by U.S. troops in May 2011.

- Al-Qaeda has conducted attacks against U.S. targets since 1992, when it bombed hotels where U.S. soldiers were staying in Yemen. It attacked U.S. embassies in Kenya and Tanzania in 1998. Al-Qaeda also masterminded commuter train attacks in Madrid, Spain, in 2004, and London, England, in 2005, and it attempted the bombing of a Northwest Airlines flight out of Amsterdam bound for Detroit, Michigan, in 2009. Al-Qaeda was also behind a host of insurgent (rebel) attacks on both troops and civilians in Iraq after the United States began occupying that country in 2003.
- U.S. troops have had a presence in the Middle East since 1990, when they were stationed in Saudi Arabia just before the start of the Persian Gulf War (1990–91), a war in which the U.S.-led international forces stopped Iraq from overtaking Kuwait, another Middle Eastern country.
- The other clerics who signed the statement are leaders of Islamic groups within their own countries.

• • •

Jihad Against Jews and Crusaders

23 February 1998

Shaykh Usamah Bin-Muhammad Bin-Ladin, Ayman al-Zawahiri, **amir** of the Jihad Group in Egypt, Abu-Yasir Rifa'i Ahmad Taha, Egyptian Islamic Group, Shaykh Mir Hamzah, secretary of the Jamiat-ul-Ulema-e-Pakistan, Fazlur Rahman, amir of the Jihad Movement in Bangladesh.

Praise be to **Allah**, who revealed the **Book**, controls the clouds, defeats **factionalism**, and says in His Book: "But when the forbidden months are past, then fight and slay the **pagans** wherever ye find them, seize them, **beleaguer** them, and lie in wait for them in every stratagem (of war)"; and peace be upon our Prophet, **Muhammad Bin-'Abdallah**, who said: I have been sent with the sword between my hands to ensure that no one but Allah is worshipped, Allah who put my livelihood under the shadow of my spear and who inflicts humiliation and scorn on those who disobey my orders.

The Arabian Peninsula has never—since Allah made it flat, created its desert, and encircled it with seas—been stormed by any forces like the **crusader armies** spreading in it like locusts, eating its riches and wiping out its plantations. All this is happening at a time in which nations are attacking Muslims like people fighting over a plate of food. In the light of the grave

Shaykh: Also spelled sheikh; an Arab tribal leader.

Amir: Also spelled emir; a ruler, chief, or commander in some Islamic countries.

Allah: The Arabic word for God.

Book: A reference to the Koran (also spelled Qur'an or Quran); the holy book of Islam.

Factionalism: Infighting among groups.

Pagans: Nonbelievers, in this case, those who do not follow the religion of Islam.

Beleaguer: Harass or persecute.

Muhammad Bin-'Abdallah: Usually referred to simply as Muhammad; the founder of Islam (c. 570–632).

Crusader armies: U.S. soldiers specifically, but with reference also to Christian soldiers, called crusaders, who participated in a series of military campaigns ordered by the Roman Catholic Church between 1095 and 1291 with the main goal of taking the Holy Land from the Muslims.

situation and the lack of support, we and you are obliged to discuss current events, and we should all agree on how to settle the matter.

No one argues today about three facts that are known to everyone; we will list them, in order to remind everyone:

First, for over seven years the United States has been occupying the lands of Islam in the holiest of places, the Arabian Peninsula, plundering its riches, dictating to its rulers, humiliating its people, terrorizing its neighbors, and turning its bases in the Peninsula into a spearhead through which to fight the neighboring Muslim peoples.

If some people have in the past argued about the fact of the occupation, all the people of the Peninsula have now acknowledged it. The best proof of this is the Americans' continuing aggression against the Iraqi people using the Peninsula as a staging post, even though all its rulers are against their territories being used to that end, but they are helpless.

Second, despite the great devastation inflicted on the Iraqi people by the **crusader-Zionist** alliance, and despite the huge number of those killed, which has exceeded 1 million . . . despite all this, the Americans are once against trying to repeat the horrific massacres, as though they are not content with the protracted blockade imposed after the ferocious war or the fragmentation and devastation.

So here they come to annihilate what is left of this people and to humiliate their Muslim neighbors.

Third, if the Americans' aims behind these wars are religious and economic, the aim is also to serve the Jews' petty state Israel and divert attention from its occupation of Jerusalem and murder of Muslims there. The best proof of this is their eagerness to destroy Iraq, the strongest neighboring Arab state, and their endeavor to fragment all the states of the region such as Iraq, Saudi Arabia, Egypt, and Sudan into paper statelets and through their disunion and weakness to guarantee Israel's survival and the continuation of the brutal crusade occupation of the Peninsula.

All these crimes and sins committed by the Americans are a clear declaration of war on Allah, his messenger, and Muslims. And **ulema** have throughout Islamic history unanimously agreed that the **jihad** is an individual duty if the enemy destroys the Muslim countries. This was revealed by Imam Bin-Qadamah in "Al- Mughni," Imam al-Kisa'i in "Al-Bada'i," al-Qurtubi in his interpretation, and the shaykh of al-Islam in his books, where he said: "As for the fighting to repulse an enemy, it is aimed at defending **sanctity** and religion, and it is a duty as agreed by the ulema. Nothing is more sacred than belief except repulsing an enemy who is attacking religion and life."

On that basis, and in compliance with Allah's order, we issue the following **fatwa** to all Muslims:

The ruling to kill the Americans and their allies—civilians and military—is an individual duty for every Muslim who can do it in any country in which it is

Crusader-Zionist: A reference to Israel, which was formed by Zionists, who wanted to create a Jewish national homeland in Palestine. Also a comparison of Zionists to the Christian crusaders.

Ulema: The community of Islamic scholars.

Jihad: Armed struggle against unbelievers.

Sanctity: Holiness.

Fatwa: Islamic religious decree.

possible to do it, in order to liberate the **al-Aqsa Mosque** and the holy mosque in **Mecca** from their grip, and in order for their armies to move out of all the lands of Islam, defeated and unable to threaten any Muslim. This is in accordance with the words of Almighty Allah, "and fight the pagans all together as they fight you all together," and "fight them until there is no more tumult or oppression, and there prevail justice and faith in Allah."

This is in addition to the words of Almighty Allah: "And why should ye not fight in the cause of Allah and of those who, being weak, are ill-treated (and oppressed)?—women and children, whose cry is: 'Our Lord, rescue us from this town, whose people are oppressors; and raise for us from thee one who will help!'"

We—with Allah's help—call on every Muslim who believes in Allah and wishes to be rewarded to comply with Allah's order to kill the Americans and plunder their money wherever and whenever they find it. We also call on Muslim ulema, leaders, youths, and soldiers to launch the raid on Satan's U.S. troops and the devil's supporters allying with them, and to displace those who are behind them so that they may learn a lesson.

Almighty Allah said: "O ye who believe, give your response to Allah and His Apostle, when He calleth you to that which will give you life. And know that Allah cometh between a man and his heart, and that it is He to whom ye shall all be gathered."

Almighty Allah also says: "O ye who believe, what is the matter with you, that when ye are asked to go forth in the cause of Allah, ye cling so heavily to the earth! Do ye prefer the life of this world to the hereafter? But little is the comfort of this life, as compared with the hereafter. Unless ye go forth, He will punish you with a grievous penalty, and put others in your place; but Him ye would not harm in the least. For Allah hath power over all things."

Almighty Allah also says: "So lose no heart, nor fall into despair. For ye must gain mastery if ye are true in faith."

• • •

What happened next...

In this and various other pronouncements and fatwas, bin Laden tried to inspire Muslims to rise up against the West and Israel, in order to create an Islamic world free of outside interference and dedicated to Islamic values. Islamism (a fundamentalist movement characterized by the belief that Islam should provide the basis for political, social, and cultural life in Muslim nations) became the dominant revolutionary philosophy in the Middle East—and in countries with majority Muslim

al-Aqsa Mosque: An Islamic place of worship and holy site in Jerusalem.

Mecca: The holiest site in Islam, located in Saudi Arabia.

U.S. president Barack Obama, vice president Joe Biden, secretary of state Hillary Clinton, and other officials watch the mission against Osama bin Laden in the White House situation room. Some observers suspected that bin Laden's death at the hands of U.S. troops in May 2011 would further inflame Islamists. © WHITE HOUSE PHOTO/ALAMY.

populations—beginning in the 1990s. Islamist groups challenged government power in Algeria, Sudan, and Nigeria in the 1990s. In 1996 the Taliban (a fundamentalist Islamic group) took power in Afghanistan and established an Islamic state.

Bin Laden and al-Qaeda followed through on their threats to use violence against the United States wherever they could. Al-Qaeda militants bombed a U.S. Navy destroyer, the USS *Cole*, in Yemen on October 12, 2000, killing seventeen U.S. sailors. The most dramatic attack occurred on September 11, 2001, and claimed more than three thousand lives. The attacks, however, only increased the U.S. presence in the Muslim world. In December 2001 U.S. president George W. Bush (1946–) sent troops to Afghanistan to remove the Taliban from power, because it had been harboring bin Laden. In 2003 a U.S.-led coalition invaded Iraq, based on the belief (which later proved false) that Iraq had weapons of mass destruction. The Iraq War continued until December 2011 as coalition forces battled insurgents and worked to establish a democratic government in Iraq.

By the early 2000s, it was still not clear how powerful the Islamist view would be in shaping events in the Middle East. Some observers noted that Islamism influenced suicide bombers, who believe that they are serving Allah when they participate in suicide attacks. (A suicide bombing is an attack intended to kill others and cause widespread damage, carried about by someone who does not hope to survive the attack.) In Palestinian attacks against Israel, in Iraqi insurgent attacks against U.S. forces in that country, and in al-Qaeda strikes against Western targets, suicide bombers are considered by many to be heroic martyrs, or people who die for their religion. In 2011, a series of prodemocracy uprisings known as the Arab Spring occurred throughout the Middle East and North Africa, and observers debated the role of Islamists in those events. Some suspected that bin Laden's death at the hands of U.S. troops in May 2011 would further inflame Islamists.

Did you know . . .

- The Taliban, a strict Islamist group, held power in Afghanistan from 1996 to 2001. This group banned all television and music in the country, restricted laughing in public, and used strict punishments such as cutting off hands and feet or stoning people to death to enforce government laws. Under Taliban rule, women could not obtain the same education as men, and were required to wear head-to-toe veils.

- In Turkey and Morocco, an Islamist group called the Justice and Development Party has modified its views to try to bring Islamic religious values into a democratic political system.

- Saudi Arabia follows a version of Islam called Wahhabism, which promotes strict observance of sharia and insists on a literal interpretation of the Koran (also spelled Qur'an or Quran; the holy book of Islam). As one of the world's leading oil producers, Saudi Arabia has also tried to maintain political friendships with the United States and other large, oil-consuming nations.

Consider the following...

- "Jihad Against Jews and Crusaders" calls on Muslims to kill Americans. Is there any way to justify such a command from a group of religious leaders? Can you find any other instances in history in which religious or political leaders have made such demands?

- Using the arguments put forth in the "Jihad Against Jews and Crusaders," explain how the Islamist approach to Middle East politics offers solutions to the problems of the region. Then, consider whether there might be more moderate ways to solve those problems.

- Compare and contrast the "Jihad Against Jews and Crusaders" to one or more of the other documents in this chapter. How do these visions for the Middle East differ? Are they compatible or contrary to each other? To what extent do these visions still shape politics in the region?

For More Information

BOOKS

Bergen, Peter. *Holy War, Inc.* New York: Touchstone, 2002.

Burke, Jason. *Al-Qaeda: Casting a Shadow of Terror.* New York: I.B. Tauris, 2003.

Loehfelm, Bill. *Osama bin Laden.* Farmington Hills, MI: Lucent Books, 2003.

Martin, Richard C., and Abbas Barzegar, eds. *Islamism: Contested Perspectives on Political Islam.* Palo Alto, CA: Stanford University Press, 2010.

Mockaitis, Thomas R. *Osama bin Laden: A Biography.* Santa Barbara, CA: Greenwood, 2010.

Randal, Jonathan. *Osama: The Making of a Terrorist.* New York: Alfred A. Knopf, 2004.

Scheurer, Michael. *Osama bin Laden.* Oxford and New York: Oxford University Press, 2011.

PERIODICALS

"Is Islamism a Threat? A Debate." *Middle East Quarterly*, no. 4 (December 1999). Available online at http://www.meforum.org/article/447 (accessed on November 30, 2011).

Wilson, Scott, Craig Whitlock, and William Branigin. "Osama bin Laden Killed in U.S. Raid, Buried at Sea." *The Washington Post* (May 2, 2011).

World Islamic Front. "Jihad against Jews and Crusaders." *Al-Quds al-Arabi* (February 23, 1998).

WEB SITES

Burke, Jason. "The Making of Osama bin Laden." *Salon.com* (November 1, 2001). http://dir.salon.com/news/feature/2001/11/01/osama_profile/index.html (accessed on November 30, 2011).

"Hunting Bin Laden." *PBS Frontline*. http://www.pbs.org/wgbh/pages/frontline/shows/binladen (accessed on November 30, 2011).

The Contribution of Islam to a Global Ethic

Excerpt from "The Contribution of Islam to a Global Ethic"

A speech by Shirin Ebadi

Delivered at the University of Tübingen, Germany

October 20, 2005

"[A] correct and dynamic interpretation of Islam allows a person to be both a Muslim and to respect and comply with human rights."

Shirin Ebadi (1947–) was born in Iran, and she grew up in a time when girls and women in that nation had better opportunities for education and careers than they would by the time Ebadi reached her thirties. Ebadi was raised and educated during the reign of Mohammad Reza Pahlavi (1919–1980), the shah of Iran, whose secular (nonreligious) government enacted a series of social and economic reforms (including increased rights for women) known as the White Revolution. Pahlavi worked toward modernizing Iran and increasing its global influence. Ebadi completed college with a law degree, became a judge, and was the first woman in Iran to lead a court that reviewed laws passed by the government. In 1979, however, the Iranian Revolution (also known as the Islamic Revolution) resulted in an overthrow of the shah in favor of a government led by Islamic clerics (ordained religious officials) who ruled according to a strict interpretation of Islam. In their view, Islamic law forbade women to be judges. Ebadi was reduced to being a legal assistant, despite her education, experience, and accomplishments.

Ebadi did not practice law again for nearly fifteen years. In the 1990s she began providing legal assistance to families and speaking out

Shirin Ebadi. © JEFF
MORGAN 13/ALAMY.

for the rights of women and children. Her heroic and dangerous struggle for civil rights and freedoms in Iran, a country dominated by strict laws and harsh punishments, made her controversial. Through her speeches, interviews, and writings, Ebadi generated international publicity about repression in Iran. In 2003, Ebadi was honored with the Nobel Peace Prize.

Winning the prestigious Nobel Peace Prize made Ebadi internationally famous, and she was invited to speak by many organizations around the world. In 2005 she was asked to give a lecture sponsored by the Global Ethic Foundation. The organization promotes international peace through "ethical awareness" and the appreciation of basic values common in major religions and philosophical traditions. The Global Ethic Foundation sponsors a major event about once a year that features a world leader as the speaker. For her speech, Ebadi chose the topic, "The Contribution of Islam to a Global Ethic."

Things to remember while reading the excerpt from "The Contribution of Islam to a Global Ethic." 5th Global Ethic lecture, October 20, 2005:

- An "ethic" is defined as a set of principles of conduct and a theory or a system of moral values. By addressing the contributions of Islam to a global ethic, Ebadi is focusing on values of Islam that are common among religions.

- In the beginning of her lecture, Ebadi describes differences among people around the world, including customs, physical features, clothing, and lifestyles. After providing several examples of differences, Ebadi notes that many cultures share a common set of myths and principles based on respect for human rights.

- Democracy, according to Ebadi, is fundamental to human rights, because democracy invites many voices with multiple and sometimes opposing viewpoints, which contributes to continual social and moral development and improvements. Ebadi contrasts this approach with non-democratic states that do not allow different interpretations and opinions.

- Ebadi compares the strict interpretation of Islam by Iranian leaders to a dictatorship (a form of government led by a dictator, a ruler with unrestricted power) that suppresses freedom. A more dynamic interpretation of Islam, she argues, is compatible with democracy and human rights.

• • •

The Contribution of Islam to a Global Ethic

. . . My dear friends!

We all believe that on this earth, which is here for all of us, many different people live, with many different cultures. People have different ways of living, and their cultures differ from each another. People speak different languages, and religions guide people in different ways. People are born with different skin colours and different traditions give their lives its "colour". People dress differently, and different guiding principles help them adapt to their **respective** different environmental conditions. People express their opinions and convictions in different ways; their music, art and literature follow different styles. Yet, despite all these differences, all people share something basically in common. They are all human beings; no one is more than a human being and no one is less.

And different cultures also have something basically in common. People everywhere in the world, whether in the East or in the West, people of every skin colour and race, every religion and conviction have the same needs in common.

One proof of this **allegation** is the astonishing similarity of the myths of different nations. They are the bedrock for the different cultures, which are later formed based on these myths. Moreover, **philologists** tell us that the roots of many words are very similar, as though a single person or group of people had created them.

If then, there are such common or even identical roots of life on this earth for all persons and groups of people, why should we doubt that there are also universal rules and values, which are valid for all mankind?

Different cultures can also go in search of what they have in common while maintaining their own distinctive features and discover their common needs, setting up the same rules for them and adhering to them—all of them.

Every culture and religion respects the life, dignity and property of persons. In contrast, terror and violence against people and their humiliation are considered reprehensible by every society and in every order of society.

Around 60 years ago, that is, just after the end of the **Second World War**, **jurists** and scholars from different nations and cultures came together and attempted to determine the basic common needs of mankind and to list them. This formed the basis for the **Universal Declaration of Human Rights**, which, in its turn, depended on a Global Ethic. As this ethic is the basis for laws, no state can now violate human rights by **invoking** the principle of non-interference in internal affairs and laws.

Those who refuse to comply with human rights, citing cultural differences and the **relativity** of values are in truth **antiquated** oppressors who hide their **tyrannical** nature under the mask of culture and, in the name

Respective: Individual, unique.

Allegation: Claim.

Philologists: Those who study written texts or records.

Second World War: World War II (1939–45).

Jurists: Those who study the law.

Universal Declaration of Human Rights: A declaration adopted by the United Nations in 1948 stating that all people have certain basic rights including life, liberty, equality, justice and self determination.

Invoking: Calling on or referring to.

Relativity: The absence of absolute, universal standards.

Antiquated: Obsolete, out of date.

Tyrannical: Oppressive and controlling.

of a national or religious culture, wish to oppress and terrorize their own nation.

The world will only become peaceful and the peace will be of longer duration when human rights are applied comprehensively and universally.

. . . The relativity of cultural norms and values must not be used to justify the violation of human rights. We cannot refuse to comply with human rights by invoking religion. For, as I already explained, there is no religion, which condones oppression, war, discrimination, the murder of innocent people or the looting of national property, etc.

Sadly, non-democratic **Islamic states** avail themselves of this excuse and believe that, since the people in their countries are Muslim, the state must enforce and apply the laws of Islam and that compliance with human rights is only possible, insofar as human rights are compatible with Islamic law. In cases where there is a contradiction, for example with regard to women's rights or democracy, an Islamic state cannot and should not comply with human rights. Such states only recognize their own interpretations and constructions of Islamic law. Interpretations by other Muslims are not accepted and rejected in their entirety. Everyone who does not share their interpretation and construction of religion is, in their eyes, an **apostate** and has forfeited his life. Or these states impose an extensive censorship whereby such a person is not permitted to **promulgate** his thoughts and ideas.

In 1980, the **Universal Islamic Declaration of Human Rights** was proclaimed in Cairo at the Islamic Conference of Foreign Ministers. If we take this Declaration as a sign among Muslims that internationally applicable human rights should be complied with, there is no problem. But it would be wrong to perceive this Declaration as a counterpart to the Universal Declaration of Human Rights. Because if Muslims wish to exclude themselves from the applicability of the Universal Declaration of Human Rights with the excuse that they are Muslims and set up their own rules based only on their religion (which is based on the interpretation of Islamic states), then they would naturally also have to grant the same right to other religions. Under these circumstances, we would end up with as many declarations of human rights as there are religions in the world, in other words, with around 5000 declarations. This would be **tantamount** to an **obliteration** of human rights. And Islamic states would suffer more from this, because they are not strong at an international level.

The truth is that a correct and dynamic interpretation of Islam allows a person to be both a Muslim and to respect and comply with human rights.

But the significant problem is the following. Non-democratic Islamic states are, for various reasons, not prepared to allow an interpretation and concept of Islam, which would be compatible with democracy and human rights. Such an interpretation would rock the foundations of their dictatorial rule and shake them to its core. So far, no **dictator** in the world has voluntarily agreed, without pressure from the masses, to a limitation of his own powers.

Islamic states: Nations governed by the belief that Islam should provide the basis for political, social, and cultural life in Muslim nations.

Apostate: One who abandons or rejects his religion.

Promulgate: Declare, make known.

Universal Islamic Declaration of Human Rights: A document restating basic human rights in terms of Islamic law.

Tantamount: Equivalent.

Obliteration: Complete destruction.

Dictator: A ruler with unrestricted power.

The non-democratic Islamic states are hiding behind the name of Islam and justify their oppression by abusing the name of Islam. Admittedly, the abuse and misuse of religion and, generally speaking, the abuse of ideology is not limited to Muslims. The Middle Ages was an **apogee** of oppression on the part of the Roman Catholic Church. The Roman Catholic Church also claimed that it was applying and carrying out Christian **precepts** and commandments. And how could we forget the terrible **internment** camps in Siberia under Stalin's rule or the blood bath among the students on Tiananmen Square in Beijing. There too, it was claimed that **Socialist** principles were being applied and implemented.

We need to shine the light of knowledge on the religion used as a shield or, more generally, on the shield of ideology behind which states hide, to ensure that everyone learns the truth, so that everyone will know that religion is being abused. The establishment of a "united front" of Muslims from different countries to fight against totalitarian states while adhering to the holy values of Islam is good news for the liberation of Muslims. This "united front" has no name, no leader, no headquarters and no offices. Its place is in the consciousness and spirit of every thinking Muslim who respects democracy while preserving the religion of his forefathers and ancestors, who does not wish to act on unethical teachings and does not tolerate violence and oppression.

Another point, which must be considered is the manner in which the Global Ethic is adapted to national ethics. Let us assume that something would finally happen and all laws and regulations would be drawn up on the basis of human rights. In many societies it will become apparent that people are not able to immediately accept these cultural changes. They might even rebel against them. In Afghanistan, for example, the wearing of a **burkha** was an unconditional obligation laid upon all women. Moreover, the **Taliban** did not permit girls to go to school. Taliban rule has ended, but despite the fact that several years have passed since then, many Afghan men sadly still do not permit their daughters to go to school and still force them to wear a burkha.

We should not forget that cultural changes and changes of ethics require time. What is important is the necessity for cultural change and the striving for a Global Ethic, that is, after the basic principles of human rights. Let me give you an example. During the first years at school, a child learns the four basic arithmetical operations. The child slowly learns to solve simple mathematical problems. In the last years at high school the child is capable of solving difficult and complex problems. The subject taught was always referred to as mathematics. But there is a big difference between adding up two numbers and solving complicated mathematical equations.

The same applies to the cultural development of a society. We cannot apply Sweden's laws for women to Saudi-Arabia overnight or laws based on democratic principles in all African countries. What is important is the

Apogee: High point.

Precepts: Directions, rules.

Internment: Imprisonment.

Socialist: Based on socialism, a system in which the government owns the means of production and controls the distribution of goods and services.

Burkha: A garment that covers the entire body, with an opening for the eyes, worn by some Muslim women.

Taliban: An Islamist militant group that controlled Afghanistan from 1996 to 2001.

development of a society towards a higher culture, and in this context laws play an important role. One of the functions of the law is its role as a spearhead. The law must stand above culture, one step ahead, in order that it can help develop and elevate the culture. If we take the example of Afghanistan, we would have to teach the people that education is a requirement for everyone. It would be necessary to ensure that families whose daughters go to school would benefit, for example through receiving cheap loans or preferential hiring for governmental positions. After a certain time, forbidding children to attend school or forbidding women to be educated would be declared illegal. A punishment would have to be devised for fathers who forbid their daughters to attend school. This means it will be necessary to proceed slowly, step by step.

A further point, which needs to be pointed out when developing and elevating a culture, is that this development must not take too long. This means that it is necessary to attempt to reach international standards as quickly as possible. Proceeding too slowly in the direction of international standards must not become a means in the hand of non-democratic states of obtaining more time for themselves.

And finally, I would like to state that invoking democracy and human rights must not be misused. One cannot take democracy as a pretext to attack a country. It is not possible to bring human rights to people with bombs. Nor is it acceptable to take the struggle against a **dictatorship** as an excuse to rob a nation of its resources. Democracy and human rights can only be achieved together with and in accordance with the will of people and not against it.

A civil society and freedom-loving people must take up the struggle against dictatorship and take their fate into their own hands. Only in this way can a society become peaceful and achieve a lasting peace. . . .

● ● ●

What happened next . . .

Ebadi's international fame and her continued outspokenness against laws and punishments that violated human rights were considered dangerous by authorities in Iran, and she was threatened with arrest many times. Nevertheless, Ebadi became a leading force for the One Million Signatures campaign. The campaign began after a peaceful demonstration in June 2006 protesting legal restrictions against women in Iran was forcefully broken up by police. Demonstrators began a petition drive to demand that the Iranian parliament (legislature) grant equal rights to women. Despite gathering hundreds of thousands of signatures and

Dictatorship: A form of government led by a dictator.

calling for reform, Iranian women continued to have fewer legal rights than men.

Ebadi helped open the Center for Protecting Human Rights in Tehran, the capital city of Iran, to provide free legal representation to journalists, students, and protestors who faced prosecution for criticizing the government. One of the co-founders of the center was jailed for several months and then sentenced to five years in prison for opposing the state. In 2009 Ebadi was forced to leave the country for her safety. She lived in Great Britain and then in Canada. The Iranian government continued to crack down on protestors, especially after many men and women demonstrated against what they believed were rigged elections in 2009 that essentially reelected the same government officials and clerics already in power.

In 2011, Ebadi published *The Golden Cage: Three Brothers, Three Choices, One Destiny.* Set in Iran after the 1979 revolution, the novel follows three brothers, each of whom becomes committed to a certain political or religious philosophy. Developing themes similar to those she expressed in "The Contribution of Islam to a Global Ethic," the novel shows each of the brothers becoming rigid in his beliefs, leading to tragedies in their lives. Their sister, who is more compassionate and is involved in practical matters and daily struggles, emerges as the book's wisest character.

Did you know...

- Ebadi sued the U.S. government in 2004 because her book, *Iran Awakening: A Memoir of Revolution and Hope*, was not allowed to be published and distributed in the United States. Because of trade sanctions against Iran, the importation of items from Iran into the United States was prohibited.
- Ebadi's tireless defense of those accused of political crimes and her continued criticism of human rights violations resulted in many acts of intimidation against her and her family. In 2008, her documents and computer were confiscated during a raid of her office by government authorities; her home was vandalized by government supporters; and in 2009, her Nobel Prize medal was confiscated and her bank accounts were frozen by the Iranian government.
- Ebadi has written many books on law, covering such varied areas as medicine and construction and the rights of children and refugees.

Shirin Ebadi stands in front of a bookshelf in her basement law offices in Tehran, Iran, in 2009, where she has received death threats. Ebadi's activism has resulted in many acts of intimidation against her and her family. SCOTT PETERSON/GETTY IMAGES.

Consider the following...

- At the beginning of her lecture, Ebadi lists some differences among people around the world, but also notes common themes in myths and religions. Make a short list of things important to you and conduct some research into how these values are approached in two or three different religions.

- In her lecture, Ebadi states that cultural changes and changes of ethics require time. Consider some important changes in laws and ethics in U.S. history, such as the abolition of slavery or granting women the right to vote. Write an essay about why changes in laws often also require cultural changes, and why some take longer than others.

- Near the end of her lecture, Ebadi states, "One cannot take democracy as a pretext to attack a country. It is not possible to bring human rights to people with bombs. Nor is it acceptable to take the struggle against a dictatorship as an excuse to rob a nation of its resources." Given this point of view, what do you think her opinion is of the U.S. involvement in Iraq during the Persian Gulf War (1990–91) and the Iraq War (2003–11)?

For More Information

BOOKS

Ebadi, Shirin. *The Golden Cage: Three Brothers, Three Choices, One Destiny.* Carlsbad, CA: Kales Press, 2011.

Ebadi, Shirin, and Azadeh Moaveni. *Iran Awakening: A Memoir of Revolution and Hope.* New York: Random House, 2006.

Hubbard-Brown, Janet. *Shirin Ebadi: Champion for Human Rights in Iran.* New York: Chelsea House, 2007.

PERIODICALS

"An Iranian Family Torn Apart." *Times* (London; July 16, 2011): 22.

Khaleeli, Homa. "Top 100 Women: Activists and Campaigners." *The Guardian* (London; March 7, 2011): 18.

Kirpalani, Anita. "Shirin Ebadi: The Activist in Exile." *Newsweek International* (January 18, 2010).

Nordlinger, Jay. "Iran's Lawyer and Laureate: A Sit-down with Shirin Ebadi." *National Review* (June 6, 2011): 28.

"Who's Afraid of Shirin Ebadi?" *New York Times* (August 15, 2006). Available online at http://www.nytimes.com/2006/08/15/opinion/15iht-ediran.2491544.html (accessed on November 30, 2011).

WEB SITES

Ebadi, Shrin. "The Contribution of Islam to a Global Ethic." *Global Ethic Foundation* October 20, 2005). http://classic.weltethos.org/dat-english/00-lecture_5-ebadi.htm (accessed on November 30, 2011.

"Shirin Ebadi: Autobiography." *Nobel Prize.org.* http://www.nobelprize.org/nobel_prizes/peace/laureates/2003/ebadi-autobio.html (accessed November 30, 2011).

"Shirin Ebadi." *Oslo Freedom Forum.org* (May 9–10, 2011). http://www.oslofreedomforum.com/speakers/shirin_ebadi.html (accessed on November 30, 2011).

"Profile: Shirin Ebadi." *BBC News* (November 27, 2009). http://news.bbc.co.uk/2/hi/middle_east/3181992.stm (accessed on November 30, 2011).

Obama's Cairo Speech

Excerpt from President Barack Obama's Cairo Speech

Published in The New York Times

June 4, 2009

"America and Islam are not exclusive and need not be in competition. Instead, they overlap, and share common principles—principles of justice and progress; tolerance and the dignity of all human beings."

In June 2009, a few months after he was inaugurated as president of the United States, Barack Obama (1961–) delivered a highly anticipated speech in which he addressed the strained relations between the United States and many nations in the Middle East. The U.S. occupation (physical and political control of an area seized by a foreign military force) of Iraq and Afghanistan, ongoing conflict between Israel and the Palestinians, and Iran's growing nuclear capabilities were among the political and policy issues contributing to those strained relations. During his campaign for the presidency, Obama had promised to seek ways to relieve tension and suspicion between Americans and Muslims worldwide and to improve prospects for peace and cooperation.

Relations between Muslim nations and the United States and Israel, the closest U.S. ally in the Middle East, are characterized by distrust and sometimes violence. Attacks on the United States on September 11, 2001, by members of al-Qaeda, a terrorist group, were followed by U.S.-led wars in Afghanistan and Iraq. Even before those events, however, strained and sometimes hostile relations between the United States and Muslim nations had been occurring for decades. People around the world were interested in hearing how Obama's approach to the Middle East would be different than those of past U.S. presidents and how the

U.S. president Barack Obama delivers his landmark speech to the Muslim world at Cairo University in Egypt, on June 4, 2009. Obama titled his speech "A New Beginning." SAUL LOEB/AFP/GETTY IMAGES.

president would maintain deep U.S. ties with Israel while reaching out to Muslims. To emphasize his different approach, Obama called his speech "A New Beginning."

In the speech, Obama sets a friendly and personal tone from the outset. He extends a greeting of peace and goodwill from Americans, including Muslims and other people of Middle Eastern heritage who live in the United States. He announces that he has come to seek a new beginning and intends to emphasize common principles shared by Americans and Muslims, those living in the United States and elsewhere around the world, and he refers to his personal heritage, noting that he is Christian but his father, who came from Kenya, was from a family that included generations of Muslims. He is careful to emphasize that both Americans and people living in Muslim countries are at fault for problems between them.

Obama made his speech in Cairo, Egypt. The event was hosted by two universities: al-Azhar, which is over one thousand years old and steeped in Muslim traditions, and Cairo University, a modern college founded one century ago. Obama's speech was broadcast live and translated throughout the Middle East.

Things to remember while reading the excerpt from President Barack Obama's Cairo Speech:

- The speech refers to the "Road Map" for peace, which is a phased plan with many provisions intended to move Israel and the Palestinians towards a resolution that includes the creation of a Palestinian state and an end to violence. (Palestinians are an Arab people whose ancestors lived in the historical region of Palestine, comprising parts of present-day Israel and Jordan, and who continue to lay claim to that land.) Specifically, the Roadmap called for an end to violence between Israel and the Palestinians, the creation of a Palestinian constitution, the withdrawal of Israelis from the occupied territories (lands under the political and military control of Israel), and commitment on both sides to a two-state solution. The Roadmap was created by mediators from the United States, the European Union, Russia, and the United Nations, and it was formally announced by President George W. Bush (1946–) in 2003. In the month prior to delivering the Cairo speech, Obama met with Israeli president Shimon Peres (1923–) and Prime Minister Benjamin Netanyahu (1949–), as well as Palestinian Authority president Mahmoud Abbas (1935–), to discuss progress in the ongoing conflict.

- Obama does not use the term "terrorism" in his speech. He refers to violence inflicted on innocent human beings as a result of extremism and notes that the Koran (also spelled Qur'an or Quran; the holy book of Islam) regards violence against the innocent as violence against all humanity.

- White House press secretary Robert Gibbs (1971–) told reporters in a May 2009 White House press briefing that Obama chose to deliver the speech in Egypt because "it is a country that in many ways represents the heart of the Arab world." Indeed, nearly 79 million Muslims live in Egypt, and the nation has long been a critical player in ongoing peace talks in the region. Furthermore, in contrast to many other Muslim nations, the United States has maintained generally strong diplomatic ties with Egypt based on shared security and economic interests.

• • •

President Barack Obama's Cairo Speech

. . . We meet at a time of tension between the United States and Muslims around the world—tension rooted in historical forces that go beyond any current policy debate. The relationship between Islam and the West includes centuries of co-existence and cooperation, but also conflict and religious wars. More recently, tension has been fed by **colonialism** that denied rights and opportunities to many Muslims, and a **Cold War** in which Muslim-majority countries were too often treated as **proxies** without regard to their own aspirations. Moreover, the sweeping change brought by modernity and globalization led many Muslims to view the West as hostile to the traditions of Islam.

Violent extremists have exploited these tensions in a small but potent minority of Muslims. The attacks of September 11th, 2001 and the continued efforts of these extremists to engage in violence against civilians has led some in my country to view Islam as inevitably hostile not only to America and Western countries, but also to human rights. This has bred more fear and mistrust.

So long as our relationship is defined by our differences, we will empower those who **sow** hatred rather than peace, and who promote conflict rather than the cooperation that can help all of our people achieve justice and prosperity. This cycle of suspicion and discord must end.

I have come here to seek a new beginning between the United States and Muslims around the world; one based upon mutual interest and mutual respect; and one based upon the truth that America and Islam are not exclusive, and need not be in competition. Instead, they overlap, and share common principles—principles of justice and progress; tolerance and the dignity of all human beings. . . .

Part of this conviction is rooted in my own experience. I am a Christian, but my father came from a Kenyan family that includes generations of Muslims. As a boy, I spent several years in Indonesia and heard the call of the **azaan** at the break of dawn and the fall of dusk. As a young man, I worked

Colonalism: The establishment of colonies in one territory by people from another nation as a means of expanding that nation's power.

Cold War: A period of intense political and economic rivalry between the United States and the Soviet Union that lasted from 1945 to 1991.

Proxies: Substitutes or representatives.

Sow: Plant.

Azaan: Muslim prayer.

in Chicago communities where many found dignity and peace in their Muslim faith.

As a student of history, I also know civilization's debt to Islam. It was Islam—at places like Al-Azhar University—that carried the light of learning through so many centuries, paving the way for Europe's **Renaissance** and **Enlightenment**. It was innovation in Muslim communities that developed the order of algebra; our magnetic compass and tools of navigation; our mastery of pens and printing; our understanding of how disease spreads and how it can be healed. Islamic culture has given us majestic arches and soaring spires; timeless poetry and cherished music; elegant calligraphy and places of peaceful contemplation. And throughout history, Islam has demonstrated through words and deeds the possibilities of religious tolerance and racial equality.

I know, too, that Islam has always been a part of America's story. The first nation to recognize my country was Morocco. In signing the Treaty of Tripoli in 1796, our second President John Adams wrote, "The United States has in itself no character of **enmity** against the laws, religion or tranquility of Muslims." And since our founding, American Muslims have enriched the United States. They have fought in our wars, served in government, stood for civil rights, started businesses, taught at our Universities, excelled in our sports arenas, won Nobel Prizes, built our tallest building, and lit the Olympic Torch. And when the first Muslim-American was recently elected to Congress, he took the oath to defend our Constitution using the same Holy **Koran** that one of our Founding Fathers—Thomas Jefferson—kept in his personal library.

So I have known Islam on three continents before coming to the region where it was first revealed. That experience guides my conviction that partnership between America and Islam must be based on what Islam is, not what it isn't. And I consider it part of my responsibility as President of the United States to fight against negative stereotypes of Islam wherever they appear.

But that same principle must apply to Muslim perceptions of America. Just as Muslims do not fit a crude stereotype, America is not the crude stereotype of a self-interested empire. The United States has been one of the greatest sources of progress that the world has ever known. We were born out of revolution against an empire. We were founded upon the ideal that all are created equal, and we have shed blood and struggled for centuries to give meaning to those words—within our borders, and around the world. We are shaped by every culture, drawn from every end of the Earth, and dedicated to a simple concept: E pluribus unum: "Out of many, one." . . .

That does not mean we should ignore sources of tension. Indeed, it suggests the opposite: we must face these tensions squarely. And so in that spirit, let me speak as clearly and plainly as I can about some specific issues that I believe we must finally confront together.

Renaissance: A rebirth of learning and culture that blossomed in fourteenth-century Italy and spread across Europe through the seventeenth century.

Enlightenment: Known as the Age of Reason, the eighteenth-century European cultural movement that stressed intellectual inquiry and valued reason over emotion.

Enmity: Hostility.

Koran: Also spelled Qur'an or Quran; the holy book of Islam.

The first issue that we have to confront is violent extremism in all of its forms.

In **Ankara**, I made clear that America is not—and never will be—at war with Islam. We will, however, relentlessly confront violent extremists who pose a grave threat to our security. Because we reject the same thing that people of all faiths reject: the killing of innocent men, women, and children. And it is my first duty as President to protect the American people.

The situation in Afghanistan demonstrates America's goals, and our need to work together. Over seven years ago, the United States pursued al Qaeda and the **Taliban** with broad international support. We did not go by choice, we went because of necessity. I am aware that some question or justify the events of 9/11. But let us be clear: al Qaeda killed nearly 3,000 people on that day. The victims were innocent men, women and children from America and many other nations who had done nothing to harm anybody. And yet Al Qaeda chose to ruthlessly murder these people, claimed credit for the attack, and even now states their determination to kill on a massive scale. They have affiliates in many countries and are trying to expand their reach. These are not opinions to be debated; these are facts to be dealt with.

Make no mistake: we do not want to keep our troops in Afghanistan. We seek no military bases there. It is agonizing for America to lose our young men and women. It is costly and politically difficult to continue this conflict. We would gladly bring every single one of our troops home if we could be confident that there were not violent extremists in Afghanistan and Pakistan determined to kill as many Americans as they possibly can. But that is not yet the case.

That's why we're partnering with a coalition **coalition** of forty-six countries. And despite the costs involved, America's commitment will not weaken. Indeed, none of us should tolerate these extremists. They have killed in many countries. They have killed people of different faiths—more than any other, they have killed Muslims. Their actions are **irreconcilable** with the rights of human beings, the progress of nations, and with Islam. The Holy Koran teaches that whoever kills an innocent, it is as if he has killed all mankind; and whoever saves a person, it is as if he has saved all mankind. The enduring faith of over a billion people is so much bigger than the narrow hatred of a few. Islam is not part of the problem in combating violent extremism—it is an important part of promoting peace.

We also know that military power alone is not going to solve the problems in Afghanistan and Pakistan. That is why we plan to invest $1.5 billion each year over the next five years to partner with Pakistanis to build schools and hospitals, roads and businesses, and hundreds of millions to help those who have been displaced. And that is why we are providing more than $2.8 billion to help Afghans develop their economy and deliver services that people depend upon.

Ankara: The capital city of Turkey. Obama addressed the Turkish parliament (legislature) there in April 2009.

Taliban: An Islamist militant group that controlled Afghanistan from 1996 to 2001.

Coalition: Alliance.

Irreconcilable: Unable to bring into harmony with; incompatible with.

Let me also address the issue of Iraq. Unlike Afghanistan, Iraq was a war of choice that provoked strong differences in my country and around the world. Although I believe that the Iraqi people are ultimately better off without the tyranny of Saddam Hussein, I also believe that events in Iraq have reminded America of the need to use diplomacy and build international consensus to resolve our problems whenever possible. Indeed, we can recall the words of Thomas Jefferson, who said: "I hope that our wisdom will grow with our power, and teach us that the less we use our power the greater it will be."

Today, America has a dual responsibility: to help Iraq forge a better future—and to leave Iraq to Iraqis. I have made it clear to the Iraqi people that we pursue no bases, and no claim on their territory or resources. Iraq's **sovereignty** is its own. That is why I ordered the removal of our combat brigades by next August. That is why we will honor our agreement with Iraq's democratically-elected government to remove combat troops from Iraqi cities by July, and to remove all our troops from Iraq by 2012. We will help Iraq train its Security Forces and develop its economy. But we will support a secure and united Iraq as a partner, and never as a **patron**.

And finally, just as America can never tolerate violence by extremists, we must never alter our principles. 9/11 was an enormous trauma to our country. The fear and anger that it provoked was understandable, but in some cases, it led us to act contrary to our ideals. We are taking concrete actions to change course. I have **unequivocally** prohibited the use of torture by the United States, and I have ordered the prison at **Guantanamo Bay** closed by early next year.

So America will defend itself respectful of the sovereignty of nations and the rule of law. And we will do so in partnership with Muslim communities which are also threatened. The sooner the extremists are isolated and unwelcome in Muslim communities, the sooner we will all be safer.

The second major source of tension that we need to discuss is the situation between Israelis, Palestinians and the Arab world.

America's strong bonds with Israel are well known. This bond is unbreakable. It is based upon cultural and historical ties, and the recognition that the aspiration for a Jewish homeland is rooted in a tragic history that cannot be denied.

Around the world, the Jewish people were persecuted for centuries, and **anti-Semitism** in Europe culminated in an **unprecedented Holocaust**. Tomorrow, I will visit Buchenwald, which was part of a network of camps where Jews were enslaved, tortured, shot and gassed to death by the Third Reich. Six million Jews were killed—more than the entire Jewish population of Israel today. Denying that fact is baseless, ignorant, and hateful. Threatening Israel with destruction—or repeating vile stereotypes about Jews—is deeply wrong, and only serves to evoke in the minds of Israelis this most painful of memories while preventing the peace that the people of this region deserve.

Sovereignty: State of self-government or independence.

Patron: One with more power who provides support with money or influence to one who is less powerful.

Unequivocally: Absolutely and totally.

Guantanamo Bay: A bay on the southeastern coast of Cuba that is the site of a U.S. naval base and detention facility where suspected members of al-Qaeda and the Taliban are held.

Anti-Semitism: Prejudice against Jews.

Unprecedented: Never before seen or experienced.

Holocaust: The mass murder of European Jews and other groups by the Nazis during World War II (1939–45).

The World Trade Center on fire after the September 11, 2001, terrorist attack on New York City. Barack Obama mentioned the attacks in his Cairo speech, noting that "9/11 was an enormous trauma to our country." © RICHARD LEVINE/ALAMY.

On the other hand, it is also undeniable that the Palestinian people—Muslims and Christians—have suffered in pursuit of a homeland. For more than sixty years they have endured the pain of dislocation. Many wait in refugee camps in the West Bank, Gaza, and neighboring lands for a life of peace and security that they have never been able to lead. They endure the daily humiliations—large and small—that come with occupation. So let there be no doubt: the situation for the Palestinian people is intolerable. America will not turn our backs on the legitimate Palestinian aspiration for dignity, opportunity, and a state of their own.

For decades, there has been a **stalemate**: two peoples with legitimate aspirations, each with a painful history that makes compromise **elusive**. It is easy to point fingers—for Palestinians to point to the displacement brought by Israel's founding, and for Israelis to point to the constant hostility and attacks throughout its history from within its borders as well as beyond. But if we see this conflict only from one side or the other, then we will be blind to

Stalemate: A situation in which no progress can be made.

Elusive: Unable to be achieved.

the truth: the only resolution is for the **aspirations** of both sides to be met through two states, where Israelis and Palestinians each live in peace and security.

That is in Israel's interest, Palestine's interest, America's interest, and the world's interest. That is why I intend to personally pursue this outcome with all the patience that the task requires. The obligations that the parties have agreed to under the **Road Map** are clear. For peace to come, it is time for them—and all of us—to live up to our responsibilities.

Palestinians must abandon violence. Resistance through violence and killing is wrong and does not succeed. For centuries, black people in America suffered the lash of the whip as slaves and the humiliation of segregation. But it was not violence that won full and equal rights. It was a peaceful and determined insistence upon the ideals at the center of America's founding. This same story can be told by people from South Africa to South Asia; from Eastern Europe to Indonesia. It's a story with a simple truth: that violence is a dead end. It is a sign of neither courage nor power to shoot rockets at sleeping children, or to blow up old women on a bus. That is not how moral authority is claimed; that is how it is surrendered.

Now is the time for Palestinians to focus on what they can build. The Palestinian Authority must develop its capacity to govern, with institutions that serve the needs of its people. **Hamas** does have support among some Palestinians, but they also have responsibilities. To play a role in fulfilling Palestinian aspirations, and to unify the Palestinian people, Hamas must put an end to violence, recognize past agreements, and recognize Israel's right to exist.

At the same time, Israelis must acknowledge that just as Israel's right to exist cannot be denied, neither can Palestine's. The United States does not accept the legitimacy of continued Israeli **settlements**. This construction violates previous agreements and undermines efforts to achieve peace. It is time for these settlements to stop.

Israel must also live up to its obligations to ensure that Palestinians can live, and work, and develop their society. And just as it devastates Palestinian families, the continuing humanitarian crisis in Gaza does not serve Israel's security; neither does the continuing lack of opportunity in the West Bank. Progress in the daily lives of the Palestinian people must be part of a road to peace, and Israel must take concrete steps to enable such progress.

Finally, the Arab States must recognize that the **Arab Peace Initiative** was an important beginning, but not the end of their responsibilities. The Arab-Israeli conflict should no longer be used to distract the people of Arab nations from other problems. Instead, it must be a cause for action to help the Palestinian people develop the institutions that will sustain their state; to recognize Israel's legitimacy; and to choose progress over a self-defeating focus on the past.

Aspirations: Goals.

Road Map: A political plan to implement a lasting peace between Israelis and Palestinians.

Hamas: A Palestinian Islamic fundamentalist group and political party operating primarily in the Gaza Strip and West Bank with the goal of establishing a Palestinian state and opposing the existence of Israel.

Settlements: Communites established and inhabited in order to claim land.

Arab Peace Initiative: A plan introduced in 2002 to end the Arab-Israeli conflict.

America will align our policies with those who pursue peace, and say in public what we say in private to Israelis and Palestinians and Arabs. We cannot impose peace. But privately, many Muslims recognize that Israel will not go away. Likewise, many Israelis recognize the need for a Palestinian state. It is time for us to act on what everyone knows to be true.

Too many tears have flowed. Too much blood has been shed. All of us have a responsibility to work for the day when the mothers of Israelis and Palestinians can see their children grow up without fear; when the Holy Land of three great faiths is the place of peace that God intended it to be; when Jerusalem is a secure and lasting home for Jews and Christians and Muslims, and a place for all of the children of Abraham to mingle peacefully together as in the story of Isra, when Moses, Jesus, and Mohammed (peace be upon them) joined in prayer.

The third source of tension is our shared interest in the rights and responsibilities of nations on nuclear weapons.

This issue has been a source of tension between the United States and the Islamic Republic of Iran. For many years, Iran has defined itself in part by its opposition to my country, and there is indeed a **tumultuous** history between us. In the middle of the Cold War, the United States played a role in the overthrow of a democratically-elected Iranian government. Since the **Islamic Revolution**, Iran has played a role in acts of hostage-taking and violence against U.S. troops and civilians. This history is well known. Rather than remain trapped in the past, I have made it clear to Iran's leaders and people that my country is prepared to move forward. The question, now, is not what Iran is against, but rather what future it wants to build.

It will be hard to overcome decades of mistrust, but we will proceed with courage, **rectitude** and resolve. There will be many issues to discuss between our two countries, and we are willing to move forward without preconditions on the basis of mutual respect. But it is clear to all concerned that when it comes to nuclear weapons, we have reached a decisive point. This is not simply about America's interests. It is about preventing a nuclear arms race in the Middle East that could lead this region and the world down a hugely dangerous path.

I understand those who protest that some countries have weapons that others do not. No single nation should pick and choose which nations hold nuclear weapons. That is why I strongly reaffirmed America's commitment to seek a world in which no nations hold nuclear weapons. And any nation—including Iran—should have the right to access peaceful nuclear power if it complies with its responsibilities under the nuclear **Non-Proliferation Treaty**. That commitment is at the core of the Treaty, and it must be kept for all who fully abide by it. And I am hopeful that all countries in the region can share in this goal.

The fourth issue that I will address is democracy.

I know there has been controversy about the promotion of democracy in recent years, and much of this controversy is connected to the war in Iraq.

Tumultuous: Marked by violence or disorder.

Islamic Revolution: Uprising in Iran in 1979 that led to the overthrow of the monarchy and the establishment of an Islamic republic in that nation.

Rectitude: Moral rightness.

Non-Proliferation Treaty: International treaty originally signed in 1970 to limit the spread of nuclear weapons.

So let me be clear: no system of government can or should be imposed upon one nation by any other.

That does not lessen my commitment, however, to governments that reflect the will of the people. Each nation gives life to this principle in its own way, grounded in the traditions of its own people. America does not presume to know what is best for everyone, just as we would not presume to pick the outcome of a peaceful election. But I do have an unyielding belief that all people yearn for certain things: the ability to speak your mind and have a say in how you are governed; confidence in the rule of law and the equal administration of justice; government that is transparent and doesn't steal from the people; the freedom to live as you choose. Those are not just American ideas, they are human rights, and that is why we will support them everywhere. . . .

• • •

What happened next . . .

Obama's speech was generally well received. Although he introduced no new policies, many people who listened to the speech in the audience or by broadcast were encouraged by his positive tone and his emphasis on shared principles, instead of differences, between America and Muslim nations. The speech contributed to Obama being awarded the prestigious Nobel Peace Prize later in 2009. In the Nobel Prize press release issued when the award was announced, the selection committee said that it honored Obama for what it called his "extraordinary efforts to strengthen international diplomacy and cooperation between peoples." Those were the main goals of his Cairo speech.

Similarly, another important theme of the speech—the promise of democracy as a means for expanding and protecting human rights—indirectly played out in real events. During the spring of 2011, a series of prodemocracy uprisings spread throughout the Middle East and North Africa. Dubbed the Arab Spring, the first successful revolt was in Cairo, the capital city of Egypt and site of the Obama's speech. Syria and Libya were among other predominantly Muslim nations where people began protesting for democratic reforms and more freedom.

Yet, the Middle East continues to be a hotbed of tension and violence. While Israel and the Palestinian Authority (the recognized governing institution for Palestinians in the West Bank and the Gaza Strip) continue to negotiate terms of peace and recognition, the cycle of violent attacks and retaliation has yet to be broken. Iran continues to build a nuclear energy

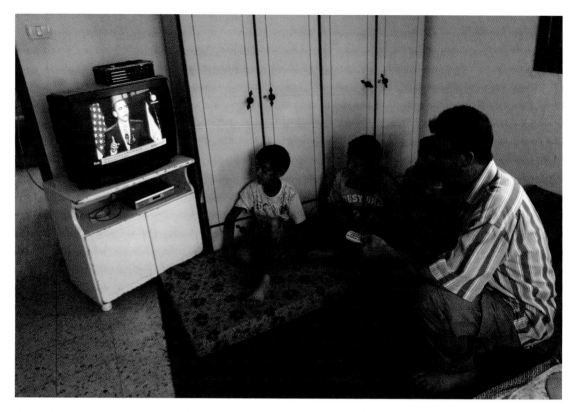

A Palestinian family watches from their home in the Gaza Strip as U.S. president Barack Obama delivers his Cairo speech. Many people who listened to the speech were encouraged by Obama's positive tone and his emphasis on shared principles. SAID KHATIB/ AFP/GETTY IMAGES.

program despite objections from the United States and the United Nations, which suspect that Iran is pursuing the development of nuclear weapons. Although Iran has repeatedly insisted that its nuclear program will be used for peaceful purposes, it conducted tests of medium- and long-range missiles in 2009, much to the concern of other nations. Mistrust and tension among nations and Christians, Jews, and Muslims persist in modern times, as they have for centuries, only now on a global scale.

Did you know...

- Within his Cairo speech, Obama used phrases from the great books of the three major religions associated with the Middle East, quoting from the Koran, the Talmud (the authoritative, ancient body of Jewish teachings and tradition), and the Bible.

- The Cairo speech followed other efforts by Obama to reach out to Muslims, including visits to Turkey and Iraq. After the speech, Obama traveled to France and Germany, and he toured Buchenwald, one of many concentration camps where Jewish people were systematically killed during World War II (1939–45).
- Some critics objected to Obama delivering his speech in Egypt, where the government was known to crack down on political opposition. After the protests and revolution in Egypt less than two years, later, Obama gave what some called his second Cairo speech. In that second speech he called for the resignation of Egyptian president Hosni Mubarak (1928–).

Consider the following...

- Some commentators assessed Obama's speech as being positive in tone, but they criticized it for not providing specific policies and actions. Do you think that speeches by political leaders can provide enough inspiration to motivate change if they are not accompanied by new rules and guidelines? Explain why or why not.
- Before the speech, Obama met with Egyptian president Hosni Mubarak. The two leaders discussed two of the tensions Obama addressed in his speech: the ongoing conflict and prospects for peace between Israel and the Palestinians and Iran's nuclear goals. Mubarak was widely criticized for suppressing human rights in his own country. Why would a U.S. president choose to have political discussions with leaders known to compromise the ideals of democracy?
- Research Egypt's role in conflict and peace in the Middle East and the history of its relationship with the United States. Write an essay explaining why Obama chose Cairo as the location to deliver "A New Beginning," as opposed to another Middle Eastern nation or the White House.
- Obama gave his speech the hopeful title of "A New Beginning." Do you think the speech indeed marked a fresh start in improving relations between the United States and the Muslim world? Why or why not?

For More Information

PERIODICALS

DeAtkine, Norvell B. "President Obama's Pitch to the Muslim World: Public Diplomacy or Policy?" *American Diplomacy* (June 23, 2009).

Fallows, James. "Belatedly, on the Cairo Speech and Obama Rhetoric in General." *The Atlantic* (June 15, 2009). Available online at http://www.theatlantic.com/technology/archive/2009/06/belatedly-on-the-cairo-speech-obama-rhetoric-in-general/18770 (accessed on November 30, 2011).

Packer, George. "Rights and Wrongs." *The New Yorker* (May 2010): 35.

"Religious Leaders Praise Obama Speech." *America* (June 2009): 8.

"Text: Obama's Speech in Cairo." *The New York Times* (June 4, 2009). Available online at http://www.nytimes.com/2009/06/04/us/politics/04obama.text.html (accessed on November 30, 2011).

WEB SITES

Gibbs, Robert. "Press Briefing by Press Secretary Robert Gibbs." The White House (May 8, 2009). http://www.whitehouse.gov/the_press_office/Briefing-by-White-House-Press-Secretary-Robert-Gibbs-5-8-09/ (accessed on November 30, 2011).

"The Nobel Peace Prize 2009 Press Release." Nobelprize.org (October 9, 2009). http://www.nobelprize.org/nobel_prizes/peace/laureates/2009/press.html (accessed on November 30, 2011).

"Reaction to President Obama's Cairo Speech." *PBS NewsHour* (June 4, 2009). http://www.pbs.org/newshour/updates/middle_east/jan-june09/reaction_0604.html (accessed on November 30, 2011).

Personal Accounts of Middle East Conflict

M any people who do not live in the Middle East learn about the conflicts that have disrupted life in that region over the last century through news reports. They rely on newspapers, magazines, and television to explain what is happening. News about the Middle East tends to focus on the big picture. It reports on opposing claims to land; on sharia (Islamic religious law) in government and secular (nonreligious) laws in government; on tensions between people who hold conservative Islamic values and those who hold liberal ones; on conflicts between people who want to be independent of western influence and those who promote changes brought by Western practices; and on the hatred many Arabs have toward the West because of its long history of involvement in Middle Eastern affairs. Mostly these news reports focus on groups rather than ordinary individuals. They describe troop movements, bombings, and responses by political leaders. The news rarely describes what individuals face on a daily basis.

However, to those people who live in the Middle East, have relatives in Middle Eastern countries, or have recently visited the region, these conflicts are not merely stories in a newspaper or on the evening news. They are daily events that shape and change lives in dramatic ways. To a Palestinian living in a village in Israeli-occupied territory, these conflicts are personal encounters with soldiers in the area or security officials at a checkpoint on the road to a neighbor's house. To an Israeli mother whose son has gone off to serve his required time in the army, each newscast is a chance to understand what her son may be experiencing. To a journalist or aid worker taken hostage by Islamic fundamentalists (people who stress adherence to a strict or literal interpretation of religious principles), the conflicts are not global but personal. That imprisoned person faces the real threat of not being able to go home again.

In this chapter, the conflict in the Middle East is presented through the personal narratives of several different people who have experienced it

A Palestinian boy talks to Israeli soldiers in Hebron. To the people who live in the Middle East, the conflicts of the region are daily events that shape and change lives in dramatic ways. © PETER TURNLEY/CORBIS.

firsthand. Some of these people try to carry out violent acts in response to events in the Middle East. Soha Bechara (1967–) is a Christian Lebanese woman who was imprisoned for her attempted assassination of a military leader in Lebanon. Era Rapaport (1945–) is an Israeli settler jailed for helping to plant a bomb under the vehicle of a Palestinian town mayor. Others turned to political means to make a personal impact on the Middle East conflict. Meir Kahane (1932–1990) was an American-born Jew whose belief in Zionism (an international political movement that called for the creation of an independent Jewish state in Palestine) brought him to Israel. There he became convinced of the necessity for a radical solution to the Arab-Israeli conflict. His solution got him elected to the Israeli Knesset (legislature) and then thrown into an Israeli prison. Sumaya Farhat-Naser (1948–) is a Palestinian activist whose efforts to bring about peace were frustrated by Israeli occupation (the physical and political control of an area seized by a foreign military force). Still others were drawn into the conflict in the Middle East as participants in the larger events that have torn the region apart. Terry Anderson (1947–) is an American journalist who was held hostage in Lebanon for more than six years by an Iranian-supported Islamic terrorist group. Manal M. Omar (1975–) is a Saudi-born American who traveled to Iraq in 2003 to help women whose relatively progressive lifestyles (by Middle Eastern standards) were torn apart by war and the fallout of U.S. occupation of their country. It is through these accounts that the true personal impacts of the various conflicts in the Middle East can be seen.

Resistance

Excerpt from *Resistance: My Life for Lebanon*

Written by Soha Bechara

Printed in 2003

"Inevitably, I would be arrested. But what would they do to me? Torture me? Execute me on the spot?"

Born in Lebanon on June 15, 1967, Soha Bechara remembered her childhood as happy and peaceful, filled with playtime with her cousins and village-wide festivals and celebrations. In her memoir, *Resistance: My Life for Lebanon*, Bechara describes her village of Deir Mimas as "like paradise to me." By the time Bechara was a teenager, however, her sense of the situation had changed. From the early 1970s, Bechara was increasingly aware of the troubles that plagued her country.

Jews began immigrating to Palestine in the nineteenth century with the goal of establishing a Jewish state there, in the land that had been home to an ancient Jewish kingdom. Unfortunately, the region was already home to Arabs (people who speak the Arab language) who had lived there for hundreds of years. (Palestine is a historical region in the Middle East on the eastern shore of the Mediterranean Sea, comprising parts of present-day Israel and Jordan.) Thus, when Jews declared the establishment of the state of Israel in Palestine in 1948, neighboring Arab countries attacked Israel in an attempt to take back the land which they believed had been stolen from Arab Palestinians. Israel emerged victorious from the 1948 Arab-Israeli War, and thousands of Arab Palestinians became refugees, people who flee their country to escape violence or persecution. Many Palestinian refugees fled to Lebanon, among other countries.

Soha Bechara, author of
Resistance: My Life for
Lebanon. © ERIC FOUGERE/
SYGMA/CORBIS.

Palestinians continued to press their claim to the former territory of
Palestine. Palestinian refugees and the Palestine Liberation Organization
(PLO) were involved in cross-border attacks into Israel both before
and after PLO headquarters were established in Lebanon in 1971.

(The PLO is a political and military organization formed to unite various Palestinian Arab groups with the goal of establishing an independent Palestinian state.) Palestinian raids into Israel from southern Lebanon brought counterattacks by Israeli planes dropping bombs near Bechara's hometown.

Bechara also experienced firsthand the political differences among the Lebanese people that led to a civil war in 1975. The Lebanese government was sectarian, meaning that the various religious sects (groups) were represented based on the proportion of the population each sect claimed. The majority of the power was held by Christians, but by 1970 Muslims were an estimated 60 percent of the total population. Soon both Christian and Muslim groups formed their own militias, or armed civilian military forces. These militias lead Lebanon into a civil war that would last from 1975 to 1990. During the war Bechara's family was forced to travel back and forth between their village and shelters in Beirut. "We were refugees in our own city," she recalls in *Resistance: My Life for Lebanon*. By 1976, "the daily reality was war."

In 1978 Israeli troops invaded southern Lebanon in an attempt to secure its borders from Palestinian attacks and remove the PLO from Lebanon. Israel briefly occupied a portion of Lebanon that included Bechara's childhood village. (Occupation is the physical and political control of an area seized by a foreign military force.) By now Bechara had already become accustomed to war. In 1982 Israeli planes dropped leaflets on Beirut advising people to flee, because the Israelis were about to invade Lebanon once again. Despite the warnings in the leaflets Bechara decided to stay. In time she became politically active. She volunteered at Red Cross clinics and joined the Communist Party. (Communism is a system of government in which the state plans and controls the economy and a single political party holds power.)

A sense of devotion to the interest and culture of Lebanon blossomed in her. "I could not stop thinking about Israel and my duty as a Lebanese," she wrote in *Resistance*, recalling her experiences in the early 1980s. She was humiliated and angered by Israel's occupation of her homeland. Eventually, her nationalist beliefs culminated in her desire to do "anything" for her country. The following excerpt from Bechara's memoir, *Resistance: My Life for Lebanon*, describes her decision to become an assassin, as well as her terrible experiences in prison.

A Lebanese woman fighter during the Battle of Beirut in 1975. Many Lebanese women, like Soha Bechara, fought to free portions of Lebanon from Israeli control. © ALAIN DEJEAN/SYGMA/CORBIS.

Things to remember while reading the excerpt from *Resistance: My Life for Lebanon*:

- The resistance movement to which Bechara refers throughout her memoirs was a group of militant political activists who attempted to oust Israel from Lebanon throughout the late 1970s and 1980s.

Israel invaded Lebanon in 1978 and again in 1982. Israeli forces occupied parts of southern Lebanon from 1982 until 2000.

- The South Lebanon Army (SLA) was a militia, or armed civilian military force, that served as an Israeli ally in Lebanon. The SLA sometimes worked with the Israeli Defense Forces (IDF), Israel's army.
- Rabih was the only name by which Soha Bechara knew her superior in the resistance movement. She met him in 1986, and he was her main contact with the resistance movement as she prepared for and attempted the assassination of the SLA leader Antoine Lahad (1927–) in 1988.
- Bechara had earned the trust of Lahad by working as an aerobics instructor for his wife Minerva. The position enabled her to enter the Lahad household as a guest and offered her the opportunity to spend time alone with the Lahads.
- Issam is the name of Soha Bechara's cousin, with whom she lived in Marjayoun, in the area occupied by Israelis in southern Lebanon. Issam had no idea of his cousin's activities for the resistance movement prior to her imprisonment.
- On November 7, 1988, Bechara was arrested by the SLA, and, after being interrogated in Israel, she was sent to Khiam prison in southern Lebanon without being officially charged or put on trial for her attempted assassination of SLA chief Antoine Lahad.

• • •

Resistance: My Life for Lebanon
Chapter 8: The Operation

I met again with my contact at the heart of the resistance.

Rabih listened as I told him about my first interview with Antoine Lahad. Right away, he made it clear that we would have to plan for me to be replaced by someone whose job it would be to eliminate the militia chief. I answered that, considering the circumstances, I myself was in the best position to succeed. Rabih was not very taken with this idea. He admitted its efficiency, but he seriously doubted that I was capable of carrying out the operation. But faced with my stubbornness, he resigned himself to taking the risk. There was still the question of the weapon. . . .

Time was short, so Rabih and I decided to meet in a discreet spot, a café where couples often went on dates. That day, he secretly brought with him a 5.5 mm revolver. In a few words he told me how it worked, pointing out the safety catch. . . .

I took my role of aerobics instructor very seriously. Little by little, I became quite close to Minerva. . . . So I found myself going again and again to her house, either to bring her videocassettes or to work out problems with the classes. When she was busy or indisposed and I had to wait, I would play with her little son, whose affection I easily gained.

Step by step, I fine-tuned my plan. . . .

Wearing a white shirt, blue pants, and black ballet slippers, I made it once again without difficulty into the couple's beautiful house. I had been dropped off by Issam, who, to kill time, liked to join the nightly **cavalcade** of cars that filled the streets of Marjayoun. Before leaving, I had taken the revolver from its **cache** and hid it among a few other little things in my purse. The SLA chief's bodyguards let me pass without suspicion.

The usual routine.

I found Minerva in the garden with a Spanish friend. We moved inside, where we met her friend's husband, César, the director of a television station. Later, Antoine Lahad joined us. The atmosphere was pleasant. We spoke in French. Minerva lamented once again the small-mindedness of people in the **occupied zone**. We moved into the living room. The militia chief sat down near the telephone, with me to his right, as I had imagined. The conversation **idled** along. I kept myself a bit behind it all.

I listened.

After a half-hour, our hostess asked us what we'd like to drink. I murmured my thanks, but said that it was late and I had to go. Her husband insisted, and I made as if I was staying out of politeness. The militia chief turned on the television. It was the nightly news, on the station of the occupied zone. There was a report on the **Intifada**. On the screen, I had time to see a young Palestinian throwing a stone. Antoine Lahad watched distractedly, playing with the remote control. Suddenly, the telephone rang. He picked it up. His face darkened. Whoever he was talking to was obviously bringing up an unpleasant subject.

I stole a glance at the living room clock.

It was nearly eight. Sitting to my left, Antoine Lahad continued his conversation. His gaze rested on me for a moment. He examined me, as if curious. I drew towards me the bag lying at my feet. I was extraordinarily calm. I slid my hand into the opening, telling Minerva that I had brought the keys and videotapes she wanted. My hand, hidden from sight, closed on the handle of the gun. Still sitting, I took the weapon from the bag like it was the most natural thing in the world. Instantly, I pointed it towards the militia chief, supporting my fist with my left hand.

I struggled to aim at the **condemned** man's heart.

I pulled the trigger once and thought I saw the bullet bury itself in his khaki shirt. Antoine Lahad, taken aback, shot to his feet, as Rabih had predicted. An insult sprang from his lips . . . . I fired a second time, as planned.

Cavalcade: Procession of vehicles.

Cache: Hiding place.

Occupied zone: The part of Lebanon occupied by Israeli troops.

Idle: Went slowly.

Intifada: The Palestinian uprising against Israeli occupation in the West Bank and the Gaza Strip.

Condemned: Doomed.

He staggered.

For a second, life in the living room froze. Minerva, lying on the ground, let out a scream, shattering the silence. She cried for a gun to settle me and a helicopter to evacuate her husband. I threw a sweeping glance around me. The Spanish woman, her face ashen, looked at me fixedly, like a madwoman. Her husband, paralyzed with terror, was staring at me like he would be next. I took the chance to throw the gun into the bedroom off the living room, trying to gain a little time. The bodyguards would look for the weapon as soon as they burst into the room, which would be soon enough. Six feet away from me, the militiaman's body had rolled to the floor and lay there, motionless.

Chapter 9: The Arrest

It was done. I had completed my mission.

What would happen to me now?

I had asked myself the question a thousand times since deciding to carry out the operation, and I had never found an answer. We had made no plans for me to escape, or for someone to rescue me. It would have been too dangerous. Antoine Lahad's house was like a fortified camp. I had been able to enter an hour earlier, fooling the guards one last time, then fire on the leader of Israel's **proxy** militia. But now the two shots had sounded the alert.

Inevitably, I would be arrested. But what would they do with me? Torture me? Execute me on the spot? . . .

Chapter 10: Khiam

Khiam, or hell with no name, with no existence.

The Khiam prison, set up in an old military installation, was created in 1985. . . . Khiam sat on a **promontory** that was strategically important for the occupied zone. It was far from any fighting, quite close to Israel, and difficult to access. Officially, the SLA was responsible for the prison, although the Israelis had managed it directly when it was created and then gradually shifted the interrogation work to Lebanese **mercenaries**. Shin Bet, the Israeli internal security agency, kept files on all the detainees, and now and then its agents would come to inspect the premises. The squat buildings of Khiam looked down upon the village of the same name. They consisted of interrogation rooms and two sets of usually overcrowded collective cells, one set for men and one for women. A few other buildings housed the guards, and that was all. The prison was encircled by watchtowers and surrounded by a minefield. It would have been extraordinarily difficult, if not impossible, to escape.

When I landed there, its reputation was already well established. . . .

The prison fed on two kinds of prey. First there were the resistance fighters, myself among them, captured in battle or exposed by the security

Proxy: A person authorized to act with the authority of another.

Promontory: A high point of land overlooking a lowland or a body of water.

Mercenaries: Hired soldiers.

forces. We all suffered the same fate. Interrogation and torture to start, then seclusion without trial or sentence, the length of detention set by the whims of the jailers. Israel did not want to appear responsible for these **cumbersome** detainees. Probably, a part of the Israeli public would not accept such human rights violations committed under the **auspices** of their country. The proof: when Lebanese were detained on Israeli soil, kept as hostages in exchange for information about soldiers missing in action, or even more **macabre**, in exchange for the bodies of those killed and abandoned to the enemy, Israeli and Palestinian human-rights groups and lawyers would struggle tirelessly for the prisoners. In comparison, Khiam was perfect for Israel. No laws, no judges, no lawyers. Prisoners in Khiam were negated, buried, conveniently wiped from the world of the living.

But the security forces were not satisfied with locking up the ones who fought them. The prison was often bursting with people who had no relation to the **guerrillas**. Women, children, and the elderly, from all backgrounds, were also transferred to Khiam for the purposes of intimidation, pressure, and torture. For the SLA, it was a means to get information about people judged to be suspicious, and a way to blackmail or threaten the prisoners into **collaborating** with the security services in the occupied zone. For these prisoners, too, detention became a kind of lottery. No one knew, on going into Khiam, if he would be released the next week or many years later.

And no one could be sure of coming out alive, particularly the women—the daily routine wore down even the most healthy. In part, this was because of the climate. The prison, located to the south of Beirut but at a high altitude, was **stifling** hot in summer and freezing cold in winter. Snow would fall at that height, and the buildings, like all those in hot countries, were designed without the slightest protection against the cold. The cells, which naturally had no running water, were **spartan**. The detainees slept under sheets on old foam mattresses. Blankets were rare. Because of poor construction, the floors of the jail were never clean. Moisture rose from the ground and seeped through the mattresses at night, chilling you to the bone. Apart from these pallets and some iron water-tanks, the detainees shared a plastic bucket, often without a lid, as a **latrine**. It was emptied twice a day, in the heat of summer as in winter. The buckets were usually constructed out of kitchen-oil jugs.

In Khiam, the rhythm never changed.

The women detainees were woken at dawn and given a **frugal** breakfast. They then had to clean their cell, come out by turns and empty the bucket, quickly wash themselves in the cramped room designated for that purpose, and fill up their water-cans. Time outside the cell was limited to five minutes, measured by stopwatch in a quasi-military fashion. Tardiness was severely punished. At noon, a scanty lunch was brought into the cells. In mid-afternoon, a few pieces of food were also served. These three moments were the only times of day when the prison became somewhat animated.

Cumbersome: Burdensome, awkward.

Auspices: Guidance or authority.

Macabre: Horrific.

Guerrillas: Fighters who use unconventional combat tactics against a more powerful foe.

Collaborating: Working with.

Stifling: Airless, oppressive.

Spartan: Simple, without comforts.

Latrine: Toilet.

Frugal: Minimal.

At all other times, silence was the rule, and any raised voices were subject to punishment. Coughing, or clearing one's throat, was also prohibited. The detainees could talk in low voices with other women inside the same cell, but communication between cells was not allowed.

The prisoners, shut up in their cells, were cut off from all contact with the outside world. Visits were forbidden, even for families who lived only a few miles from Khiam. Nothing came to lighten the dull **monotony**. Whether they had been captured during an operation or torn unsuspecting from their beds, the women were all in the same boat. . . .

The mediocre food and uncomfortable cells encouraged sickness in bodies already tired out by interrogations and intensive torture. In the prison, where the detainees (men and women) sometimes numbered over two hundred, there were supposed to be two medical orderlies, of extremely limited competence and means, but usually there was only one. In Khiam, you were better off not getting sick. It was very difficult to get permission from the camp authorities to be transferred to the nearest hospital in Margayoun. You were also better off not complaining too much or breaking the rules. **Reprisals** were instant. Beatings and time in solitary subdued the more rebellious.

. . . For the male prisoners, living conditions were even harsher than for the women, partly because of overcrowding and the constant beatings administered by the guards. This was especially true of the solitary cells. A woman confined to solitary was locked up in a sort of box, two and a half feet wide by six and a half feet long and eight feet high, in which she could still move a little. For the men, the solitary was a nightmare; the cell was a cube, measuring less than three feet a side, pierced by a tiny hole. The prisoner, swallowed up, compressed, folded over on himself, was of course unable to stand and could barely move except to eat. He was sometimes taken out so that he could hurriedly wash himself. Yet somehow prisoners survived in that half-light for many months, though they often suffered heavy consequences: skeletal disorders and problems of vision. One of them held out for a year and a half of this inhuman treatment.

• • •

What happened next . . .

Antoine Lahad survived Soha Bechara's assassination attempt, and Bechara spent ten years in the prison at Khiam. The mistreatment of prisoners at Khiam came to international attention, and several groups rallied in their calls for better treatment of Khiam's prisoners and for Bechara's freedom in particular. The horror of her imprisonment continues to haunt Bechara. Freed on September 3, 1998, Bechara confessed

Monotony: Sameness.

Reprisals: Retaliatory actions.

A prison cell at Khiam Prison in southern Lebanon. Bechara and other Lebanese resistance fighters were held for interrogation by the Israeli army at Khiam Prison. © THOMAS HARTWELL/CORBIS.

in her memoir that "I have not spent a single day since I was freed without thinking of the camp, of those men and women who suffered there." In 2000, when the Israeli forces left southern Lebanon, Khiam closed. Bechara wrote of the time as "a rare moment of unity for the Lebanese," who had been divided for so long.

That moment, however, was short-lived. Although the enemies had changed since Bechara first took up her fight for freedom, Lebanon remained divided in the 2000s. Religious and political differences continued to cause conflict in the nation. In addition, the neighboring country of Syria, which had become a strong political force in Lebanon since sending troops to support various factions in the civil war in 1976, maintained its troops in Lebanon even after the civil war ended in 1990, and tried to gain control of the Lebanese government.

On March 14, 2005, an estimated one million Lebanese, representing a mix of the various cultures and religions found in that country, demonstrated for national unity and against Syria. Demonstrators in the March 14 Movement (later called the Cedar Revolution) called for the withdrawal of Syrian troops and an investigation into the deaths of Lebanese officials perceived to be at odds with Syria, including the assassination of Lebanese prime minister Rafiq Hariri (1944–2005) just one month prior to the demonstrations. Syrian troops withdrew from Lebanon that April, ending Syria's twenty-nine-year military presence there.

In 2006 Lebanon was once again engaged in conflict with Israel. Hezbollah, a Shiite militant group and political party based in Lebanon, had become a powerful political force in the nation, with strong representation in the Lebanese parliament (legislature). One of the foundations of Hezbollah was its opposition to Israel. In July 2006 Hezbollah attacked a small force of Israeli troops who were patrolling the Israel-Lebanon border. Israel responded with extreme force, launching air, naval, and ground attacks at Hezbollah targets in Lebanon. Hezbollah, in turn, fired about four thousand rockets into northern Israel. During that conflict, which lasted just over a month, the building that had been the Khiam prison was destroyed. The government of Lebanon remains in turmoil, as influence from other nations—including Syria, Iran, Saudi Arabia, and Western nations—continue to support opposing political factions vying for power. Bechara's desire for "a free Lebanon, a country at peace," which she wrote about in *Resistance*, has yet to be achieved, but it continues to be the quest for millions of its citizens.

Did you know...

- Of Bechara's ten years in prison, six were spent alone in a cell that measured six feet by two feet. During this time she was allowed only ten minutes to eat the one meal served each day.
- Israeli troops forced the Palestine Liberation Organization (PLO) out of Lebanon in 1982, but Israel remained an occupying force in Lebanon until 2000.
- In 1989, Khiam prisoners revolted against their poor treatment. The uprising resulted in the deaths of two inmates and only a few improvements, such as blankets and sanitary buckets.
- In 1994, the International Committee of the Red Cross (ICRC) won the prisoners of Khiam many rights once denied, including communication with relatives and limited visits; the ability to

receive packages of clothing, food, and toiletries; and access to news and books.

- Upon her release from Khiam on September 3, 1998, Soha Bechara found it difficult to adjust to life outside of prison, especially because she was overwhelmed by questions from thousands of journalists and visitors. To adapt to her new life away from the public eye, she moved to France. Now based in Geneva, Switzerland, she lectures on her experiences and remains active in support of Palestinians.

Consider the following...

- Soha Bechara's personal account of conflict is unusual because most prison memoirs have been written by men. Identify the details in her story that are unique because of her gender.

- Female participants in revolutionary movements are often characterized as acting out plans designed by men without being fully knowledgeable about the consequences of their activities. Describe Soha Bechara's knowledge of her own activities. Use specific examples from the excerpt to support the description.

- Soha Bechara describes inmates' poor treatment at Khiam. Imagine that the world has just learned of Khiam inmates' miserable conditions during its years of operation. Write a persuasive letter to the United Nations requesting international support for the humane treatment of prisoners. Possibly do extra research on the historical treatment of prisoners to make the letter more convincing.

For More Information

BOOKS

Bechara, Soha. *Resistance: My Life for Lebanon.* Brooklyn, NY: Soft Skull Press, 2003.

Gelvin, James L. *The Modern Middle East: A History,* 3rd ed. New York: Oxford University Press, 2011.

PERIODICALS

Fattah, Hassan M. "Syrian Troops Leave Lebanon After 29-Year Occupation." *New York Times* (April 26, 2005).

Lebanon: The Israel-Hamas-Hezbollah Conflict. CRS Report for Congress. U.S. Library of Congress, Congressional Research Service (September 15, 2006). Available online at http://www.fas.org/sgp/crs/mideast/RL33566.pdf (accessed on November 30, 2011).

Petrou, Michael. "Middle East War Clouds: The Next Deadly Clash Between Israel and Hezbollah Is Brewing." *MacLean's* (May 10, 2010).

Shadid, Anthony, and David D. Kirkpatrick. "In Tumult, New Hope for Palestinian Cause." *New York Times* (August 10, 2011).

They Must Go

Excerpt from *They Must Go*
Written by Meir Kahane
Published in 1981

"A time bomb in the Holy Land ticks away relentlessly."

American-born Meir Kahane (1932–1990) became a political radical in Israel during the 1970s and 1980s. As a young man growing up in New York City, Kehane was a fervent Zionist, a supporter of an international political movement that called for the creation of an independent Jewish state in Palestine. (Palestine is a historical region in the Middle East on the eastern shore of the Mediterranean Sea, comprising parts of present-day Israel and Jordan.) Zionism originated in the late nineteenth century as Jews around the world began to feel that the only way to protect themselves from the extensive anti-Semitism (prejudice against Jews) they had long been facing was to establish a Jewish state. Palestine was the site of the ancient Jewish kingdom. But it was also home to Arabs (people who speak the Arab language) who had lived in the region for hundreds of years. As Jews began immigrating to Palestine in large numbers, conflict between Arabs and Jews was unavoidable. When the state of Israel was established in 1948, Arab Palestinians continued to lay claim to the region and were supported in their cause by neighboring Arab nations. Several Arab-Israeli wars followed, with Israel successfully defending itself in each conflict.

Kahane was a young man when the state of Israel was established, but he had already became an advocate for Zionism. As a teenager he was a member of a Zionist youth group called Betar. He completed his education and became a rabbi (a Jewish scholar, teacher, and religious leader) in 1958. He was an Orthodox Jew, adhering to a strict interpretation and application of Jewish religious texts and traditions. In the late 1960s,

Kahane founded the Jewish Defense League (JDL), an organization founded to defend Jews against anti-Semitism.

Kahane moved to Israel in the early 1970s. Once there, he became convinced that a Jewish homeland must restrict and limit Arab participation. He noticed a detail in the Israeli constitution that he considered fatal to the survival of the Jewish state, namely that Arabs were allowed to coexist in Israel as full citizens. Kahane was not afraid to voice his opinions on this point. Kahane envisioned an Israel created for Jews alone. Labeled a racist by some Israelis, Kahane was embraced by others as the Jewish radical the nation needed to combat Palestinians who threatened Israel. His position drew support from those in Israeli politics who were very conservative, even as he encouraged violent acts against Arabs. For those hoping to resolve the problem of conflicting Jewish and Arab claims to the land once called Palestine, however, Kahane seemed dangerous.

Kahane gained his reputation, for good and for bad, when he was detained on numerous occasions by Israeli police and became involved in several trials throughout the 1970s and 1980s. Along with his political rallying, his most infamous activities included a plan to avenge the Israeli athletes killed by a group of Palestinians called Black September at the 1972 Olympic Games, an attempted assassination of the Soviet ambassador, and a plot to explode a bomb at the Iraqi Embassy in Washington, D.C. None of these plans were successfully carried out, but the publicity of the various trials made Kahane a popular figure among extremists in Israel.

On May 13, 1980, Kahane was imprisoned in Israel's maximum security prison at Ramle without being formally charged with a crime. In his prison cell, Kahane wrote *They Must Go*, a book detailing his philosophy against the coexistence of Arabs and Jews in Israel and presenting his argument about what he called the "ultimate contradiction" in the Israeli constitution. The following excerpt from *They Must Go* illustrates Kahane's powerful voice and his extreme opinions.

Things to remember while reading the excerpt from Meir Kahane's *They Must Go*:

- Meir Kahane was born Martin David Kahane on August 1, 1932, in Brooklyn, New York.
- In his teens, Kahane joined a militant Zionist youth group called Betar, which trained its members in military tactics in order to fight for a Jewish state.

Meir Kahane was known for his extreme views against Arabs living within Israel, which he wrote about in They Must Go.
© HULTON-DEUTSCH COLLECTION/CORBIS.

- Kahane was highly educated; he became a rabbi at the Yeshiva Mirrer seminary in St. Paul, Minnesota, and attended New York Law School in the 1950s.
- Kahane wrote several books, all about his views on the creation of a Jewish state free of Arabs in Israel.

• • •

They Must Go
Introduction: Arabs and Jews—Only Separation

Some years ago I was arrested by the Israeli police and charged with "**incitement** to revolution." The grounds? I had reached the conclusion that it was impossible to find a solution for the Arab-Jewish confrontation in the Land of Israel (both the State of Israel and the lands liberated in **1967**;) that the Jewish state was inevitably headed towards a situation like that in Northern Ireland; that the only possible way to avoid or to **mitigate** it was the **emigration** of Arabs. Consequently, I had sent letters to several thousand Arabs offering them an opportunity (funds and visas) to emigrate voluntarily. The fact that many Arabs replied positively and that a major Arab village in the **Galilee**, Gush Halev, offered to move all its inhabitants to Canada in return for a village there did not prevent the worried Israeli government from arresting me.

Four long years and one important war later, a scandal broke in Israel. It was revealed that Yisrael Koenig, a high official in the Ministry of the Interior who is in charge of the northern region of Israel, had drafted a secret memorandum in which he warned of the increasing danger of Arab growth (which would make Arabs in the Galilee a majority by 1978) as well as of increasing Arab national militancy. His solution included several measures that he hoped would lead to Arab emigration.

The pity is that vital years have passed since my original proposal, wasted years that saw the **Yom Kippur War** produce a major psychological change in Arab thinking. In the aftermath of that war and its political consequences, vast numbers of Arabs, who in 1972 were depressed and convinced that Israeli **sovereignty** could not be destroyed, are today just as convinced that time is on their side, that it will not be long before the **Zionist** state collapses. Then they—the Arabs—will hold sway over all that will be "Palestine." The necessary **corollary** is, of course, that hundreds of thousands who were potential voluntary **émigrés** nine years ago are now determined to stay and await the day of Arab victory. *But they must go.*

It is in order to convince the Jew of this that I have written this book.

The problem with so many people who proclaim the virtues of coexistence between the Jewish majority of the Jewish state and its Arab minority is that they hold the Arab, as well as his intelligence, and his national pride, in contempt.

There is an ultimately **insoluble** contradiction between a Jewish state of Israel that is the fulfillment of the 2,000-year-old Jewish-Zionist dream and a state in which Arabs and Jews possess equal rights—including the right of the Arabs democratically and peacefully to put an end to the Jewish state. Those

Incitement: Encouragement.

1967: The 1967 Arab-Israeli War (known in Israel as the Six-Day War), in which Israel captured portions of land that are now called the occupied territories.

Mitigate: Lessen.

Emigration: Departure from one's country or region to live elsewhere.

Galilee: A region in northern Israel.

Yom Kippur War: The Israeli name for the 1973 Arab-Israeli War between Israel and the allied Arab nations of Egypt and Syria.

Sovereignty: Supreme authority and control.

Zionist: Jewish.

Corollary: Result.

Émigrés;: People who have left their native country, especially for political reasons.

Insoluble: Having no solution.

who refuse to give the Arab that right but tell him he is equal think he is a fool. He is not.

The reality of the situation is therefore, clear. The Jews and Arabs of the Land of Israel ultimately cannot coexist in a Jewish-Zionist state. A time bomb in the **Holy Land** ticks away relentlessly.

A Jewish state means Jewish orientation and ties. It means Jewish culture and a Jewish spirit in the Jewish **body politic**. But above all, a Jewish spirit in the Jewish body politic. But above all, a Jewish state means Jewish sovereignty and control of its destiny. That can be accomplished only by a permanent Jewish majority and a small, insignificant, and **placid** Arab minority. But the Arabs believe that the Jews are thieves who stole their land. The Arabs feel no ties to or emotions for a state that breathes "Jewishness." And they grow, **quantitatively and qualitatively**. They will surely make violent demands for more power, including "autonomy" in various parts of the land. Eventually, the very majorityship of Jews will be threatened by the Arab birthrate. The result will be bloody conflict.

If we hope to avoid this terrible result, there is only one path for us to take: the immediate transfer of Arabs from **Eretz Yisrael**, the Land of Israel, to their own lands. For Arabs and Jews of Eretz Yisrael there is only one answer: separation, Jews in their land, Arabs in theirs. Separation. Only separation. . . .

Chapter 6: The Ultimate Contradiction

There is an ultimate insoluble contradiction between the State of Israel that is the fulfillment of the 2,000-year-old Jewish-Zionist dream and the modern nation-state that sees all its citizens as possessing equal rights and privileges. There is an ultimately **immutable** clash between that part of Israel's Declaration of Independence that created the *Jewish* state and the part that promised "complete equality of social and political rights to all its citizens," even though they be Arabs and not Jews. There is—let it be said once and for all—a potential confrontation between the Jewish-Zionist state that was the **millennial** dream of the Jewish people and modern concepts of democracy and citizenship.

We are pained, embarrassed, thrown into intellectual agony. We hasten to avoid such talk. It is unnecessary, dangerous, irresponsible, better left unspoken. Nonsense! Far better to meet the issue, deal with it boldly and courageously, explain it to our children and ourselves, than to have it explode in our faces tomorrow.

There is nothing for which the Jew need apologize. A people that has suffered **ecumenical agony** and that has been deprived of the rights that other nations demand for themselves owes no one an explanation. The Middle East sees **Islamic republics** in which the Arabic quality and the Muslim character of the state are inscribed in the constitution; who shouts about Arabic "racism"? Africans insist upon the blackness of their state, and

Holy Land: Roughly the present-day territory of Israel, the Palestinian territories, and parts of Jordan and Lebanon. This area includes sacred sites for Jews, Christians, and Muslims.

Body politic: The people of a nation considered together as an organized group of citizens.

Placid: Peaceful, mild.

Quantitatively and qualitatively: In number and in strength of belief.

Eretz Yisrael: "Land of Israel" in Hebrew; the ancient kingdom of the Jews.

Immutable: Not able to be changed, permanent.

Millenial: Relating to a millennium, or one thousand years.

Ecumenical agony: Religious persecution worldwide.

Islamic republics: Nations based on the principles of the religion of Islam.

exclusiveness of culture and identity are the foundations of scores of nations. Who apologizes? The Zionist state *is* Judaism, the need for a land of the Jews where the people can escape **Holocaust** and build a distinctive Jewishness that will flourish.

The very kernel of Jewish longing for a homeland through nearly 2,000 years of exile was the belief that the Jews were a separate and distinct people. In a world in which we recognize the right of self-determination for **Papua**, who will challenge Jewish rights?

Moreover, the Jews constituted a unique people in that they were at one and the same time a religion and a nation, a religio-nation, which had lived as a unique society and culture in its own land—Eretz Yisrael. On the one hand they suffered unparalleled horrors and massacres in their wanderings in foreign lands. They knew no peace in any country in which their numbers grew large and their quality shone through. There was no society, religion, or economic or social system that gave them permanent haven and rest. Jews were burned to death, drowned, cut to pieces, converted to death, **Inquisitioned** to death, **Crusaded** to death, **Islamized** to death, **pogromed** to death, and **Auschwitzed** to death. The Jews learned a bitter lesson in their twenty centuries of being strangers, of existing as a minority. The lesson? It is not good to be a stranger. Never be a minority. Never again!

As impolite as it may sound, the Jews learned, after rivers of blood, not to trust to the tolerance and mercies and hospitality of others. They no longer wished to rely on the armies and the police and the swords of others to protect them from holocausts. Enough of being strangers. The Jews wanted to live. The Jews wanted their own armies, their own protection, *their own home.* . . .

If the Arab is unhappy about this one can understand. It is never easy to be a lodger in someone else's home. But his unhappiness will not be resolved, for the Jew will not turn a lodger into an owner. If the Arab would rather live in his own home and atmosphere, he is welcome in any of the twenty-plus Arab states that exist. Israel cannot, and morally dare not, change its Jewish character. For Israel to change that Jewish character would be to turn those who created it on the basis of the Jewish historical right into liars and thieves.

It would be more than admitting that "Jewishness" was used in the past only in order to take away Arab land. It would be a cynical slap in the face to world **Jewry** which gave of its energies, funds, and in many cases, lives for the dream of a Jewish state. It would be a **despicable** cutting off of all obligations to oppressed and persecuted Jews who see in today's Israel their trustee and defender. The Israeli who was once in need of a home and who found it in a state that was pledged to help him would now—no longer in need—selfishly cut the lifeline for others.

The Jew has no moral right to an Israel that is a non-Jewish state. But in a Jewish state let no one insult the Arab by insisting that he is equal and that it is "his" state, too. It is this ultimate contradiction between the Jewish character of Israel and the democratic right of the Arab to aspire to all the rights that

Holocaust: The mass murder of European Jews and other groups by the Nazis during World War II (1939–45).

Papua: The southeast portion of the island of New Guinea.

Inquisitioned: Investigated; a reference to the Inquisition, the Roman Catholic court system for the discovery and punishment of heresy that began in the twelfth century.

Crusaded: To engage in a crusade; a reference to the series of military campaigns ordered by the Roman Catholic Church between 1095 and 1291 with the main goal of taking the Holy Land from the Muslims.

Islamized: Forced to follow the faith of Islam.

Pogromed: The targeted victim of mob attack.

Auschwitzed: The name of a death camp used as a verb, meaning murdered; Auschwitz was one of the largest Nazi concentration camps used during the Holocaust.

Jewry: Jews as a group.

Despicable: Appalling, disgraceful.

Jews have—including to have an Arab majority in the land—that will never give the Arab rest or allow him to accept the status quo. . . .

• • •

What happened next . . .

After his six-month detention in 1981, Kahane resumed his political activities with great enthusiasm. He formed a right-wing political party called the Kach Party. The Kach political goal was to establish a Jewish state in Israel for Orthodox Jews. Kahane spoke of the removal of Arabs from Israel as an apocalypse, a catastrophic event that would end the rule of evil on earth. Kahane drew critics within Israel as well as from the international community. Calling his views racist, some compared his policies to those promoted by the Nazi Party in Germany in the 1930s and 1940s, which carried out the Holocaust, the mass murder of European Jews and other groups by the Nazis during World War II (1939–45). At the same time, Kahane also gained supporters.

In 1984, he won a seat in the Israeli Knesset, or legislature. His victory spurred a national debate about whether Israel was a state made up of racists. Were Israelis really unable to compromise with Arabs as Kahane so strongly believed? As his critics worried, Kahane gained more political support. By 1988, polls indicated that the Kach Party had almost 6 percent of the vote, enough to seize a good deal of power in the Knesset. Before the elections, however, the Israeli Supreme Court removed Kahane from his Knesset seat and banned the Kach Party from the vote, claiming that the party was racist and anti-democratic.

Nevertheless, Kahane continued on his same path, speaking out even more frequently about the removal of Arabs from Israel as the only real way to secure a Jewish state. After one such speech, given on a fund-raising trip in New York, in November 1990, Kahane was shot and killed by El Sayyid A. Nosair (1955–), an Arab.

Did you know . . .

- To avenge Meir Kahane's death, an Israeli supporter gunned down two Palestinians the next day.
- The Kach Party remains active to the early 2000s and is suspected of sponsoring attacks on Palestinians in the occupied territories,

Meir Kahane speaks at a rally in Jerusalem in 1984. Kahane founded the Kach Party in the 1980s and was elected to the Israeli Knesset in 1984. DAVID RUBINGER/TIME & LIFE PICTURES/GETTY IMAGES.

lands under the political and military control of Israel, especially the West Bank and Gaza Strip.

- Kahane's son, Binyamin (1966–2000), founded a group similar to his father's Kach Party, called Kahane Chai (meaning "Kahane Lives") in 1990. Binyamin Kahane and his wife were killed in 2000.
- The U.S. State Department listed both the Kach Party and Kahane Chai as terrorist organizations in 2004.
- Prior to national elections in 2009, Israeli politician Avigdor Lieberman (1958–) was accused by *Haaretz*, an Israeli news

organization, of being a former member of the Kach Party. Lieberman's Yisrael Beiteinu party won fifteen seats in that year's election, making it the third largest party in the Knesset. Lieberman became Israel's deputy prime minister and minister of foreign affairs.

Consider the following...

- How does Kahane justify ridding Israel of Arabs? Use specific examples from the text.

- Several groups, both political and militant, worked to secure Israel's independence. If Kahane's *They Must Go* formed the basis of such a group, would this group be considered a legitimate freedom fighting group or a terrorist group? Explain.

- Was Kahane's suggestion that Arabs could move to the twenty-plus Arab states of the world legitimate? Write two arguments: one that supports this suggestion as reasonable and another that argues that this suggestion is racist. Evaluate each argument. Is it possible to make each convincing? Why or why not?

For More Information

BOOKS

Friedman, Robert I. *The False Prophet: Rabbi Meir Kahane, from FBI Informant to Knesset Member.* New York: Lawrence Hill Books, 1990.

Kahane, Libby. *Rabbi Meir Kahane: His Life and Thought.* Jerusalem: Institute for the Publication of the Writings of Rabbi Meir Kahane, 2008.

Kahane, Meir. *Never Again! A Program for Survival.* New York: Pyramid Books, 1972.

Kahane, Meir. *They Must Go.* New York: Grosset & Dunlap, 1981.

Mergui, Raphael, and Philippe Simonnot. *Israel's Ayatollahs: Meir Kahane and the Far Right in Israel.* London: Saqi Books, 1987.

PERIODICALS

Hewitt, Bill. "After a Career of Preaching Hatred for Arabs, Rabbi Meir Kahane Is Cut Down by an Assassin's Bullet." *People Weekly* (November 19, 1990): 65–66.

Lewis, Neil A. "Appeals Court Upholds Terrorist Label for a Jewish Group." *The New York Times* (October 18, 2006).

WEB SITES

"Kach, Kahane Chai" *Council on Foreign Relations* (March 20, 2008). http://www.cfr.org/israel/kach-kahane-chai-israel-extremists/p9178 (accessed on November 30, 2011).

Shyovitz, David. "Rabbi Meir Kahane." *Jewish Virtual Library.* http://www.jewishvirtuallibrary.org/jsource/biography/kahane.html (accessed on November 30, 2011).

Letters from Tel Mond Prison

Excerpt from *Letters from Tel Mond Prison: An Israeli Settler Defends His Act of Terror*

Written by Era Rapaport

Published in 1996

> "Where did I get the nerve to do what I did? I dislike any type of violence.... Here I was doing what I've abhorred."

Certain events in life inspire ordinary people to do extreme things. As Era Rapaport's prison memoir, *Letters from Tel Mond Prison: An Israeli Settler Defends His Act of Terror*, attests, a threat against one's home can be one such event. In 1980 Era Rapaport (1945–) was a Jewish settler living in the West Bank, an area between Israel and Jordan on the west bank of the Jordan River that was occupied by Israel after the 1967 Arab-Israeli War (known in Israel as the Six-Day War). The West Bank is largely populated by Palestinians, an Arab people whose ancestors lived in the historical region of Palestine, comprising parts of present-day Israel and Jordan, and who continue to lay claim to that land. After 1967, Palestinians in the region were subject to Israeli military rule. Israel began establishing settlements in the West Bank, as well as other territories occupied after the 1967 Arab-Israeli War, an act that violated international law. (Settlements are communities established and inhabited in order to claim land.) Palestinians resisted Israeli rule and settlement in the occupied territories (lands under the political and military control of Israel), sometimes violently.

One of the Jewish settlements established in the West Bank was at the town of Hebron. On May 2, 1980, six Jews were killed by Palestinians in Hebron. Although it was rumored that Palestinian mayors had given

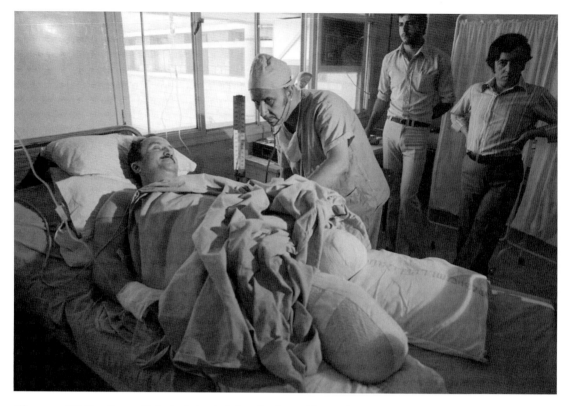

The mayor of Nablus, Bassam Shaka, in the hospital after a bomb attack by Jewish terrorists in 1980. Shaka lost both of his legs when the bomb that Era Rapaport set went off. © DAVID RUBINGER/CORBIS.

the order to kill these Jews, the Israeli government did not retaliate or punish the Palestinians. Feeling no support from the Israeli government, Rapaport and others planned and executed the bombing of several Palestinian mayors' automobiles on June 2, 1980. The bomb Rapaport planted destroyed the legs of Bassam Shaka (1930–), the mayor of Nablus, a town about thirty miles north of Jerusalem.

Era Rapaport was raised in an Orthodox Jewish family in New York City. (Orthodox Jews adhere to a strict interpretation and application of Jewish religious texts and traditions.) Family members gave him a deep faith in and devotion to the teachings of the Torah, the Jewish scripture. Additionally, his father had been born in Jerusalem, Palestine, and he instilled a great love of that land in his son. Rapaport first visited Israel in 1966 to study at a yeshiva (an Orthodox Jewish rabbinical seminary). When the 1967 Arab-Israeli War broke out, Rapaport served as a medic for the wounded in Jerusalem. Although he returned to the United States to complete a master's degree in social work, Rapaport felt that his future was in Israel, and he moved there permanently in 1971. After marrying an Israeli woman, he moved to the West Bank. There Rapaport worked to establish the first Jewish settlement on land he considered to be the ancient capital of the Jews nearly three thousand years before. In the settlement of Shilo, his family grew to include six children.

After taking part in the car bombing that injured Shaka in 1980, Rapaport became a fugitive in Israel. In 1983, Rapaport fled to the United States with his family, where he tried to persuade more Jews to settle in Israel. Upon his return to Israel in December 1986, he was arrested for his part in the car bombing. He was tried and jailed in January 1987.

"How does a nice Jewish boy from East Flatbush, Brooklyn, a gifted social worker, a marcher for civil rights, a loving husband and father, end up blowing off the legs of the PLO mayor of Nablus?" William B. Helmreich asked in his introduction to *Letters from Tel Mond Prison*. Rapaport struggled with that very question, considering his actions and their consequences carefully in letters and musings he wrote during his two-year prison term.

Things to remember while reading the excerpt from *Letters from Tel Mond Prison: An Israeli Settler Defends His Act of Terror*:

- Many of the letters Rapaport wrote in prison serve as a way for him to recount the events that led to his imprisonment; in them, he attempts to explain how he changed from a pacifist (someone opposed to violence as a means of settling disputes) standing up for Israeli rights to one who used violence as a way to influence change.

- While Rapaport wrote most of these letters while serving his sentence in Tel Mond Prison, the first letter was written just after the car bombing in 1980. This letter was never sent, but it does capture Rapaport's frame of mind shortly after the violent act.

• • •

Letters from Tel Mond Prison: An Israeli Settler Defends His Act of Terror

May 1980

Shilo

Dear Avi,

I don't know that I'll ever mail this to you. It may be too problematic to do so. But more than ever before, I need your advice.

It's Sunday night now, forty-eight hours after the murders in Hevron [also spelled Hebron]. Some of the funerals were today. Besides the anger and the public cries for revenge, you could hear the **recriminations**: "Had we acted before, after the attack on Solomon, this never would have happened. Now we must react, we must prevent another attack."

What can I tell you? Who knows when one is prepared for life-or-death decisions? Never in my days in the States, and never here, would I have imagined myself dealing with the problem before me. This is not a question of what kind of car to buy, or where to purchase a house, or to what school to send the kids. I remember when we hassled with the question of participating in marches for the freedom of Soviet **Jewry**, rabbis published positive and negative responses to the question. Yes, it was a difficult decision, but it wouldn't necessarily change your life. In this situation, Avi, I don't really have any illusions. My government is not going to act. That is a given fact. Yes, we'll try to persuade them, but we've had the experience in the past. So I know that I have to act.

But, Avi, there are huge **ramifications** to such a decision, some personal and some national. Truthfully, I am not sure which is more important. This is not pre-1948 when the **Underground** acted against the British. We are a **sovereign** government, and we are a sovereign state. Do I have the right to assume responsibility for what my government is doing? Would an action by myself and others not be a **desecration** of the honor of Medinat Yisrael (the State of Israel)? I couldn't do that, Avi; I love my country too much to disgrace it publicly. Even when I come to the States to talk about the situation here, I won't talk negatively about **Aretz**. You know better than I that there is a halachah [law] against speaking lashon harah [evil speech] about our land. If I were to act, I'd be doing more than speaking lashon harah. All my life I've been taught by my **Abba** and **Ema** about the special honor that one must have for Medinat Yisrael and its leaders and elders. Could it be that by one act of mine, I'll throw all of that out the window? Is it also possible that my action will be the basis for others to act as well? Who knows where it would end? Everyone has his "red line." My red line is the present situation, and therefore I feel that something has to be

Recriminations: Criticisms, accusations.

Jewry: Jews as a group.

Ramifications: Consequences.

Underground: Jews working in secret for a Jewish homeland in Palestine prior to 1948, when the land was under the control of the British.

Sovereign: Having total authority and control.

Desecration: Violation of something that is sacred or holy.

Aretz: A reference to Eretz Yisrael, the ancient kingdom of the Jews.

Abba: Father.

Ema: Mother.

done. Someone else's red line can be something else, and then he'll act. It'll be a situation of no law and order. I have grown up to be a law-and-order person. What right do I have to possibly hurt our country on a national level?

Then there is the personal level. I know, Avi, that if I am to act, there is a good chance, almost guaranteed, that I'll be spending time in jail. Possibly even ten years or more. That will, to an extent, destroy our family. Do I have a right to force Orit [Rapaport's wife] into being a living widow? That's exactly what it would be. My kids will grow up basically without a father. Don't they have to be asked? You know that's a **rhetorical question**; they're too young to understand. Who knows how many years this could take from my parents' lives? And myself? You know me, Avi. I love kids so much. Just the thought of being in jail without them for two weeks or a month, I go crazy. I can't even begin to imagine how I'll live without them. Also, I love the outdoors, working, being active, building Eretz Yisrael. All that will stop. . . .

March 1987

Tel Mond Prison

. . . Orit and I held each other tight, sensing, together, the serious-ness of the action that we were going to undertake in just one short hour or so. I looked in her eyes and said to her, "Thank you for all you've given me."

I rechecked my gear to see if everything was in place and then went to the kids' room for two last kisses. Oh, how I love them! I told Orit to get some sleep. Then I slipped out the door.

Noos [Rapaport's accomplice] and I met some fifty yards from the entrance to **Shilo**. We walked swiftly to a waiting car. With us, in a plastic bag, was a wooden box carrying the bomb.

[After riding in a car for several miles Era Rapaport and Noos arrived close to the Arab village of Yutma.]

. . . [W]e asked Moshe [the driver] to turn onto a side road and turn off his motor and lights.

Quickly Noos and I jumped out and opened our army bags. We had practiced doing this over and over at night in the mountains surrounding Shilo. At any moment a car could pass by; we had to work fast. Three minutes, and we were on our way, dressed as soldiers in army fatigues, gloves on our hands, and knitted caps ready to be pulled over our faces. . . .

We guided Moshe to a side street about three blocks from the **Bassam** house. He parked between two cars about one-third of the way up the street.

Rhetorical question: A question asked merely for effect with no answer expected.

Shilo: An Israeli settlement in the northern West Bank.

Bassam: Bassam Shaka is Rapaport's target.

This way a passing car couldn't make out the Israeli license plate. We both quickly stepped out of the car. We told Moshe that if we were not back in twelve minutes he should leave, or if he heard shots and we were not back within three minutes, he should also leave. We checked our watches, and then Noos and I were on our way. . . .

A small light was on in Shaka's house, but I detected no movement. My **M16** was loaded, cocked with the safety off. In all our stakeouts we never encountered a guard, but we didn't intend to be surprised by one now.

Noos was under Bassam's car. A wrong move, and the bomb would go off with Noos beneath it. Seconds passed slowly. I squelched the need to ask him how things were going. Noos had attached the bomb by magnet to the car and was stretching the trip wire. The slightest mishap, and it was all over. I heard him placing the rock on the wire and slipping out from under the car. He had successfully attached the bomb. . . . Within a minute we had left the area and were heading, via side streets, toward south Shechem, on our way back to Shilo. From what we could tell, no one had seen us, and everything went off well. Now we had to wait and see if everything worked as well in the morning. . . .

I was dead tired, but my mind was racing. The main thought and hope was that the explosive would go off. We had done intensive information gathering and knew that Bassam drove the car by himself to his office. The explosive was built to maim only. Would it go off? Would it do the job?

Now, I was a bit scared. The action was over. How long would it take until the police would find me? Yet, I said to myself, you made a decision. But I was floored at my action. Where did I get the nerve to do what I did? I dislike any type of violence. As a social worker, I constantly tried to influence youth to reject violence. Here I was, doing what I've **abhorred**.

Yet I know, as **Ecclesiastes** says, "There is a time for everything under the sky . . . a time to throw stones and a time to gather them . . . a time for war and a time for peace . . . a time to kill and a time to heal." We would all prefer to be nonviolent all the time, and that day will come. . . .

M16: A gas-operated assault rifle.

Abhorred: Hated, despised.

Ecclesiastes: A book of wisdom in Jewish and Christian scriptures.

April 1987

Tel Mond Prison

. . . After services, around 7:00 A.M., a few of us gathered around, as usual, for a few moments of what's new. Noos and I acted quite normal. The bombs were set to go off at 8:00 A.M., and I was a bit anxious but was careful not to mention a word that could be misinterpreted.

At home, after getting Moriyah and David off to kindergarten, Orit and I took a short walk, and I filled her in. "Beep, beep, beep," began the radio. " . . . It is 9:00 A.M. and here is the news. Bassam Shaka, the Mayor of Shechem, was seriously wounded this morning when a bomb blew up his car. Karim Chalef, Mayor of Ramallah, was injured when his car also blew up." . . .

March 1988

Tel Mond Prison

It seems to me that the newspapers are purposely not emphasizing that the Arabs are out to kill us. Their weapons are as deadly as ours. Your press presents it as a **David and Goliath** reversed. We are Goliath with modern arms and army, and the Arabs are David with slingshot and pebbles. What a lot of garbage! The roads that we drive are twisting and winding. Around every bend a terrorist with a **Molotov cocktail** or large stone can be waiting. They hide behind trees and boulders and wait until they see the "white of our eyes." There is no way to know where and when they'll appear.

If the situation sounds like the **Wild Wild West**, then, to an extent, it is. Yes, it's more dangerous than before to ride the roads. It is a difficult period. For me, also, it is a frustrating time—for many reasons. I acted against the same terrorist organization that is presently terrorizing a good part of our country and people. Yet I am sitting in prison, and they are free to continue their terrorist activities. Second, Orit and the children travel the roads often, and I can't even be out there to protect them if something happens. . . .

I can only begin to imagine the difficult time that you people are going through: being bombarded by the terrible press, hearing such frightening reports of the situation here and seeing it all on TV. You are where it is really hard to be. I know that I have written this to you before, but I'll repeat it again. Being in Israel during these years has been an amazing experience, both difficult and happy. Above all is the fact and the feeling that we are continuing in the ways of our people. There is a weight on our shoulders—a weight of generations. It is as if the millions of Jews from all the thousands of years of our wandering are all standing around us watching, waiting to see our actions. I'm not imagining it, my Brother. I feel it. . . .

Love ya,

Era

P.S. Come soon.

• • •

David and Goliath: A biblical story about a boy named David, who uses his slingshot to kill the giant Goliath.

Molotov cocktail: A crude bomb consisting of a bottle filled with a flammable liquid with a rag stuck in it to serve as a fuse.

Wild Wild West: Western part of the United States during the nineteenth century, a region that was dangerous and virtually lawless.

What happened next . . .

Upon his release from prison in 1989, Rapaport returned to the settlement he had started with eight other families, and he eventually served as its mayor. Life in the settlement areas remained difficult, as Jews and Palestinians had yet to resolve their differences. Even Jews were divided over the settlements in the occupied territories. Some believed that the occupied territories could be used as offerings to the Palestinians in a "land for peace" deal. Others firmly believed that the occupied territories were part of the ancient Jewish kingdom and should remain theirs forever.

In 1992, the editor of *Letters from Tel Mond Prison*, William Helmreich, contacted Rapaport to arrange for a tour of the West Bank. Rapaport picked up his guest in a car with reinforced windows and an M16 rifle, saying "We don't take chances here." In the early 2000s, Jewish settlement in the occupied territories remained a point of conflict. In 2004 Israeli prime minister Ariel Sharon (1928–) announced the disengagement plan, a plan to evacuate all the settlements in the Gaza Strip and some in the West Bank by the end of the following year. By September 2005, these settlements had been evacuated and destroyed, despite protests from the settlers.

Did you know . . .

- In early 2005, prior to the Israeli evacuation later that year, there were approximately 21 Jewish settlements in the Gaza Strip and more than 140 in the West Bank.
- Rapaport had been an activist in an underground group known as the Jewish Underground, which planned to destroy Palestinian governing bodies and holy places.
- After the assassination of Israeli prime minister Yitzhak Rabin (1922–1995) in 1995, twenty-seven members of the Jewish Underground were identified. Israel and the world learned that terrorist acts had been committed by these respected members of society, including establishers of settlements, teachers, and war heroes.

Consider the following . . .

- Era Rapaport writes of loving his family and the pain he would feel without them in jail. Nevertheless he decides that his convictions outweigh the personal pain he would feel without his family. How does Rapaport justify his act of terror? Are his arguments convincing? Explain why.

- Rapaport writes "We would all prefer to be nonviolent all the time, and that day will come." Explain how his actions helped or hindered the coming of this time of peace. What other means could he have used to reach his objective?

- Rapaport based his decision to commit a violent act on a belief that the land of Israel belonged to Jews in ancient times and should again be theirs. Did this idea come across in his letters as he explained his actions? Explain using specific examples.

For More Information

BOOKS

Gunderson, Cory Gideon. *The Israeli-Palestinian Conflict*. Edina, MN: Abdo, 2004.

Harms, Gregory, and Todd M. Ferry. *The Palestine Israel Conflict: A Basic Introduction*, 2nd ed. London: Pluto Press, 2008.

Rapaport, Era. *Letters from Tel Mond Prison: An Israeli Settler Defends His Act of Terror*. New York: Free Press, 1996.

Tessler, Mark. *A History of the Israeli-Palestinian Conflict*, 2nd ed. Bloomington: Indiana University Press, 2009.

WEB SITES

"In a Nutshell: Israeli Palestinian Conflict." *Mideastweb.org.* http://www.mideastweb.org/nutshell.htm (accessed on November 30, 2011).

"Transcript: Troubled Lands." *PBS: NOW with Bill Moyers.* http://www.pbs.org/now/transcript/transcript_settlers.html (accessed on November 30, 2011).

Daughter of the Olive Trees

Excerpt from *Daughter of the Olive Trees*
Written by Sumaya Farhat-Naser
Published in 2003

"Everywhere...there are checkpoints. Soldiers bar the way and carry out inspections; they are a serious obstacle to everyone on the road."

Born in a tiny village called Bir Zeit near Jerusalem in 1948, the same year that the state of Israel was established, Palestinian activist Sumaya Farhat-Naser (1948–) never experienced the freedoms of her Arab ancestors who had lived in Palestine for centuries. (Arabs are people who speak the Arabic language or who live in countries in which Arabic is the dominant language; Palestine is a historical region in the Middle East on the eastern shore of the Mediterranean Sea, comprising parts of present-day Israel and Jordan.) The year she was born, nearly 700,000 Palestinian refugees fled, or were expelled from, their homes during the 1948 Arab-Israeli War. (Refugees are people who flee their country to escape violence or persecution.) The growing Jewish population forced these Palestinians off their land and sometimes raided their villages and burned their homes.

Sumaya Farhat-Naser and her family did not flee. Her village was located in the West Bank, an area between Israel and Jordan on the west bank of the Jordan River. In 1948, Jordan assumed control of this land, including her village. Then Israel occupied the area after the 1967 Arab-Israeli War. Farhat-Naser never experienced life in her village without the presence of an occupying power.

A Palestinian mother and her two children at a refugee camp in Jordan, in 1949. When Israel took over the West Bank in 1967, many families such as Sumaya Farhat-Naser's were forced to live in refugee camps like this one. © HULTON-DEUTSCH COLLECTION/CORBIS.

Although her childhood was marked by poverty and hunger, Farhat-Naser grew up in a strong, loving family. Possessed of a quick mind and a strong will, Farhat-Naser rejected her grandfather's attempt to marry her off at age fourteen and instead persuaded him to allow her to get an education. After completing her doctorate in botany at a German university, Farhat-Naser returned to teach at Bir Zeit University in her hometown from 1982 to 1997. During her time in Germany, she learned of the Nazi Party's extermination of the Jews during the Holocaust, the mass murder of European Jews and other groups by the Nazis during World War II (1939–45). This knowledge gave her an appreciation for her occupiers' position. Indeed, Jews had struggled to establish a Jewish state as a means of protecting themselves from the anti-Semitism

Sumaya Farhat-Naser, author of Daughter of the Olive Trees. © VARIO IMAGES GMBH & CO.KG/ALAMY.

(prejudice against Jews) and violence they had experienced throughout the world.

Dismayed at the difficulties in finding peace with Israel, Farhat-Naser began a quest of her own in the 1980s. She sought out Israeli peace activists from whom she could learn the mindset of her occupiers. In turn, she told the story of her people. In the following excerpt from *Daughter of the Olive Trees*, Farhat-Naser explains in detail what life was like in her hometown.

Things to remember while reading the excerpt from *Daughter of the Olive Trees*:

- At the time *Daughter of the Olive Trees* was first published in Germany in 2002, Farhat-Naser had not been able to contact the Israeli peace activists with whom she had discussed peace. The Palestinian uprising against Israel, called the Second Intifada, which began in 2000, ended their discussions.
- Farhat-Naser wrote in the introduction to her book that her decision to write it was an attempt to continue her efforts for peace in the Middle East.
- *Daughter of the Olive Trees* documents not only the difficulties of living under occupation, but also the successful steps toward peace that Farhat-Naser has experienced over the years.

• • •

Daughter of the Olive Trees

In recent years I had seen from my balcony how the lights of **Bet El** were increasing. At first they were only on one hill, a few years later on two, and then they spread to three and today to four hills. The settlement has been built round the village of Doura, which is really surrounded by it. Doura is a breathtakingly beautiful village that used to live from **terrace** market-gardening. The village women used to work on the terraces every day, singing and telling stories, and the next day before the sun was up they would take the vegetables to market in Ramallah. I was often in this village working on projects for the women, for instance **literacy** courses. . . . I often went to Doura to visit my friends Izz, Jamila, Umm Muhammad and others and to buy vegetables.

When a large plot of land belonging to the village of Doura was **confiscated** five years ago, there was a big protest. I was among the demonstrators and had to look on with the others as **settlers** shot at students, killing two of them. One was Ibrahim, my friend Izz's cousin. After the deaths of the two students it was reported that a committee would investigate the incident. A week later we were told that it was only a water reservoir which was being built and the agitation over the confiscation of land was unnecessary. Today the second hill behind the water reservoir has already been built on. At the moment the settlement of Bet El is being connected with other settlements by a road. It runs through the fields of the farmers of Doura and is destroying the foundation of the village's life. I, too, can no longer go to Doura, although it is only three kilometres from Birzeit [Bir Zeit]. . . .

Separate roads are built for the settlers. Everywhere where the settlers' roads cross Palestinian roads there are **checkpoints**. Soldiers bar the way and carry out inspections; they are a serious obstacle to everyone on the road. . . .

Sometimes there is a checkpoint in the middle of a Palestinian village or town where Israelis never come. For instance in Samiramis, the first checkpoint before Ramallah, soldiers block the road. On the 14-kilometre long stretch to Jerusalem there are also the checkpoints at Qalandia and al-Ram. It is pretty well impossible to drive round the checkpoints; any way round them is blocked off with concrete obstacles. Yet thousands of cars try to find another way, for instance across fields and through the labyrinth of streets in Kufr Aqab and the Qalandia refugee camp, between houses and along unasphalted roads. Cars often have to reverse back along the road from the point they have struggled to reach because a lorry or bus is coming from the other direction. There is a danger of plunging over the unfenced verge into the field below. And all the time we see before us the settlements which are expanding from one hill to the next. In the evening the increasing number of lights from the nearest confiscated hill proclaim their presence over a wide area.

Bet El: A Jewish settlement in the West Bank.

Terrace: A flat shelf of land cut into a hill or mountain for growing crops.

Literacy: The ability to read and write.

Confiscated: Taken without payment.

Settlers: Newcomers who establish homes; in this context, Israelis who move into territory once occupied by Palestinians to form settlements.

Checkpoints: A place, usually along a border, where travelers are subject to security checks.

One feels enormous pain and rage when one arrives back on the road beyond the soldiers' checkpoint, only fifty metres after all those detours. . . .

One Friday I, my husband Munir and our daughter Ghada had to drive to Ramallah to do some shopping, get an exit visa, go to the bank and do other things which had been accumulating for weeks. We were glad that that day traveling by car was permitted. But on the way back there were hundreds of cars and people waiting at the checkpoint; no car was allowed to pass. I went over to one of the soldiers and said: "This morning you let us through. Now we want to go home." He replied that new regulations had arrived that the journey was only allowed in one direction. No argument helped, no entreaties. The people stood there furious. A few were weeping.

• • •

What happened next . . .

Farhat-Naser offered a unique perspective on life for Palestinians living under Israeli occupation, and she has not stopped working for peace. She served as director of the Jerusalem Center for Women from 1997 to 2001, working in partnership with Bat Shalom, an Israeli women's peace organization. She continues to lecture on daily life in Palestine under Israeli occupation, and she advocates for the training and education in conflict resolution, human rights, and leadership skills for the women of Palestine.

Farhat-Naser has stated her dream of witnessing an end to the conflict between Palestinians and Israelis. However, despite Israel's withdrawal from Gaza and parts of the West Bank in 2005, a lasting peace had not been secured as of 2011, and peace talks alternated with periods of violence and military action.

Did you know . . .

- The Oslo Accords of 1993 introduced the idea of "land for peace." Upon signing the agreement, Palestinians agreed that Israel existed within borders that comprised nearly 78 percent of the land of Palestine once governed by the British mandate, a system that gave Great Britain the authority to administer Palestine after World War I (1914–18). Palestinians also hoped that Israel would turn over control of the occupied territories, which made up the remaining 22 percent of the mandate, to them. This idea of land for peace had yet to be resolved when Farhat-Naser wrote her book.

- Without an agreement with the Palestinians, Israeli prime minister Ariel Sharon (1928–) decided to withdraw troops and evacuate settlements from some of the occupied territories. By September 2005, Israel's planned withdrawal from the Gaza Strip and parts of the West Bank was complete.
- Elections to establish a Palestinian parliament (legislature) in 2006 were dominated by members of the Islamist party Hamas, a major blow to the ruling party, Fatah. Subsequent conflict between Hamas and Fatah has further complicated peace efforts. However, in 2011 the two factions agreed to a reconciliation, with the aim of working toward the establishment of an independent Palestinian state.

Consider the following...

- Farhat-Naser considers herself a peace activist. Given her account of life under occupation, what aspects of life for Palestinians are the most important ones for her to impress upon the Israeli peace activists she knows?
- Farhat-Naser describes the Israeli settlements as seen from the village of Doura. Imagine what a Jewish settler looking from the other direction at Doura would see. Explain in detail the scene from a Jewish settler's position and how that person might feel about the situation.
- Farhat-Naser wrote her book in part because her dialogue with fellow peace activists had been cut off by the Second Intifada in 2000. What other means could she have used to continue to work for peace? Explain how they compare to the effectiveness of writing her book.

For More Information

BOOKS

Farhat-Naser, Sumaya. *Daughter of the Olive Trees.* Basel, Switzerland: Lenos Verlag, 2003.

Harms, Gregory, and Todd M. Ferry. *The Palestine Israel Conflict: A Basic Introduction,* 2nd ed. London: Pluto Press, 2008.

Tessler, Mark. *A History of the Israeli-Palestinian Conflict,* 2nd ed. Bloomington: Indiana University Press, 2009.

PERIODICALS

Black, Ian, and Conal Urquhart. "Palestinian Joy as Rivals Fatah and Hamas Sign Reconciliation Pact." *The Guardian* (May 4, 2011).

"Israeli Cabinet OKs Gaza Withdrawal." *Los Angeles Times* (February 21, 2005).

Weymouth, Lally. "No Guts, No Glory, No Peace." *Newsweek,* (December 6, 2004): 32.

WEB SITES

"In a Nutshell: Israeli Palestinian Conflict." *Mideastweb.org.* http://www.mideastweb.org/nutshell.htm (accessed on November 30, 2011).

Jaffer, Mehru. "Dreaming Amidst Despair." *Boloji.com.* http://www.boloji.com/index.cfm?md=Content&sd=Articles&ArticleID=6260 (accessed on November 30, 2011).

Den of Lions

Excerpt from *Den of Lions*

By Terry Anderson

Published in 1993

"My mind seemed to stall for a few seconds, and by the time I realized what was happening, one of the men was beside the driver's door of my car, yanking it open and pushing his pistol at my head."

The impact of ongoing conflicts in the Middle East has not been restricted to those living there. American journalist Terry Anderson (1947–) learned firsthand that all people can be targets during times of war. Anderson was assigned to cover Beirut, the capitol of Lebanon, for the Associated Press (AP) in 1982. That year Israeli troops invaded from southern Lebanon in an effort to remove the Palestine Liberation Organization (PLO) from the region. (The PLO is a political and military organization formed to unite various Palestinian Arab groups with the goal of establishing an independent Palestinian state.) Anderson followed the U.S. Marine Corps throughout the country on a peacekeeping mission. He wrote a series of articles about Lebanon's attempts to rebuild itself after the destruction caused by Israel's attack. Anderson grew accustomed to moving freely through checkpoints as a member of the press. (Checkpoints are places, usually along a border, where travelers are subject to security checks.) He recalled in his memoir *Den of Lions* that the late fall of 1982 and the early part of 1983 was a time of optimism, when "everyone saw an end to the war, an end finally to the bad times."

Soon after Anderson was promoted to chief Middle East correspondent for the AP, violence in Lebanon surged once again. Religious factions within Lebanon fought for political power. The international peacekeeping force changed the focus of its mission and began to act in support of

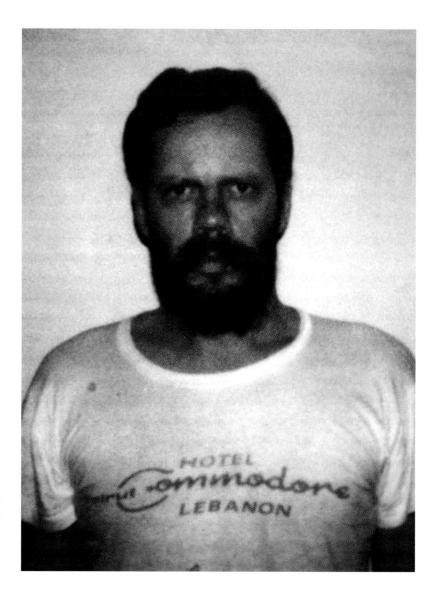

This photograph of Terry Anderson was released in April 1988, proving that he was still alive. Anderson would not be released for another four years.
© CORBIS.

the Lebanese government. Israeli troops occupied the south of Lebanon as Syrian troops increased from the north. As violence grew, reporters who had once been treated by all groups as neutral observers were increasingly singled out and harassed according to their nationalities. Sometimes caught in the crossfire of others' battles and sometimes direct targets, journalists were no longer safe. Americans in particular were scorned by the Lebanese, as evidenced by the bombing of the 1983 U.S. embassy in Beirut and the kidnapping of American scholars and journalists.

The Lebanese government collapsed in February 1984, and the United States removed its marines from Lebanon the next month. On March 12, 1985, the United States ordered Americans working for international agencies to leave Beirut. Anderson and other journalists delayed, ignoring the call. Four days later, Terry Anderson's life was forever changed. The following excerpt from his book *Den of Lions* recounts his kidnapping and his years in captivity.

Things to remember while reading the excerpt from *Den of Lions*:

- Terry Anderson had served with the U.S. Marines as a combat correspondent during the Vietnam War (1954–75).

- Hezbollah, a militant group based in Lebanon, was responsible for Anderson's kidnapping. In the early 1980s, Hezbollah received money from Iran in order to wrest political power from the Christians.

- At the time of Anderson's kidnapping, Lebanon was engaged in a civil war that lasted from 1975 to 1990. Lebanon's government is sectarian, meaning that the various religious sects (groups) were represented based on the proportion of the population each sect claimed. The majority of the power was held by Christians, but Muslims had grown to make up the majority of the population. In large part, the civil war was a battle for power between Muslim and Christian factions.

- On March 15, 1985, the day before he was kidnapped, Anderson mentioned to his news editor that four men in a Mercedes had followed him during his lunch hour. He did not report the incident to authorities.

- Anderson was held for nearly seven years, during which time he was interrogated and treated as a prisoner of war, even though he had very little information that could help his kidnappers.

- Anderson tells of being forced to write a note that refers to the actions of "the detained persons of Kuwait." In December 1983, Islamic extremists executed a series of bombings in Kuwait in retaliation for support of Iraq by that nation, as well as the United States and France. Those detained for the bombing became known as the "Kuwait 17."

- Anderson was able to communicate with several fellow hostages during his time in captivity. One hostage was Terry Waite (1939–), a British humanitarian who was in Lebanon to help negotiate the release of four hostages when he was taken hostage himself.

• • •

Den of Lions

Beirut. 8 A.M. March 16, 1985

The green Mercedes, sparkling clean in the weak morning sunlight, drifted to a gentle halt in the narrow road, just a few yards up the hill from the graffiti-covered monument to **Gamal Abdel Nasser**. Don Mell, the young AP photographer I was dropping off at his apartment after our tennis game, had noticed it earlier at the sports club but hadn't mentioned it—it didn't seem important. Now, though, it struck him as odd, especially the curtains drawn over the rear window.

. . . [T]hree unshaven men threw open the doors and jumped out, each holding a 9mm pistol in his right hand, hanging loosely by his side.

My mind seemed to stall for a few seconds, and by the time I realized what was happening, one of the men was beside the driver's door of my car, yanking it open and pushing his pistol at my head. "Get out," he said fiercely. "I will shoot. I will shoot."

"Okay," I answered quickly. I pulled the keys from the ignition and dropped them between the seats. "Okay, no problem. No problem."

He reached in and pulled the glasses from my face. As I slid out of the seat, half crouched, he put his hand around my shoulders, forcing me to remain bent over.

"Come, come quickly."

I glanced up at Don, just a vague blur on the other side of the car, willing him to run, but not daring to shout the words. He just stood, frozen.

The young man, dark and very Arab-looking, perhaps twenty or twenty-five, pulled me along beside him toward the Mercedes, just four or five yards away, still forcing me to remain half bent.

"Get in. I will shoot," he hissed at me, pushing me into the backseat. "Get down. Get down."

I tried to crouch in the narrow space between the front and back seats. Another young man jumped in the other door and shoved me to the floor, throwing an old blanket over me, then shoving my head and body down with both his feet. I could feel a gun barrel pushing at my neck. "Get down. Get down."

The car lurched into gear and accelerated madly up the hill. . . .

Gamal Abdel Nasser: The longtime president of Egypt and champion of Arab causes (1918–1970).

After fifteen or twenty minutes, the car turned off the main highway straight into what seemed to be a garage. A metal door clanged down, cutting off the street noise. The doors were yanked open and hands grabbed at me, pulling me upright, but careful to keep the blanket over my head. There were mutterings in Arabic, short, guttural, incomprehensible.

Someone slipped the blanket away, slipping a dirty cloth around my head at the same time, then wrapping plastic tape around and around. Other hands grabbed at my tennis shoes, yanking them off. . . .

"What is your name?" a voice asked, heavily accented.

"Terry Anderson. I am a journalist."

"Your company?"

"The Associated Press. A wire service."

The man seemed uninterested in my answers. . . .

Beirut. April 1985.

Hours, days, nights, weeks. Blank nights. Gray dawn after gray dawn.

An English-speaking man came in today and dictated a short letter to me. At least I know why I've been kidnapped, or at least what the "official" reason is. He was abrupt, but not threatening. Simply gave me a pen and a piece of paper, then told me what to write:

"I am fine. I received your message. You should know that I am a victim of the American policy that favors Israel and which forced the detained persons in Kuwait to do what they did. My freedom is tied to the freedom of the detained over there. The American government still does not care about us. I ask you to do your best to pressure the American government to release the detained people over there because we are very close to being hanged in the case that this term is not met." . . .

The days begin to settle into a kind of routine: Sleepless nights, watching the dawn light grow slowly on the ceiling, shifting and turning, trying to ease the stiffness and pain of lying on a bed twenty-four hours a day. Listen to the roaches, occasionally watch one or two or three, two inches long, crawl slowly up the wall. Hear the stirring and muttering in Arabic as the guards awaken. Food—usually a sandwich of Arabic bread and dry, yellow cheese. Brief trip down the hall to the filthy bathroom. One guard unlocks the chains. Another stands against the wall holding a small automatic pistol with a silencer. Back to the cot. Read the Bible for a while. Lunch—perhaps a bowl of soup, or cold rice with canned vegetables dumped on top. The evenings are sometimes enlivened by short visits from one or two of the young men, sometimes to ask questions in broken English, sometimes just to amuse themselves. Occasionally, one or two will kneel or sit on my chest, poke their guns in my ear or neck, and hiss threats: "You dead. I kill you." . . .

Beirut. April 1990.

All good, but we're still chained to the wall in this dammed room. . . .

I pray a great deal, mostly at night, and read the Bible, in English or French. It helps keep me calm, and able to accept whatever happens. . . .

Beirut. August 1990.

Brian's gone home! And we're back with John. No warning, no indication that something was going to happen. The guards just came in, ordered us to stand up, taped our arms and around our eyes, then dumped us in a car trunk for a ten-minute ride, apparently just a few blocks.

When we were unwrapped in our new abode, another apartment in the southern suburbs of Beirut, John was sitting against the wall, bearded and grinning with relief.

It seems Brian and he had been together, along with Frank Reed, for more than a year. Suddenly, Reed was taken out nearly four months ago; then two days ago, they came for Brian. . . .

The apartment is the same one I was kept in with Fontaine, and again later. The blood mark from beating my head on the wall is still there, a little faded but obvious.

John says Reed was in very bad shape when they were put together with him, and didn't get much better. He had been abused badly, and was being treated with contempt by the guards until John and Brian protested. They said he had gone off his head—believed he had a radio in his head and could talk with the U.S. embassy in East Beirut.

John also said there was another prisoner in the apartment, in the next room, and both he and Brian believed it was Terry Waite. They had communicated sporadically and vaguely with knocks on the wall, but couldn't really exchange information. Both he and Brian were chained on the opposite side of the room from the wall between the two rooms, and could tap on it only during exercise periods. . . .

September 5, 1990. My two thousandth day.

I've established contact with Terry Waite. He is next door, as John and Brian thought. I began by tapping on the wall and, when he tapped back, painstakingly tapped out the series 1-2-3-4- . . . to 26. Then, using numbers for the alphabet (1=a, 2=b, and so on) I tapped out our names. It took a while, but he caught on. I spent all one night tapping out a summary of all the news: Brian's release, Frank's release; the comments and promises of Iran, Syria, and others on hostages over the past year. Then the world news: the Berlin Wall's falling, communism's demise in eastern Europe, free elections in the Soviet Union, work toward multiracial government in South Africa. All the incredible things that have happened since he was taken nearly three years ago. He thought I was crazy.

He's been in isolation all that time, without even a scrap of news. . . .

Baalbek, Lebanon. December 4, 1991.

The 2,454th day, and the last. The two new subchiefs came in this morning to say that I would be going home tonight. They talked with me awhile about various things. Strangely, they seemed mostly concerned with justifying themselves, and the last seven years. They said that their group now realized that this had all been a mistake, and they had gotten little out of it. They knew that the release last year of their brothers in Kuwait, the main goal they'd had in the beginning and for all those years, had nothing to do with the hostages they had held so long. "This tactic [kidnapping] is not useful. We will not do it again," one of them said. "We are not giving up. But we will use other means."

He did not explain what that meant, and I was not interested enough to pursue the subject. . . .

It's dark outside now. They always prefer to wait for darkness to fall before making any move. The door opens. Several guards come in. I'm already dressed—I put on my new clothes two hours ago. Mahmoud says, as he has so many times, "Stand up."

No tape this time. Just the blindfold. The new subchiefs are there. One of them hands me a small bouquet. Half a dozen carnations. "Give this to your wife, and tell her we're sorry."

Someone takes my arm, guides me through the door, outside, and into a car. Another Mercedes, just like the one they forced me into so long ago. . . .

The car stops. I'm pulled out. Someone puts his hand on my shoulder. "I'm a Syrian colonel. You're free."

• • •

What happened next...

On December 4, 1991, Terry Anderson was released, the last of the American hostages to be freed in Lebanon. He was greeted by his love, Madeleine, and their six-year-old daughter, Sulome. After a recuperation period spent on the island of Antigua, Anderson regained his life. He and Madeleine married on April 18, 1993. About his terrible years in captivity, Anderson concluded, as German philosopher Friedrich Wilhelm Nietzsche (1844–1900) once wrote, "That which does not destroy me, makes me stronger."

After his release, Anderson eagerly sought out new opportunities. He took a professorship at Ohio University in Athens, Ohio, from which he retired in 2002. Next he joined the faculty at the University of Kentucky in 2009 to teach a course in international journalism, and in 2011, he accepted visiting professorship at Syracuse University. In addition to his work as a

Terry Anderson in 1993. AP PHOTO.

teacher and lecturer, he opened a restaurant in Athens and another in the Caribbean and bought a 200-acre horse ranch. In 2004, he made an unsuccessful run for a seat in the Ohio senate. He hoped to be remembered as more than "the guy who was kidnapped," as he told the *Akron Beacon Journal.*

Did you know . . .

- Throughout Anderson's captivity the U.S. government and other international organizations tried to secure the release of the American hostages. The U.S. government's attempts to free American hostages even included a secret arms deal with Iran in 1986, but no American hostages were released from Lebanon between 1986 and 1989.
- Anderson attributed his survival in captivity to reading the Bible and to writing poetry.
- While Anderson emerged from captivity in relative good health, some of the other American hostages suffered permanent nerve damage and hearing loss. One hostage had a dented skull from the torture he endured in captivity.
- Anderson sued the Iranian government, a key Hezbollah sponsor, seeking compensation for his time as a hostage, and in 2000, he was awarded a multimillion-dollar settlement to be paid out of Iranian assets frozen by the U.S. government. Anderson used some of the settlement money to fund his business and charitable ventures; however, in 2009, he filed for bankruptcy after his businesses failed.

Consider the following . . .

- The U.S. government refused to negotiate directly with Anderson's kidnappers. It is the policy of the U.S. government not to give in to terrorist demands. Is this policy valid? Based on what happened to Anderson, explain why such a policy should stand or why it should be revised.
- Should journalists be able to move freely throughout areas of conflict? Consider how their jobs might be compromised if journalists were not allowed access to firsthand information.

For More Information

BOOKS

Anderson, Terry. *Den of Lions.* New York: Crown, 1993.

PERIODICALS

Bugeja, Michael J. "Terry Anderson and the Truth." *Editor & Publisher* (June 26, 2000): 18.

"Delivered from Evil." *Time* (December 16, 1991): 16.

Gersh, Debra. "Journalists Recall the Allure of Beirut." *Editor & Publisher,* (April 6, 1991): 9.

Smolowe, Jill. "Lives in Limbo." *Time,* (December 16, 1991): 18.

"Terry Anderson Seeks Legacy of Rural Public Servant Over Foreign Hostage." *Beacon Journal* (Akron, Ohio; October 18, 2004).

WEB SITES

Alessi, Ryan. "Former Middle East Hostage Terry Anderson to Teach at UK." *Kentucky.com* (December 19, 2008). http://www.kentucky.com/2008/12/19/631076/former-middle-east-hostage-terry.html (accessed on November 30, 2011).

"Terry Anderson Begins Sixth Year of Captivity." *Congressional Record: Senate.* March 20, 1990, p. S2709. http://www.fas.org/irp/congress/1990_cr/s900320-anderson.htm (accessed on November 30, 2011).

Barefoot in Baghdad

Excerpt from *Barefoot in Baghdad: A Story of Identity—
My Own—and What It Means To Be a Woman in Chaos*
By Manal M. Omar
Published by Sourcebooks, Inc., in 2010

"In every case, the women bore the brunt of any violence and
all the poverty."

Between the 1960s and the early 2000s, Iraqi women experienced significantly more rights than women in other Middle Eastern countries. In 1968, the Ba'ath Party (a secular [nonreligious] political party founded in the 1940s with the goal of uniting the Arab world and creating one powerful Arab state) seized power in Iraq, enacting programs to unite its authority and to promote rapid economic growth in the midst of ongoing labor shortages. The party recognized that the social and economic contributions of women were essential for attaining both of these goals. As a result, laws specifically aimed at improving the status of women were passed. In 1970, the Iraqi Constitution was adopted. It granted equal rights to all men and women. The constitution recognized Iraq's Personal Status Laws, which were originally adopted in 1959 to regulate issues of marriage, divorce, child custody, and inheritance outside the influence of religious courts and which codified the rights of women in those situations. The party made further moves to modernize Iraqi society by adopting national programs to end illiteracy and to provide free education and health care to all citizens. When the Iran-Iraq War (1980–88) began in September 1980, a severe shortage in the male workforce resulted, and many women took jobs outside the home. Women's status in Iraq had improved markedly.

Despite this progress, the rights of women often conflicted with traditions that call for a male-dominated family structure, adherence to

Iraqi women walk past a mural of Saddam Hussein in Baghdad. Under Saddam, women's rights and freedoms lost further ground. © IMAGESTATE MEDIA PARTNERS LIMITED - IMPACT PHOTOS/ALAMY.

religious principles, and defense of family honor and reputation. In the last years of the war, a backlash against women entering the workforce arose. This movement grew significantly when men came home from the war in 1988 to a failing economy. After the Persian Gulf War (1990–91), many of the positive steps that had been taken to advance the status of women in Iraqi society were in jeopardy. Support for Saddam Hussein (1937–2006), who rose through the ranks of the Ba'ath Party in the 1970s to assume power in 1979, was beginning to wane, and he began appealing to conservative Sunni religious groups and tribal leaders to increase his popularity. (Sunnis are followers of the Sunni branch of Islam.) As a result, women's rights and freedoms lost further ground. Women found their ability to move freely in public severely restricted, and reports of violence against women increased.

In March 2003, the U.S.-led coalition forces invaded Iraq and ended Saddam's rule. The ensuing years of occupation (the physical and political control of an area seized by a foreign military force) and the establishment of a new government in Iraq brought about countless changes to the country's political and cultural environment. Although the war certainly affected all Iraqis, women in particular saw many of the rights they once enjoyed severely restricted, despite the U.S. and coalition presence. Kidnappings, rapes, and honor killings increased, making women fearful of going out in public and therefore limiting their ability to work and go to school. (An honor killing is the killing of a relative, especially a female, who is perceived to have brought dishonor upon their family.) Violence also increased at home. The United Nations reported that one in five married Iraqi women has been a victim of physical domestic violence, while one in three has been subject to emotional violence. Of the female victims of physical domestic violence, 14 percent have been subject to violence during pregnancy.

These were the circumstances that brought Manal M. Omar (1975–) to Iraq in 2003 as part of a humanitarian mission with Women to Women International, a group that helps women in war-torn countries rebuild their lives. Omar was born in Saudi Arabia to Palestinian parents. (Palestinians are an Arab people whose ancestors lived in the historical region of Palestine, comprising parts of present-day Israel and Jordan, and who continue to lay claim to that land.) Her family moved to Texas when she was six months old. Although surrounded by a loving family, she struggled with identity while growing up as an Arab-American Muslim. By her teenage years, she came to the conclusion that her multicultural heritage was her strength. Having spent most of her summers in the Middle East, Omar had a deep affection for the region. Her desire to aid its people was rooted in this love. After earning a bachelor's degree in international development and a master's degree in

Manal Omar, author of Barefoot in Baghdad: A Story of Identity—My Own—and What It Means To Be a Woman in Chaos. AP PHOTO/ JEREMY PIPER.

Arab studies, she began a career that took her to Iraq shortly after the Persian Gulf War. The following excerpt from *Barefoot in Baghdad: A Story of Identity—My Own—and What It Means to Be a Woman in Chaos* is an account of some of Omar's experiences during her two years in Iraq. She found that despite their hardships Iraqi women are hopeful and committed to improving their lot in life.

Things to remember while reading the excerpt from *Barefoot in Baghdad: A Story of Identity—My Own—and What It Means to Be a Woman in Chaos*:

- Many Iraqi women believe life was better for them under Saddam Hussein's rule that it was after the 2003 invasion by U.S. and coalition troops.

- Despite her intentions to improve the lives of other women, Omar would not have gone to Iraq if her father had not given his approval.

- Resolution 137, a bill to cancel Iraq's Personal Status Law, was a proposed in late 2003 by conservatives in the Iraqi legislature. The resolution declared that religious institutions would be the authority for personal and family matters such as marriage and divorce, as opposed to civilian courts. The bill was defeated in March 2004.

- The excerpt below is from "The Negotiation Chips," Chapter 10 of *Barefoot in Baghdad.*

● ● ●

Barefoot in Baghdad: A Story of Identity—My Own—and What It Means to Be a Woman in Chaos

The Negotiation Chips

. . . My six months on the ground had demonstrated what I had known by instinct. Iraqi women were powerful. Through my relationship with Reema Khalaf, the chairperson of the Independent Nahrain Women's Association, I met regularly with the heads of various organizations. These women were predominately engineers, doctors, lawyers, and professors. They were considered the elite of their communities, and often they had their own informal networks that they were willing to use to strengthen the women in their communities. Some of these women had attained the highest level of decision maker.

At the same time, I was able to communicate with women on the ground. I was traveling in and out of the most ghettoized areas of Iraq, including the **marginalized** areas of Baghdad. Like most of the world's poor, these communities suffered because they were stereotyped as being infested with drug dealers, pimps, and thugs. In some cases the stereotype was true. In most cases, however, the areas were populated with families that were struggling to make ends meet. In every case, the women bore the **brunt** of any violence and all the poverty.

Marginalized: Pushed to the margin or outside, made powerless.

Brunt: The main force of something.

Downtrodden: Beaten down, oppressed, and discouraged.

Refurbish: Renovate, restore.

Grassroots: Common people.

Sanctions: Punitive measures adopted by the international community against a nation that has violated international law, usually in the form of diplomatic, economic, or social restrictions.

Naive: Simple, inexperienced.

Patriarchal: Male-dominated.

Iran-Iraq War: A war between Iran and Iraq that lasted from 1980 to 1988.

Invasion of Kuwait: Iraq invaded Kuwait on August 2, 1990.

First Gulf War: The Persian Gulf War (1990–91), a war in which coalition forces forced Iraq's withdrawal from Kuwait.

Second Gulf War: The Iraq War (2003–11), a war in which U.S.-led forces removed Saddam Hussein from power.

Machiavellian: Typical of Italian statesman and philosopher Machiavelli (1469–1527), that is, purposely dishonest and manipulative.

The majority of women I worked with were widows and divorcees, and some were just teenagers. Despite their difficult circumstances, these women were determined to carve out a better future. I was amazed at their outspoken nature, their candid list of needs, and their resolution to create change for themselves. In the short span of a few months I watched countless women who had entered my office **downtrodden** emerge from it full of optimism.

Such was the case of Saadiyah. She had learned of our program through word of mouth. Several women in her neighborhood were already enrolled, and as a widow with six children, she felt she had nothing to lose by visiting our office in Karbala. Saadiyah attended the first few sessions reluctantly. Over time, she became more easily involved in the work of the women's center. Not only was she an active participant in the rights awareness workshops, but she signed up for the carpentry class. Saadiyah introduced an innovative way of earning money through carpentry. Each morning she would go to the fruit and vegetable market and collect empty wooden crates. She would then break the crates and use the wood to **refurbish** furniture.

The women ranged from the elite to the **grassroots**, and it was an honor to work with each of them. They particularly embodied for me all that our shared culture could accomplish. It was easy to see why their strength was legendary in the Middle East. They had paved the way for women in the region by being among the first to vote, the first to participate in the judiciary system, and the first to demonstrate their economic power. Women from the rural areas became legendary for devising methods to survive the **sanctions** of the 1990s. The women I met were proud of their ability to survive, and although they were exhausted, they were willing to continue the struggle for a better future.

Nonetheless, these women were not **naive**. Regardless of their economic status, they were well aware of their violent **patriarchal** history. They often spoke of the internal conflicts that led to the execution of the king that ended the monarchy in 1958. That was quickly followed by the coup of Gen. Abdul Karim Kassem and five years later to the Baathist regime and then the overthrow of Gen. Ahmed Hassan al-Bakr by Saddam Hussein in 1979. I heard from women of all socioeconomic backgrounds that Saddam's ascension was the beginning of the end. Although the country enjoyed prosperity on one level, the Saddam regime would also lead to hundreds of executions, the **Iran-Iraq War** in the 1980s, the **invasion of Kuwait**, the **First Gulf War**, thirteen years of sanctions, and the **Second Gulf War**.

For the past few decades, women in Iraq had been forced into the backdrop of Saddam's theatrics. They were used as props when needed. Saddam's approach on women's issues epitomized his **Machiavellian** quest for power. On the one hand, Saddam was well known for his promotion of women in the workplace and the education of women. On the other hand, he was quick to use women as a negotiating chip to gain local tribal support. For example, Saddam promoted **secular** laws, but he was willing to turn a blind eye during the 1990s to promoted **honor killings** in order to appease the tribes. Under the pretext of fighting prostitution in 2000, Saddam's **Fedayeen** forces beheaded two hundred women "**dissidents**" and dumped their heads on their families' doorsteps for public display.

By now, Iraqi women realized they needed to take matters into their own hands. Many argued that for too long power had been left unquestionably in the hands of men. They recognized a void had been created, and many were determined to be part of whatever power structure would step up to fill it. Women were focused on the endgame. They were strategizing ways to leap forward, and they refused to be discouraged by the signs surrounding them.

These signs were plenty. Nine months after the fall of the regime, the dust from the war was just beginning to settle down. It was clear that women's rights were not going to be defended from the outside. It was the responsibility of the Iraqi women to take action from within. Iraqi politicians and the leaders of the American occupying forces made speeches that promised women's rights, but they took no action beyond offering consolation prizes. The threat to women's legal and social status demanded—and received—a response at all levels, from the grassroots to the ruling elite. When the U.S.-led **Coalition Provisional Authority** refused to swear in a female judge who had been appointed, citing religious and cultural grounds, she fought for her right to the judgeship by using Islamic teachings as her weapon.

Women took these setbacks in stride and still had confidence that their interests rested with the **CPA**. That is, until **Fern**'s prediction turned into reality.

On December 29, 2003, with less than a thirty-minute debate, the Interim Governing Council (IGC) voted for **Resolution 137**. The primary advocate for Resolution 137 was Abdel Aziz Hakim, the leader of the Supreme Council for Islamic Revolution in Iraq (SCIRI). The council was an important political player, and many other political parties that supported women's issues did not want to lose the SCIRI as an ally.

Fern and other women's rights activists around the country went into a frenzy. Resolution 137 would push women's rights back centuries. Whereas Iraqi women had been looking for ways to leap forward, they now found themselves in the unenviable position of fighting for the status quo.

Iraqi women united against the resolution and even took to the streets in one of the first public protests in over thirty years in the streets of Baghdad. These women were among the first members of civil society to immediately practice democratic and transparent management, and they quickly formed the Iraqi Women's Network to fight the resolution. They elected a steering committee, and the network swiftly organized protests and petitions against the repeal of the 1959 personal status laws.

Secular: Nonreligious.

Honor killings: The killing of a relative, especially a female, who is perceived to have brought dishonor on the family.

Fedayeen: An Arabic term meaning one who sacrifices for a cause; used to describe several distinct militant groups that have formed in the Arab world at different times. Opponents of the fedayeen use the term to describe members of Arab terrorist groups.

Dissidents: Those who disagree with an established religious or political system.

Coalition Provisional Authority: A transitional government established after the invasion of Iraq by U.S. and coalition forces.

CPA: Coalition Provisional Authority.

Fern: Fern L. Holland (1970–2004), an American civilian who worked for the CPA on women's rights in Iraq. She was murdered on March 9, 2004.

Resolution 137: A proposed bill to cancel Iraq's Personal Status Law.

Fern and other international women's rights activists held the U.S. government responsible. They claimed that the IGC was an extension of the Coalition Provisional Authority in Iraq since the IGC had been appointed by the United States. As a result, if the resolution were passed into law, it would be an infringement of international law as defined by the 1907 **Hague Regulations**. The Hague Regulations forbade any changes to the civil law by an occupying power. Under the Hague Conventions, the IGC's **mandate** was only to restore public order and safety.

Fern made good on her promise of taking the issue to the public media. She worked closely with Iraqi women leaders to send out reports of the U.S. government's supporting the decay of women's rights, which used terms such as "sexual harassment" and "women's oppression" to get as much attention as possible. She even helped leak an email from a State Department official that referred to Safia Suhail, one of the leading women's rights activists in Iraq, as a loud-mouthed reformist. This email further tied the U.S. government's support and tolerance to the IGC's marginalization of women.

The result of Resolution 137 was far more catastrophic for the women's movement than Fern and the others could have imagined. For the previous six months, women's organizations had been demonstrating the power of cooperation across religious and ethnic divides. I had helped organize a few meetings among women's groups from across the country, and I was always amazed at the mosaic of Iraqi cultures that responded. Secular women shared a round table with their more conservative counterparts; Arabs eagerly expressed interest in learning from the Kurds.

Although all women were united against Resolution 137, the **rhetoric** of defending women's rights became divisive. International women's groups began to attack core Islamic values. The secular elite from within Iraq joined their voices, and the slogans in the protests could easily be turned into anti-Islamic sentiments. The conservative political parties, such as SCIRI, seized on the opportunity to denounce the protests against Resolution 137 as being orchestrated by Western feminists, therefore reducing the significance of the organic outrage among Iraqi women at this assault on their rights. At the same time, women in the conservative areas believed they were being pushed into a defensive position. They believed firmly in Islamic law, and they were confident that Islamic law was the best vehicle to protect their rights. They instantly jumped to the other side of the spectrum and called for all personal status laws to be rooted in Islamic law. The debate began the division between two extremes: secular versus Islamic law, pro-women versus pro-family.

Women's rights, which had once been a unifying factor, became a source of conflict.

Both extremes were in the minority, and the majority of Iraqi women were torn. When political parties would present the debate as simply

Hague Regulations: International treaties negotiated at the Hague, Netherlands that were among the first formal statements of laws of war.

Mandate: Directive, authority.

Rhetoric: Exaggerated discussion or commentary.

choosing Islam over secularism, the vast majority chose Islam. When secularists would outline the rights that would be lost to them, the women grew fearful. Iraqi women wanted to protect their rights, but they did not want to lose their Islamic identity. Most important, as the attacks linking women's humiliation to Islam grew, even the most liberal women felt a powerful, prideful urge to debunk the anti-Islamic myths.

I joined the women in the middle. After all, this was a struggle I had faced my entire life. The balance between my Islamic beliefs and my identity with the Western concepts of democracy and freedom was a trapeze act. For Iraqi women these values were being presented as mutually exclusive. Women were being told they could only make one choice. In the true spirit of the American dream, I wanted it all. I wanted Iraqi women to be able to protect their rights through the rule of law based on the best global practices. I also saw the need for their rights to be defended by using Islamic interpretations to ensure **traction** on the community level. In other words, what good did it do to have a law that set the marriage age at sixteen when there was no way the government could enforce it? In addition to the law, there needed to be an awareness that demonstrated the need to protect girls from the dangers that early marriage could bring to them and their families.

The problem with Resolution 137 was not simply that **Shari'a** law was being introduced into personal status matters; the core problem was that there was no attempt to define Shari'a law. Whose interpretations were going to be used? Women would be left **vulnerable** to the educational limitation and understanding of the local religious **clerics**. A well-versed religious cleric in Najaf could make a liberal pro-women judgment on inheritance, while a cleric in Basra would deny any women any rights. Without an agreement on the system to be implemented, judgments on women's affairs would be completely **arbitrary**.

The term Shari'a law was being used as if it had a predefined **monolithic** classification. There was a legitimate fear that this understanding could lead to serious violations of women's rights, such as denial of education, forced early marriage, domestic violence, execution by stoning, and public flogging.

The division over Resolution 137 caused the Iraqi women's rights movement to lose its comparative advantage of having a wide membership base. Whereas the first few months of the occupation had required only a distinction between Baathist and non-Baathist, finger wagging over sectarian and ethnic divides was now becoming finger wagging over religious and ethnic divides. She is a **Shia**. She is a **Sunni**. She is a **Kurd**. These phrases were becoming more and more frequent and often took on a derogatory tone.

In some instances, the divide centered on attire. Women would quickly label one another based on how much or how little the other wore. A woman who was covered from head to toe would be dismissed as a backward puppet

Traction: The ability to catch on.

Shari'a: Also spelled sharia; Islamic religious law.

Vulnerable: Without adequate protection.

Clerics: Ordained religious officials.

Arbitrary: Random or without reason.

Monolithic: Solid and unbroken.

Shia: A follower of the Shia branch of Islam.

Sunni: A follower of the Sunni branch of Islam.

Kurd: A member of a non-Arab ethnic group who live mainly in present-day Turkey, Iraq, and Iran.

of the Shia conservatives, whereas women who were uncovered were seen as pawns of the Western feminists.

Over time, one's clothing began to play an even greater role. The magnificence of Iraqi civil society in the early months had been the coexistence of women from different backgrounds, each dressed in a unique way to symbolize her individual comfort level. Now the same women who, a few months earlier, had been sitting next to one another and debating everything from integrating women into the political system to revamping the curriculum in the primary schools were openly attacking one another. It only made it more and more difficult for women to identify their true allies.

One of the strongest Iraqi women to emerge in this charged political scene was Salama Al-Khafaji. She wore the traditional black **abaya**. With the trend of labeling based on physical appearance, her appointment to the IGC received a strong backlash and protests by leading Iraqi women's groups. Over time, however, Salama proved to be an independent woman who was ready to make her own sacrifices for the new Iraq. This would later include the life of her seventeen-year-old son, who was killed during an assassination attempt on her life.

I felt that the debate over Islamic and secular values greatly minimized the larger danger of the resolution. The issue was being minimized as a women's issue alone, but it struck at the very fabric of the newly emerging civil society in Iraq. I would often reiterate to U.S. officials that women should be used as a barometer of success inside Iraq. The status of women highlighted the progress, or lack thereof, of Iraqi society on several levels. Nothing better exemplified this than Resolution 137. In the early months on the ground, any talk of Iraq's becoming another Islamic state, such as Saudi Arabia or Iran, had been dismissed by political analysts and local Iraqis alike. Iraq's history boasted a strong secular legacy, with the understanding that religion belonged in the home, not in the public sphere, and particularly not in the political sphere.

Resolution 137 strongly challenged that assumption.

At the same time, the introduction of the resolution in December 2003 highlighted the beginnings of rising tensions between the ethnic and sectarian divides. The impact on the women's movement was a **microcosm** of the larger impact on the country as a whole. The introduction of laws being interpreted by each sect foreshadowed the future divides between Iraqi nationals. The 1959 personal status laws had been rooted in secular law, but this whole situation foreshadowed an internal struggle for the entire country. It was the first introduction of formal sectarianism as the foundational base of social and political life in Iraq.

Abaya: A loose-fitting full-length robe worn by some Muslim women.

Microcosm: Small version of something larger.

In the end, Resolution 137 was repealed. But over subsequent years it would reappear in new forms, making it clear that Iraqi women had won only a minor battle. The war was yet to begin.

• • •

What happened next...

Iraq's turn toward more a religiously and socially conservative society continues to affect the role of women in politics and daily life. Only one woman served as a cabinet member in 2011. In the two previous governments, women held from four to six positions. Bushra Hussein, the only woman in the cabinet, was named a minister of state in 2010, a position with little power and no budget. Another female lawmaker, Vyan Dakheel, declined the offer to become minister of state for women's affairs, because she felt it was a position without real power to serve women. The position is now being filled temporarily by a man. The current Iraqi constitution does require that 25 percent of parliament members be women, but critics state that this only guarantees women a place in government, not a real voice.

Tension also exists about Article 2 of the current Iraqi constitution. In essence, Article 2 states that Islam is the religion of the state and the foundation of legislation. It also states that no law can be enacted that goes against the established provisions of Islam. Many Iraqi women are apprehensive because Islamic law has often been used to limit their rights. Thus, the form of Islamic law that will be adopted in Iraq is an important factor in determining the fate of women's rights. Will it be moderate, like it is in Morocco? Or, will it be of stricter interpretation, as in Saudi Arabia?

Omar notes that her book "takes its title from a popular Iraqi-Turkmen proverb that says, 'Walk barefoot and the thorns will hurt you.' It is often used as a warning to those who challenge societal norms." Many Iraqis fear that if the current trends continue, women will lose more of their freedoms, while others are hopeful that because of those who are willing to "walk barefoot," women will regain the rights they have lost since 2003. As of 2011, many non-governmental organizations existed in Iraq to assist individual women and the overall cause of women's rights. Whatever happens, it is a certainty that the plight of Iraq's women will be part of the larger fight over Iraq's future.

Did you know...

- Manal Omar joined the United States Institute of Peace (USIP) in 2008, eventually serving as its director of programs in Iraq, Iran, and North Africa as part of its Post-Conflict Peace and Stability Operations unit.

Young Iraqi women walk on campus at Al-Mustansiriyah University in Baghdad. In 2007 the United Nations estimated that women in Iraq were twice as likely as men to be illiterate. ALI YUSSEF/AFP/GETTY IMAGES.

- Although reports indicate that security in Iraq is still unstable, U.S. president Barack Obama (1961–) has promised that all U.S. troops will leave Iraq before the end of 2012.
- The United Nations estimated in 2007 that women were twice as likely as men to be illiterate and made up only 18 percent of the nation's workforce.

Consider the following...

- Omar states that she can neither attack nor defend the United States, although she wants to do both. Why might she feel this way?
- The Iraqi constitution stipulates that laws cannot be enacted that violate Islamic law. In the future, what impact could this

have on an Iraqi democratic society, specifically upon women's rights?

- It has been estimated that approximately 750,000 Iraqi women have been widowed during the Iraq War. Many widows and their children have been reduced to begging on the streets to survive. Assume you are a humanitarian aid worker. What ideas do you have about how to begin to address this situation?

For More Information

BOOKS

Al-Ali, Nadje. *Iraqi Women: Untold Stories from 1948 to the Present.* London: Zed Books, 2007.

Al-Ali, Nadje. *What Kind of Liberation? Women and the Occupation of Iraq.* Berkeley: University of California Press, 2009.

Asquith, Christina. *Iraqi Women: Untold Stories from 1948 to the Present.* New York: Random House, 2009.

Coleman, Isobel. *Paradise Beneath Her Feet: How Women Are Transforming the Middle East.* New York: Random House, 2010.

Omar, Manal M. *Barefoot in Baghdad: A Story of Identity—My Own—and What It Means To Be a Woman in Chaos.* Naperville, IL: Sourcebooks, Inc., 2010.

PERIODICALS

Goldenberg, Suzanne. "Crime Puts Iraqi Women Under House Arrest." *The Guardian* (October 11, 2003). Available online at http://www.guardian.co.uk/world/2003/oct/11/iraq.suzannegoldenberg (accessed on November 30, 2011).

Kiefer, Francine. "Despite Democracy in Iraq, Women Actually Losing Freedoms." *Christian Science Monitor* (March 15, 2011). Available online at http://www.csmonitor.com/Commentary/Editorial-Board-Blog/2011/0315/Despite-democracy-in-Iraq-women-actually-losing-freedoms (accessed on November 30, 2011).

Rubin, Elizabeth. "Fern Holland's War." *New York Times* (September 19, 2004).

Susskind, Yifat. "U.S. Must Help End Tyranny Against Iraqi Women." *The Progressive* (March 5, 2007).

WEB SITES

"Background on Women's Status in Iraq Prior to the Fall of the Saddam Hussein Government." *Human Rights Watch* (November 2003). http://www.hrw.org/legacy/backgrounder/wrd/iraq-women.htm (accessed on November 30, 2011).

"Iraqi Women Make Rare Trip to U.S. to Tell Their Stories of Life Under Occupation." *Democracy Now* (March 6, 2006). http://www.democracynow.org/2006/3/6/iraqi_women_make_rare_trip_to (accessed on November 30, 2011).

"The Road Ahead, Women's Rights and the Future of Iraq." *The Majalla* (February 15, 2011). http://www.al-majalla.com/en/ideas/article263887.ece (accessed on November 30, 2011).

7

Artists' Perspectives on the Middle East Conflict

United Nations Security Council resolutions, memoirs of prisoners and terrorists, declarations of war, statements of political vision, reports from British Royal commissions—these are the documents that historians and students typically use to understand the complicated issues relating to the long-standing and ongoing Middle East conflict. In most cases, these documents are attempts to establish the truth, to state a political program, to promote change, or to account for past actions. They tell a large part of the story, but not the entire story.

Artists have also sought to interpret the political problems that exist in the Middle East. Through their sculptures, paintings, poems, novels, and even graphic novels, they offer different perspectives on the major events in the region. Artists bring a unique approach to understanding the world. They emphasize the senses, such as sight, sound, and touch; they examine the emotional elements of issues; and they urge people to open themselves to the difficulty and complexity of human problems. The documents in this chapter present three artists' interpretations of Middle East conflicts.

The excerpt from Joe Sacco's (1960–) graphic novel *Palestine* and selections from the poetry of Mahmoud Darwish (1941–2008) both focus on the conflict between Arabs (people who speak the Arab language) and Israelis over who should control the territory that was once known as Palestine, a historical region in the Middle East on the eastern shore of the Mediterranean Sea, comprising parts of present-day Israel and Jordan. The selection from *Persepolis* by Marjane Satrapi (1969–), tells the story of the 1979 Iranian Revolution (also known as the Islamic Revolution) through the eyes of a young girl. Like most works of art, these selections present the viewpoints of their respective artists rather than attempting to present a balanced perspective. However,

A Palestinian artist painting a large banner featuring Palestinian president Yasser Arafat. Artists often used Arafat as a symbol for Palestinian nationalism. © SUHAIB SALEM/REUTERS/CORBIS.

they are compelling in both their creativity and honesty, and they offer an alternative way of learning about and understanding Middle Eastern conflicts.

Palestine

Excerpt from *Palestine*

> *Written and illustrated by Joe Sacco*
>
> *Originally published as individual comics between 1993 and 1996*
>
> *Republished as a collection by Fantagraphics Books in 2001*

"Look, on your side there are some extremists, and on our side there are some extremists."

During the winter of 1991–92, Maltese-American comic artist Joe Sacco (1960–) traveled to the Middle East, where he spent several months in Israel and in the occupied territories (lands under the political and military control of Israel) of the West Bank and the Gaza Strip. (The West Bank is an area between Israel and Jordan on the west bank of the Jordan River; the Gaza Strip is a narrow strip of land along the eastern shore of the Mediterranean Sea, west of Israel and bordering Egypt in the southwest.) Sacco arrived in the occupied territories near the end of the First Intifada, an Arabic word for "uprising." The First Intifada was a Palestinian effort to use street protests, strikes (work stoppages), and minor violence, such as throwing stones at Israeli tanks, to draw international attention to the unjust ways Palestinians had been treated by their Israeli occupiers. (Palestinians are an Arab people whose ancestors lived in the historical region of Palestine, comprising parts of present-day Israel and Jordan, and who continue to lay claim to that land.)

In January 1993, Sacco published a comic book about his experience in the Middle East. He went on to publish a total of nine issues between 1993 and 1996, eventually combining them to create the

271

graphic novel *Palestine* (2001). Through black-and-white illustrations, a strong plot, and plenty of dialogue from the dozens of characters in the book, Sacco explored his arrival in the occupied territories, a visit to Israel, and the encounters he had with Palestinians, Arabs from other countries, Israelis, and Americans and Europeans traveling in the region. The book offers a history of the Palestinian-Israeli conflict, bringing readers into the complicated world of Middle Eastern politics. In each issue Sacco focused more closely on the nature of the Palestinian experience, using a wide range of characters to tell different aspects of the story.

Palestine is unlike any other work published on the Israeli-Palestinian conflict, an ongoing conflict between Jews in Israel and Arab Palestinians over the control of land and government of the territory known as Palestine. Other works on the conflict have been contributed by journalists, scholars, or people who want to persuade others of their position on the conflict. Sacco provides an entirely different approach. He let his characters speak, and they report all sides of the story (although Sacco sympathizes particularly with the Palestinians living in the occupied territories). According to Palestinian scholar Edward Said, writing in the introduction to *Palestine*, readers see these stories "through the eyes and persona of a modest-looking ubiquitous [present everywhere] crew-cut young American man who appears to have wandered into an unfamiliar, inhospitable [unfriendly] world of military occupation, arbitrary [random] arrest … torture and sheer brute force generously, if cruelly applied."

Sacco's work was immediately praised for its imaginative approach to depicting the complex conflict. An *Utne Reader* review noted that that "Sacco uses the comic book format to its fullest extent, creating bold perspectives that any photojournalist would envy." Ty Burr stated in an *Entertainment Weekly* review, "It figures that one of the first books to make sense of this mess would be a comic book." Sacco won the 1996 American Book Award for his work.

In the excerpt below, Sacco offers his unique artistic perspective on the clashes between Israelis and Palestinians in the occupied territories. First Sacco visits a village that he calls in *Palestine* a "veritable gold mine of Palestinian misery" to hear one family's story of how Israeli soldiers cut

Joe Sacco

Comic book artist Joe Sacco was born in 1960 on the island nation of Malta and lived in Australia as a child before settling permanently in the United States. He studied journalism at the University of Oregon. After graduating from college he worked in several journalistic jobs but spent most of his time working on comic books.

In a *January Magazine* interview with Rebecca Tuhus-Dubrow, Sacco refers to himself as "Just a cartoonist, I mean, doing journalism in comics form." Critics have praised Sacco's ability to use an artist's attention to physical detail to highlight specific elements of the stories he tells, yet they have also noted that his works provide a good understanding of the nature of the issues he covers.

Sacco has said that his biggest hero is the British journalist and novelist George Orwell (1903–1950), who had a unique ability to insert himself into the nonfiction stories that he told without compromising his ability to describe events. Asked what his goals were in writing *Palestine*, Sacco told Tuhus-Dubrow that he hoped people would "just pay a little more attention to the news, or just understand a little more from reading the book what's going on, or get involved in activism, or get involved in reading, you know, really get involved in the subject itself."

TUHUS-DUBROW, REBECCA. "JOE SACCO." *JANUARY MAGAZINE.* HTTP://WWW.JANUARYMAGAZINE.COM/PROFILES/JSACCO.HTML (ACCESSED ON NOVEMBER 30, 2011).

Graphic novelist Joe Sacco in the Gaza Strip, in 2003. AP PHOTO/KHALIL HAMRA.

down their family's beloved olive trees. Next he visits a village that had just been attacked by Israeli settlers.

Things to remember while reading the excerpt from *Palestine*:

- Joe Sacco has said that *Palestine* was written primarily for an American audience.
- Israel took control of the occupied territories during the 1967 Arab-Israeli War, when it occupied lands previously held by Egypt and Jordan. The war forced many thousands of Palestinians to live in refugee camps in countries such as Jordan and Syria or in temporary shelters for people forced to relocate because of war. Many of these refugee camps became permanent homes for Palestinians. As of 2011, the United Nations Relief and World Agency for Palestinian Refugees counted 1.4 million people living in 58 camps in Jordan, Lebanon, Syria, the West Bank, and the Gaza Strip.
- The narrator makes reference to Greek Orthodox Christmas. The Orthodox religion is a Christian religion. The Roman Catholic Church and the Orthodox Church split apart in the eleventh century over issues of religious law. While the religions share many aspects, including holidays, each religion follows its own religious calendar that dictates when specific religious holidays are celebrated. Hence, Greek Orthodox Christmas and Catholic Christmas may occur on different days, depending on the year.
- Olive trees are a symbol of Palestinian land ownership.
- Hebrew is the ancient language of the Jewish people and the official language of present-day Israel, although many Jews also speak English. Arabic is the language commonly spoken by Palestinians.
- A Molotov cocktail is a crude bomb made by filling a bottle with a flammable liquid and using a rag as a fuse.
- The Homestead Act was a nineteenth-century U.S. law that gave pioneers the right to claim lands in the western United States that appeared unoccupied, even though they were often home to Native American tribes.

Palestine

And speaking of settlements, Sami drives us to the village outskirts...

ALL THE LAND ON THIS SIDE OF THE ROAD HAS BEEN CONFISCATED BY THE ISRAELIS FOR SETTLEMENT...

It's scores of acres of farmland and pasture we're looking at... again, just drops in the bucket... Israel has expropriated two-thirds of the West Bank for its own use, including the settlement of Jews... (and I'm not counting annexed "Greater Jerusalem")...but like Prime Minister Shamir says:

IF WE ESTABLISH A SETTLEMENT HERE OR EXPAND A SETTLEMENT THERE, THIS IS ONLY NATURAL. WE ARE OPERATING ACCORDING TO THE UNDERSTANDING THAT THE LAND BELONGS TO US.

And with that "understanding" in mind, the World Zionist Organization's 'Master Plan 2010' points out that only five percent of the West Bank is "problematic for settlement..."

I suppose what makes it "problematic" is that hundreds of thousands of Palestinians still live here — in the countryside, though, they're mostly confined within village boundaries set under British rule in 1942... and the Israelis routinely reject rural building applications, forcing tens of thousands of Palestinians to build and live in "illegal" dwellings, hundreds of which are leveled every year... in fact, according to some official Israeli figures, in '87 and '88 the Israelis demolished more Palestinian homes than they granted building licenses...

But if a Jew wants to join a settlement on occupied Arab land, it's full steam ahead! Incentives to make your head spin! A government grant to offset moving expenses! Eligibility for higher loans at lower interest! Cheaper housing than in Israel! A seven percent income tax deduction! You get the idea — the yuppie version of the Homestead Act...

63

© 2005 JOE SACCO.
COURTESY OF
FANTAGRAPHICS BOOKS.

What happened next...

Near the conclusion of *Palestine*, Sacco depicts three Israeli soldiers questioning a thirteen-year-old Palestinian boy who is forced to stand in the rain. Sacco wonders what will happen to the Palestinians and Israelis, caught in a seemingly unending conflict, as a result of the violence and hatred between them. He wonders "what can happen to someone who thinks he has all the power... [and] what becomes of someone when he believes himself to have none?"

In July 2001, when he wrote the preface to the collected edition of *Palestine*, Sacco was still unsure about the prospects for peace: "As I write these words, a second Intifada is taking place because, in short, Israeli occupation, and all the consequences of the domination of one people by another, has not ceased." In the years since Sacco made those remarks, the relationship between the Palestinians and Israelis has seen both progress and setbacks. Palestinians elected Mahmoud Abbas (1935–) as president Palestinian Authority (the recognized governing institution for Palestinians in the West Bank and the Gaza Strip) in 2005. Serious peace talks were renewed between the two sides. In September 2005, Israel withdrew settlers from all of the Gaza Strip and parts of the West Bank. After that, peace talks alternated with periods of violence and military action, both between Israel and Palestine and between Palestine's rival political factions, Hamas and Fatah. Meanwhile, Palestinians continued to push for an independent Palestinian state. Despite these developments, the questions raised by Sacco in *Palestine* remain: How will the Palestinians and Israelis, whose entire culture has been shaped by years and years of conflict, learn to set aside their anger and hostility to live in peace?

Did you know...

- In 2005, prior to the Israeli withdrawal, over 4 million Palestinians lived in the occupied territories.
- In addition to *Palestine*, Sacco has published *Safe Area Gorazde: The War in Eastern Bosnia, 1992–1995* (2000), *Notes from a Defeatist* (2003), *I Live Here* (2009), which benefited Amnesty International, and *Footnotes in Gaza* (2010), a graphic novel based on two 1956 incidents of mass killings of Palestinians in the cities of Rafah and Khan Younis.

Consider the following...

- In the introduction to *Palestine*, Edward Said wrote, "Joe Sacco can...transmit a great deal of information, the human context and historical events that have reduced Palestinians to their present sense of stagnating [unchanging] powerlessness." Point to several instances in Sacco's work where he uses visual images to convey information about people and events.

- *Palestine* uses such literary devices as metaphors, similes, and imagery to help its audience understand the story. Locate examples of these devices in Sacco's work and explain how they help to heighten the effect of the story.

- Compare Sacco's work on Palestine with historical or journalistic depictions. What are the strengths and weaknesses of each type of work? Is one better at conveying the "truth" about a situation? Explain in detail.

- Identify some of the important questions raised by Sacco's work. Identify other sources that can be used to further explore these issues.

For More Information

BOOKS

Sacco, Joe. *Palestine*. Introduction by Edward Said. Seattle, WA: Fantagraphics Books, 2001.

PERIODICALS

Blincoe, Nicholas. "Cartoon Wars." *New Statesman* (January 6, 2003): 26.

Burr, Ty. "Palestine: A Nation Occupied." *Entertainment Weekly* (October 7, 1994): 71.

Cooke, Rachel. "Eyeless in Gaza." *The Guardian/The Observer* (November 21, 2009). Available online at http://www.guardian.co.uk/books/2009/nov/22/joe-sacco-interview-rachel-cooke (accessed on November 30, 2011).

Crain, Liz. "Joe Sacco." *The Progressive* (July 2011).

Gilson, Dave. "Joe Sacco: The Art of War." *Mother Jones* (July/August 2005).

Utne Reader. Unsigned review of *Palestine* by Joe Sacco. (March/April 1995): 111.

WEB SITES

"Artist Bio: Joe Sacco." *Fantagraphics Books*. http://www.fantagraphics.com/artist-bios/artist-bio-joe-sacco.html (accessed on November 30, 2011).

Tuhus-Dubrow, Rebecca. "Joe Sacco." *January Magazine*. http://www.january magazine.com/profiles/jsacco.html (accessed on November 30, 2011).

The Poetry of Mahmoud Darwish

Select poems from *Unfortunately, It Was Paradise*
> *Includes the poems "On This Earth," "I Belong There,"*
> *"Athens Airport," and "I Talk Too Much"*
> *Published in 2003*

Poem from *The Adam of Two Edens*
> *Includes the poem "As He Walks Away"*
> *Published in 2000*

"Our flutes would have played a duet / if it weren't for the gun."

Mahmoud Darwish (1941–2008) is widely considered to be the most significant Palestinian poet and one of the most important poets to write in the Arabic language. Munir Akash and Carolyn Forché, translators and editors of Darwish's poetry collection *Unfortunately, It Was Paradise*, wrote in the introduction to that book that Darwish was "beloved as the voice of his people... an artist demanding of his work continual transformation" as well as a "legend whose lyrics are sung by fieldworkers and schoolchildren." Darwish spoke about Palestinian issues throughout the world, and he was cheered by huge crowds when he made appearances in the Middle East. His poems are considered some of the most moving to emerge from the Arab-Israeli conflict.

Mahmoud Darwish was born on March 13, 1941, in the Arab village of Birwa in what was then the British-controlled territory of Palestine. (Palestine is a historical region in the Middle East on the eastern shore of the Mediterranean Sea, comprising parts of present-day Israel and Jordan.) In 1948 the state of Israel was established in the former territory of

Palestinian poet Mahmoud Darwish. AP PHOTO/ REUVEN KOPICHINSKY.

Palestine. Darwish and his family were driven from their homes to clear the way for Jewish settlement. Other Palestinians became refugees (people who flee their country to escape violence or persecution) during the violence of the 1948 Arab-Israeli War. Darwish and his family settled in Deir el Asad where Darwish's father worked as a common laborer and the family eventually attained status as Arab residents of Israel. (Arabs are people who speak the Arabic language or who live in countries in which Arabic is the dominant language.) Darwish was constantly offended by how Arab Palestinians were treated as second-class citizens in the land of their birth. When he was in elementary school, he began to write poetry that expressed his anger and sense of loss, and he continued to write throughout his life.

Darwish's anger at Israel—expressed in poetry and political protest—led to his frequent arrest by Israeli police, and in 1970, Darwish fled his home to avoid further time in prison. For the next twenty-five years, he was a poet in exile and a spokesman for Palestinian causes. His work was published in Arabic-language literary journals, magazines, and newspapers, and he was a supporter of the Palestine Liberation Organization (PLO), a political and military organization formed to unite various Palestinian Arab groups with the goal of establishing an independent Palestinian state. In 1996, Darwish returned to his homeland, settling in the city of Ramallah, a town in the Israeli-occupied West Bank. Darwish's works won several prestigious literary prizes, and with the translation and publication of his work into English, Darwish become known internationally.

Darwish wrote poems about olive trees, women he has loved, bread, an airport, speaking at conferences, and many other subjects. Yet his best-loved poems are on the subject of Palestine. Darwish told the *New York Times* in 2001 that he saw Palestine as a metaphor "for the loss of Eden, for the sorrows of dispossession and exile, for the declining power of the Arab world in its dealings with the West."

Darwish's poetry provides a unique way of seeing the world. For example, in Darwish's poetry, an olive tree represents the Palestinians' desire to cling persistently to their homes, as the roots of an olive tree hold to the soil. It also represents the desire for peace and for the prophet Muhammad (c. 570–632), the most important prophet in the Islamic faith.

The poems excerpted below illustrate some of the different ways that Darwish expressed his sadness, longing, and sense of loss about Palestine. They come from two of his collections, *Unfortunately, It Was Paradise*, which was published in 2003 but includes poems written as early as 1986, and *The Adam of Two Edens*, published in 2000.

Things to remember while reading the poetry of Mahmoud Darwish:

- Although his work has been acclaimed in Arabic communities for some years, Darwish only became well known to English-speaking readers after the publication of the works from which the following poems are taken.
- Darwish's early poetry was angry, lashing out at Israel for its occupation of lands that Palestinians claim as their own. Look for traces of anger in the poems appearing below.

- Athens Airport, in the Greek capital, is a common transfer point for travelers visiting or leaving the Middle East, and it has also been the site of several terrorist attacks associated with Palestinians.
- "I Talk Too Much" references the right of return, which is the right, claimed by a dispossessed people, to return to their historic homeland. In this case, the right of return is the desire of Palestinian refugees to return to their homes.

• • •

On This Earth

We have on this earth what makes life worth living: April's
hesitation, the aroma of bread
at dawn, a woman's point of view about men, the works of
Aeschylus [ancient Greek dramatist], the beginning
of love, grass on a stone, mothers living on a flute's sigh and the
invaders' fear of memories.

We have on this earth what makes life worth living: the final
days of September, a woman
keeping her apricots ripe after forty, the hour of sunlight in
prison, a cloud reflecting a swarm
of creatures, the peoples' applause for those who face death
with a smile, a tyrant's fear of songs.

We have on this earth what makes life worth living: on this
earth, the Lady of Earth
mother of all beginnings and ends. She was called Palestine.
Her name later became
Palestine. My Lady, because you are my Lady, I deserve
life.

I Belong There

I belong there. I have many memories. I was born as everyone is
born.
I have a mother, a house with many windows, brothers,
friends, and a prison cell
with a chilly window! I have a wave snatched by seagulls, a
panorama of my own.
I have a saturated meadow. In the deep horizon of my word,
I have a moon,
a bird's sustenance, and an immortal olive tree.

I have lived on the land long before swords turned man into prey.

I belong there. When heaven mourns for her mother, I return
heaven to her mother.

And I cry so that a returning cloud might carry my tears.

To break the rules, I have learned all the words needed for a trial
by blood.

I have learned and dismantled all the words in order to draw
from them a single word: *Home*.

Athens Airport

Athens airport disperses us to other airports. *Where can I fight?*
asks the fighter.

Where can I deliver your child? a pregnant woman shouts back.

Where can I invest my money? asks the officer.

This is none of my business, the intellectual says.

Where did you come from? asks the customs official.

And we answer: *From the sea!*

Where are you going?

To the sea, we answer.

What is your address?

A woman of our group says: *My village is the bundle on
my back*.

We have waited in the Athens airport for years.

A young man marries a girl but they have no place for their
wedding night.

He asks: *Where can I make love to her?*

We laugh and say: *This is not the right time for that question*.

The analyst says: *In order to live, they die by mistake*.

The literary man says: *Our camp will certainly fall*.

What do they want from us?

Athens airport welcomes its visitors without end.

Yet, like the benches in the terminal, we remain, impatiently
waiting for the sea.

How many more years longer, O Athens airport?

I Talk Too Much

I talk too much about the slightest nuance [subtle differences]
between women and trees,

about the earth's enchantment, about a country with no
passport stamp.

I ask: *Is it true, good ladies and gentlemen, that the earth of
Man is for all human beings*

*as you say? In that case, where is my little cottage, and where
   am I?*

The conference audiences applaud me for another three
   minutes,

three minutes of freedom and recognition.

The conference approves our right of return,

like all chickens and horses, to a dream made of stone.

I shake hands with them, one by one. I bow to them. Then I
   continue my journey

to another country and talk about the difference between a
   mirage and the rain.

I ask: *Is it true, good ladies and gentlemen, that the earth of
   Man is for all human beings?*

As He Walks Away

The enemy who drinks tea in our hovel
has a horse in smoke, a daughter with
thick eyebrows, brown eyes and long hair
braided over her shoulders
like a night of songs.

He's never without her picture
when he comes to drink our tea,
but he forgets to tell us about her nightly chores,
about a horse of ancient melodies
abandoned on a hilltop.

Relaxing in our shack, the enemy
slings his rifle over my grandfather's chair,
eats our bread like any guest,
dozes off for a while on the wicker couch.
Then, as he stoops to pat our cat on the way out,
says: *"Don't blame the victim."*
"And who might that be?" we ask.
"Blood that won't dry in the night."

His coat-buttons flash as he walks away.
Good evening to you! Say hello to our well!
Say hello to our fig trees! Step gingerly
on our shadows in the barley fields.
Greet our pines on high. But please
don't leave the gate open at night.
And don't forget the horse's terror of airplanes.
And greet us there, if you have time.

That's what we want to say at the doorstep.
He hears it well enough,
but muffles it with a cough,
and waves it aside.

Then why does he visit the victim every evening,
memorize our proverbs by heart, as we do,
repeat our songs about our
specials holidays in the holy place?

Our flutes would have played a duet

if it weren't for the gun.

As long as the earth turns around itself inside us

the war will not end.
Let's be good then.
He asked us to be good while we're here.
He recites Yeats's [Irish poet William Butler Yeats (1865–1939)]
    poem about the *Irish Airman*:
"Those that I fight I do not hate,
Those that I guard I do not love."
Then he leaves our wooden ramshackle hut
and walks eighty meters to our old stone house
on the edge of the plain.

Greet our house for us, stranger,

The coffee cups are the same.
Can you smell our fingers still on them?
Can you tell your daughter
with the braid and thick eyebrows
she has an absent friend
who wishes to visit her, to enter her mirror
and see his secret.

How was she able to trace his age in this place?

Say hello to her, if you have time.

What we want to tell him

he hears well enough, but muffles with a cough
and waves aside.

His coat buttons flash

as he walks away.

• • •

What happened next...

Poetry does not have consequences in the same way that a declaration of war or a peace treaty has consequences. No one has ever claimed that one of Darwish's poems sparked a military victory or encouraged a soldier to lay down his weapon. Yet many who read Darwish's poetry remark that they emerge from that reading with a different sense of the world, that they feel a new compassion for Palestinians. Salma Khadra Jayyusi, editor of the anthology *Modern Arabic Poetry*, writes that "poetry is the main vehicle for expressing the emotional experience of a people, and for revealing their deeper consciousness of the world, and it may bring the reader into a more intimate knowledge of other people's actual life situations." In this subtle way, poetry can have consequences of its own.

Darwish told *The Progressive* in 2002, "I thought that poetry could change everything, could change history and could humanize, and I think that the illusion is very necessary to push poets to be involved and to believe, but now I think that poetry changes only the poet." For Darwish personally, his poetry certainly had very real consequences. He was punished for writing a poem as a schoolboy, imprisoned for his poetry and protest as a young man, and later revered for his work and heralded as a spokesman for his people.

Did you know...

- Darwish won the Lannan Foundation Award for Cultural Freedom in 2001, which included a $350,000 prize. He also received the Sultan bin Ali al Owais Cultural Award for cultural and scientific achievement, as well as other prominent literary honors.
- After Darwish's death in Houston, Texas, on August 9, 2008, Palestinian president Mahmoud Abbas (1935–) declared three days of national mourning in the poet's honor, and Darwish was given what amounted to a state funeral in Ramallah.
- Darwish's last collection of poems, *The Impression of Butterflies*, was published in 2008.
- Darwish was not the only poet writing about the Arab-Israeli conflict. Many poets and other writers on both sides of the conflict such as Palestinian poet Kemal Nasir and Israeli poet Aharon Shabtai (1939–) have offered their own perspectives.

Palestinian President Mahmoud Abbas salutes the coffin of Mahmoud Darwish during the poet's funeral in Ramallah. Darwish was given the what amounted to a state funeral. © JIM HOLLANDER/EPA/CORBIS.

Consider the following...

- Darwish's work is often interpreted as making political statements, athough in a very subtle way. Select one of Darwish's poems and write a short essay pointing out how the poem engages with political issues.
- Pick one of Darwish's poems and discuss the ways he used figures of speech such as metaphor or simile to enhance his meaning.
- Salma Khadra Jayyusi, editor of *Modern Arabic Poetry*, writes that "poetry is the main vehicle for expressing the emotional experience of a people." In what ways does Darwish's poetry express the emotional experience of his people?
- Read the work of another poet who has written about politics in the Middle East. How is his or her view of the situation different from that of Darwish?

For More Information

BOOKS

Darwish, Mahmoud. *The Adam of Two Edens: Selected Poems.* Syracuse, NY: Syracuse University Press, 2000.

Darwish, Mahmoud. *Unfortunately, It Was Paradise: Selected Poems.* Translated and edited by Munir Akash and Carolyn Forché. Berkeley: University of California Press, 2003.

Jayyusi, Salma Khadra, ed. *Modern Arabic Poetry: An Anthology.* New York: Columbia University Press, 1987.

PERIODICALS

Assadi, Mohammed. "Palestinians Plan Big Funeral for Poet Darwish." *The Washington Post* (August 10, 2008).

Handal, Nathalie. "Mahmoud Darwish: Palestine's Poet of Exile." *The Progressive* (May 2002): 24–27.

Shatz, Adam. "A Poet's Palestine as a Metaphor." *New York Times* (December 22, 2001).

WEB SITES

"Mahmoud Darwish." *Khalil Sakakini Culture Centre.* http://www.sakakini.org/literature/mdarwish.htm (accessed on November 30, 2011).

"Mahmoud Darwish: In the Presence of Absence." *Mahmoud Darwish.com.* http://www.mahmouddarwish.com/ui/english/ShowContent.aspx?ContentId=1 (accessed on November 30, 2011, 2011).

"Palestinian Poet Derides Factions." *BBC News* (July 16, 2007). http://news.bbc.co.uk/2/hi/middle_east/6900624.stm (accessed on November 30, 2011, 2011).

Persepolis

Excerpt from *Perseoplis*
By Marjane Satrapi
Originally published in 2000
English translation published by Pantheon Books, 2003

"We didn't really like to wear the veil, especially since we didn't understand why we had to."

In 1979, the Iranian Revolution (also known as the Islamic Revolution) resulted in the overthrow of Iran's monarchy, led by Shah Mohammad Reza Pahlavi (1919–1980). In its place, an Islamic regime run by clerics (ordained religious officials) claimed power. At the time, Marjane Satrapi (1969–) was a lively, privileged ten-year-old growing up in Tehran, Iran's capital city. Her intellectual, leftist parents raised young Marjane to be curious and opinionated, and they had actively protested against the shah's rule.

Under the shah, Iran had a secular (nonreligious) government. The new government was Islamist, meaning that it was based on the belief that Islam should provide the basis for political, social, and cultural life in Muslim nations. The new Islamist government imposed many changes on the lives of the Iranian people based on religious law. Satrapi went from attending a French school that taught both boys and girls to an Islamic all-girls school. She and the other females in her family were forced to wear a veil in public, and her favorite uncle was executed on suspicion of being a communist spy. (Communism is a system of government in which the state plans and controls the economy and a single political party holds power.) One year after the revolution, Iran and Iraq went to war, and missile attacks and death became a part of daily life for Satrapi. At the same time, she was becoming increasingly rebellious, wearing Western clothes and listening to Western music, even though she knew such actions could get her arrested. Fearing for her safety, Satrapi's parents sent her to Vienna, Austria, at age fourteen to attend high school.

After four years, Satrapi returned to Iran to study graphic arts, but soon she was back in Europe, where she continued to study art in France. After receiving a copy of *Maus*, a Holocaust-themed graphic novel, she decided that she would present her memoir in similar form. (The Holocaust was the mass murder of European Jews and other groups by the Nazis during World War II [1939–45].) The result was *Persepolis*, which was published in France in 2000. It was released in the United States in 2003 and was subsequently translated into more than twenty languages.

The illustrations and narration in *Persepolis* are simple and concise, reflecting a child's point of view about growing up during times of revolution, oppression, and war. In the excerpt below, from a chapter titled "The Veil," Satrapi matter-of-factly presents the political

Marjane Satrapi wrote about her experiences growing up during the Iranian Revolution in the graphic novel Persepolis.
KEVIN SCANLON/GETTY IMAGES).

developments that led to her and her classmates being segregated in school and forced to wear veils, as well as their confused, sometimes humorous reactions to these changes.

While *Persepolis* is certainly a personal story, it is also the story of a nation and its people. In the book's introduction, Satrapi notes that since the revolution in Iran, "this old and great nation has been discussed mostly in connection with fundamentalism, fanaticism, and terrorism. . . . I know this image is far from the truth." In addition to showing a different side of her country, she is also committed to honoring her countrymen who suffered from repression or died fighting for freedom. In 2003 she told the *New York Times*, "The period between '80 and '84 is a little taboo in Iran. People don't like to talk about it. That's why I think this book is important. I would have died of sadness if all these people had been forgotten."

Things to remember while reading the excerpt from *Persepolis*:

- Forces that were active in the revolution that toppled the shah included both the conservative Islamists who opposed Western influences in their nation and the liberals who demanded social justice. Ultimately, the Islamists, led by Ayatollah Ruhollah Khomeini (1902–1989), assumed control of Iran.
- Satrapi was not a reader of comics or graphic novels before she chose the format for her memoir.
- Satrapi is descended from Iranian royalty. Her great grandfather was the emperor of Persia from 1848 to 1896. However, because her great grandfather had approximately one hundred wives, she is among several thousand of his descendants.

• • •

Persepolis

FROM *PERSEPOLIS: THE STORY OF A CHILDHOOD* BY MARJANE SATRAPI, TRANSLATED BY MATTIAS RIPA & BLAKE FERRIS, TRANSLATION COPYRIGHT © 2003 BY L'ASSOCIATION, PARIS, FRANCE. USED BY PERMISSION OF PANTHEON BOOKS, A DIVISION OF RANDOM HOUSE, INC.

FROM *PERSEPOLIS: THE STORY OF A CHILDHOOD* BY MARJANE SATRAPI, TRANSLATED BY MATTIAS RIPA & BLAKE FERRIS, TRANSLATION COPYRIGHT © 2003 BY L'ASSOCIATION, PARIS, FRANCE. USED BY PERMISSION OF PANTHEON BOOKS, A DIVISION OF RANDOM HOUSE, INC.

• • •

What happened next...

Satrapi wrote about her teenage years in Vienna in three additional *Persepolis* volumes, which were combined and released under the title *Persepolis 2* in the United States in 2004. Three years later, Satrapi directed an animated film version of *Persepolis*, which made its debut at the 2007 Cannes Film Festival despite protests from the Iranian government. The film was met with critical acclaim and was nominated for an Academy Award.

In addition to her work as a writer and film director, Satrapi is an outspoken advocate for reform in her native country. In 2009, she publicly protested the results of Iran's national elections, alleging that the victory of President Mahmoud Ahmadinejad (1956–) was rigged. She maintains, however, that her criticism of Iran is ultimately based in her love for it. As she noted in a September 2004 radio interview for *The Leonard Lopate Show*, "If I did not care about my country, I would not spend my time saying this is not good and we should not do this. All that comes from the fact that I want my country to be a better place and I want definitely to go back to my country and live in my country."

Did you know . . .

- Satrapi has not been back to Iran since the publication of *Persepolis*. Although she says she has not received any direct threats, she is fearful that she would be arrested.
- *Persepolis* borrows its title from the name of an ancient Persian city. The country of Iran was known as Persia until 1935.
- That Satrapi chose to tell her story through drawings is in violation of Islam's anti-iconic teachings, which prohibit the representation of a living being in art.

Consider the following . . .

- In a 2004 radio interview for *The Leonard Lopate Show*, Satrapi said, "Because I love my country so much, I criticize it." What do you think that this statement means? How does *Persepolis* exemplify this idea?
- Satrapi said in an interview for the *Powells Books* Web site, "Image is an international language." Review the drawings in *Persepolis* and locate examples of how different moods are portrayed.
- Compare Satrapi's work on life in Iran after the revolution with historical or journalistic sources. What are the strengths and weaknesses of these types of work? Is one better at conveying the "truth" about a situation? Explain in detail.

For More Information

BOOKS

Satrapi, Marjane. *Perseoplis*. Pantheon Books, 2003.

Schroeder, Heather Lee. *A Reader's Guide to Marjane Satrapi's "Persepolis"*. Berkeley Heights, NJ: Enslow, 2010.

PERIODICALS

Addley, Esther. "Rebel in Exile." *The Guardian* (May 14, 2003).

Arnold, Andrew D. "An Iranian Girlhood." *Time,* (May 16, 2003). Available online at http://www.time.com/time/arts/article/0,8599,452401,00.html (accessed on November 30, 2011).

Bahrampour, Tara. "A Memoir Sketches an Iranian Childhood of Repression and Rebellion." *New York Times* (May 21, 2003): E1.

Hattenstone, Simon. "Confessions of Miss Mischief." *The Guardian* (March 28, 2008).

Walt, Vivienne. "Never Mind the Mullahs: Iranian Exile Marjane Satrapi." *Mother Jones* (January-February 2008): 74.

WEB SITES

Welch, Dave. "Marjane Satrapi Returns." *Powells Books* (October 10, 2006). http://www.powells.com/blog/interviews/marjane-satrapi-returns-by-dave/ (accessed on November 30, 2011).

OTHER SOURCES

Marjane Satrapi interview with guest host Jeffrey Toobin. *The Leonard Lopate Show*. WNYC New York Public Radio (September 8, 2004). Transcript available at http://mapage.noos.fr/marjane.persepolis/paroles/wnyc.html (accessed on November 30, 2011).

The Arab Spring

In December 2010, protesters in Tunisia took to the streets to demonstrate the lack of political freedom and economic opportunity in their country under President Zine el-Abidine Ben Ali (1936–), who had ruled the North African nation since 1987. Like the leaders of many Arab nations, Ben Ali ran an authoritarian regime that jailed political opponents, controlled the media, tolerated corruption, and repressed personal freedoms, often with brutality. (An authoritarian regime is a type of leadership in which power is consolidated under one strong leader, or a small group of elite leaders, who do not answer to the will of the people.) Mohamed Bouazizi (1984–2011), a street vendor in the city of Sidi Bouzid, set himself on fire outside of a government office on December 17, in a desperate act of defiance against constant harassment by local police. Bouazizi's supporters staged a peaceful protest that turned into a riot. Additional anti-government demonstrations quickly gained momentum in other cities, as people fed up with living under repression and fear, and enabled by social networking technology, demanded change. By the following month, Ben Ali had stepped down from power.

Almost immediately, a similar but larger-scale scene played out in Egypt, where weeks of protests centered in Cairo's Tahrir Square led to the February 2011 ouster of President Hosni Mubarak (1928–), who had ruled that nation for thirty years. These revolutions inspired a series of prodemocracy uprisings across the Middle East and North Africa, which together became known as the Arab Spring. The leaders of numerous nations in the region saw the hold on their power threatened by a call for democratic reform that came from the streets. Regimes have responded to protesters with both violent crackdowns and the promise of concessions. Many countries with interests in the region, including the United States, have been forced to navigate these developments carefully, as resentment

Protestors in Tahrir Square, Cairo, in February 2011. © HANNIBAL HANSCHKE/EPA/CORBIS.

of their long-standing involvement in the affairs of the region are often among the protesters' grievances.

The concept of democratic reform is not new to the Middle East, but the timing, scale, relative success, and potential impact of the Arab Spring have brought the events international attention. Equally compelling is the fact that the Arab Spring is as much about the actions of ordinary people as it is about the practices and reactions of those in power. The makeup of the protesters tends to be one of inclusion. Men and women, young students and older citizens, and people of various ethnicities, faiths, and socioeconomic levels have risked arrest, brutality, and even death to voice their demands. Indeed, as the Arab Spring uprisings continued throughout 2011, thousands were killed, injured, and jailed. Their savvy use of social media to organize and share information with each other and the rest of the world was an essential tool in sustaining the protesters' efforts.

The excerpts included in this chapter reflect the efforts of groups and individuals to effect change in the Middle East in the years leading up to and during the Arab Spring. In the *Damascus Declaration for Democratic National Change*, written in 2005, activists from many walks of Syrian life come together to call for democratic reform from one of the Middle East's most repressive regimes. An Egyptian mother relates the story of what motivated her to take on election corruption in her country in "Taking to the Street." Finally, Norwegian journalist Asne Seierstad profiles several Syrian citizens caught up in the 2011 movement to oust President Bashar Assad (1965–) in an excerpt from "Out of the Shadow of Fear." While the ultimate outcomes of the Arab Spring remain uncertain, the people of the region will likely find themselves newly empowered by their ability to take a stand against oppression.

The Damascus Declaration

Excerpt from the *Damascus Declaration for Democratic National Change*

October 16, 2005

"Establishment of a democratic national regime is the basic approach to the plan for change and political reform. It must be peaceful, gradual, founded on accord, and based on dialogue and recognition of the other."

Although its history is rooted in one of the world's most ancient civilizations, modern Syria was established as an independent nation in 1946. The region of Syria and Lebanon had been governed under French mandate (administrative authority) since the end of World War I (1914–18). After gaining independence, Syria experienced many changes of leadership and much turmoil as a result, including a 1963 coup (overthrow of the government) that brought the Ba'ath Party to power. (The Ba'ath Party is a secular [nonreligious] political party founded in the 1940s with the goal of uniting the Arab world and creating one powerful Arab state.) From 1970 into the second decade of the twenty-first century, however, Syria has had only two leaders: Hafez Assad (also spelled al-Assad, 1930–2000), a military leader from the Ba'ath Party whose forces took over the nation in 1970, and his son, Bashar Assad (also spelled al-Assad, 1965–), who was elected as president after the elder Assad's death in 2000.

Syria has operated under emergency law since 1963. Emergency law allows the government to suspend certain constitutional rights and gives it the ability to arrest, detain, and question citizens without making any

Syrian president Bashar Assad.
© RIA NOVOSTI/ALAMY.

formal criminal charges. The Syrian government under Hafez Assad used this power regularly to arrest and jail citizens for not supporting government policies and to intimidate members of opposing political parties. When Bashar Assad became president, some government restrictions were eased for a short period, but authoritarian rule (in which power is consolidated under one strong leader, or a small group of elite leaders, who do not answer to the will of the people) soon predominated. Political opposition continued to be suppressed by government security forces.

In 2005, over 250 members of opposition parties representing the different religious and ethnic groups of Syria signed the *Damascus Declaration for Democratic National Change.* The document, named after the capital city of Syria, was a formal protest to government repression. In a public show of unity, some signers of the document held a press conference that had not been authorized by the Syrian government, which strictly controlled public and media events. Identifying the Syrian government as authoritarian, the *Damascus Declaration* called for reforms and the institution of democratic processes, beginning with a dialogue among diverse political and ethnic groups as the basis for forming a new government. In advocating for a peaceful change of power, the document

Middle East Conflict: Primary Sources, 2nd Edition

also called for an end to emergency law and the release of political prisoners.

Almost as significant as the contents of the document itself is the broad range of groups and individuals that supported it. Those who signed the document included the National Democratic Gathering, the Kurdish Democratic Alliance, the Committees of Civil Society, the Kurdish Democratic Front, and the Future Party, as well as prominent intellectuals and public figures. Although the signers and other supporters varied in ethnic background, religious affiliation, political interest, and social standing, they all expressed a desire to improve the future of their nation.

Things to remember while reading the excerpt from the *Damascus Declaration for Democratic National Change*:

- The *Damascus Declaration* stresses the importance of having different political and ethnic groups participating in reforming the Syrian government. The idea of including people with diverse opinions and backgrounds was contrasted with the actual makeup of the current government, which was referred to as a clique—a group that has exclusive membership and acts primarily in its own self-interest.

- Islam is recognized as the most important cultural component of Syria. Islam is defined in the declaration as a religion with higher intentions and values and more tolerance than the policies and actions of the Syrian government. The government is described as violent and exclusive and, therefore, not representative of Islamic values.

- The Kurdish issue addressed in the document refers to the Kurds, the largest ethnic minority in Syria. (Kurds are a non-Arab ethnic group.) Kurds make up about 10 percent of the Syrian population. Parts of Syria, Iran, Iraq, and Turkey were once known as Kurdistan, homeland of the Kurdish people. To maintain authority over the Kurds, the Syrian government banned the teaching of the Kurdish language and history in schools. The *Damascus Declaration*, by contrast, invites Kurdish participation in forming a new government.

- The document refers specifically to Law 49, an emergency law adopted in 1980 that made punishable by death membership in the

A Syrian Kurdish farmer. Kurds make up about 10 percent of the population in Syria, and the Damascus Declaration *invites Kurdish participation in forming a new government.* © SHERI LAIZER/ ALAMY.

Muslim Brotherhood, an Islamic fundamentalist group organized in opposition to Western influence and in support of Islamic principles and opposed to the Assad government. It also refers to the Universal Declaration on Human Rights, which was originally compiled in 1948 under the leadership of the United Nations as a definition of the basic rights to which all people worldwide are entitled. (The United Nations is an international organization of countries founded in 1945 to promote international peace, security, and cooperation.)

- In addition to the repression to which it subjected its own people, the Syrian government was also accused of hostile actions involving neighboring countries. Months prior to the introduction and publication of the *Damascus Declaration* in 2005, the former prime minister of Lebanon, Rafiq Hariri (1944–2005), was killed in a massive explosion in a heavily secured area of Beirut, Lebanon. Many authorities in Lebanon and other nations believed Hariri was executed by political opponents with ties to Syria. Also, before the *Damascus Declaration* was made public, the United States issued economic sanctions against Syria. (Sanctions are punitive measures adopted by the international community against a nation that has violated international law, usually in the form of diplomatic, economic, or social restrictions.) The United States accused the Syrian government of allowing anti-American fighters to pass into and out of Iraq during the Iraq War (2003–11).

• • •

Damascus Declaration for Democratic National Change

Self-appraisal: The act of truthfully assessing one's own situation.

Monopoly: Complete control.

Cliquish: Operating as an exclusive group in which only certain members are allowed.

Rending: Tearing apart.

Exacerbating: Making worse.

Syria today is being subjected to pressure it had not experienced before, as a result of the policies pursued by the regime, policies that have brought the country to a situation that calls for concern for its national safety and the fate of its people. Today Syria stands at a crossroad and needs to engage in **self-appraisal** and benefit from its historical experience more than any time in the past. The authorities' **monopoly** of everything for more than 30 years has established an authoritarian, totalitarian, and **cliquish** [fi'awi] regime that has led to a lack of [interest in] politics in society, with people losing interest in public affairs. That has brought upon the country such destruction as that represented by the **rending** of the national social fabric of the Syrian people, an economic collapse that poses a threat to the country, and **exacerbating** crises of every kind, in addition to the stifling isolation which the regime has brought upon the country as a result of its destructive, adventurous, and short-sighted policies on the Arab and regional levels, and especially in Lebanon. Those policies were founded on **discretionary** bases and were not guided by the higher national interests.

All that—and many other matters—calls for **mobilizing** all the energies of Syria, the homeland and the people, in a rescue task of change that lifts the country out of the mold of the security state and takes it to the mold of the political state, so that it will be able to enhance its independence and unity, and so that its people will be able to hold the reins of their country and participate freely in running its affairs. The transformations needed affect the various aspects of life, and include the State, the authorities, and society, and lead to changing Syrian policies at home and abroad.

In view of the **signatories**' feeling that the present moment calls for a courageous and responsible national stand, that takes the country out of its condition of weakness and waiting that is poisoning the present political life, and spares it the dangers that loom in the horizon, and in view of their belief that a clear and **cohesive** line on which society's various forces agree, a line that projects the goals of democratic change at this stage, acquires special importance in the achievement of such change by the Syrian people and in accordance with their will and interests, and helps to avoid **opportunism** and extremism in public action, they have reached an accord on the following bases:

Establishment of a democratic national regime is the basic approach to the plan for change and political reform. It must be peaceful, gradual, founded on accord, and based on dialogue and recognition of the other.

Shunning totalitarian thought and severing all plans for exclusion, custodianship, and **extirpation** under any **pretext**, be it historical or realistic; shunning violence in exercising political action; and seeking to prevent and avoid violence in any form and by any side.

Islam—which is the religion and ideology of the majority, with its lofty intentions, higher values, and tolerant **canon law**—is the more prominent cultural component in the life of the nation and the people. Our Arab civilization has been formed within the framework of its ideas, values, and ethics and in interaction with the other national historic cultures in our society, through moderation, tolerance, and mutual interaction, free of fanaticism, violence, and exclusion, while having great concern for the respect of the beliefs, culture, and special characteristics of others, whatever their religious, confessional, and intellectual affiliations, and openness to new and contemporary cultures.

No party or trend has the right to claim an exceptional role. No one has the right to shun the other, persecute him, and **usurp** his right to existence, free expression, and participation in the homeland.

Adoption of democracy as a modern system that has universal values and bases, based on the principles of liberty, **sovereignty** of the people, a

Discretionary: Optional or subject to personal judgment.

Mobilizing: Moving into action.

Signatories: Signers.

Cohesive: Connected.

Opportunism: The practice of taking advantage of a situation without regard to negative consequences for others.

Exterpation: Destruction or elimination.

Pretext: False reason, made-up excuse.

Canon law: Religious law.

Usurp: Take away by force.

Sovereignty: Supreme power or authority.

State of institutions, and the transfer of power through free and periodic elections that enable the people to hold those in power accountable and change them.

Build a modern State, whose political system is based on a new social contract, which leads to a modern democratic Constitution that makes citizenship the **criterion** of **affiliation**, and adopts **pluralism**, the peaceful transfer of power, and the rule of law in a State all of whose citizens enjoy the same rights and have the same duties, regardless of race, religion, ethnicity, sect, or clan, and prevents the return of tyranny in new forms.

Turn to all the components of the Syrian people, all their intellectual trends and social classes, political parties, and cultural, economic, and social activities, and give them the opportunity to express their views, interests, and aspirations, and enable them to participate freely in the process of change.

Guarantee the freedom of individuals, groups, and national minorities to express themselves, and safeguard their role and cultural and linguistic rights, with the State respecting and caring for those rights, within the framework of the Constitution and under the law.

Find a just democratic solution to the Kurdish issue in Syria, in a manner that guarantees the complete equality of Syrian Kurdish citizens with the other citizens, with regard to nationality rights, culture, learning the national language, and the other constitutional, political, social, and legal rights on the basis of the unity of the Syrian land and people. Nationality and citizenship rights must be restored to those who have been deprived of them, and the file must be completely settled.

Commitment to the safety, security, and unity of the Syrian national [? union] and addressing its problems through dialogue, and safeguard the unity of the homeland and the people in all circumstances, commitment to the liberation of the **occupied territories** and regaining the **Golan Heights** for the homeland, and enabling Syria to carry out an effective and positive Arab and regional role.

Abolish all forms of exclusion in public life, by suspending the emergency law; and abolish martial law and extraordinary courts, and all relevant laws, including Law 49 for the year 1980; release all political prisoners; [allow] the safe and honorable return of all those wanted and those who have been voluntarily or involuntarily **exiled** with legal guarantees; and ending all forms of political persecution, by settling **grievances** and turning a new leaf in the history of the country.

Strengthen the national army and maintain its professional spirit, and keep it outside the framework of political conflict and the democratic game, and confine its task to protecting the country's independence, safeguarding the constitutional system, and defending the homeland and the people.

Criterion: Standard or defining requirement.

Affiliation: State of being tied to or associated with something.

Pluralism: The acceptance of more than one idea or approach.

Occupied territories: The lands under the political and military control of Israel.

Golan Heights: A mountainous region located on the border of Syria and Israel, northwest of the Sea of Galilee, that has been occupied by Israel since the 1967 Arab-Israeli War.

Exiled: Banished from a country.

Grievances: Complaints or charges.

Liberate popular organizations, federations, trade unions, and chambers of commerce, industry, and agriculture from the **custodianship** of the State and from party and security **hegemony**. Provide them with the conditions of free action as civil society organizations.

Launch public freedoms, organize political life through a modern party law, and organize the media and elections in accordance with modern laws that ensure liberty, justice, and equal opportunities for everyone.

Guarantee the right of political work to all components of the Syrian people in their various religious, national, and social affiliations.

Emphasize Syria's affiliation to the Arab Order, establish the widest relations of cooperation with the Arab Order, and strengthen strategic, political, and economic ties that lead the [Arab] nation to the path of unity. Correct the relationship with Lebanon, so that it will be based on liberty, equality, sovereignty, and the common interests of the two peoples and countries.

Observe all international treaties and conventions and the Universal Declaration on Human Rights, and seek within the framework of the United Nations and in cooperation with the international community to build a more just World Order, based on the principles of peace and mutual interest, warding off aggression, and the right of nations to resist occupation, and to oppose all forms of terrorism and violence directed against civilians.

The signatories to this declaration believe the process of change has begun, in view of its being a necessity that **brooks** no postponement because the country needs it. It is not directed against anyone, but requires everyone's efforts. Here we call on the Ba'thist citizens of our homeland and citizens from various political, cultural, religious, and confessional groups to participate with us and not to hesitate or be apprehensive, because the desired change is in everyone's interest and is feared only by those involved in crimes and corruption. The process of change can be organized as follows:

1. Opening the channels for a comprehensive and equitable national dialogue among all the components and social, political, and economic groups of the Syrian people in all areas and on the following premises:

The need for radical change in the country, and the rejection of all forms of cosmetic, partial, or **circumspection** reform.

Seek to stop the deterioration and the potential collapse and anarchy which could be brought upon the country by a mentality of fanaticism, revenge, extremism, and objection to democratic change.

Rejection of the change that is brought from abroad, while we are fully aware of the fact and the objectivity of the link between the internal and the external in the various political developments that are taking place in our contemporary world, without pushing the country toward isolation, adventure, and irresponsible stands, and anxiousness to safeguard the country's independence and territorial **integrity** reform.

Custodianship: Control.

Hegemony: Dominating influence or rule.

Brooks: Tolerates.

Circumspection: Careful or cautious consideration.

Integrity: Wholeness or completeness.

2. Encourage initiatives for the return of society to politics, restore to the people their interest in public affairs, and activate civil society.

3. Form various committees, salons, forums, and bodies locally and throughout the country to organize the general cultural, social, political, and economic activity and to help it in playing an important role in advancing the national consciousness, giving vent to frustrations, and uniting the people behind the goals of change.

4. A comprehensive national accord on a common and independent program of the opposition forces, which charts the steps of the stage of transformation and the features of the democratic Syria of the future.

5. Pave the way for convening a national conference in which all the forces that aspire to change may participate, including those who accept that from among the regime, to establish a democratic national regime based on the accords mentioned in this declaration, and on the basis of a broad and democratic national coalition.

6. Call for the election of a Constituent Assembly that draws up a new Constitution for the country that foils adventurers and extremists, and that guarantees the separation of powers, safeguards the independence of the judiciary, and achieves national integration by consolidating the principle of citizenship.

7. Hold free and honest parliamentary elections that produce a fully legitimate national regime that governs the country in accordance with the Constitution and the laws that are in force, and on the basis of the view of the political majority and its program.

These are broad steps for the plan for democratic change, as we see it, which Syria needs, and to which its people aspire. It is open to the participation of all the national forces: political parties, civilian and civil bodies, and political, cultural, and professional figures. The plan accepts their commitments and contribution, and is open to review through the increase in the collectivity of political work and its effective societal forces.

We pledge to work to end the stage of **despotism**. We declare our readiness to offer the necessary sacrifices for that purpose, and to do all what is necessary to enable the process of democratic change to take off, and to build a modern Syria, a free homeland for all of its citizens, safeguard the freedom of its people, and protect national independence.

• • •

What happened next . . .

Government crackdowns against opposing political groups did not end after the *Damascus Declaration* was issued. In 2006, twelve signers of the document were arrested for anti-government political activities. They

Despotism: Rule by absolute authority.

were sentenced to two-and-a-half years in prison. Meanwhile, Syrian president Bashar Assad rewarded his most loyal followers, helping to further consolidate his power. In 2007, he won a second seven-year term as president. As in 2000, he was the only candidate.

Forces committed to bringing democracy to Syria continued to take action despite the threat imposed by the government. In 2008, a group of political opponents to Assad elected a leadership committee. A week later, many of the leaders of the opposition were among thirty people arrested for working for political change, which is outlawed under Syria's emergency law, since any group not connected with the government is banned from forming a political party. Three of the most outspoken opposition leaders remained in custody for an extended period of time. Among many crackdowns, the Syrian government shut down the ability for its citizens to access Facebook and other social media sites because some Syrians were using them for political debate and for making remarks critical of the president.

In 2011 a wave of prodemocracy uprisings swept across North Africa and the Middle East, including successful uprisings against authoritarian governments in Tunisia, Egypt, and Libya, among other nations. Called the Arab Spring, the events inspired demonstrations in several Syrian cities, including Damascus. Syrian security forces responded with violence. By December 2011, the United Nations estimated that more than five thousand people had been killed since the uprising began. In addition, fourteen thousand protesters had been arrested and jailed. Whether the Assad regime could withstand the increasingly bold public demand for the ideals expressed in the *Damascus Declaration* remained in question in late 2011.

Did you know . . .

- Syrian activist Michel Kilo (1940–), who wrote the draft of the *Damascus Declaration*, is a Christian and a journalist. In 2006 he signed the *Beirut-Damascus Declaration*, which urged Syria to recognize the independence of neighboring Lebanon. Kilo was arrested for signing the *Beirut-Damascus Declaration* and spent three years in jail.
- Hafez Assad ruled Syria from 1970 to 2000. When he died, the Syrian parliament amended the nation's constitution, reducing the minimum age of the president from forty years old to thirty-four

An anti-government protest in Hama, Syria, in July 2011. The Arab Spring uprisings inspired demonstrations in several Syrian cities. -/AFP/GETTY IMAGES.

years old. The amendment allowed Assad's son Bashar to become eligible to be nominated for president. Bashar Assad ran unopposed and was elected to succeed his father.

- Damascus was settled about 2500 BCE, making it one of the oldest continuously inhabited cities in the world.

Consider the following...

- The *Damascus Declaration* describes a "security state" as a clique and a "political state" as a country run by people with diverse beliefs and backgrounds. Consider the characteristics of a clique. In a political setting, what do you think would be the positive and negative outcomes of a government that operates as a clique?
- Many of the signers of the *Damascus Declaration* spent time in jail for having openly expressed opposition to the Syrian government.

Research two or three other figures throughout history who have been detained after declaring their political opinions and compare and contrast their experiences with those who signed the *Damascus Declaration*.

- Why is it considered significant, and perhaps even historic, that the *Damascus Declaration* was supported by a diverse mix of organizations and individuals? In what ways does this diversity strengthen the document's message? In what ways might some use this diversity as a reason to criticize its message?

For More Information

BOOKS

Wright, Robin. *Dreams and Shadows: The Future of the Middle East.* New York: Random House, 2008.

PERIODICALS

Alami, Mona. "Syrian Opposition Unites in Face of Oppression." *USA Today* (April 19, 2011): 6A.

"Bashar Goes Ballistic; Syria's Uprising." *The Economist* (August 20, 2011): p. 44.

Giglio, Mike. "The Republic of Fear." *Newsweek* (April 11, 2011): p. 30.

Zoepf, Katherine. "Syria's Opposition Unites Behind a Call for Democratic Changes." *New York Times* (October 20, 2005): A15.

WEB SITES

Damascus Declaration for Democratic National Change (October 16, 2005). http://faculty-staff.ou.edu/L/Joshua.M.Landis-1/syriablog/2005/11/damascus-declaration-in-english.htm (accessed on November 30, 2011).

"Profiles: Syrian Opposition Figures." *Al Jazeera* (June 27, 2011). http://english.aljazeera.net/indepth/2011/06/201162764247546667.html (accessed on November 30, 2011).

Taking to the Street

"Taking to the Street"

By Ghada Shahbandar

Published in Al Ahram Weekly *(Cairo)*

March 14, 2007

"Later in the day, when I watched television footage and saw photographs of the incident I understood why my friend was so angry. I was enraged by what I could only see as a flagrant and brutal attack on our beliefs, norms and values."

On May 25, 2005, members of a political activist group known as Kifaya (also spelled Kefaya; which means "enough") gathered in Cairo, Egypt, to protest a referendum (a direct public vote on a single proposal) posed by the government of President Hosni Mubarak (1928–). Mubarak, who had retained his power for the previous twenty-four years based on an election system built around a yes-or-no vote for a single presidential candidate, proposed a constitutional change that would allow multi-candidate elections. While the proposal sounded like a positive step towards election reform, critics pointed out that the conditions other parties would need to meet in order to get a candidate on the ballot were nearly impossible to achieve and called the proposal a sham. On the day that the referendum was put to a vote, Kifaya members launched a demonstration to voice their opposition.

The protesters were met by a violent attack by government supporters. These were not soldiers or police, but instead were young men dressed in dark street clothes who began beating the protesters, particularly the women, many of whom were groped and sexually assaulted in the midst of the fray. Police who were at the protest did nothing to stop the attacks,

Protestors from the Kifaya movement are surrounded by riot police in Cairo, on May 25, 2005. © MONA SHARAF/ REUTERS/CORBIS.

and video images of the brutal incident were broadcast on the Arabic news network Al Jazeera and other news outlets worldwide.

The event got the attention of Ghada Shahbandar, a forty-two-year-old housewife, university professor, and mother of four teenagers. After receiving a frantic phone call from her friend Bosayna Kamel, a television journalist who witnessed the protests, and watching the violent images on television for herself, Shahbandar was horrified. She was equally bothered by the reaction of her children, who expressed their belief that change was a hopeless cause. The brutality of that day, combined with her children's apathy, prompted Shahbandar into action. Along with Kamel and Engi Haddad, a marketing manager, Shahbandar organized a campaign demanding a government apology for the attack on the women protesters, and they chose a simple white ribbon as the symbol of their cause. Within days, the group had distributed five thousand ribbons. They asked supporters to wear them at a government demonstration that was planned for June 1, one week after the original attack. They also asked that supporters wear the white ribbons while going about their daily lives as a show of solidarity against the government's actions.

Although the efforts of Shahbandar, Kamel, and Haddad did not result in an apology from the Egyptian government, they felt empowered to take a broader stand. As Shahbender describes in the article "Taking to the Street," the result was the creation of Shayfeen.com (also known as Shafeencom or Shayfeen). The organization's name is a reference to the word "shayfeenkum" which means "we see you" in Arabic. (Shayfeen.com is an organization, not a Web site. The ".com" is a play on the Arabic word) The group's first mission was to monitor Egypt's presidential elections in September 2005. Volunteers used video cameras to capture images suggesting fraud or voter intimidation, and the group collected information on similar violations by phone and online. Over one thousand incidents were reported on the day of the election. Upon making public the information it had gathered on the alleged violations, the organization quickly gained the attention of ordinary Egyptian citizens, the government, and the media.

Things to remember while reading "Taking to the Street":

- In 1958 Egypt enacted Emergency Law No. 162, which puts strict limits on political activities not endorsed by the government. Egypt has functioned under Emergency Law almost constantly since the 1967 Arab-Israeli War. In addition to allowing for government censorship and the suspension of constitutional rights, the law prohibits groups larger than five people from coming together to discuss issues related to Egyptian politics. As a result, both the large public protests and the small meetings put together by Shahbandar and her fellow activists were considered illegal.

Ghada Shahbandar talks to the media at a Shayfeen.com press conference in Cairo, August 2005. CRIS BOURONCLE/ AFP/GETTY IMAGES.

- Prior to the events of May 25, 2005, Shahbandar was not politically active. While she kept herself informed of current events and aware of political issues, she had never participated in a demonstration or lent her support to any particular political cause.
- Shahbandar's husband (whom she later divorced) and children were deeply opposed to her activism. Furthermore, her Syrian grandfather had been killed in a political assassination, and as a result her father had raised her to steer clear of any political involvement.
- The National Democratic Party was Egypt's ruling political party under Mubarak. The Muslim Brotherhood is an Islamic fundamentalist group organized in opposition to Western influence and in support of Islamic principles. It opposed Mubarak's government and was outlawed for a time in Egypt.

• • •

Taking to the Street

It has been almost two years since I unexpectedly became more involved in "public life". I had not taken a **premeditated** decision to do so, nor did I expect to be involved for so long. I reacted **spontaneously** to the events that took place on 25 May 2005, or what's now labelled "Black Wednesday".

Premeditated: Planned.

Spontaneously: Impulsively or without planning.

On that day, I was submitting my final research paper for my Masters degree at the American University in Cairo. I was not going to cast a vote on the suggested amendment of Article 76 of the constitution, nor was I going to participate in demonstrations objecting to the referendum. I was simply going on with my daily life like the majority of Egyptians who had lost faith in the political system.

Standing outside my professor's office, I received a text message from a friend who was covering the events of the day as a reporter for an international news agency. She described an all-too-familiar scene of riot police cracking down on demonstrators and chasing them from the Saad Zaghloul **mausoleum** to the staircase of the Press Syndicate, Cairo's unofficial demonstration venue. How upset my normally composed and professional friend sounded when I called her back later astounded me. She described the new infamous scene of hired thugs attacking and sexually harassing female demonstrators with the explicit permission of the police.

Later in the day, when I watched television footage and saw photographs of the incident I understood why my friend was so angry. I was enraged by what I could only see as a flagrant and brutal attack on our beliefs, norms and values. I was further infuriated by the lack of response from our government and the National Democratic Party. No one was going to be held accountable and we, the people, appeared to find that perfectly acceptable.

One week later, for the first time in my life, I was standing at a demonstration on the Press Syndicate staircase, the venue of the violent events of Black Wednesday. By 1 June, I was one of 10 people who had decided that we could no longer stand on the sidelines and allow such happenings to go unchecked. We worked on defining our vision and mission and founded *Shayfeencom*, a popular monitoring movement that would allow for the participation of Egyptians in public life and empower them with monitoring wrongdoing. The 10 founding members all came from professional backgrounds. There were more women than men, and when we agreed on role distribution, women were chosen to speak on behalf of the movement.

Since then, *Shayfeencom* has monitored presidential and parliamentary elections, rallied support for the independence of the judiciary, campaigned for freedom of the press and launched an anti-corruption campaign. Its founding members were challenged in many ways. We were all newcomers to the arena of political activism and had to work hard to gain credibility, gather and research information, train as monitors, convince people to join the movement and maintain contact with those who did join.

More importantly, the founding members were challenged by the Egyptian political system and legislation governing civil society. The media, politicians and activists were all suspicious of our intentions. Most important of all, State Security did not welcome our existence. We were questioned,

Mausoleum: A building that serves as a tomb and a memorial to the dead.

labelled and harassed for a variety of reasons, some of which were contradictory and most of which were unjustified—at least by any activity we had undertaken or declaration we had made about our identity and intentions.

We were assigned to the officer in charge of "**socialist movements**" at State Security and were named the feminine (not feminist) velvet movement by the state-owned press. We were simultaneously accused of being an offshoot of the National Democratic Party, champions of the **Muslim Brotherhood**, and Western agents. We were considered inadequate and were held to account for not intervening in the Bird Flu crisis!

We became subject to State Security's unlimited scrutiny and inquiry into all of our activities; some of us were intimidated while others were fed misinformation about their colleagues. Professionally, we were **ostracised** by the business community and the governmental and non-governmental institutions we had associated with for years because no one wants to do business with the "opposition" (another label attached to our movement).

While I had intended this article to be about female participation in public life in Egypt, the truth is that participation is a challenge for both men and women. The socio-political environment, legislation, practices, and most importantly the political will of the government, are not conducive to participation.

Surprisingly, or maybe not, of the 10 founding members of *Shayfeencom* only three *women* remain active today.

• • •

What happened next . . .

Mubarak won the vote, as expected. However, despite the government's attempt to discredit and dismiss its activities, Shayfeen.com's involvement marked a new era of grassroots political involvement by Egyptian citizens. (The grassroots is the common people, as opposed to the political leadership.) After the presidential election, the group turned its attention to monitoring the parliamentary elections later that year, which were marked by episodes of intimidation of and violence against voters. Shayfeen.com's findings of election fraud caught the attention of many judges, who demanded that they be able to conduct their election-monitoring duties independent from state control. The group's efforts gained international attention in the media, and the U.S. State Department referred to data compiled by Shayfeen.com in its 2005 human rights report. Shayfeen.com's activities during the election were the subject of a 2007 documentary titled *Shayfeen.com: We're Watching You.*

Socialist movements: Movements in support of socialism, a system in which the government owns the means of production and controls the distribution of goods and services.

Muslim Brotherhood: An Islamic fundamentalist group organized in opposition to Western influence and in support of Islamic principles.

Ostracised: Excluded or shunned.

Shahbandar has remained an active voice in Egyptian politics. In 2008, she was elected to the board of the Egyptian Organization for Human Rights (EOHR), a nonprofit, non-governmental watchdog group. As both a citizen and a member of EOHR, she participated in protests in Cairo's Tahrir Square, beginning with what was termed a "Day of Anger" on January 25, 2011. The protests turned into a revolution that led to the end of Mubarak's rule weeks later. This time, Shahbandar's children joined her and the thousands of other Egyptians who demanded government reform. As a member of EOHR, Shahbandar reported on incidents of government brutality and other developments during the protests to the international press. Among the demonstrators were an unprecedented number of women. In media reports, Shahbandar herself estimated the crowds to be approximately 20 percent female, while other estimates ranged as high as 50 percent; furthermore, women were among the organizers of the demonstrations.

In March 2011, Shahbandar told *Evetalkonline.net*, "On Tahrir I saw all the barriers I had resented throughout my life come down. Barriers between men and women came down, and the girls forced every man to treat them with respect and equality; even during times of violence." As for the future, she expressed optimism. "I am optimistic because we have started a change and a reform process has been triggered and there's no going back. We have made gains that no one predicted. Most importantly there is an unprecedented level of awareness and engagement in public life."

Did you know...

- Egypt became a republic in 1952, after a revolution led by army officer Gamal Abdel Nasser (1918–1970) overthrew the ruling monarchy. From 1952 to 2011, Egypt was ruled by four different presidents, all of whom arose to power through the military.

- Mubarak was president of Egypt for nearly thirty years. He came to power in 1981 after President Anwar Sadat (also spelled al-Sadat; 1918–1981) was assassinated.

- Although the 2011 protests in Cairo's Tahrir Square were largely nonviolent on the part of the demonstrators, the participants risked beatings, arrest, and detention.

Consider the following...

- Shahbandar told *Evetalkonline.net* in March 2011, "I can respect any political opinion or ideology. The one thing I don't respect is apathy." In what ways can people demonstrate respect for political ideas that are different from or perhaps even in conflict with their own?

- Why do you think Shahbandar and her associates were successful in gaining public attention and support for their causes, first with the Black Wednesday protest, then through the activities of Shayfeen.com? Would they have had the same impact if they had decided to pursue their causes a decade ago? Why or why not?

- Shahbandar closes the article by noting that, at the time of its writing, only three of the ten founding female members were still active in Shayfeen.com. Why is this significant?

For More Information

BOOKS

Bradley, John R. *Inside Egypt: The Land of the Pharaohs on the Brink of a Revolution.* New York: Palgrave Macmillan, 2008.

Marsot, Afaf Lutfi Al-Sayyid. *A History of Egypt: From Arab Conquests to the Present.* 2nd ed. Cambridge: Cambridge University Press, 2007.

Wright, Robin. *Dreams and Shadows: The Future of the Middle East.* New York: Random House, 2008.

PERIODICALS

Hiel, Betsy. "Activists Crying Foul in Egyptian Election Landslide." *Pittsburgh Tribune-Review* (December 1, 2010).

McGrath, Cam. "Eerie Silence Follows 'Unprecedented Brutality'." *IPS* (January 28, 2011). Available online at http://ipsnews.net/news.asp?idnews=54275 (accessed on November 30, 2011).

Shahbandar, Ghada. "Taking to the Street." *Al Ahram Weekly* (Cairo; March 14, 2007). Available online at http://weekly.ahram.org.eg/2007/835/sc151.htm (accessed on November 30, 2011).

Slackman, Michael. "Egyptian Vote Again Marred by Intimidation." *New York Times* (November 27, 2005): A14.

WEB SITES

Abdel-Hamid, Hoda. "Bold Protests Against Mubarak Administration." *ABC News* (June 1, 2005). http://abcnews.go.com/International/story?id=809474&page=1&singlePage=true (accessed on November 30, 2011).

Hill, Evan. "Egypt's Crackdown Now Wears Camoflage." *Aljazeera* (May 21, 2011). http://english.aljazeera.net/indepth/features/2011/05/2011519172611166398.html (accessed on November 30, 2011).

"From the Living Room to Tahrir Square." *Evetalkonline.com* (March 2011). www.evetalkonline.net/site/article/188/1/1 (accessed on November 30, 2011).

Krajeski, Jenna. "Women Are Substantial Part of Egyptian Protests." *Slate.com* (January 27, 2011). http://aicwomen.wordpress.com/2011/01/31/slate-women-are-a-substantial-part-of-egyptian-protests/ (accessed November 30, 2011).

"Shayfeen.com: We're Watching You Discussion Guide." *Independent Television Service* http://www.pbs.org/independentlens/classroom/women/resources/shayfeen_discussion.pdf (accessed on November 30, 2011).

Out of the Shadow of Fear

Excerpt from "Out of the Shadow of Fear"

By Asne Seierstad
Published in Newsweek
June 5, 2011

"The authorities' aim is obvious: to strangle the protests at birth."

Beginning in December 2010, a series of prodemocracy uprisings known as the Arab Spring spread throughout the Middle East and North Africa. Risking arrest, beatings, or even death at the hands of police, government troops, or plainclothes thugs, people fed up with living under the oppressive rule of authoritarian leaders took to the streets. They demanded personal and political freedom, economic reform, and an end to government corruption. In Tunisia and Egypt, weeks of protests and labor strikes forced the presidents of those nations to step down, and inspired similar popular uprisings in Yemen, Bahrain, Libya, Jordan, and other Arab (Arabic-speaking) nations, including Syria.

Syrian president Bashar Assad (also spelled al-Assad; 1965–) came to power in 2000 after the death of his father, Hafez Assad (also spelled al-Assad; 1930–2000), who had ruled the country since assuming power in a 1970 coup, or sudden overthrow of the government. The elder Assad, a former military leader and a member of the ruling Ba'ath Party (a secular [nonreligious] political party founded in the 1940s with the goal of uniting the Arab world and creating one powerful Arab state), is credited with bringing structure and stability to the Syrian government and with enacting policies to modernize the Syrian economy and society. He is also infamous for his harsh, often violent approach to addressing any opposition to his rule. Bashar Assad, who ran unopposed in the 2000 election, eased some government restrictions and promised reforms, but his rule remained authoritarian, and political opposition continued to be suppressed by government security forces.

When pro-democracy advocates in Syria began voicing their demands in early 2011 as likeminded protesters had done in Tunisia, Egypt, and other nations in the previous weeks and months, it was no surprise that Syrian authorities responded with extreme force, propaganda, false information, and vague promises of concession. (Propaganda is material distributed for the purpose promoting a cause or viewpoint.) Reports of government forces shooting protesters in the streets made international news, and videos showing several incidents of violence were posted on the Internet. While the government worked to drum up support for Assad and blamed the unrest on terrorists, armed gangs, Islamist extremists, and foreign conspiracies, the international community was growing increasingly critical of the Syrian government. The United States and several European nations were prompted to impose sanctions against Syria. (Sanctions are punitive measures adopted by the international community against a nation that has violated international law, usually in the form of diplomatic, economic, or social restrictions.) Members of the North Atlantic Treaty Organization (NATO; an international organization created in 1949 for purposes of collective security) and the United Nations (UN; an international organization of countries founded in 1945 to promote international peace, security, and cooperation) paid close attention to ongoing developments to determine a possible course of action against Syria.

In the excerpt from "Out of the Shadow of Fear," which appeared in *Newsweek* magazine in June 2011, Norwegian journalist Asne Seierstad (1970–) conveys the experiences of several people from different walks of life in and around Damascus, Syria's capital, in the midst of the Syrian uprisings. Seierstad's account refers to key points in Syria's political history as well as the events that inspired the surge of protests in that country. She profiles a determined dissident, a frustrated shopkeeper, a conflicted businesswoman, and a brave group of young women as they reflect on the atmosphere of fear, suspicion, and secrecy under which ordinary Syrians live and the impact of the protest movement upon their outlook.

Syrians protest outside the Syrian Embassy in London, England, speaking out against the violent crackdown on anti-government demonstrators in Syria. © ROB PINNEY/DEMOTIX/DEMOTIX/CORBIS.

Things to remember while reading the excerpt from "Out of the Shadow of Fear":

- While the majority of Syrians are Sunnis (followers of the Sunni branch of Islam), the Assad family is part of a minority Muslim sect (group) known as Alawis. (Also spelled Alawites; followers of a sect of Shia Islam that live in Syria whose belief system and practices vary from Shiites in several ways). Most of those who serve on the government security forces in Syria are also Alawis, and some speculate that their loyalty to the Assads is grounded in their desire to keep their power despite their minority status. Another key part of Assad's power base is his relationship with wealthy Sunnis and others from the elite classes who have benefited socially and financially during the Assads' rule.

A woman walks past a poster of Bashar Assad in Damascus, Syria. LOUAI BESHARA/AFP/GETTY IMAGES.

- Syria has operated under emergency law since 1963. Emergency law allows the government to suspend certain constitutional rights and gives it the ability to arrest, detain, and question citizens without making any formal criminal charges. It has been used to limit the activities of groups and individuals who oppose the government, and the end of emergency law is among the demands of reform activists.

- Hafez Assad had groomed his oldest son, Basil, to succeed him as president, while Bashar pursued a career as an ophthalmologist in London. (An ophthalmologist is a medical doctor who specializes in eye care.) When Basil was killed in an automobile accident in 1994, the elder Assad ordered Bashar to return to Syria to begin military training so that he could eventually assume power.

• • •

Out of the Shadow of Fear

Posters of Bashar al-Assad are everywhere in Damascus. "Paste him up," people are ordered. . . .

Surveillance dominates every aspect of life. The secret police—the Mukhabarat—is divided into an intricate system of departments and subdepartments; no part of society is left unexamined. A network of agents spans Syria. Some have **tenure**; others work part time. Who could be a better observer than the greengrocer by the mosque or the hospital night watchman? Who can better keep tabs on a family than the schoolteacher who asks what Daddy says about the man on the posters?

The man on the posters has pale, close-set eyes, is well groomed, and has a curiously long neck. On one variant he wears sunglasses and a uniform. On others, he looks like a banker. An **ophthalmologist**, he was reeled in at his father's death to replace him as Syria's **dictator**. His name is Bashar al-Assad. His **desposition** is the goal of the **nascent** upheaval.

One Friday Abid found the resolve to join a demonstration after prayers. He hardly saw they were surrounded before he felt a stinging pain on his neck. The electric shocks chased through his body. He fell, lost consciousness. When he awoke, several others were lying around him.

The Mukhabarat had appeared, in plain clothes, from nowhere. Now they dragged him, and a hundred others, to waiting white vans. The demonstrators were taken to the outskirts of Damascus.

"We sat in rows in a *riad*, a courtyard, surrounded by high walls. Our hands were tied behind our backs, and we were forced to kneel. I counted the prayer calls from the mosque to keep track of time. Our legs became numb. When told to stand up after the last call from the mosque, none of us could. I buckled over, was beaten, forced to stand, and fell again. At night, we were stuffed into a cell. We stood upright, 12 men, on a few square meters. Next morning we were taken out to the *riad* again. After three days we were tender, and the interrogations could start."

Some were tortured for hours and came back bloodied. The one who suffered the most was an **Alawite**, a man belonging to the same Shia minority as the al-Assads, and considered a **turncoat**. Abid was more fortunate. "I am a member of the **Baath Party**. The beatings I received were not as harsh."

Abid became a party member while growing up in Daraa, the city where the revolt began. Holding a membership is sometimes required to get into college, to get a job, or to rise in the power structures.

But Abid had had enough. With only one year left of his engineering studies, he risked it all in order to take part in the **Syrian Spring**. "It's now or never. The train of freedom is leaving. We can jump on it, or we can let it go by." . . .

Tenure: A permanent position.

Ophthalmologist: A medical doctor who specializes in eye care.

Dictator: A ruler with unrestricted power.

Desposition: Removal.

Nascent: New or developing.

Alawite: Also spelled Alawi; a follower of a sect of Shia Islam whose belief system and practices vary from Shiites in several ways.

Turncoat: Traitor.

Baath Party: Also spelled Ba'ath; a secular (nonreligious) political party founded in the 1940s with the goal of uniting the Arab world and creating one powerful Arab state.

Syrian Spring: An uprising in Syria inspired by the Arab Spring, a series of prodemocracy uprisings in the Middle East and North Africa.

The authorities' aim is obvious: to strangle the protests at birth. Not to do as in Cairo and wait until the squares get crowded. Whereas the gatherings in Tunisia and Egypt rapidly grew to number in the thousands, Syrian authorities mercilessly beat down on groups of 25, 50, or 100.

"Getting a thousand people out on the streets here is like getting a million people out in Cairo," says Abid's host. . . .

Syrian political life revolves around Bashar al-Assad. The real power figures are Bashar and his younger brother, Maher, commander in chief of the Republican Guard, an Alawite-dominated elite force, the only army allowed inside Damascus. Their father, Hafez al-Assad, the Air Force pilot who took power in 1970, is remembered as a shrewd politician. Belonging to the Alawite minority—merely 12 percent of the population—he built a power base of mainly his own clan. His son has lacked the experience to navigate in the national and regional political terrain and has lost some support. . . .

Daraa, a sleepy town in the desert on the Jordanian border, was where it all started. One afternoon in March, some boys wrote antigovernment graffiti on a wall. They were detained by the security forces and taken to the local police station. And then silence.

Their parents searched for them, asked around. Nobody knew. They went to the authorities and were sent packing. The local sheik joined the fathers at the office of the head of security in town.

"Give us our children back," said the religious leader. He removed his headband—called an *ogal*—and placed it on the table, a symbolic gesture to indicate the importance of the request. If you ask for something, be prepared to give something in return, says the **Quran**.

"Forget your children. Go get new ones," the head of security allegedly replied. . . .

The disappeared children. The staggering insults. More and more people gathered around the building. They were turned away, but they came back.

A week passed before the children were released. They had been severely maltreated. Skin and flesh had been beaten off the knuckles of their hands. Some were said to have had their fingernails pulled out. **YouTube** videos of the kids were distributed on the Net [Internet]. The protests spread to other cities.

Damascus remained an island of calm until the end of March, when spontaneous protests started occurring even there. There was no coordination, no defined leadership. The time and place for the demonstrations had to be transmitted from mouth to mouth, from friend to friend. And they had better be real friends. . . .

This Friday the Umayyad Mosque is stage to a modern drama. The mosque is the only legal gathering place, and still strictly monitored by the security forces. Every word from the **imam**'s mouth is noted.

Quaran: Also spelled Koran or Qur'an; the holy book of Islam.

YouTube: A video sharing Web site.

Imam: Muslim religious leader.

The **bazaar** is empty. The stalls are closed. Iron shutters protect glass jars and baskets. A whiff of cardamom rests over the spice market. The leather craftsman has left behind a faint **tang** of hide, the soapmaker a trace of lavender. The tourists have gone; only the locals are left, small boys on bicycles, grandfathers on their chairs. Police units on motorcycles have closed off several streets. Some plan a protest after prayers.

The silence is oppressive. The area **teems** with Mukhabarat. Everyone knows who they are, even though they act like normal men. They squat on curbsides, lean against walls, sit on benches or together by doorways. They're dressed in shirts and trousers, like other men. Though they might be more broad-shouldered than the average Syrian, and certainly have a stronger **proclivity** for leather jackets, the clothes aren't what set them apart. It's their glance.

They possess a way of looking that is inquisitive but not curious. It's one-way; they want to take, not meet. Their conversation, or lack thereof, is the other giveaway. Between most people there is at least a little chitchat. These men hardly talk, and when they do, they do it without facial expressions, without a jab in the side, a poke on the shoulder. They don't talk like people really talk. They are on assignment.

As prayers are about to end, a cold wind trembles. The sky above the mosque darkens, splits, and rain starts hammering down. Water splashes on canopies that give way under the weight. A man tries to keep the water out of his entrance with a broom. Suddenly white frozen pearls drum on roofs and tarps, make the jasmine fall off the trees and drown in puddles. "God is great," says a man who follows the hailstorm from his doorway. "I've never seen this in Damascus before. It is protection from God. People will stay calm. So they won't get killed today," he says with a sigh.

It's as if the deserted street, shuttered stores, and everything that drowns in the storm **emboldens** the man. He talks about his brother, who narrowly avoided a government **sniper** last Friday. "It brushed by him here," Tarek says, pointing to the side of his throat. The bullet peeled off the outermost layer of skin during a demonstration in Zamalka. Several people were killed.

The snipers shoot to kill. Not many, just enough to frighten. The orders are said to be no more than 20 a day, but many Fridays the numbers have been higher.

Like other Syrians, he talks about The Fear.

"It's injected into us at birth," he says softly, demonstrating an imaginary needle. "It makes us bow our heads, turn away, distrust each other. Everyone can be reported. If you happen to be rude to a policeman or he doesn't like your face, you can disappear for years. Do you know when I've been most frightened? When I've seen the Assads on TV. I ordered my sons to sit and listen in reverence. You had to be careful around the children. But everything changed in March. I told my boys what is happening in our country. The oldest one came with me to the protest last week. But my 5-year-old

Bazaar: Marketplace.

Tang: Odor.

Teems: Swarms.

Proclivity: Preference or tendency.

Emboldens: Encourages.

Sniper: A marksman who shoots targets from concealed positions.

daughter cried when I said Bashar had to go. 'I love Bashar,' she cried. The way we've taught her. 'No, you should hate him,' I explained. 'But I love him,' she sobbed."

Tarek points to the poster above the door. "They came with him 10 days ago. 'Paste him up,' they ordered. I was afraid not to. This is my living, after all. Others pasted him up too. No wonder my daughter is confused."

In the fashionable shopping district of Damascus the atmosphere is somber. Elegant, minimally clad mannequins view passersby with an arrogant **mien**. The cashiers stand listlessly with resigned expressions. There are no pictures of the president. The regime does not paste over the clean windows of the upper class. The poorer the district, the more posters.

Shirin paces the floor of her fashion store in tight jeans and flat suede **Uggs**. She had planned for a spring sale, but then came the bloodbath in Daraa. "Advertising while people are being killed felt wrong," she says.

But the successful businesswoman has little sympathy for the protesters—"Some young rebels running around making trouble'—and supports Bashar al-Assad. "We have an excellent foreign policy. We are independent, and produce all we need, except for some spare parts for airplanes. The **sanctions** have taught us self-reliance. We don't need foreign intervention, as in Libya. And what's so wrong about **Gaddafi**? I always thought he made a lot of sense.'

But as a **matriarch** with three sons, she is upset about the arrests of the youngsters in Daraa. "The president should have ordered the hanging of the local chief of security,' she **opines**. "The way he treated the parents was a declaration of war. They're **Bedouins** down there, divided into clans. I worry extremists will exploit the situation and wind people up.'

She sighs. "I really love this country. This is where I want to live. Live now. . . ."

The next day, there are more girls than usual on a specific Damascene shopping street. They walk in pairs. To those in the know, discerning who is there on an assignment is not difficult. They look around nervously. They keep tossing their heads. They have flat-soled shoes. Like the men outside the mosque, they talk without facial expressions. One pair here, another one there. Three. Four. A small gathering. A larger one.

Suddenly, they open their purses and hold up their banners. Some written on cloth, some on paper. Each woman has her slogan.

Stop the Killing. Stop the Violence.

They start walking silently to the square with the looming bronze statue of Hafez al-Assad. None of the bystanders says a word. They pay attention, in disbelief. The girls cross the roundabout to get to the statue. A minute passes. Two. Maybe three. They are surrounded. White vans and scores of men in plain clothes pop up from nowhere. They tear posters out of the girls' hands, throw the women to the ground. "Whores," the men shout. "Cows!" Some

Mien: Appearance or disposition.

Uggs: Sheepskin boots; the term usually refers to those made by the footwear company UGG.

Sanctions: Punitive measures adopted by the international community against a nation that has violated international law, usually in the form of diplomatic, economic, or social restrictions.

Gaddafi: Mu'ammar al-Qaddafi (also spelled Moammar al-Gad-dafi; 1942–2011), Libya's long-term head of state, who was ousted and killed in October 2011.

Matriarch: Female head of a family.

Opines: Declares.

Bedouins: Nomadic Arabs.

lie on the ground. One refuses to release her poster and screams as her finger is broken.

But most have fled. They disappeared over the square, into the side alleys. Every girl for herself. As they had planned. It's all over in a matter of minutes. A white van drives away with four of the girls. The other vehicles depart from the scene.

The square appears as if nothing has happened. But something has happened. Something has begun.

• • •

What happened next...

Protesters in other countries had also faced violent crackdowns by police and government troops that resulted in arrest, injury, or death. For example, in Tunisia, approximately 300 people were killed during the weeks of protest and revolution; in Egypt, approximately 850 were killed. By December 2011, the United Nations estimated that more than five thousand people had been killed and fourteen thousand had been arrested since the uprising began. Although protests in smaller towns continued to build, government forces were particularly active in combating revolt in Damascus and Aleppo, Syria's two largest cities, and other areas considered strategically important for maintaining Assad's hold on his power.

The ongoing violence prompted the United Nations to order an investigation into human rights violations. The United States and other nations called for Assad to step down and expanded sanctions against Syrian business interests. Meanwhile, some activists reported cases where government troops were killed for refusing orders to fire upon civilians. In November 2011 the Arab League (a regional political alliance of Arab nations formed in 1945 to promote political, military, and economic cooperation within the Arab world) suspended Syria from membership in the League, because of Syria's violent suppression of anti-government demonstrations.

Whereas the Syrian government's brutal tactics have successfully suppressed various protests and uprisings in the past, in this case, it seems to have further inspired pro-democracy advocates to continue their fight and prompted others tired of living in oppression to join the effort. As of late 2011, however, Assad remained in office, refusing to bow to the calls from both within and outside of his country to either enact true reforms or step aside.

A view of the city of Hama, Syria. In 1982 Syrian president Hafez Assad order the massacre of thousands of protestors in Hama.
© ELIO CIOL/CORBIS.

Did you know...

- In 1982 Hafez Assad ordered the massacre of over ten thousand Sunni Muslim protesters in the city of Hama (some reports put the number of dead closer to twenty thousand). Most of the protesters were members of the Muslim Brotherhood, an Islamic fundamentalist group organized in opposition to Western influence and in support of Islamic principles.

- On February 9, 2011, the Syrian government announced it was lifting its four-year ban on the social networking Web site *Facebook* and the video sharing Web site *YouTube*. Although the move was promoted as a gesture in favor of open communication among Syrian citizens, some critics suspected that the government's true motive was to monitor the online activities of opposition activists. Three months later, the government was once again cracking down on the use of *Facebook* and other social media sites, and some activists had reported being forced to relinquish their passwords and instances of their personal web pages being hacked.

- The antigovernment graffiti that the boys wrote on the wall in Daraa translates as "The people want the fall of the regime."

Consider the following...

- The United States and other nations imposed sanctions on Syria in hopes of pressing its government to end the violence against political opponents or to give up power altogether. Research the types of sanctions that were imposed and the impact that they were intended to have. Do you think sanctions are effective in making a government change its policies? Why or why not?

- Foreign journalists were banned from Syria, and the media within the country was largely under government control. Activists relied heavily upon social media, the Internet, and other technology to mobilize supporters and report on events. What are the advantages and shortcomings of information gathered through social media and the Internet? In what ways was the 2011 uprising different than an uprising that may have occurred ten years before it?

- Seierstad's article includes profiles of Syrians from various walks of life. How might people's status in Syrian society influence their opinion of the Assad regime and their likeliness to actively participate in a protest movement?

For More Information

BOOKS

Leverett, Flint. *Inheriting Syria: Bashar's Trial by Fire.* Washington, DC: Brookings Institution Press, 2005.

PERIODICALS

Badran, Tony. "A Spreading Revolt in Syria; Is Assad Losing His Grip?" *The Weekly Standard* (April 25, 2011).

Giglio, Mike. "The Republic of Fear." *Newsweek* (April 11, 2011): 30.

Razaq, Rashid. "Syrian Forces Kill Seven as Protests Break Out on Eid." *The Evening Standard* (London, England; March 26, 2011): 24.

Slackman, Michael. "With Thousands in Streets, Syria Kills Protesters." *New York Times* (March 26, 2011): A1.

Seierstad, Asne. "Out of the Shadow of Fear." *Newsweek* (June 5, 2011). Available online at http://www.thedailybeast.com/newsweek/2011/06/05/out-of-the-shadow-of-fear-in-syria.html (accessed on November 30, 2011).

Stack, Liam, and Katherine Zoepf. "Dozens of Protests Across Syria Are Said to Be Largest and Bloodiest to Date." *New York Times* (April 9, 2011): A9.

"Syria's Assad Talks of Reform as Protests Loom." *Washington Times* (February 1, 2001): A07.

Zakaria, Fareed. "A New Middle East." *Time Magazine* (May 1, 2011). Available online at http://www.time.com/time/magazine/article/0,9171,2069033,00.html#ixzz1YdK7wKlx (accessed on November 30, 2011).

WEB SITES

"Profile: Syria's Bashar al-Assad." *BBC News* (March 10, 2005). http://news.bbc.co.uk/2/hi/middle_east/2579331.stm (accessed on November 30, 2011).

Where to Learn More

Books

Al Aswany, Alaa. *On the State of Egypt: What Made the Revolution Inevitable.* New York: Vintage Books, 2011.

Anderson, Sean, and Stephen Sloan. *Historical Dictionary of Terrorism.* Lanham, MD: Scarecrow Press, 2002.

Barr, James. *A Line in the Sand: Anglo-French Struggle for the Middle East.* New York: W.W. Norton and Co., 2012.

Brown, Nathan J. *Palestinian Politics after the Oslo Accords: Resuming Arab Palestine.* Berkeley: University of California Press, 2003.

Carew-Miller, Anna. *Palestinians.* Philadelphia: Mason Crest, 2010.

Cleveland, William L. *A History of the Modern Middle East.* Boulder, CO: Westview Press, 2004.

Council on Foreign Relations/Foreign Affairs. *New Arab Revolt: What Happened, What It Means, and What Comes Next* . New York: Council on Foreign Relations, 2011.

Currie, Stephen. *Terrorists and Terrorist Groups.* San Diego, CA: Lucent Books, 2002.

DeFronzo, James. *The Iraq War: Origins and Consequences.* Boulder, CO: Westview Press, 2009.

Drummond, Dorothy. *Holy Land Whose Land: Modern Dilemma Ancient Roots.* Seattle, WA: Educare Press, 2002.

Encyclopedia of the Modern Middle East and North Africa. 4 vols. New York: Macmillan Reference USA, 2004.

Engel, David. *Zionism.* Harlow: Pearson/Longman, 2009.

Etheredge, Laura S., ed. *Persian Gulf States: Kuwait, Qatar, Bahrain, Oman, and the United Arab Emirates.* New York: Rosen/Britannica Educational Publishing, 2011.

Farsoun, Samih K., with Christina E. Zacharia. *Palestine and the Palestinians.* Boulder, CO: Westview Press, 1997.

Finkel, Caroline. *Osman's Dream: The History of the Ottoman Empire.* New York: Basic Books, 2007.

Gelvin, James L. *The Modern Middle East: A History,* 3rd ed. New York: Oxford University Press, 2011.

Gunderson, Cory Gideon. *The Israeli-Palestinian Conflict.* Edina, MN: Abdo, 2004.

Hirst, David. *Beware of Small States: Lebanon, Battleground of the Middle East.* New York: Nation Books, 2010.

Hourani, Albert. *A History of the Arab Peoples.* Cambridge, MA: Belknap, 1991.

Kalin, Ibrahim. "Roots of Misconception: Euro-American Perceptions of Islam before and after September 11." In *Islam, Fundamentalism, and the Betrayal of Tradition: Essays by Western Muslim Scholars.* Edited by Joseph E.B. Lumbard. Bloomington, IN: World Wisdom, 2004, pp. 144–187. Available online at http://www.worldwisdom.com/uploads/pdfs/58.pdf (accessed on November 30, 2011).

Karsh, Efraim. *The Arab-Israeli Conflict: The 1948 War.* New York: Rosen Publishing, 2008.

———. *The Iran-Iraq War: 1980–1988.* Oxford, UK: Osprey, 2002.

Kennedy, Hugh. *The Great Arab Conquests: How the Spread of Islam Changed the World We Live In.* Cambridge, MA: Da Capo Press, 2008.

Khalidi, Rashid. *The Iron Cage: The Story of the Palestinian Struggle for Statehood.* Boston, MA: Beacon, 2006.

Kherdian, David. *The Road from Home: The Story of an Armenian Girl.* New York: Greenwillow Books, 1979.

Kinross, Lord. *The Ottoman Centuries: The Rise and Fall of the Turkish Empire.* New York: Morrow Quill Paperbacks, 1979.

Kort, Michael. *The Handbook of the Middle East.* Brookfield, CT: Twenty-First Century Books, 2002.

Lewis, Bernard. *The Middle East: A Brief History of the Last 2,000 Years.* New York: Scribner, 1995.

Mackey, Sandra. *Mirror of the Arab World: Lebanon in Conflict.* New York: W.W. Norton, 2009.

Miller, Debra A. *The Arab-Israeli Conflict.* San Diego, CA: Lucent Books, 2005.

Milton-Edwards, Beverly, and Stephen Farrell. *Hamas: The Islamic Resistance Movement.* Cambridge, England: Polity Press, 2010.

Myre, Greg, and Jennifer Griffin. *This Burning Land: Lessons from the Front Lines of the Transformed Israeli-Palestinian Conflict.* Hoboken, NJ: Wiley, 2010.

Nardo, Don. *The Islamic Empire.* Detroit, MI: Lucent Books, 2011.

Polk, William R. *Understanding Iran: Everything You Need to Know, from Persia to the Islamic Republic, from Cyrus to Ahmadinejad.* Basingstoke, United Kingdom: Palgrave Macmillan, 2011.

Ra'ad, Basem L. *Hidden Histories: Palestine and the Eastern Mediterranean.* London: Pluto Press, 2010.

Rabinovich, Itamar. *The Lingering Conflict: Israel, Arabs, and the Middle East, 1948–2011.* Washington, DC: Brookings Institution Press, 2011.

Rapoport, David C. "Terrorism." In *Encyclopedia of Violence, Peace, & Conflict.* Vol. 3. 2nd ed. Edited by Lester Kurtz. San Diego, CA: Academic Press, 2008.

Shindler, Colin. *A History of Modern Israel.* Cambridge: Cambridge University Press, 2008.

Schneer, Jonathan. *The Balfour Declaration: The Origins of the Arab-Israeli Conflict.* New York: Random House, 2010.

Shlaim, Avi. *Israel and Palestine: Reappraisals, Revisions, Refutations..* London and New York: Verso, 2010.

Slavicek, Louise Chipley. *Israel.* New York: Chelsea House, 2008.

Smith, Charles D., ed. *Palestine and the Arab-Israeli Conflict: A History with Documents,* 7th ed. Boston MA: Bedford/St. Martin's, 2009.

Taheri, Amir. *The Persian Night: Iran Under the Khomeinist Revolution.* New York: Encounter Books, 2010.

Wingate, Katherine. *The Intifadas.* New York: Rosen, 2004.

Wright, Robin. *Dreams and Shadows: The Future of the Middle East.* New York: Penguin, 2008.

Young, Michael. *The Ghosts of Martyrs Square: An Eyewitness Account of Lebanon's Life Struggle.* New York: Simon and Schuster, 2010.

Periodicals

Anderson, Jon Lee. "Who Are the Rebels?" *New Yorker* (April 4, 2011). Available online at http://www.newyorker.com/talk/comment/2011/04/04/110404taco_talk_anderson (accessed on November 30, 2011).

Beinin, Joel. "Is Terrorism a Useful Term in Understanding the Middle East and the Palestinian-Israeli Conflict?" *Radical History Review* no. 85 (Winter 2003): 12–23. Available online at http://www.why-war.com/files/85.1beinin.pdf (accessed on November 30, 2011).

"A Bitter Stalemate." *Economist* (September 24, 2011): 58.

Diamond, Larry. "Why Are There No Arab Democracies?" *Journal of Democracy* 21, no. 1 (January 2010).

"Gaza Strip," *New York Times* (August 11, 2011). Available online at http://topics.nytimes.com/top/news/international/countriesandterritories/gaza_strip/index.html (accessed on November 30, 2011).

Ghosh, Bobby. "Islamophobia: Does America Have a Muslim Problem?" *Time* (August 19, 2010). Available online at http://www.time.com/time/print out/0,8816,2011936,00.html (accessed on November 30, 2011).

Hogan, Matthew."The 1948 Massacre at Deir Yassin Revisited." *Historian* 63, no. 2 (Winter 2001).

Huntington, Samuel P. "The Clash of Civilizations?" *Foreign Affairs* 72, no. 3 (Summer 1993). Available online at http://www.polsci.wvu.edu/faculty/ hauser/PS103/Readings/HuntingtonClashOfCivilizationsForAffSummer 93.pdf (accessed on November 30, 2011).

Khouri, Rami G. "Drop the Orientalist Term 'Arab Spring.'" *Daily Star* (August 17, 2011). Available online at http://www.dailystar.com.lb/Opinion/ Columnist/2011/Aug-17/Drop-the-Orientalist-term-Arab-Spring.ashx#axzz 1ZMX0FZfe (accessed on November 30, 2011).

Lebanon: The Israel-Hamas-Hezbollah Conflict. CRS Report for Congress. U.S. Library of Congress, Congressional Research Service (September 15, 2006). Available online at http://www.fas.org/sgp/crs/mideast/RL33566.pdf (accessed on November 30, 2011).

Masoud, Tarek. "The Upheavals in Egypt and Tunisia: The Road to (and from) Liberation Square." *Journal of Democracy* Vol. 22, No. 3 (July 2011). Available online at http://www.journalofdemocracy.org/articles/gratis/ Masoud-22-3.pdf (accessed on November 30, 2011.

Shapiro, Samantha. "Revolution, Facebook Style." *New York Times* (January 22, 2009). Available online at http://www.nytimes.com/2009/01/25/magazine/ 25bloggers-t.html (accessed on November 30, 2011).

Steavenson, Wendell. "Roads to Freedom: The View from within the Syrian Crackdown." *New Yorker* (August 29, 2011): 26–32.

Web Sites

"Al-Qaeda (a.k.a. al-Qaida, al-Qa'ida)." *Council on Foreign Relations* (June 17, 2011). http://www.cfr.org/terrorist-organizations/al-qaeda-k-al-qaida-al- qaida/p9126 (accessed on November 30, 2011).

Asser, Martin. "The Muammar Gaddafi Story." *BBC News* (October 21, 2011). http://www.bbc.co.uk/news/world-africa-12688033 (accessed on November 30, 2011).

"Background Note: Lebanon." *U.S. Department of State* (May 23, 2011). http:// www.state.gov/r/pa/ei/bgn/35833.htm#history (accessed on November 30, 2011).

"Bahrain News: The Protests (2011)." *New York Times* (September 26, 2011). http://topics.nytimes.com/top/news/international/countriesandterritories/ bahrain/index.html (accessed on November 30, 2011).

"The Battle for Libya: Killings, Disappearances, and Torture." *Amnesty International* (September 2011). http://www.amnesty.org/en/library/asset/ MDE19/025/2011/en/8f2e1c49-8f43-46d3-917d-383c17d36377/mde 190252011en.pdf (accessed on November 30, 2011).

Beinin, Joel, and Lisa Jajjar. "Palestine, Israel and the Arab-Israeli Conflict: A Primer." *Middle East Research and Information Project.* http://www. merip.org/palestine-israel_primer/intro-pal-isr-primer.html (accessed on November 30, 2011).

Brown, Nathan J. "U.S. Policy and the Muslim Brotherhood." *Carnegie Endowment for International Peace* (April 13, 2011). http://carnegieendow ment.org/2011/04/13/u.s.-policy-and-muslim-brotherhood/i6 (accessed on November 30, 2011).

"Bullets to Ballet Box: A History of Hezbollah." *Frontline World.* www.pbs.org/ frontlineworld/stories/lebanon/history.html (accessed on November 30, 2011).

Collelo, Thomas, ed. "Syria." *Country Studies.* (1987). http://countrystudies.us/ syria/ (accessed on November 30, 2011).

El Mansour, Mohammed. "The U.S.-Middle East Connection: Interests, Attitudes, and Images." *Teach Mideast* (2004). http://teachmideast.org/ essays/28-history/110-the-us-middle-east-connectioninterests-attitudes-and-images (accessed on November 30, 2011).

"Foreign Terrorist Organizations." *U.S. Department of State.* (May 19, 2011). http://www.state.gov/s/ct/rls/other/des/123085.htm (accessed on November 30, 2011).

Grace, Francie. "Munich Massacre Remembered." *CBS News.* (February 11, 2009). http://www.cbsnews.com/stories/2002/09/05/world/main520865.shtml (accessed on November 30, 2011).

"The Gulf War." *Harper's Magazine.* http://www.harpers.org/GulfWar.html (accessed on November 30, 2011).

"The Gulf War: an In-Depth Examination of the 1990–1991 Persian Gulf Crisis." *PBS Frontline.* http://www.pbs.org/wgbh/pages/frontline/gulf/ (accessed on November 30, 2011).

"A History of Conflict—Israel and the Palestinians: A Timeline." *BBC News.* http://news.bbc.co.uk/2/shared/spl/hi/middle_east/03/v3_ip_timeline/html/ (accessed on November 30, 2011).

"Hunting Bin Laden." *PBS Frontline..* http://www.pbs.org/wgbh/pages/front line/shows/binladen/ (accessed on November 30, 2011).

Internet Islamic History Sourcebook. Fordham University, http://www.fordham. edu/halsall/islam/islamsbook.html#Islamic%20Nationalism (accessed on November 30, 2011).

"Iran: A Brief History." *MidEast Web..* http://www.mideastweb.org/iranhistory. htm (accessed on November 30, 2011).

"Guide to the Middle East Peace Process." *Israeli Ministry of Foreign Affairs.* http://www.mfa.gov.il/MFA/Peace+Process/Guide+to+the+Peace+Process/ (accessed on November 30, 2011).

The Islamic World to 1600. Applied History Research Group, University of Calgary. http://www.ucalgary.ca/applied_history/tutor/islam/ (accessed on November 30, 2011).

"Islamophobia." *Council on American-Islamic Relations (CAIR)*. http://www.cair.com/Issues/Islamophobia/Islamophobia.aspx (accessed on November 30, 2011).

The Ottomans.org. http://www.theottomans.org/english/history/index.asp (accessed on November 30, 2011).

"Profile: Egypt's Muslim Brotherhood." *BBC News Middle East*. http://www.bbc.co.uk/news/world-middle-east-12313405 (accessed on November 2, 2011).

The Question of Palestine and the United Nations. United Nations Department of Public Information (March 2003). http://www.un.org/Depts/dpi/palestine/ (accessed on September 16, 2011).

Slim, Randa. "Hezbollah's Most Serious Challenge." *Foreign Policy* (August 5, 2011). http://mideast.foreignpolicy.com/posts/2011/05/03/hezbollah_s_most_serious_challenge (accessed on November 30, 2011).

"The Suez Crisis: An Affair to Remember." *Economist* (July 27, 2006). http://www.economist.com/node/7218678 (accessed on November 30, 2011).

"Zionism and the Creation of Israel." *MidEast Web*. http://www.mideastweb.org/zionism.htm (accessed November 3, 2011).

Index

Bold type indicates major entries. Illustrations are marked by (ill.).

O